Introductio
COMPUT
SIMULAT

A. WAYNE BENNETT

Virginia Polytechnic Institute and State University

Introduction to COMPUTER SIMULATION

WEST PUBLISHING COMPANY

St. Paul • New York • Boston

Los Angeles • San Francisco

Library of Congress Catalog Card Number: 74–4509

ISBN: 0–8299–0017–9

1st Reprint—1975

To Shirley, Beth and David
in gratitude and affection

Preface

The rapid development of electronic computers and their widespread use for simulation have made computer simulation an important subject in many disciplines. Unfortunately, analog, hybrid and digital simulation are often taught separately with little emphasis on interrelations. Also, students frequently receive several "introductions" to simulation which lead to overlaps and gaps in coverage.

The purpose of this book is to provide a comprehensive introduction to analog, hybrid and digital simulation. An elementary knowledge of differential equations is assumed and used as background for a gradual development of basic simulation concepts.

The book is divided into three sections. The first section, devoted to analog simulation, introduces the basic analog computing elements and illustrates their use in a series of simple example problems. Although some electronic circuit details are

provided, they are not essential to the presentation   and   may
be omitted.   The fundamentals of analog simulation are extended
to include time and magnitude scaling (Chapter 4) and nonlinear
system simulation (Chapter 5).   The last two chapters in   the
analog section discuss transfer function simulation (Chapter 6)
and state variable simulation (Chapter 7).   Both chapters **are**
intended to supplement material on control systems.

The second section of the book is devoted to hybrid   computation.   In Chapter 8, Hybrid computing elements are introduced
along with a general discussion of hybrid computers.   Since
hybrid elements are used to link analog and digital computers,
digital signals and digital computing elements are introduced
next.   The discussion of digital computing elements includes
combinational digital logic (Chapter 9) and sequential digital
logic (Chapter 10).   Several example problems are included   to
illustrate hybrid simulation techniques.   Chapter 11 presents
hybrid optimization techniques.   The last chapter in the hybrid
section introduces the digital computer and discusses its   use
in hybrid computation.

The last section of the book presents digital simulation.
The first chapter in this section (Chapter 13) discusses   numerical integration and some of the approximations required to
simulate continuous systems on a digital computer.   Chapter 14
is devoted to digital simulation of continuous systems.   The
chapter discusses continuous system languages and provides
several illustrations of CSMP.   In Chapter 15, digital simulation
of discrete systems is presented.   Several discrete system   simulation languages are discussed and an example problem is ᵣre-
sented to illustrate GPSS.

Whenever possible, the same example problems   are   used to
illustrate the different simulation techniques.   This   approach
permits the student to focus full attention on the techniques
being illustrated rather than the problems used in the illustration.
Hopefully, this also provides additional insight into the inter-
relationships of the various simulation techniques.   The book
includes more than five hundred fifty (550) exercises of varying
degrees of difficulty.   The problems are keyed to the appropriate

section number to assist in identifying the background material. In addition, references to more than one hundred other sources of information are provided.

The organization of the book enables it to be used in a variety of ways. The first five chapters can be used as source material for a one-quarter, two-credit course on analog simulation. The inclusion of Chapters 6 and 7 should provide enough material for a one-quarter, three-credit course or a one-semester, two-credit course on analog simulation with control system applications. The exercises at the end of each chapter suggest a number of laboratory experiments that could be used for a one-credit laboratory to accompany the course. If control system theory is of little interest, a one-quarter, three hour or one-semester, two-credit course could be built around Chapters 1-5, 8, 9 and 10. In addition to analog simulation, this would provide coverage of hybrid and digital computing elements and their use in system simulation. If Chapters 1-10 are covered, then a two-quarter or two-semester sequence is recommended.

Since the optimization techniques of Chapter 11 are of considerable practical value, the two-quarter/semester sequence may be expanded to include this material. However, it may be necessary to omit certain portions of Chapters 5, 6 or 7.

The digital computer is introduced in Chapter 12, along with its role in hybrid computation. This material should be useful to individuals interested in the programming and interfacing of mini-and micro-computers as well as hybrid computation. If this material is included in a two-quarter/semester course, it may be necessary to omit material from earlier chapters.

Chapters 13, 14 and 15 deal with digital simulation and can be treated separately. Chapter 13, presents the background of digital integration and can be omitted. However, this material provides valuable information on sample rate and integration interval. Therefore, individuals planning additional work in digital simulation should understand these basic concepts.

Chapter 14 is devoted to digital simulation of continuous systems. The simulation techniques are related to transfer function simulation (Chapter 6) and state variable simulation

(Chapter 7). A number of the more popular simulation languages are discussed and several example problems are simulated by means of CSMP. Since much of the work on digital simulation of continuous systems is an outgrowth of earlier work on analog computers, the material of the first section provides an excellent background for digital simulation. Also, many of the hybrid simulation techniques of Chapters 9 and 10 are illustrated with CSMP. Thus, digital simulation can be presented along with appropriate analog and hybrid material. A one-quarter/semester course on digital simulation of continuous systems might include material from Chapters 1-3, 8-10, 13 and 14 with selected topics from Chapters 7 and 12.

A very limited introduction to discrete system simulation is presented in Chapter 15. The primary intent is to introduce the concept of discrete systems and acquaint the student with another type of digital simulation. The material in this chapter is not intended to serve as a full course on discrete system simulation and should be supplemented with additional material if a thorough treatment of discrete system simulation is desired.

The entire book can be covered in a three-quarter or two-semester course. As noted previously, the exercises at the end of each chapter suggest a series of experiments to accompany the course. Hopefully, coverage of the material provides an appreciation for the scope of computer simulation as well as simulation techniques. The book is intended to serve as an introduction to computer simulation and the level and pace are set to facilitate self study. Therefore, portions of the book could be covered in a basic course and the remainder of the book covered by self study. This approach also facilitates the omission of selected portions of the book without serious loss of continuity.

A. Wayne Bennett

Acknowledgements

I want to acknowledge the help and support of many people throughout the development of the material for this book. Former students, too numerous to list, have contributed many ideas and suggestions. Since a great deal of the material was developed in the Computer Engineering Laboratory at VPI&SU, I am especially indebted to Bob Amundson, John Ayres, Mike Batchelder, Marty Cacioppo, Mike Doering, John Evans, John Hind, Dan Osecky, Jim Price, Alvin Schmitt and Roy Sykes. I also would like to thank Dr. William A. Blackwell, Chairman of the Electrical Engineering Department at VPI&SU, and Dr. W. J. Fabrycky, Associate Dean of Engineering at VPI&SU, for their support and interest.

In addition to many hours of typing and proofreading, my wife, Shirley, has provided invaluable encouragement and inspiration. To her, I owe my heartfelt thanks and loving appreciation. A special acknowledgment is due Mrs. Juanita Marlett for her assistance in typing the manuscript. Her willing cooperation has been priceless.

To my daughter, Beth, and son, David, I owe a debt of gratitude for their patient understanding throughout the writing of this book. As always, I owe more to my parents, Mr. and Mrs. A. Conrad Bennett, than words can express.

Contents

†

1

Introduction

1.1 INTRODUCTION

In recent years, the use of computers has increased at a phenomenal rate. In less than twenty-five years the computer has grown from a laboratory curiosity to a major industry affecting most every phase of life. One of the most important applications of computers is in simulation. Although it is difficult to determine a precise definition of the term "simulation",[1] techniques have been developed for computer simulation of a wide variety of systems. Applications range from biological systems to business and industrial systems. Computer simulation is now used in most every field of endeavor. With such widespread use, it is important to understand basic simulation techniques and gain experience in their application.

The purpose of this book is to introduce the fundamentals of analog, hybrid and digital simulation. The techniques will

be illustrated with a variety of examples. Also practice problems of increasing difficulty are included with each chapter.

The first portion of this chapter is devoted to a discussion
of simulation. A brief history of computer simulation is
presented in the next section to provide background for the
remainder of the material. Additional historical details will
be presented later to indicate the manner in which computer simulation has developed. This chapter also includes a discussion
of analogies and an outline of the remaining chapters of the book.

1.2 SIMULATION

As indicated earlier, a precise definition of simulation is
difficult to obtain. The term is used to cover a wide variety
of activities ranging from the development of mathematical relations describing a system, to the construction of a physical
model or mock-up. For the purposes of this book, the term simulation will be used to describe the process of formulating a
suitable mathematical model of a system, the development of a
computer program to solve the equations of the model and operation of the computer to determine values for system variables.

The emphasis will be on the computer aspects of the process
and the phrase "modeling and simulation" will be encountered
frequently. Although this seems to imply that modeling is not a
part of simulation, this is not the case, modeling is a very
important phase of the simulation process. Modeling involves
the development of mathematical relations describing the
system variables. This usually requires linearization of
certain terms and omission of minor effects. Since the equations
of the model are the basis for simulation, the results are only
as good as the model.

1.3 A BRIEF HISTORY

The use of electronic computers to simulate physical sys-
ems has grown quite rapidly since World War II. The electronic
analog computer was the first computer to be widely used for
simulation. The first published paper on a general purpose
electronic analog computer was by J. R. Raggazzini, R. H.
Randall, and F. A. Russell.[2] It appeared in 1947, and was the
result of earlier work on antiaircraft fire control systems.

Also involved in the early work on analog computers was G. A. Philbrich. In the years following the introduction of the analog computer, utilization grew quite rapidly. By 1955, a wide variety of analog equipment was being manufactured by several companies.

The success of analog simulation and the rapid growth and development of the digital computer led to its use for simulation. The approaches ranged from direct digital simulation,[3] to special purpose digital programs that simulate an analog computer on the digital computer.[4,5] In the latter approach, the system equations are first programmed in analog computer form. The resulting analog diagram is then programmed for the digital computer using certain basic building blocks. This method takes advantage of the ease with which the equations of physical systems can be programmed for the analog computer. Other methods of digital simulation are more difficult to program but frequently result in more efficient utilization of the digital computer. These methods are discussed in the latter portion of this book.

In comparing analog and digital computers, it should be noted that they each have certain distinct advantages and disadvantages. The analog computer is a parallel device which operates on problem variables simultaneously. It is capable of direct integration of system variables in a straightforward manner and has an intimate relation to the variables of the physical system. As a result, it is an excellent tool for teaching dynamic systems. On the other hand, the digital computer is a sequential device capable of storing vast amounts of data. The outstanding features of the digital computer are accuracy and the ease with which it can change from one application to another.

The complementary nature of analog and digital computers has led to the hybrid computer which is a combination of the two technologies. Hybrid computers were first developed in the aerospace industry in the late 1950's. Since that time, a wide variety of hybrid computers have been built. These range from special purpose simulators to general purpose machines with many applications.

Recent development of mini-and micro-computers has already
had an impact on computer simulation. The advent of practical
parallel processors and higher execution rates indicate an even
brighter future for computer simulation.

1.4 ANALOGIES

The application of analogies in engineering and science
has a long history. The use of scaled models, equivalent
circuits, and mechanical devices to represent a physical system
are examples of such analogies.

Computer simulation can be looked upon as the solution of
a set of equations that represent the physical system under
study. In analog simulation, the computer produces voltages
that are analogous to problem variables. In a digital computer
simulation, the "output" is a numerical value computed for a
particular variable at some point in time or space. One of the
big problems in analog simulation is understanding the relation
of a problem variable to computer voltage. Many people, particularly those not electrically oriented, have trouble with
this initially. Actually, it is not a serious problem and
will be presented in a manner that <u>does</u> <u>not</u> require an
electrical background.

1.5 OUTLINE OF THE BOOK

This book has been organized to provide an orderly introduction to analog, hybrid and digital simulation. Chapter 1 is
an introduction and the remaining chapters are outlined as
follows:

Chapter 2: <u>Basic Linear Analog Components,</u> introduces the
operational amplifier and demonstrates the use of the operational amplifier for summation and integration. The chapter
also discusses potentiometers and the control and operation of
an analog computer.

Chapter 3: <u>Analog Simulation of Linear Systems</u>, demonstrates
the basic programming techniques for simulating linear, stationary, differential equations. The methods include both implicit
and explicit handling of the highest-order derivatives. The
generalized, linear, second-order differential equation is

introduced and illustrated with a physical example.   The programming methods are extended to simultaneous differential equations.   Finally, the use of a static check is presented.

Chapter 4: <u>Magnitude and Time Scaling</u>, presents the need and methods for magnitude and time scaling.   In order to provide appropriate background, some approximate methods for estimating the range of system variables are presented. The unit method for magnitude scaling is introduced and illustrated with examples.   Time scaling is presented as a simple gain change and then developed as an alteration of the differential equation. Guides for time scaling are included along with several examples.

Chapter 5: <u>Simulation of Nonlinear Systems</u>, presents the computer components used in the simulation of nonlinear systems. The chapter discusses the use of diodes, function generators and function multipliers. Also, the characteristics of nonlinear systems and special considerations for their simulation are included.

Chapter 6: <u>Transfer Function Simulation</u>, introduces block diagram and transfer function representation of dynamic systems. With this background, methods for simulating systems represented in transfer function form are presented and illustrated.   The chapter discusses the advantages of the various techniques and cites likely sources of difficulty. The presentation builds on the generalized, linear, second-order differential equation presented in an earlier chapter and a different simulation diagram is developed. Portions of this discussion lead naturally to the state variable approach presented in Chapter 7.

Chapter 7: <u>State Variable Simulation</u>, introduces the concept of state variables and develops programming methods for simulating systems expressed in state variable form. The chapter begins with a discussion of matrix-vector operations. The state variable equations are developed and the relationships between transfer function representation and state variables are presented. The chapter summarizes the benefits of state variable representation and illustrates state variable programming with several numerical examples.

Chapter 8: <u>Introduction to Hybrid Computers and Hybrid Computing Elements</u>, presents the concept of hybrid computing elements. The chapter summarizes the characteristics of analog and digital computers and cites the advantages of combining the two types of computers. A brief history of hybrid computers is included. The chapter also presents computing elements that are analog <u>and</u> digital in nature and demonstrates their use in simulation.

Chapter 9: <u>Combinational Digital Logic in System Simulation</u>, introduces combinational digital logic and its use in system simulation. The chapter includes brief discussions of gates, logical expressions, and the realization of logic functions. With this background, techniques are presented for including logic, analog switches, track-store units and comparators in system simulation.

Chapter 10: <u>Sequential Digital Logic in System Simulation</u>, presents sequential digital logic and its use in system simulation. The flip-flop is discussed along with its use as a memory element in registers, counters and shift registers. The chapter also includes a discussion of timing and synchronization problems, and the control of the digital elements. Several example problems are used to illustrate the use of sequential logic in systems simulation.

Chapter 11: <u>Optimization</u>, discusses optimization techniques and computer implementation with illustrations of the operations. The chapter includes a discussion of cost functions and methods for their evaluation. Also, the optimal control problem is discussed briefly.

Chapter 12: <u>The Digital Computer and Hybrid Computation</u>, presents the basic operation of a digital computer and the problems associated with the interconnection of an analog computer to a digital computer. The chapter discusses digital-to-analog conversion, analog-to-digital conversion and other requirements of the interface. The operating fundamentals of a full hybrid system are presented along with desirable hybrid software. A typical system is presented and discussed.

Chapter 13: <u>Fundamentals of Digital Simulation</u>, presents the basic approaches to numerical integration and digital computer realization. The chapter discusses methods for state variable and transfer function representation.

Chapter 14: <u>Digital Simulation of Continuous Systems</u>, includes a brief history of digital simulation of continuous systems. The chapter presents a simulation language, CSMP, and illustrates its use by means of several examples. The use of CSMP to simulate hybrid systems is also included. The chapter discusses two other simulation languages briefly.

Chapter 15: <u>Digital Simulation of Discrete Systems</u>, provides a brief history of discrete system simulation and a survey of available languages. Two of the more popular discrete system simulation programs are discussed and illustrated with example problems.

1.6   REFERENCES FOR CHAPTER 1:

(1) Naylor, T. H.: <u>Computer Simulation Techniques</u>, John Wiley & Sons, Inc., New York, 1966.

(2) Ragazzini, J. R., R. H. Randall, and F. A. Russell: "Analysis of Problems in Dynamics by Electronic Circuits," Proc. IRE, pp. 444-452, May, 1947.

(3) Hurt, J. R.: "New Difference Equation Technique for Solving Nonlinear Differential Equations," Proceedings of the Spring Joint Computer Conference, 1964.

(4) Selfridge, R. G.: "Coding a General-Purpose Digital Computer to Operate as a Differential Analyzer," Proceedings 1955, Western Joint Computer Conference, IRE, 1955.

(5) Brennan, R. D. and H. Sano: "Pactolus - A Digital Analog Simulator Program for the IBM 1620," Proceedings of the Fall Joint Computer Conference, 1964.

(6) Brennan, R. D. and R. N. Lineberger: "A Survey of Digital Simulation: Digital Analog Simulator Programs," <u>Simulation</u>, Vol. 3, No. 6, pp. 22-36, December, 1964.

A

ANALOG
SIMULATION

2

Basic Linear
Analog Components

2.1 INTRODUCTION

In this chapter, the basic linear components of the analog computer are presented. The elements form the basis for all analog computation. The presentation will be general in nature since the actual connection details will vary among the available analog computers. Also, technical details that are not essential to utilizing the analog computer will be omitted. Readers interested in additional information are referred to the reference list at the end of this chapter.

2.2 THE OPERATIONAL AMPLIFIER

The fundamental component of the analog computer is the operational amplifier. It is the basic element that enables the computer to sum, integrate and multiply <u>by a constant</u>. A thorough understanding of the electrical characteristics of the operational amplifier is not required in order to use the analog computer.

However, some information of this nature is useful and this section will include a brief summary of operational amplifier
characteristics.

The operational amplifier is an inverting, high-gain, direct-
coupled amplifier. Ideally, it should have an infinite gain at
all frequencies. However, typical values of gain are on the order
of -1×10^7, where the negative sign indicates inversion. In
addition, the ideal operational amplifier should have an infinite
input resistance or impedance and an output impedance of zero.
Presently available operational amplifiers have input impedances
of several megohms and output impedances of less than 100 ohms.
The ideal operational amplifier should also have zero phase shift
to all frequencies. The amplifiers on most analog computers have
very little phase shift for the frequencies used in normal computing. Another important characteristic of the ideal operational
amplifier is zero offset (i.e., zero volts at the input should
produce zero volts at the output). The amplifiers presently available have excellent offset characteristics and adjustment of the
balance level to assure that the amplifier is properly zeroed is
seldom required. However, the amplifier balance should be checked
each time the computer is used.

The characteristics of the ideal operational amplifier can be
summarized as follows: infinite gain, infinite bandwidth, infinite
input impedance, zero output impedance, zero drift or offset, and
zero phase shift. The operational amplifiers for analog computers
operate over a ±10 or ±100 volt range. The maximum voltage (±10
and ±100) is usually referred to as the reference voltage.

The symbol that will be used for the operational amplifier is
shown in Figure 2-2-1. The number at the output apex of the symbol

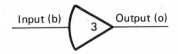

Figure 2-2-1. The operational amplifier

is an identification number assigned to each amplifier of the computer (amplifier No. 3 is shown). The letter "b" at the input
stands for base and relates to the input of the transistor amplifier. The "o" at the output is obvious. Notice the curved line

on the input side of the symbol. It will be used to distinguish
the operational amplifier from certain other computing elements.

2.3 THE SUMMING AMPLIFIER

The operational amplifier can be connected to provide arithmetic summation. The circuit for the summing amplifier is shown
in Figure 2-3-1. The characteristics of the summing amplifier

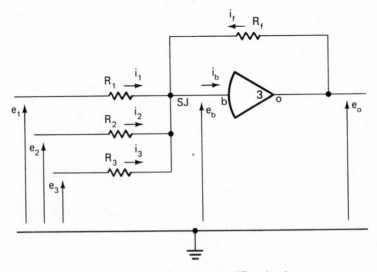

Figure 2-3-1.   Summing amplifier circuit

circuit of Figure 2-3-1 can be determined from the following analysis. Using OHM'S LAW, the electric current in the resistors can
be written

$$i_1 = \frac{e_1 - e_b}{R_1} ,$$

(2.3.1)

$$i_2 = \frac{e_2 - e_b}{R_2} ,$$

(2.3.2)

$$i_3 = \frac{e_3 - e_b}{R_3} ,$$

(2.3.3)

and

$$i_f = \frac{e_o - e_b}{R_f} .$$

(2.3.4)

By KIRCHHOFFS CURRENT LAW, the sum of the currents at the input to the amplifier is

$$i_1 + i_2 + i_3 + i_f - i_b = 0. \tag{2.3.5}$$

Substituting Equations (2.3.1,2,3,4) into (2.3.5) gives

$$\frac{e_1 - e_b}{R_1} + \frac{e_2 - e_b}{R_2} + \frac{e_3 - e_b}{R_3} + \frac{e_o - e_b}{R_f} = i_b. \tag{2.3.6}$$

Since most analog computers are designed to operate at either ±100 volts or ±10 volts, the voltages e_1, e_2, e_3, e_b and e_o must be less than 100 volts. By definition, the output of the operational amplifier is

$$e_o = - A \, e_b \,, \tag{2.3.7}$$

where $A > 10^7$ for most amplifiers. Since $|e_o| \leq 100$ volts and by equation (2.3.7), $e_b = - e_o/A$, then $e_b < 10^{-5}$ volts. Thus, the amplifier input voltage is quite small compared to the other voltages. In fact, the input voltage of the amplifier is so small it is often considered as a "virtual" ground (i.e., 0 volts).

The input current, i_b, can be written

$$i_b = \frac{e_b}{R_i} \,,$$

where R_i is the input resistance of the operational amplifier. Since most amplifiers have $R_i > 10^6$ and $e_b < 10^{-5}$, then $i_b < 10^{-11}$. Thus, the input current can be neglected in comparison to the other currents of the circuit. Since $i_b < 10^{-11}$ and $e_b < 10^{-5}$, Equation (2.3.6) can be simplified to

$$\frac{e_1}{R_1} + \frac{e_2}{R_2} + \frac{e_3}{R_3} + \frac{e_o}{R_f} \cong 0. \tag{2.3.8}$$

Neglecting i_b and e_b and solving for e_o yields the output voltage in terms of the input voltages,

$$e_o = - \left[\frac{R_f}{R_1} e_1 + \frac{R_f}{R_2} e_2 + \frac{R_f}{R_3} e_3 \right]. \tag{2.3.9}$$

This is the basic equation for the summing amplifier. The voltages e_1, e_2, e_3 and e_o are referenced to the electrical ground (i.e., 0 volts) and may be positive or negative.

A practical understanding of the summing amplifier can be obtained from Equation (2.3.8). As long as the assumptions $i_b \cong 0$ and $e_b \cong 0$ hold, Equation (2.3.8) is approximately correct and each term of the equation represents a current into the node common to all of the resistors. Since the resistor junction is connected to the amplifier input, the voltage at the resistor junction is approximately zero or a "virtual ground." Thus, the amplifier develops an output voltage, e_o, which produces a current, e_o/R_f, through the feedback resistor to cancel the currents through R_1, R_2 and R_3. In other words, the amplifier produces a current in R_f to maintain the sum of the currents at the amplifier and resistor junction equal to zero. If one of the input voltages is increased and causes more current to flow into the junction, the output voltage of the operational amplifier decreases to produce an equal reduction in the current in R_f. Thus, the action of the operational amplifier is to maintain the sum of the currents equal to zero. For this reason, the point at the input to the amplifier (the resistor junction) is often called the "summing junction." Hence, the label, SJ, in Figure 2-3-1.

Special attention should be given to the minus sign of Equation (2.3.9). Notice that if the weighted sum of the inputs e_1, e_2 and e_3 is positive, the output will be negative. Thus, the amplifier inverts (i.e., it produces a negative output for a net positive input and a positive output for a net negative input). A common problem for beginning programmers is the failure to account for the inversion feature of the amplifiers. Most computers have the resistors already connected so that the weighting factors (gains), R_f/R_n, are fixed at 0.1, 1.0 and 10.0. On ±10 volt analog computers, the resistance values are 10 Kohms and 100 KΩ (100,000Ω). On ±100 volt analog computers, 100 KΩ and 1 MΩ resistors are provided. It should be noted that the amplifier can be used as an inverter by using only one input and a "gain" of 1.

In programming the analog computer, the resistors of the circuit in Figure 2-3-1 are seldom shown on the diagram. Instead,

the symbol of Figure 2-3-2 is used.   Notice the straight-line on
the input side of a summing amplifier   in contrast to the curved
line of the operational amplifier, shown in Figures 2-2-1 and 2-3-1.

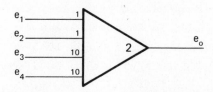

Figure 2-3-2.   Summing amplifier symbol

The numbers at each input of the symbol indicate the gain (R_f/R_n)
for that input.   The equation for the combination of gains   shown
in Figure 2-3-2 is

$$e_o = - (e_1 + e_2 + 10e_3 + 10e_4). \qquad (2.3.10)$$

Thus, the summing amplifier can be used without resorting to circuit analysis and this approach will be used throughout the book.

    To illustrate the use of the summing amplifier, assume that
the inputs x, y and z are available and it is desired   to   determine corresponding values for w using the equation

$$w = x - 2y - 10z. \qquad (2.3.11)$$

In the general form, the equation for a summing amplifier is

$$w = -(ax + by + cz). \qquad (2.3.12)$$

To implement Equation (2.3.11), the needed coefficients are a = -1,
b = 2 and c = 10.   An inverter can be utilized to provide the sign
change for the ax term.   The resulting diagram is shown in Figure
2-3-3.   Notice that the term 2y was obtained by using   two   inputs
with a gain of one.

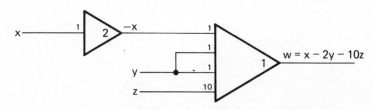

Figure 2-3-3.   Program for $w = x - 2y - 10z$

The example problem is not quite as straightforward as it might seem since nothing has been said about the range of values of the variables. Since all operational amplifiers have definite ranges of operation, the problem of limits and the scaling neces- sary to maintain linear operation are likely to occur. These problems will be discussed in Chapters 3 and 4. Also, note that input gains other than 0.1, 1.0, 2.0 and 10.0 will be needed to solve general equations. This will also be discussed later.

2.4 THE INTEGRATING AMPLIFIER

The operational amplifier can also be connected to provide integration. The circuit for the integrating amplifier is shown in Figure 2-4-1. The characteristics of the integrator can be

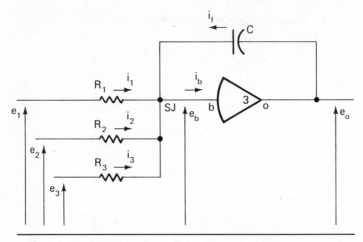

Figure 2-4-1.   The integrating amplifier

determined from the following circuit analysis. Using OHM'S LAW, the electric current in the resistors can be written

$$i_1 = \frac{e_1 - e_b}{R_1} \, , \qquad\qquad (2.4.1)$$

$$i_2 = \frac{e_2 - e_b}{R_2} \, ,$$

and

$$i_3 = \frac{e_3 - e_b}{R_3} \, . \qquad\qquad (2.4.2)$$

The current in the capacitor is

$$i_f = C \frac{d(e_o - e_b)}{dt} .$$

(2.4.3)

Writing KIRCHHOFFS CURRENT LAW at the summing junction yields

$$i_1 + i_2 + i_3 + i_f - i_b = 0.$$

(2.4.4)

In Section 2.3, it was shown that i_b and e_b can be neglected. Substitution into Equation (2.4.4) yields

$$\frac{e_1}{R_1} + \frac{e_2}{R_2} + \frac{e_3}{R_3} + C \frac{de_o}{dt} \cong 0.$$

(2.4.5)

Solving Equation (2.4.5) for e_o yields

$$\frac{de_o}{dt} = -\left[\frac{e_1}{R_1 C} + \frac{e_2}{R_2 C} + \frac{e_3}{R_3 C}\right].$$

(2.4.6)

Multiplying Equation (2.4.6) by dt and integrating gives

$$\int_{e(t_o)}^{e(t)} de_o = -\int_{t_o}^{t} \left[\frac{e_1}{R_1 C} + \frac{e_2}{R_2 C} + \frac{e_3}{R_3 C}\right] dt,$$

(2.4.7)

which yields

$$e_o(t) - e_o(t_o) = -\int_{t_o}^{t} \left[\frac{e_1}{R_1 C} + \frac{e_2}{R_2 C} + \frac{e_3}{R_3 C}\right] dt.$$

(2.4.8)

This equation can be written in the form

$$e_o = -\int_{t_o}^{t} \left[\frac{1}{R_1 C} e_1 + \frac{1}{R_2 C} e_2 + \frac{1}{R_3 C} e_3\right] dt + e_o(t_o),$$

(2.4.9)

where $e_o(t_o)$ is the initial condition on $e_o(t)$. Thus, the integrating amplifier produces the <u>negative</u> of the integral of the weighted sum of the inputs. As in the case of the summing amplifier, the integrators also exhibit sign inversion. The equation for the integrator includes a term for the output evaluated at the initial value of time. This is the familiar initial condition (IC) associated with integration and the solution of differential equations. The initial condition term is actually the initial

value of the output which is determined by the voltage (charge) on
the capacitor of the integrator at time $t = t_o$.

A practical understanding of the operation of an integrator
can be gained from Equation (2.4.5). The terms of the equation
represent currents into the summing junction. The feedback current
from the output reaches the summing junction by means of the capacitor. In order to produce a current in the capacitor branch, the
output voltage must be changing at the rate, $C(de_o/dt)$. Therefore,
in order to maintain the net summing junction currents at zero,
the amplifier output must be changing at a <u>rate</u> proportional to
the sum of input currents and inversely proportional to the capacitance. Thus, the integral of the weighted sum of the input voltages is produced.

Most computers provide the integrating capacitor in a pre-
wired integrating network and the input resistors are the same ones
provided for summing amplifier connections. Similar to the summing
amplifier, the gain or weighting factors $1/(CR_n)$ are fixed at 1.0
and 10.0. (Some computers include gains for 100 and 500). Normally,
analog computer diagrams do not show the resistors and capacitor of
Figure 2-4-1. Instead, the symbol shown in Figure 2-4-2 is used.

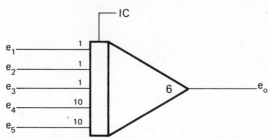

Figure 2-4-2. Integrating amplifier symbol

The numbers by each input indicate the gain $1/(CR_n)$ for that particular input. For the combination of gains shown in Figure 2-4-2,
the equation for the output is

$$e_o = -\int_{t_o}^{t} (e_1 + e_2 + e_3 + 10e_4 + 10e_5)\, dt + IC. \qquad (2.4.10)$$

In order to illustrate the use of the summing integrator, assume that values for x, y, and z are available and that it is de-

sired to determine corresponding values of w using the equation

$$w(t) = \int_{t_o}^{t} (2x - y + 10z)dt, \qquad (2.4.11)$$

where w = 1.0 at t = o. A general expression for the summing integrator is

$$w(t) = -\int_{t_o}^{t} (ax + by + cz)\,dt + w(t = o). \qquad (2.4.12)$$

For this problem, a = -2, b = 1, and c = -10. The diagram to compute values of w, from x, y and z is shown in Figure 2-4-3.

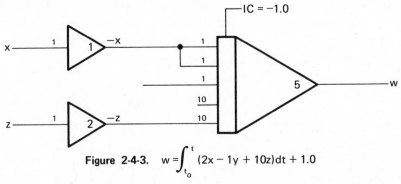

Figure 2-4-3. $w = \int_{t_o}^{t} (2x - 1y + 10z)dt + 1.0$

The inverters (1 and 2) would not be necessary if -x and -z were available. Note that although the stated initial condition on w was +1.0, the initial condition input on the integrator in Figure 2-4-3 is shown as -1.0. This is intended since the initial condition input appears inverted at the output. This inversion is associated with the amplifier and is typical of most available computers. Thus, when working with a computer that inverts the initial condition input, positive initial conditions are obtained by putting a negative value on the initial condition input. If the desired initial condition is negative, the input to the initial condition terminal must be positive.

The sign on the initial condition must be determined from the algebraic sign of the function at the integrator output and the stated initial condition of the function. For example, assume that an integrator is producing x(t) and the stated initial condition is x(0) = 4.0. The initial output of the integrator must be positive and a negative value at the initial condition input is required, IC = -4. If the initial condition were x(0) = -4.0, then the initial condition input must be positive,

IC = 4. However, if the output of the integrator is -x(t) and the stated initial condition is x(0) = 6, then -x(0) = -6. The initial value at the integrator output must be negative and therefore, the initial condition input must be positive, IC = 6. If the integrator output is -x(t) and the given initial value is x(0) = -6, then -x(0) = 6. The initial value at the integrator must be positive and the initial condition input must be negative, IC = -6. Before leaving this example, it is important to note that there are several other programs for Equation (2.4.11). Figure 2-4-4 illustrates the use of a summing amplifier before the integrator. The same result can be achieved by the diagram shown in Figure 2-4-5. The last solution has an advantage over the others since it requires only two operational amplifiers.

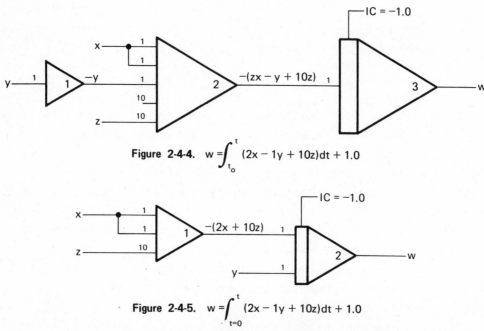

Figure 2-4-4. $w = \int_{t_o}^{t} (2x - 1y + 10z)dt + 1.0$

Figure 2-4-5. $w = \int_{t=0}^{t} (2x - 1y + 10z)dt + 1.0$

In addition to learning how to realize mathematical expressions with summing and integrating amplifiers, the student should become familiar with the action of an integrator on certain common waveforms. For example, a sudden change in the value of the integrator input [i.e., a step input, Figure 2-4-6(a)] will yield a ramp (i.e., a steadily increasing output). The slope of the output ramp will be equal to the <u>negative</u> of the product of the magnitude of the step change and the gain of the integrator. Thus, a positive step input will yield a negative ramp at the output as shown in Figure 2-4-6(c). The sign change is due to the inversion of the amplifier. The integrator and waveforms for this discussion are shown in Figure 2-4-6. If the output of the integrator of Figure 2-4-6 were fed into another integrator, the output would be a parabola with positive values.

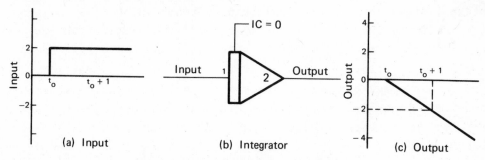

Figure 2-4-6. Step response of an integrator

The action of an integrator on the pulse input of Figure 2-4-7(a) is shown in Figure 2-4-7(c). Note the effect of the initial condition.

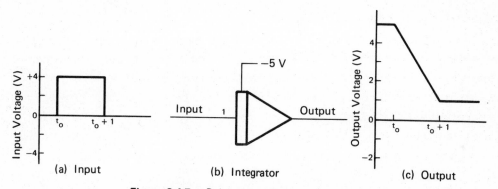

Figure 2-4-7. Pulse response of an integrator

The presence of the independent variable time, t, and the initial value of the output at t_o in the equation for an integrator imply the ability to start and stop the process of integration. Analog computers provide special circuits to place the required initial condition on the integrating capacitor and keep it there until the operator starts integration at the desired time, t_o. The state for setting the intial condition is called the "reset" or "initial condition" mode. Integration is

initiated by placing the computer in the "operate" mode.   The
mode of the integrators is controlled by a "mode control" switch.
In addition to the "reset" or "initial condition" position, most
computers provide a "hold" mode which stops the process of integration and "freezes" time.   The operator can either continue the
problem by going back to the "operate" mode or initiate a new run
by placing the mode control switch in "reset" or "IC." Most computers include an automatic switching network which will switch
back and forth from "reset" to "operate." The repeatative cycling
from "IC" to "operate" repeats a solution with sufficient speed
to provide oscilloscope display of the results.   In addition,
some larger computers permit automatic mode control from a digital
computer.   These features will be discussed in more detail later.

Earlier in this section, it was stated that most analog computers provide fixed gain ratios of 0.1, 1.0 and 10:0.   However,
in the example problems and in practice, the necessity of having
other values of gain is obvious.   This requirement can be   met
through the use of potentiometers and will be discussed in   the
next section.

2.5 POTENTIOMETERS

In order to provide the variety of gain ratios encountered
in actual problems, potentiometers are included in the basic components.   Figure 2-5-1 illustrates the   two   circuits   for potentiometers.   Physically, the potentiometer is a resistor, R_p in
Figure 2-5-1(a) and (b), with an extra contact that can be moved
along the resistor.   The moveable contact, indicated by the arrow
in Figure 2-5-1 (a) and (b), is often called the "wiper arm." The

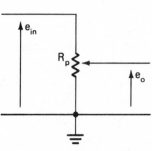

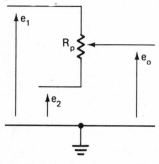

(a) Grounded potentiometer   (b) Ungrounded potentiometer

Figure 2-5-1.   Potentiometer circuits

arrow head should <u>not</u> be confused with a direction of electric current flow. In part (a) of Figure 2-5-1, one side of the potentiometer is connected to ground (0 volts) and the equation for the output, in terms of the input is

$$e_o = K \, e_{in}. \tag{2.5.1}$$

In equation (2.5.1), K is the relative setting of the wiper arm of the potentiometer and is in the range $0 < K < 1$. Thus, the output is a fraction of the input. In part (b) of Figure 2-5-1, the circuit illustrates an ungrounded potentiometer. The equation relating the output to the input is

$$e_o = K(e_1 - e_2) + e_2, \tag{2.5.2}$$

where K is in the range $0 < K < 1$.

Equations (2.5.1) and (2.5.2) do not take into account the effect of a load connected to the output of the potentiometers. When the output of a potentiometer is connected to another computing component, the effective value of K is reduced. For example, consider the potentiometer of Figure 2-5-1(a), with no load on the output and the wiper arm of the potentiometer set midway, $K = 0.5$ and the output is one-half of the input. Thus, the multiplying factor of the potentiometer is 0.5. If the output of the potentiometer is then connected to another computing element, the effective K is less than 0.5 and the output is less than one-half of the input. To avoid this problem, potentiometers <u>must be</u> set to the desired value by monitoring the output with the output <u>connected</u> to the appropriate computing element. To repeat an important point, potentiometers should be set <u>after</u> they are connected to the rest of the computing elements. The term potentiometer is often abbreviated to "pot" and the two terms will be used interchangeably.

As with the summing and integrating amplifiers, the circuit for the potentiometer is not drawn on computer diagrams. The standard symbols are shown in Figure 2-5-2. The number inside of

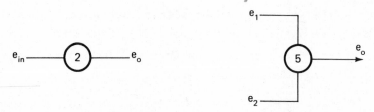

Figure 2-5-2. Potentiometer symbols

the circle is an identification number for the potentiometer. The
setting of the pot (i.e., the multiplying fraction) is usually
written near the symbol on the computer diagram.

     To illustrate the use of potentiometers, consider the equa-
tion $w = x-2y-5z$. A computer diagram implementing the equation
is shown in Figure 2-5-3. In Figure 2-5-3, the amplifier gains are

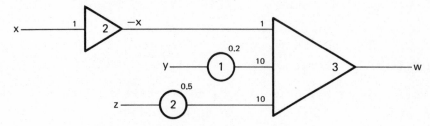

Figure 2-5-3.   Diagram for $w = x - 2y - 5z$

standard values of 1 and 10. The effective gain for a pot at the
input of an amplifier is the product of the pot setting and the
input gain of the amplifier. For example, the y input of Figure
2-5-3 has an effective gain of $(0.2)(10) = 2.0$. Again, note that
the pots should be set after they have been connected to the amplifier inputs. The use of potentiometers with an integrator is
shown in Figure 2-5-4.

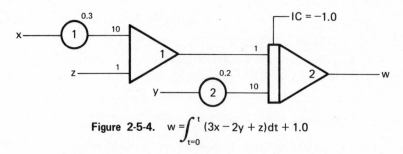

Figure 2-5-4. $w = \int_{t=0}^{t} (3x - 2y + z)dt + 1.0$

     Since the precision of most analog computers is three sig-
nificant figures, an accurate means of setting the potentiometers,

under loaded conditions, must be provided. The most convenient
method utilizes a precision, digital voltmeter. The reference
voltage (±10v or ±100v) is applied to the input of the pot. The
loaded output is monitored with the digital voltmeter (DVM) and
the wiper arm of the potentiometer moved to the desired setting.
Another approach uses a 10-turn, calibrated, precision potentiometer or a switchable resistor network as a reference for a
"null" circuit similar to Figure 2-5-5. The precision pot is
set to the desired ratio (K) and the potentiometer to be set is
turned until the meter indicates a null (i.e., zero current).
Since no current flows in the meter at null, this enables the
potentiometer to be set with only its operating load current
present. This is very important. Assume that a pot is set
while its output is connected to an amplifier input with a gain
of 1. The load on the pot is the 100 KΩ input resistor. If the
output of the pot is then moved to an amplifier input with a
gain of 10, the load on the pot is 10 KΩ. The change in load
resistance causes an increase in the output current of the pot
and hence, a decrease in the effective pot setting.

Some computers provide servo-set potentiometers which are
turned to the null point by small servo-motors and do not require

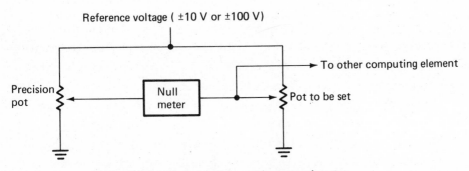

Figure 2-5-5. Null circuit for setting potentiometer

operator intervention. Also, digital/analog converter potentiometers can be set under the control of a digital computer. This
is a necessary feature for efficient parameter search studies and
for digital control of analog simulation and computation. However,
these features are not normally available on small analog computers.

2.6 CONTROL AND SET-UP

The set-up and operation of summing amplifiers, integrators, and potentiometers would be quite time consuming without some specialized control circuits. Since a number of different schemes are in existence, the actual details will not be discussed here and the reader is referred to the operating manuals for the specific machine to be used. Most computers include special techniques for the following functions:

Balancing the Amplifiers; a process for adjusting an amplifier to produce zero volts at the output when the input is at zero volts. Any unbalance present introduces error and the amplifier balance should be checked periodically, since amplifiers "drift" out of balance. Modern solid - state amplifiers have excellent drift characteristics and it is not a serious problem. Usually, all that is necessary is a check on amplifier balance and adjustments are seldom needed.

Monitoring the output of amplifiers; a means of connecting a built-in voltmeter, a recorder, or an oscilloscope to the output of a specific amplifier. The amplifier monitor switch is convenient for selecting a particular amplifier to record the solution to the problem under study. It is also useful for setting-up a problem.

Setting Potentiometers; pot setting is an important phase of programming and most computers provide one of the methods discussed previously. Specific details are given in the operation manual for each type of computer.

Integrator Switching Network; a most important feature of the analog computer. As discussed earlier, the operation of integrators is controlled by the "reset-hold-operate" selector. The nomenclature refers to the integrating network shown in Figure 2-4-1. When the selector is in "reset," the integrating capacitor is being charged to the voltage level required by the initial condition on a particular variable. When the selector is in "hold," the amplifier input is disconnected from the input summing junction and the capacitor and amplifier are holding the voltage level that was present at the output when the selector was moved to "hold." When the selector is in "operate," the summing junction is connected to the amplifier input and the amplifier operates as an integrator. Thus, the "hold" feature enables the operator to interrupt the simulation and appraise values of problem variables. Following the interruption, the operator can either "reset" and start a new run or continue the same run by switching back to "operate." Thus, the operator can continue the problem as if no interruption had occurred. This ability to "freeze" time is a valuable asset of the analog computer. Most computers include circuits for controlling the mode ("operate", "hold", or "reset") on all integrators simultaneously or individually.

Amplifier Overload Indication; provided to monitor the computing amplifiers to make certain they are operating in the linear range. This is important since overloading an amplifier or exceeding the normal range of operation can cause a reduction in amplifier gain, and possibly a serious "offset" or unbalance. Under these conditions, the assumptions ($i_f \cong 0$, $e_b \cong 0$) are no longer true and the amplifier is not producing an accurate sum or integral of the inputs. The overload indicators are usually lights (an audible alarm on some computers) which indicate a particular amplifier has exceeded the normal voltage range (± 10 or ± 100 volts) or the allowable current level.

Many other convenient features have been engineered into current analog computers. Most machines have removable patch panels. This enables an operator to patch a problem prior to putting it on the machine. It also provides a means of saving a program while the computer is being used for other problems. The layout of the patch panels is most convenient since elements used together most often are grouped. Also, frequently used connections, such as connecting an operational amplifier as a summing or integrating amplifier can be made by inserting a single patch plug.

Other features are available on most analog computers. However, since it is desired to introduce the subject gradually, further discussion will be deferred until later in the book.

2.7 PROBLEMS FOR CHAPTER 2

Problems covering the material of this chapter are identified by section.

2.2.1 Assume an operational amplifier gain of -2×10^7 and calculate the input, e_b, required to produce +10 volts at the output.

2.2.2 For the amplifier of Problem 2.2.1, calculate the output voltage, e_o, for an input, e_b, of 0.001 volts.

2.3.1 Using the equation for a summing amplifier, determine the value of the input resistors needed to produce $e_o = - (e_1 + e_2 + 10 \ e_3)$ if the feedback resistor is 100 KΩ(100,000Ω).

2.3.2 Using the equation for a summing amplifier, assume $R_1 = R_2 = 100$ KΩ and $R_3 = 10$ KΩ. Determine the equation for e_o in terms of e_1, e_2 and e_3 if $R_f = 10$ KΩ.

2.3.3 In Section 2.3 a gain of two was obtained by connecting together two input gains of one. Verify this using $R_1 = 100$ KΩ, $R_2 = 100$ KΩ and $R_f = 100$ KΩ.

2.3.4 Develop a computer diagram to solve the equation $w = 2 \ x + y - 10z$ if $-x$, y and z are available.

2.3.5 For the diagram shown, determine the output voltage w.

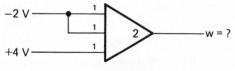

Figure 2-7-1.

2.3.6 Assume that the sum of the currents into the summing junction due to input voltages is greater than the feedback current that can be produced by the maximum amplifier output. Under these conditions, what happens to the summing amplifier?

2.4.1   Draw a computer diagram to solve the equation

$$w = \int_{t_o}^{t} (2x - 10y + z)dt + w(t{=}o)$$ if x, -y, and

z are available and if the initial condition on
w is 2.0.

2.4.2   For the diagram shown, write an equation for the
output, w(t).

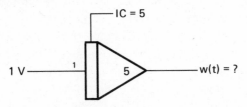

Figure 2-7-2.

2.4.3   Sketch the output response of an integrator with
a gain of 1.0 if the input is a 3—volt pulse
lasting 2 seconds.   Assume zero initial conditions.

2.4.4   Repeat Problem 3.4.3 with an initial condition of
-2 volts.

2.4.5   If the input resistors are 100 KΩ, what value of
capacitance is required to give an integrator
gain of 1.0?

2.4.6   If the capacitor determined in Problem 3-4.5 is
used in the feedback, what "gain" is produced
if a 10 KΩ resistor is used in the input?

2.4.7   If the linear range is defined to be ±10 volts,
how long can an integrator with a gain of 10
operate with a 1.0 volt input?   What happens
for values of time exceeding the answer for
part one?

2.4.8   Sketch w(t) for the diagram shown.

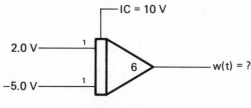

Figure 2-7-3.

2.5.1   For the diagram shown, determine the output, w.

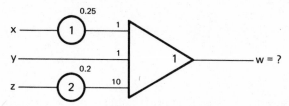

Figure 2-7-4.

2.5.2   For the diagram shown, determine the output
        equation, w(t).

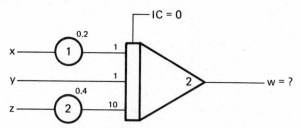

Figure 2-7-5.

2.5.3   For the diagram shown, determine the output, w.

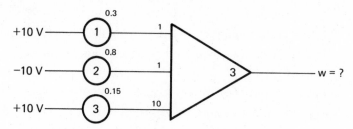

Figure 2-7-6.

2.5.4   For the diagram shown, determine the output
        equation and sketch the output versus time.

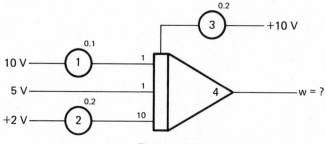

Figure 2-7-7.

2.5.5 For the diagram shown, determine the equation for the output.

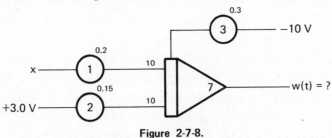

Figure 2-7-8.

2.5.6 For the diagram shown, determine the equation for the output.

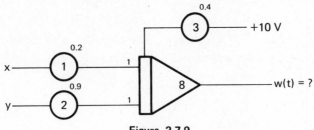

Figure 2-7-9.

2.5.7 Draw a computer diagram to solve the equation w = 2x + 4y - z, if -x, y, and z are available. Comment on the limits of values.

2.6.1 Using the instruction manual for an available analog computer, determine the procedure for balancing the amplifiers. Were adjustments required?

2.6.2 Referring to the instruction manual for an available computer, set pot 1 to 0.300, pot 2 to 0.800 and pot 3 to 0.150. Connect the plus reference to the input of pots 1 and 2. Connect the negative reference to the input of pot 3. Connect the output of pots 1 and 2 to amplifier gains of 1 on amplifier 1. Connect the output of pot 3 to a gain of 10 on amplifier 1. Use the amplifier monitoring system to check the output of the amplifier. Does the result check with an analytical solution? Reset the pots to the required values and check the output again, it should be within 0.005 volts of the analytic solution and demonstrate the necessity of setting the pots <u>after</u> patching.

2.6.3   With the analog computer in the reset mode, connect the positive reference voltage to the input of a pot and patch the output of the pot into an integrating amplifier gain of 1. Set the pot to 0.100 and use the amplifier selector system to monitor the amplifier output with a voltmeter or a recorder. Switch into the operate mode and observe the output. How many seconds before the amplifier output reaches the negative reference? How long before the overload indicator flashes?

2.8   REFERENCES FOR CHAPTER 2

(1) Howe, R. M.: <u>Design Fundamentals of Analog Computer Components</u>, Van Nostrand Co., Inc., New York, 1961.

(2) Korn, G. A. and T. M. Korn: <u>Electronic Analog and Hybrid Computers</u>, McGraw-Hill Book Co., Inc., New York, 1960.

(3) Jackson, A. S.: <u>Analog Computation</u>, McGraw-Hill Book Co., Inc., New York, 1960.

(4) Mandi, M.: <u>Fundamentals of Electronic Computers</u>: <u>Digital and Analog</u>, Prentice-Hall, Inc., Englewood Cliffs, N.J., 1967.

(5) James, M. L., G. M. Smith and J. C. Wolford: <u>Analog Computer Simulation of Engineering Systems</u>, International Textbook Co., Scranton, Pa., 1966.

(6) Blum, J. J.: <u>Introduction to Analog Computation</u>, Harcourt, Brace & World, Inc., New York, 1969.

(7) Rekoff, M. G., Jr.: <u>Analog Computer Programming</u>, Charles E. Merrill Books Inc., Columbus, Ohio, 1967.

(8) Hyndman, D. E.: <u>Analog and Hybrid Computing</u>, Pergamon Press, New York, 1970.

(9) Hausner, A.: <u>Analog and Analog/Hybrid Computer Programming</u>, Prentice-Hall, Inc., Englewood Cliffs, N.J., 1971.

(10) Johnson, C. L.: <u>Analog Computer Techniques</u>, McGraw-Hill Book Co., Inc., New York, 1956.

(11) Rummer, D. I.: <u>Introduction to Analog Computer Programming</u>, Holt, Rinehart and Winston, Inc., New York, 1969.

3

Analog Simulation of Linear Systems

3.1 INTRODUCTION

In this chapter, the procedure for programming the analog computer to solve linear, ordinary differential equations is introduced. The techniques presented here will serve as background for time and magnitude scaling discussions in Chapter 4 and for nonlinear equations in Chapter 5. The methods developed in this chapter will also be utilized for digital simulation in Chapter 14. The techniques will be illustrated with several problems and the emphasis is on a gradual introduction to analog computer programming. Additional material can be found in the references at the end of Chapter 2.

3.2 BASIC PROGRAMMING TECHNIQUES

The ease with which the analog computer can be programmed to solve differential equations was the reason for its widespread use and rapid growth. In this section, the discussions will be restricted to linear, ordinary differential equations with constant coefficients. However, the methods developed here are basic to analog and digital simulation and will be extended in later chapters.

In order to develop the basic programming technique, consider a differential equation of order n

$$a_o \frac{d^n x}{dt^n} + a_1 \frac{d^{n-1} x}{dt^{n-1}} + \ldots + a_n x = b_o f(t), \qquad (3.2.1)$$

where the coefficients $a_o, \ldots, a_n$ and b_o are constant. The first step of the procedure is to solve the equation for the highest-order derivative, $d^n x/dt^n$, in terms of the other derivatives and the forcing function $f(t)$ as shown in Equation (3.2.2),

$$\frac{d^n x}{dt^n} = - c_1 \frac{d^{n-1} x}{dt^{n-1}} - \ldots - c_n x + d_o f(t), \qquad (3.2.2)$$

where $c_1 = a_1/a_o, \ldots, c_n = a_n/a_o$ and $d_o = b_o/a_o$.

The next step is to assume that the highest-order derivative is known and available as the input to an integrating amplifier. Under these circumstances, the output of that integrator would be the integral of the input or the derivative $- d^{n-1} x/dt^{n-1}$. This is illustrated in Figure 3-2-1. Notice the inversion of the

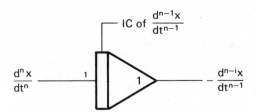

Figure 3-2-1.   Integration of $\dfrac{d^n x}{dt^n}$

integrator and the need to supply the initial condition for the output of the integrator.

To continue the process, the output of the first integrator is fed into a second integrator to produce $d^{n-2} x/dt^{n-2}$. This procedure is repeated until the dependent variable, x, is at the output of an integrator. To complete the process, the outputs of the integrators producing the derivatives of x are summed by a

summing amplifier (weighted by the appropriate coefficients) to
produce the highest-order derivative according to Equation (3.2.2).

To illustrate the procedure, consider the first-order differential equation

$$\frac{dx}{dt} + ax = f(t), \quad x(0) = b, \tag{3.2.3}$$

where a and b are constants and the time dependence of x (i.e.,
x(t))is understood. According to the procedure, solving for
the highest-order derivative yields

$$\frac{dx}{dt} = -ax + f(t). \tag{3.2.4}$$

Now assume dx/dt is available at the input of an integrator.
Since the output of an integrator is minus the integral of its
input, the output of the integrator would be -x. This is illustrated in Figure 3-2-2. According to Equation (3.2.4), the term

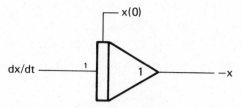

Figure 3-2-2. Integration of $\frac{dx}{dt}$

dx/dt at the input to the integrator can be produced by combining
the forcing function, f(t), with -x multiplied by a. This can be
accomplished by a summing amplifier as shown in Figure 3-2-3. By

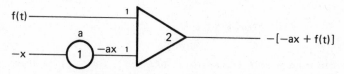

Figure 3-2-3. Summing $-ax + f(t)$

Equation (3.2.4), the output of the summing amplifier is equal
to -dx/dt. Therefore, it is necessary to include an inverter to
change -dx/dt to dx/dt. The combined computer diagram is shown
in Figure 3-2-4. Figure 3-2-4 illustrates how the assumed deri-

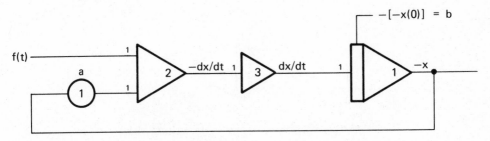

Figure 3-2-4. Computer diagram for $\dfrac{dx}{dt} = -ax + f(t)$

vative, dx/dt, is integrated to produce -x which is combined with
f(t) to produce -dx/dt. An inverter then supplies the assumed
value of dx/dt. In order to complete the process, the appropriate initial condition must be supplied to the integrator.   In
this case, the initial value is x(0) = b, since the integrator is
producing -x, the value of the integrator output should be -b
initially. However, the initial condition is inverted on most
computers. Therefore, the initial condition supplied to the IC
input of the integrator is +b as shown in Figure 3-2-4.

   In the interest of amplifier economy, a summing integrator
can be used to add f(t) to -ax and integrate simultaneously. In
order to illustrate this approach, multiply both sides of Equation
(3.2.4) by dt and integrate

$$\int dx = \int [-ax + f(t)]dt, \tag{3.2.5}$$

which is

$$x(t) - x(0) = \int_{t_o}^{t} [-ax + f(t)]dt. \tag{3.2.6}$$

Rearranging Equation (3.2.6) in the form

$$x(t) = \int_{t_o}^{t} [-ax + f(t)]dt + x(0), \tag{3.2.7}$$

yields an equation in the form of the summing integrator of Equation (2.4.9). Thus, the single summing amplifier of Figure 3-2-5
is all that is needed to solve the simple first-order equation.

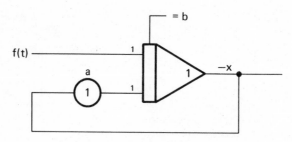

Figure 3-2-5. Solving $\dfrac{dx}{dt} = -ax + f(t)$

Since fewer amplifiers are required, the computer diagram of Figure 3-2-5 is preferred over Figure 3-2-4.

As a second illustration of the procedure, consider the second-order differential equation

$$\ddot{x} + a\dot{x} + bx = f(t), \tag{3.2.8}$$

where a and b are constants and x_o and $\dot{x}_o$ are initial conditions. The dot notation, $\dot{x} = dx/dt$ and $\ddot{x} = d^2x/dt^2$, is used here and will be used throughout this text whenever it is convenient. The first step is the solution of the equation for the highest-order derivative,

$$\ddot{x} = - (a\dot{x} + bx - f(t)). \tag{3.2.9}$$

Now, $\ddot{x}$ is assumed to be available at the input to an integrator and repeated integration is used to produce the dependent variable x. This is illustrated in Figure 3-2-6. Again, note the inversion that occurs. Also, it should be noted that the initial

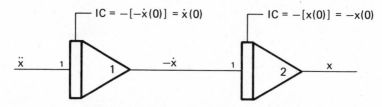

Figure 3-2-6.   Repeated integration for x

conditions x(0) and $\dot{x}$(0) must be known. This is not a restriction on the method since two initial conditions must be known before the differential equation can be solved by any method. On most computers, the initial condition is also inverted as discussed in Chapter 2.

The next step of the procedure is to sum the output of integrators 1 and 2, along with the forcing function, f(t), to yield $\ddot{x}$ as given by Equation (3.2.9). This is identical to the application of the summing amplifier illustrated in Chapter 2 and is shown in Figure 3-2-7. Since the second step of the procedure

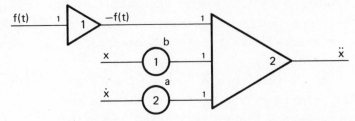

Figure 3-2-7. Program for $\ddot{x} = -[a\dot{x} + bx - f(t)]$

gave $\dot{x}$ and x from $\ddot{x}$ and the third step yields $\ddot{x}$ from $\dot{x}$ and x, the two can be combined to solve the equation. The combination of these two steps is illustrated in Figure 3-2-8. In combining

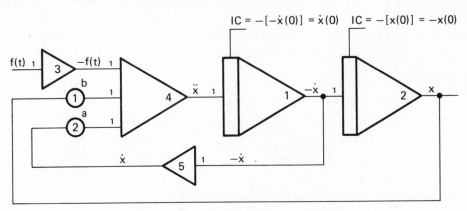

Figure 3-2-8. Program for $\ddot{x} + a\dot{x} + bx = f(t)$

Figures 3-2-6 and 3-2-7, the only extra component necessary is the inverter (amplifier number 5) which inverts $-\dot{x}$ to give $\dot{x}$ as an input to the summing amplifier.

There are several things that should be noted in Figure 3-2-8. First, there are two loops in the figure and both loops consist of an odd number of amplifiers (3). The inner loop is identified by amplifiers 4, 1 and 5. The outer loop consists of amplifiers 4, 1 and 2. Most, but <u>not all</u>, loops in analog computer programs will have an odd number of amplifiers. The reason for this is the inversion associated with operational

amplifiers.   An even number of inversions in a loop would yield
positive feedback and often lead to instability unless there   is
an off-setting signal summed into the loop.   Programs exhibiting
this instability usually oscillate and eventually saturate   the
amplifiers.   As pointed out earlier, most computers have warning
lights or alarms to indicate when the output of any amplifier has
exceeded the linear range of operation.   While an odd number   of
amplifiers in a loop is not always necessary, it is a good point
to double check.

Another point that should be made from Figure 3-2-8 is   the
input/output relationship.   There are an even number   of amplifiers (4) between the input, f(t),   and the output, x.   An even
number of inversions yields the same algebraic sign.   Therefore,
for inputs such as a positive step, f(t)= a constant, the steady-
state value of the output should likewise be positive.   Such
relationships are very useful when checking the   program   for
errors.   Note that this relationship does not hold during the
transient portion of the response since the values of $\dot{x}$ and x
are likely to affect the instantaneous value of the output.

3.3   A NUMERICAL EXAMPLE

To illustrate the procedure of the previous section, consider the numerical example described by the equation,

$$\ddot{x} + 2\dot{x} + 4x = f(t), \qquad\qquad (3.3.1)$$

where $\dot{x}(0) = 0$ and $x(0) = 2$. Solving for the highest-order derivative gives the equation,

$$\ddot{x} = - [2\dot{x} + 4x - f(t)]. \qquad\qquad (3.3.2)$$

Programming the repeated integrations and the summation as in the
previous section gives the program shown in Figure 3-3-1.   By
switching the computer from the "initial condition" mode to the
"operate" mode, the integrators begin operating   and   produce a
solution.   Recordings of x and $\dot{x}$ for f(t) = 0, (the homogeneous
case) are shown in Figure 3-3-2.   There were no units (e.g.,
meters, meters/sec) assigned to Equation (3.3.1).   Therefore, the

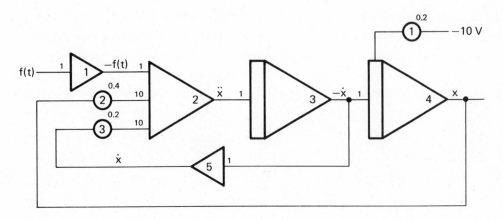

Figure 3-3-1. Program for $\ddot{x} + 2\dot{x} + 4x = f(t)$

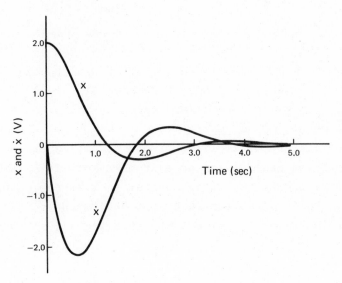

Figure 3-3-2. x and $\dot{x}$ for f(t) = 0

solution is in terms of problem "units" with a 1–volt per unit analogy. Additional details on scaling will be presented in Chapter 4. Notice that when the slope of x is negative, corresponding values of $\dot{x}$ are negative. Also, a positive slope on x yields positive values of $\dot{x}$.

In order to gain additional insight from this illustration, consider the response of the system to a forcing function. If the initial conditions are both zero, $\dot{x}(0) = x(0) = 0$, and f(t)

is a step of 4 units, f(t) = 4, the values of x and x of Figure
3-3-3 are obtained. The input step of 4 can be obtained from
the reference voltage and a pot set to 0.4 at the input of Amp.
No. 1 in Figure 3-3-1. It is important to note that the computer could be switched into the "hold" mode at any point in the

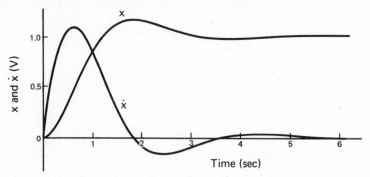

Figure 3-3-3.   x and x for f(t) = 4 with x(0) = x(0) = 0

solution to check problem variables. The solution can be continued by returning to the "operate" mode. If desired, the
problem could be started from zero again by going to the "reset"
mode before returning to "operate."

In the interest of amplifier economy, amplifier number one
can be eliminated if -f(t) is used in place of +f(t). An alternate way of saving an amplifier generates -x at the output in
place of x. The program for this approach is shown in Figure
3-3-4 and illustrates the effect of reversing all algebraic signs.

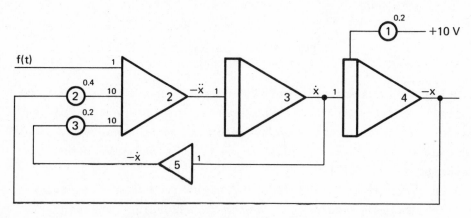

Figure 3-3-4.   Program for $\ddot{x} + 2\dot{x} + 4x = f(t)$

While the solution x(t) is the desired solution, obtaining -x(t)
is not a handicap since most recorders have a provision for
inverting the signal. This is a good point to again note the
inversion associated with each amplifier as well as the initial
condition on most computers. If the integrator is producing the
positive value of a variable, the initial condition must be the
negative of the initial value of that variable. If an integrator
is producing the negative value of a variable, the initial condition should have the same sign as the initial value of that variable.

In order to illustrate the necessary connections for a
forcing function and specific initial conditions, the same equation, $\ddot{x} + 2\dot{x} + 4x = f(t)$, will be programmed for x(0) = -3,
$\dot{x}(0)$ = -1, and f(t) = -5. The resulting computer program is
shown in Figure 3-3-5.

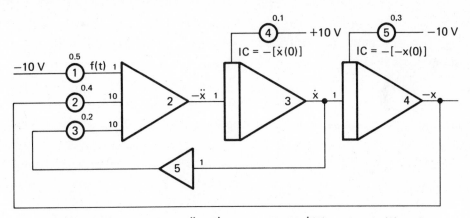

Figure 3-3-5. Program for $\ddot{x} + 2\dot{x} + 4x = -5$ with $\dot{x}(0) = -1$ and x(0) = -3

In terms of the discussion of analogies in Chapter 1, 1 volt
at the output of amplifier 4 is analogous to -1 unit of the
variable x. For example, if x is in meters, an output of 1 volt
corresponds to a negative displacement of 1 meter. In a similar
manner, 1 volt at the output of amplifier 3 is equivalent to 1
unit of $\dot{x}$. Thus, if x is a displacement measured in meters, $\dot{x}$
is velocity in meters per second and an output of 1 volt is
analogous to a velocity of 1 meter per second. Actually, choosing
the analogy is a process called scaling which is presented in
detail in the next chapter.

3.4 USING THE SUMMING INTEGRATOR

In Section 3.2, considerable amplifier economy resulted when the summing integrator was utilized in the solution of the first-order equation. In a similar fashion, the summing integrator can be used in the solution of the second-order equation. Instead of summing for $\ddot{x}$ and then integrating as in Figure 3-2-8, the summation and integration is combined in a summing integrator. The variable $\ddot{x}$ does not appear in the program.

In order to develop this approach, again consider the equation

$$\ddot{x} + a\dot{x} + bx = f(t). \qquad (3.4.1)$$

First, solve for the highest-order derivative,

$$\ddot{x} = - [a\dot{x} + bx - f(t)]. \qquad (3.4.2)$$

Next, integrate Equation (3.4.2) to form the equation of a summing integrator,

$$\int \ddot{x}\, dt = \dot{x} = - \int [a\dot{x} + bx - f(t)]\, dt. \qquad (3.4.3)$$

Equation (3.4.3) can be programmed as shown in Figure 3-4-1. Now,

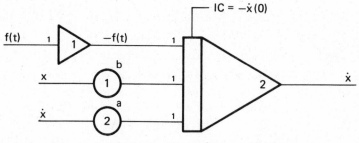

Figure 3-4-1. Program for $\dot{x} = -\displaystyle\int_{t_o}^{t} [a\dot{x} + bx - f(t)]\, dt + x(0)$

integrate $\dot{x}$ to get $-x$, invert $-x$ to x and connect as shown in Figure 3-4-2. The program of Figure 3-4-2 offers the immediate advantage of one less amplifier than the corresponding program of Figure 3-2-8. The only disadvantage is that the highest-order derivative no longer appears directly in the program.

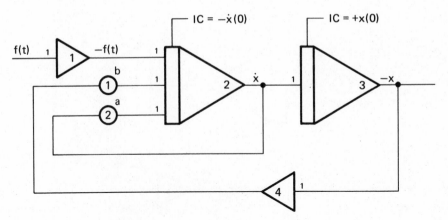

Figure 3-4-2. Program for $\ddot{x} + a\dot{x} + bx = f(t)$

An additional amplifier can be eliminated by changing the algebraic sign of Equation (3.4.3)

$$-\dot{x} = -\int [-a\overset{\circ}{x} - bx + f(t)]dt. \qquad (3.4.4)$$

This equation is programmed in Figure 3-4-3. Integrating $-\dot{x}$ to

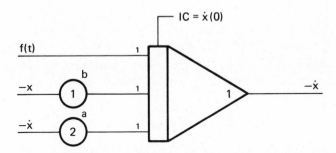

Figure 3-4-3. Program for $-\dot{x} = -\int_{t_o}^{t} [-a\dot{x} - bx + f(t)]\,dt + \dot{x}(0)$

get x and connecting the loops yields the program shown in Figure 3-4-4. This program requires fewer amplifiers (2) than the corresponding diagram of Figure 3-2-8. However, the highest-order derivative, $\ddot{x}$, is not available to be monitored. Also, if +x is not required, one amplifier could be eliminated from Figure 3-2-8 by changing algebraic signs. The amplifier inverting f(t) could also be eliminated from Figure 3-2-8 by

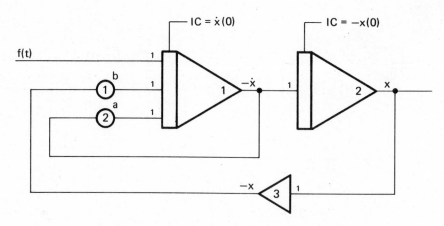

Figure 3-4-4. Program for $\ddot{x} + a\dot{x} + bx = f(t)$

putting pot 1 at the input of amplifier 5 and then using
amplifier 5 to sum f(t) and -a$\dot{x}$. However, amplifier 5 would
have to be a summing amplifier instead of an inverter.

3.5 NUMERICAL EXAMPLE

The example problem of Figure 3-3-5 can also be programmed
utilizing a summing integrator. In this case, the equation for
the summing integrator is

$$-\dot{x} = -\int[-2\dot{x} - 4x + f(t)]dt, \qquad\qquad (3.5.1)$$

where f(t) = -5.0, $\dot{x}(0)$ = 1.0 and x(0) = -3.0. The resulting
program is shown in Figure 3-5-1. The solution is similar to
the response curves shown in Figures 3-3-2 and 3-3-3.

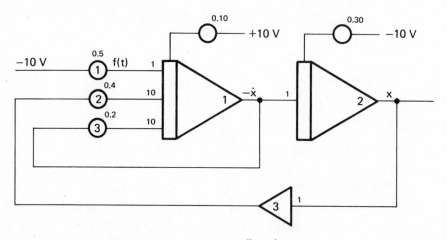

Figure 3-5-1. Program for $\ddot{x} + 2\dot{x} + 4x = 5.0$

3.6 THE GENERALIZED, LINEAR, SECOND-ORDER DIFFERENTIAL EQUATION

Since many disciplines use the generalized form of the linear, second-order differential equation, programs for solving it will be presented in this section. The equation is usually written

$$\ddot{x} + 2\delta\omega_n\dot{x} + \omega_n^2 x = \omega_n^2 f(t), \tag{3.6.1}$$

where δ is defined as the damping ratio and ω_n is the undamped natural frequency[1]. The damped natural frequency of oscillation is $\omega = \omega_n\sqrt{1 - \delta^2}$.

From the previous sections, it should be obvious that several programs to solve Equation (3.6.1) could be developed. Only two will be shown here; one with $\ddot{x}$ appearing directly in the program and another using the summing integrator approach. The programs are shown in Figures 3-6-1 and 3-6-2. Note that both programs have several pots for ω_n. In order to conserve potentiometers and simplify the process of setting and changing parameters, the function of these pots should be combined whenever possible. This is left as an exercise at the end of this chapter. Another interesting variation for the program is to separate δ and ω_n as pot settings and have one pot for damping ratio ,δ. This is left as an exercise in Section 3.12.

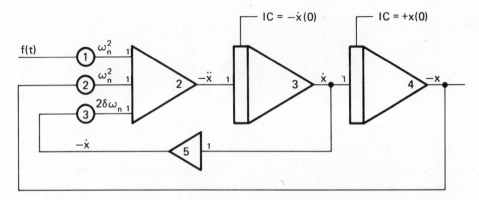

Figure 3-6-1. Program for $\ddot{x} + 2\delta\omega_n\dot{x} + \omega_n^2 x = \omega_n^2 f(t)$

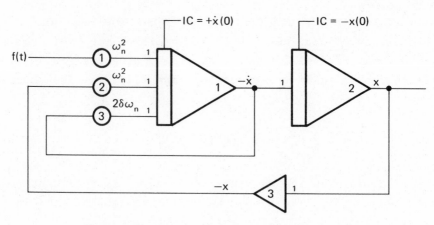

Figure 3-6-2. Program for $\ddot{x} + 2\delta\omega_n\dot{x} + \omega_n^2 x = \omega_n^2 f(t)$

The response of the generalized, linear, second-order system to a step input is frequently used to characterize a second-order system. A thorough knowledge of the effect of various values of δ are ω_n on the general response can be extended to a specific system by determining the δ and ω_n for the system under study. In order to develop an appreciation for δ and ω_n, consider the unit step response curves of Figure 3-6-3. The figure contains plots of the output, x, for $\omega_n = 1.0$ and several values of δ.

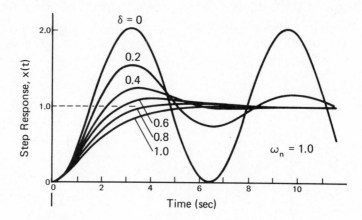

Figure 3-6-3. Step response, x(t), for different damping ratios, δ

For $\delta=0$, the response is sinusoidal with a maximum magnitude of twice the steady-state value. As the damping ratio, δ, is increased, the system becomes more damped (i.e., the overshoot decreases). For $\delta=1$, there is no overshoot. If, the damping ratio, δ, is increased further, the system exhibits even more damping. The system is said to be "overdamped" for $\delta>1$ and "underdamped" for $0<\delta<1$.

By setting the pots for $\delta=.3$ and recording the step response, x, for several values of ω_n, the effect of ω_n can be determined. This is shown in Figure 3-6-4. Increasing the

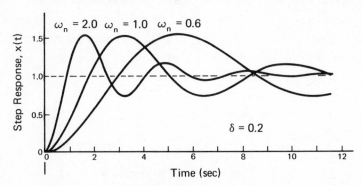

Figure 3-6-4. Step response, x(t) for differnet values of ω_n

undamped natural frequency causes the system to oscillate at a higher frequency. The actual frequency of the oscillations is $\omega = \omega_n \sqrt{1 - \delta^2}$.

In order to illustrate the use of δ and ω_n to characterize the response of a particular system, consider the equation for the numerical example of Section 3.3 which is repeated here for convenience

$$\ddot{x} + 2\dot{x} + 4x = f(t). \tag{3.6.2}$$

To simplify the discussion, let $\dot{x}(0) = x(0) = 0$. Equating the coefficients of Equations (3.6.1 and 3.6.2) yields

$$\omega_n^2 = 4, \tag{3.6.3}$$

and

$$2\delta\omega_n = 2. \tag{3.6.4}$$

Solving Equation (3.6.3) for ω_n gives $\omega_n = 2$. Using this result in Equation (3.6.4) gives $\delta=0.5$. Now, the nature of the step response of Equation (3.6.2) can be determined from the response curves of the generalized equation. The generalized curves do not include the effect of initial conditions. However, δ and ω_n

provide important insight and will be used throughout this book. Additional information will be provided in later chapters.

3.7 PHYSICAL EXAMPLE

No discussion of analog computation would be complete without a spring-mass-damper problem. Since the physics of the problem are easily understood, it can be used to illustrate the complete process of simulating the operation of a physical system. Consider the system shown in Figure 3-7-1. The object of the exercise is to write the equation of motion for the mass, M,

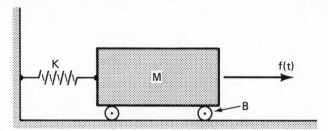

Figure 3-7-1. Spring-mass-damper system

under the influence of an applied force, f(t). The mass is connected to the wall by the ideal spring with constant K. Damping is supplied by velocity dependent friction represented by B. The positive reference direction is assumed to be to the right. For the time being, assume that the mass is initially at rest with no displacement.

The equation of motion can be written by summing the forces,

$$M\ddot{x} + B\dot{x} + Kx = f(t). \tag{3.7.1}$$

where $\dot{x}(0) = x(0) = 0$. If M = 5 Kg., B = 2.5 Nt-sec/m, K = 1.25 Nt/m, and f(t) = 2 Nt, the equation can be written in the form

$$\ddot{x} + 0.5\dot{x} + 0.25x = 0.4, \tag{3.7.2}$$

with $x(0) = \dot{x}(0) = 0$.

In order to develop the computer diagram, solve for $\ddot{x}$,

$$\ddot{x} = -(0.5\dot{x} + 0.25x - 0.4), \tag{3.7.3}$$

and apply the technique of section 3.4. The resulting diagram is shown in Figure 3-7-2. The displacement, x, and acceleration, $\ddot{x}$, in response to the applied force are shown in Figure 3-7-3.

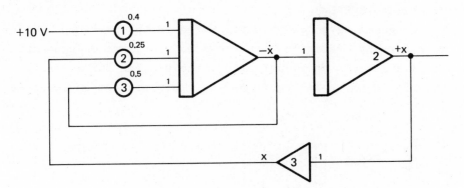

Figure 3-7-2. Spring-mass-damper problem

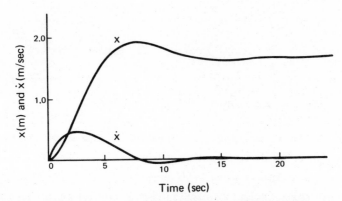

Time (sec)

Figure 3-7-3. Response of spring-mass-damper system

The analogies are: 1 volt on amplifier 2 is equivalent to 1
meter and 1 volt on amplifier 1 is equivalent to 1 meter/sec.
In order to check the steady-state response, note that at
steady state, $\ddot{x}$ and $\dot{x}$ are zero. Therefore, Equation (3.7.2)
simplifies to

$$0.25\, x = 0.4, \qquad\qquad (3.7.4)$$

at steady state. Thus, the steady-state displacement of the mass
is

$$x_{ss} = \frac{0.4}{0.25} = 1.6 \text{ meters.} \qquad\qquad (3.7.5)$$

Once the problem has been programmed, it is a simple matter to
study the response for different applied forces and parameter
values. Initial conditions on the displacement and velocity can
also be added if desired.

3.8 HIGHER-ORDER SYSTEMS

The programming procedures presented in the previous sections
will work for any order equation provided there are enough amplifiers available. As an illustration, the program for a fourth-
order system is shown in Figure 3-8-1. This problem could also

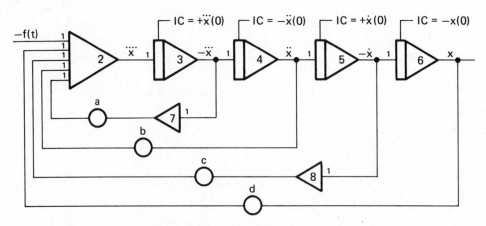

Figure 3-8-1. A fourth-order equation

be programmed with a summing integrator if the highest-order
derivative is not needed. In addition, the inversion function
of amplifiers 1, 7 and 8 could be combined in a single amplifier.
In the present form, summing amplifier 2 requires 5 gain-of-one
inputs. Most computers do not provide that many gain-of-one inputs.
Therefore, it will be necessary to use extra resistors or patch
two input resistor networks together. The operators manual for the
particular machine should be consulted for details. This program is a good illustration of the observation that most (but <u>not</u>
<u>all</u>) programs will have an odd number of amplifiers in each loop.

3.9 SIMULTANEOUS DIFFERENTIAL EQUATIONS

The techniques presented in the previous sections can also
be applied to the solution of simultaneous differential equations.
To illustrate the method, consider the two simultaneous equations.

$$\dddot{x} + a\dot{x} + b\dot{y} + cx = f(t), \tag{3.9.1}$$

and

$$\ddot{y} + d\dot{y} + e\dot{x} + fy = 0. \tag{3.9.2}$$

The first step is to solve both equations for the highest-order derivatives. This gives

$$\ddot{x} = - [a\dot{x} + b\dot{y} + cx - f(t)], \tag{3.9.3}$$

and

$$\ddot{y} = - [d\dot{y} + e\dot{x} + fy]. \tag{3.9.4}$$

The second step is to assume that both of the highest-order derivatives are known and available at the input of integrators. Now, repeated integration of both terms will yield the remaining derivatives and both dependent variables.

In the solution of a single differential equation, the next step would be to utilize a summing amplifier to sum the lower-order derivatives, the dependent variable and the forcing function. For simultaneous equations, the procedure is the same except there will be one summing amplifier for each of the highest-order derivatives (two in this case). Also, the inputs to the summers will come from more than one repeated integration sequence. The resulting program for this example is shown in Figure 3-9-1. It is interesting to note that coupling of the

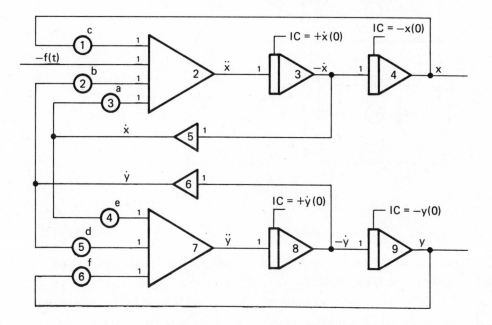

Figure 3-9-1. Simultaneous equations

two equations appears directly in the analog computer   solution.
This is an excellent way to illustrate and study the effects of
coupling in electrical, mechanical, and other types of   systems.
        Before leaving the solution of simultaneous equations,   a
few comments about amplifier economy should be made.   First,
note that summing integrators could be used as in the solution
of a single differential equation.   Also, the coupling   terms
that must be inverted can frequently share an inverter   by
forming sums and differences of terms.   Application of   these
techniques to Figure 3-9-1 yields the program shown in Figure
3-9-2.   Although this example is not very complicated,   the

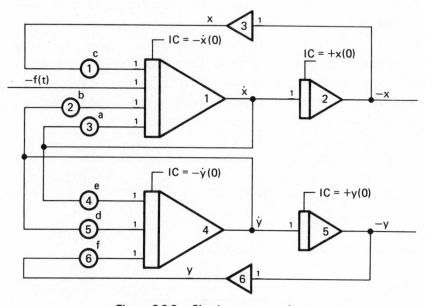

Figure 3-9-2.   Simultaneous equations

crossing of connection links make it difficult to   follow   the
diagram.   A scheme of circles and numbers has been developed
for complex problems and is illustrated for this problem   in
Figure 3-9-3.   As with single differential equations, the order
and number of simultaneous equations that can be handled   are
limited only by the number of available amplifiers.

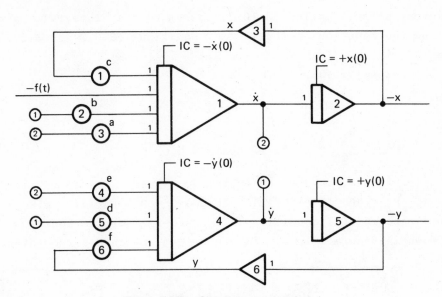

Figure 3-9-3. Simultaneous equations

3.10 NUMERICAL EXAMPLE

To illustrate the procedure for programming simultaneous equations, consider the electric circuit of Figure 3-10-1.

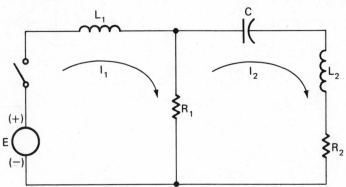

Figure 3-10-1. A two mesh electric circuit

The equations for the currents are

$$E_1 = L_1 \frac{dI_1}{dt} + R_1(I_1 - I_2),$$ (3.10.1)

and

$$0 = L_2 \frac{dI_2}{dt} + R_1(I_2 - I_1) + R_2 I_2 + \frac{1}{C}\int I_2 dt.$$ (3.10.2)

Differentiating Equation (3.10.2) to remove the integral, and writing the equation in the form of Equations (3.9.3 and 3.9.4) gives

$$\dot{I}_1 = \frac{R_1}{L_1} (I_2 - I_1) + \frac{E_1}{L_1} ,$$ (3.10.3)

and

$$\ddot{I}_2 = \frac{R_1}{L_2} (\dot{I}_1 - \dot{I}_2) - \frac{R_2}{L_2} \dot{I}_2 - \frac{1}{L_2 C} I_2.$$ (3.10.4)

For this example, assume the following values: E = 10 volts, R_1 = 4Ω, R_2 = 6Ω, L_1 = 2h, L_2 = 4h and C = 0.5 Farad. Also, assume zero initial conditions. The program for the equations is shown in Figure 3-10-2. Figure 3-10-3 presents a recording

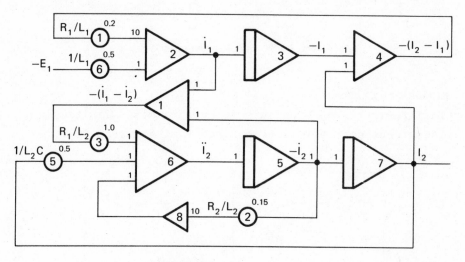

Figure 3-10-2. Computer program

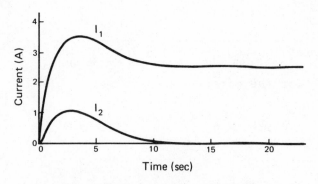

Figure 3-10-3. Mesh currents for circuit

of I_1 and I_2. The analogy for the current, I, on amplifier 3 is: 1 volt is equivalent to 1 ampere. Amplifier 7 produces I_2 and the analogy is: 1 volt is equivalent to 1 ampere. The rate of change of current, $\dot{I}_1$, also has an analogy of 1 computer volt equals 1 ampere/sec. This is also true for $\dot{I}_2$ produced by amplifier 5.

3.11 INTRODUCTION TO STATIC CHECKING

In any computational process, methods for eliminating errors are most important. In solving differential equations on the analog computer, the major sources of error are in program development, patching and equipment failure. The static check is designed to uncover errors in patching and most equipment malfunctions. Also, the setting of the coefficient potentiometers can be checked.[2]

In order to understand the procedure, consider the first-order equation used as an illustration in Section 3.2. The computer diagram of Figure 3-2-4 resulted from programming the equation,

$$\frac{dx}{dt} = -ax + f(t), \tag{3.11.1}$$

with $x(0) = 6$. If the computer is put into the reset (IC) mode, the output of amplifier 1 is held at $-x(0)$, the initial condition. This value is feedback to potentiometer 1, multiplied by (a) and summed with $f(t)$ in summing amplifier 2. The output of amplifier 2 is analogous to $-dx/dt$.

If the problem is programmed on the computer and values for the initial condition, $x(0)$, and forcing function $f(t)$, assumed, the output of amplifier 2 should agree with the value of dx/dt calculated from Equation (3.11.1). If either the initial condition, $x(0)$, or $f(t)$ are zero, portions of the diagram are not checked. Therefore, for the purpose of a static check, zero initial conditions and/or forcing functions are replaced by values that yield a valid check and avoid amplifier saturation.

In order to illustrate the procedure with a numerical example, consider the problem of Section 3.3. The equation for the diagram is

$$\ddot{x} = -[2\dot{x} + 4x - f(t)], \tag{3.11.2}$$

with $\overset{\circ}{x}(0) = 0$, $x(0) = 2$ and $f(t) = 0$. For the purpose of a
static check, let $\overset{\bullet}{x}(0) = 3.0$ and $f(t) = 9.0$. Substitution into
Equation (3.11.2) yields a value for $\overset{\cdot\cdot}{x} = -5.0$.

This can be checked on the program of Figure 3-3-4 by
patching initial conditions of $\overset{\bullet}{x}(0) = 3.0$ and $x(0) = 2.0$ with
$f(t) = 9.0$. The computer must be in the "reset" (IC) mode.
Some computers provide a special "static test" (ST) mode.
Note that $\overset{\bullet}{x}(0) = 3.0$ is achieved with a pot connected to the
minus reference voltage and set to 0.30. The $x(0) = 2.0$ is
obtained with a pot set at 0.20 and fed from the plus reference.
The forcing function of 9.0 comes from a pot set for 0.90 and
connected to the positive reference. For the static check, the
output of amplifier 4 should be -2.0 volts. Amplifier 3 should
be at +3 volts and amplifier 5 at -3 volts. If the problem is
properly patched and the pots accurately set, amplifier 2
should have -5.0 volts at its output. In general, the result
will not be an integer (e.g., 5) value and it should be checked
quite carefully with either a digital voltmeter or the precision
null circuit of the computer.

In this example, the static check should detect patching
mistakes and any error in the setting of pots 2 and 3. Also,
the summing action of amplifier 2 is verified. However, it
should be pointed out that only the IC mode of each integrator
is checked. The static check does not test the accuracy of
the integration process. It is a static check and not a dynamic check. An incorrect gain on an integrator input can be
detected on some computers which include special monitoring
circuits.

As an additional example, note that the program of Figure
3-3-5 requires no dummy initial conditions to perform a static
check. In this case, the output of amplifier 2 should be -9.0
volts.

An attempt to static check the problem as programmed in
Figure 3-4-2 may be unsatisfactory. Since a summing integrator
is utilized, the $\overset{\cdot\cdot}{x}$ term is not available at the output of an
integrator and cannot be used for checking purposes. Many
computers avoid this problem by making the "derivative" of an
integrating amplifier available. This provision enables the

operator to check the summed inputs of a summing integrator
prior to integration. However, it does not check the dynamic
operation of the integrators and is still classified as a
static check. A more complete discussion on the static check
will be presented in Chapter 4.

The static check is <u>most</u> important and should be performed
before taking data on the dynamical response of the problem.
Most computing facilities provide a detailed check list for the
static check procedure.

One important note: <u>Do</u> <u>not</u> <u>forget</u> <u>to</u> <u>remove</u> <u>the</u> <u>dummy</u>
<u>initial</u> <u>conditions</u> <u>and</u> <u>dummy</u> <u>forcing</u> <u>functions</u> <u>used</u> <u>for</u> <u>the</u>
<u>static</u> <u>check</u>.

3.12 PROBLEMS

Problems covering the material for this chapter are identified by section.

    3.2.1 Develop a computer program to solve the equation

$$2\ddot{x} + 4\dot{x} + 4x = 2, \tag{3.12.1}$$

where $\overset{\circ}{x}(0) = 0$ and $x(0) = 0$. What is the steady-
state value of x?

    3.2.2 Develop a computer program to solve the equation

$$\dddot{x} + 2\ddot{x} + 2\dot{x} + x = -3, \tag{3.12.2}$$

where $\ddot{x}(0) = \overset{\circ}{x}(0) = 0$ and $x(0) = 1$. Determine X_{ss}.

    3.2.3 Develop a computer program to solve the equation

$$\dddot{x} + 3\ddot{x} + 2\dot{x} + 4x = 2, \tag{3.12.3}$$

where $\ddot{x}(0) = 0$, $\ddot{x}(0) = 1$, $\dot{x}(0) = 4$ and $x(0) = -3$.

    3.2.4 Develop a computer program to solve

$$\ddot{x} + 2\dot{x} - 3x = 3 \tag{3.12.4}$$

where $\overset{\circ}{x}(0) = x(0) = 0$. Comment on the expected
response.

    3.4.1 Use the summing integrator to develop a program
for Problem 3.2.1 in which $\ddot{x}$ does not appear.

3.4.2   Use the summing integrator to develop a program
        for Problem 3.2.2 in which $\dddot{x}$ does not appear.

3.4.3   Use the summing integrator to develop a program
        for Problem 3.2.3 in which $\ddddot{x}$ does not appear.

3.4.4   Use the summing integrator to develop a program
        for Problem 3.2.4 in which $\ddot{x}$ does not appear.

3.6.1   Develop a program to solve the generalized,
        linear, second-order system of Section 3.6.
        Separate δ and ω_n so that they are not multi-
        plied to get one pot setting (i.e., only one pot
        determines δ).

3.6.2   Patch the program of Problem 3.6.1 on an available
        analog computer with $f(t)$ = a step input of 4.0
        (i.e., $f(t) = 4.0$), $\omega_n = 2$, $x(0) = 0$, $\dot{x}(0) = 0$
        and $\delta = 1.0$. Connect a recording device (x-y
        recorder or strip chart recorder) to monitor
        the response of x. Switch the computer from the
        "reset" or "initial condition" mode to the
        "operate" mode and record the response of x.
        Repeat the procedure for $\delta = 0.8$, $\delta = 0.6$, $\delta = 0.4$,
        $\delta = 0.2$, $\delta = 0.0$, and $\delta = -0.2$. Comment on the
        program patching required to achieve $\delta = -0.2$.
        What would you expect for larger values of
        negative damping?

3.6.3   (a) Develop a program to solve the equation

$$\ddot{x} + \omega_n^2 x = 0, \tag{3.12.5}$$

with $\dot{x}(0) = 0$, $x(0) = 5$ and $\omega_n = 2.0$.

        (b) Patch and run the problem on an analog computer
        and compare the results with an analytical solution.
        (c) Repeat part (b) with $\omega_n = 4.0$.

3.6.4   Repeat Problem 3.6.3 with $\dot{x}(0) = 5$, $x(0) = 0$ and
        $\omega_n = 2.0$. Comment on the results.

3.6.5   Repeat Problem 3.6.3 with $\dot{x}(0) = x(0) = 3.0$ and
        $\omega_n = 2.0$. Comment on the results.

3.7.1 Patch the problem of Section 3.7 on a computer and record the response of the program for $x(0) = -1.0$ meter and $\dot{x}(0) = 0$. What is this analogous to in the physical system?

3.7.2 Repeat Problem 3.7.1 with $x(0) = 1.0$ meter and $\dot{x}(0) = -1.0$ meter per second.

3.9.1 Develop a program to solve the simultaneous differential equations

$$\dddot{x} + a\ddot{x} + b\dot{x} + cx + d\ddot{y} + ey = 1.0, \qquad (3.12.6)$$

and

$$\ddot{y} + \ddot{y} + f\dot{y} - g\dot{x} + hy = 2.0, \qquad (3.12.7)$$

with zero initial conditions.

3.9.2 Develop a program to solve the simultaneous differential equations

$$\ddot{x} + 2\dot{x} + 3\dot{y} + 4x = 2.0, \qquad (3.12.8)$$

and

$$\ddot{y} + 4\dot{y} + 5y + 2x = 0, \qquad (3.12.9)$$

with $\dot{x}(0) = 0$, $\dot{y}(0) = 0$, $x(0)$ and $y(0) = 2.0$.

3.9.3 Patch the program of Problem 3.9.2 on a computer and determine the response of x and y.

3.9.4 Determine a physical system which might be represented by the equation of Problem 3.9.2.

3.10.1 Patch the program for the example problem of Section 3.10 and record the response of I_1 and I_2.

3.10.2 Change the program of Problem 3.10.1 so that resistor, R_1, is replaced with an inductor, $L_3 = 4h$. How does this affect the coupling between the two equations?

3.10.3 Patch the program of Problem 3.10.2 and determine the response of I_1 and I_2.

3.11.1 Develop a static check for Problem 3.2.1.

3.11.2 Repeat Problem 3.11.1 for Problem 3.2.2.

3.11.3 Repeat Problem 3.11.1 for Problem 3.2.3.

3.11.4   Repeat Problem 3.11.1 for Problem 3.2.4.

3.11.5   Comment on the special conditions required
         for a static check of Problems 3.4.1 through
         3.4.4.

3.11.6   Repeat Problem 3.11.1 for Problem 3.6.1, 3.6.2
         and 3.6.3.

3.11.7   Perform a static check for Problem 3.7.1.

3.11.8   Develop a static check for Problem 3.9.1.

3.11.9   Develop a static check for Problem 3.9.2.

3.11.10 Develop a static check for Problem 3.9.3.

3.11.11 Perform a static check for Problem 3.10.1.

3.11.12 Perform a static check for Problem 3.10.2.

3.13   REFERENCES FOR CHAPTER 3

(1) Gupta, S. C. and L. Hasdorff: <u>Fundamentals of
    Automatic Control</u>, John Wiley & Sons, Inc.,
    New York, 1970.

(2) Carlson, A., G. Hannauer, T. Carey and P. Holsberg:
    <u>Handbook of Analog Computation</u>, Electronic Asso-
    ciates, Inc., Princeton, New Jersey, 1965.

4

Magnitude and Time Scaling

4.1 INTRODUCTION

In previous chapters, problems with a wide range of parameters and variables have been avoided. Obviously, if the analog
computer is to be useful in the simulation of practical systems,
a method for handling these problems must be available. For
example, problem parameters are usually represented by potentiometers, which have a range of 0.05 to 0.95. Also, the output
voltage of amplifiers is analogous to the dependent variables of
the problem. Since most machines have either ±10 or ±100 volt
ranges, it is obvious that the 1 volt-per-unit analogy will not
work for all problems. The scaling problem is not always one of
scaling down problem variables and parameters. Excessively small
variables result in low voltage operation of the amplifiers with
accompanying loss of accuracy. The procedure utilized to assure
reasonable pot settings and amplifier operating ranges is called
magnitude scaling.

Another problem of equal importance to magnitude scaling is that of assuring reasonable solution times. In some applications, the process to be simulated may take days or even weeks to complete its cycle of operation. In other applications, the action takes place in seconds, microseconds or perhaps nanoseconds. In the first case, it would be uneconomical to occupy valuable equipment any longer than necessary. Also, as noted in Chapter 2, computing amplifiers are subject to drift when used for long periods of time and would introduce error. In the latter case, extremely fast systems are beyond the capability of the computer components and recording equipment. The operational amplifiers and other circuitry of the computer are not capable of properly simulating processes that have operating characteristics faster than the response of the computer amplifiers. Another reason for changing the solution rate is high speed optimization. For example, parameter search and optimization problems frequently require thousands of iterations of the simulation in order to determine the "BEST" set of parameters. Therefore, high speed simulation may save considerable time.

The procedure utilized to assure a reasonable operating time for a simulation is called time scaling. In this chapter, procedures for both magnitude and time scaling will be presented and illustrated with several example problems.

4.2   ESTIMATING THE RANGE OF VARIABLES

Before a problem can be scaled for analog simulation, the range of values for the system variables must be known. It should be emphasized that it is not necessary to know the range precisely. However, this limitation still presents a problem for most simulations.

Usually, the range of values for one or more of the system variables can be determined from known constraints of the physical structure of the system to be simulated. With this information, and certain relationships among variables, a workable program can be developed. It may be necessary to rescale the problem as more information is obtained from the simulation. Therefore, an understanding of convenient methods for estimating the maximum values of system variables is most important. In this section, some simple estimation techniques will be presented for different types of systems.

(a) **First-Order Linear Systems:** Systems described by linear, first-order differential equations are characterized by an exponential response. For example, consider the equation

$$\dot{x} + ax = b, \tag{4.2.1}$$

where $x(0) = x_o = c$. As time approaches infinity, the $\dot{x}$ term goes to zero and the steady-state value is $x_{ss} = b/a$. If $x_{ss} = b/a$ is greater than $x_o = c$, the response is an exponential rise from $x_o = c$ to $x_{ss} = b/a$ as given by the equation,

$$x(t) = (x_{ss} - x_o)(1 - e^{-at}) + x_o. \tag{4.2.2}$$

The first-order response is often characterized in terms of the time constant $\tau = 1/a$. Making this substitution yields

$$x(t) = (x_{ss} - x_o)(1 - e^{-t/\tau}) + x_o. \tag{4.2.3}$$

This is shown in Figure 4-2-1. The response makes 63.2% of the

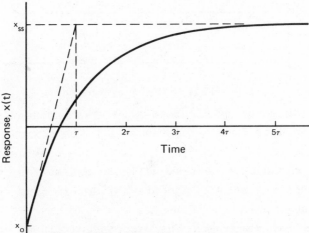

Figure 4-2-1. First-order system response

required change in a period of time equal to the time constant, τ. Thus, at $(t_o + 1/a)$ sec, the value of $x(t)$ is $x_o + (x_{ss} - x_o)(.632)$. By the end of 2 time constants, 86.5% of the required change has been made. By the passage of 3 time constants, 95% of the change has occurred and by 4 time constants, 98.2% of the change

$(x_{ss} - x_o)$ has been made. Thus, by 4 or 5 time constants, the
response can be considered to have reached x_{ss}. The maximum
value of x is the larger of $|x_{ss}|$ and $|x_o|$. Since the maximum
value of the derivative occurs at t = o, $\dot{x}_m = b - a(x_o)$. If the
output, x(t), continued to change at the initial rate, it would
reach x_{ss} in 1 time constant.

If x_{ss} is less than x_o, the response is an exponential decay
from x_o to x_{ss} given by the equation

$$x(t) = x_{ss} - (x_o - x_{ss}) e^{-at} = x_{ss} - (x_o - x_{ss})e^{-t/\tau}.$$

$$(4.2.4)$$

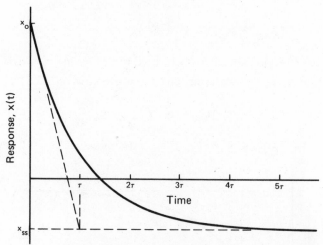

Figure 4-2-2. First-order system response

This response is shown in Figure 4-2-2. The exponential decay
is completed in 4 or 5 time constants, τ. The maximum   value of
x is the larger of $|x_{ss}|$ and $|x_o|$. As in the previous case, $\dot{x}_m$
occurs at t = o and is $\dot{x}_m = b-ax_o$. Thus, estimation of the
maximum value of the x(t) is a matter of determining the initial
and final values.

(b) **Second-Order Linear System:** The response of linear second-order
differential equations is best described in terms of the generalized equation

$$\ddot{x} + 2\delta\omega_n \dot{x} + \omega_n^2 x = \omega_n^2 f(t).$$

$$(4.2.5)$$

This equation enables the response to be characterized in terms
of the input, f(t), the damping ratio, δ, and the undamped

natural frequency ω_n. The most widely used input is the unit
step function, $f(t) = 1$ for $t>0$. For $\delta>1$, the system is
"overdamped" and the response is the combination of two expo-
nentials. Thus, the response goes from x_o to x_{ss} in an
exponential form. For $0<\delta<1$, the system is "underdamped" and
the response is a damped sinusoid. When $\delta = 0$, the response is
a sinusoid with an amplitude of $||x_{ss}|-|x_o||$. For $\delta<0$, the
system displays negative damping and is unstable. In this case,
the sinusoidal oscillations of the response increase in magnitude
and eventually will exceed the range of the computer.

For the overdamped cast $(\delta>1)$, the maximum value of x is the
larger of $|x_{ss}|$ or $|x_o|$. This is illustrated in Figure 4-2-3.

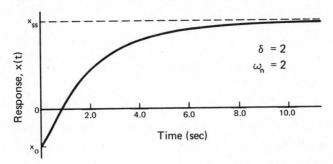

Figure 4-2-3. Second-order system step response (overdamped)

For the underdamped case $(0<\delta<1)$, the response goes from x_o to
x_{ss} in an oscillatory fashion and can overshoot x_{ss} by as much
as the magnitude of $||x_{ss}|-|x_o||$. This is illustrated in
Figure 4-2-4. For negative damping $(\delta<0)$ the oscillations grow

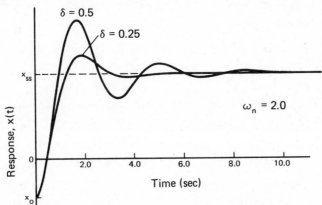

Figure 4-2-4. Second-order system step response (underdamped)

and the system can only be simulated for a few cycles before the
computing amplifiers exceed their linear range (±10 or ±100
volts) and saturate.

The underdamped case is the most difficult to scale.   In
order to determine conservative estimates for the maximum
values, assume the sinusoidal response of zero damping with
$\delta=0$. The response is of the form

$$x(t) = x_m \sin \omega_n t. \tag{4.2.6}$$

Differentiating yields

$$\dot{x}(t) = \omega_n x_m \cos \omega_n t. \tag{4.2.7}$$

Therefore,

$$|\dot{x}_m| = |\omega_n x_m| \tag{4.2.8}$$

and the maximum valued for $\ddot{x}$ (determined in a similar manner) is

$$\ddot{x}_m = \omega_n \dot{x}_m = \omega_n^2 x_m. \tag{4.2.9}$$

Thus, a knowledge of x_o, x_{ss} and ω_n enable the determination of
conservative estimates for x_m, $\dot{x}_m$ and $\ddot{x}_m$.   Also, a knowledge   of
$\dot{x}_m$ and ω_n can yield $x_m = \dot{x}_m / \omega_m$.

(c) **Higher-Order Linear Systems:**   For systems of order greater than
two, the determination of maximum values is more difficult.   Unfortunately, a set of parameters such as ω_n and δ which describe
the response have never been developed.   Therefore,   without   a
detailed knowledge of the system, determination of maximum values
is an approximation, at best.   In   order to illustrate   the techniques, consider a system described by an equation   of   the form

$$a_o \frac{d^n x}{dt^n} + \ldots + a_{n-1} \frac{dx}{dt} + a_n x = b_o f(t). \tag{4.2.10}$$

An approach similar to the method used for second-order systems
could be employed.   It would require the separation   of   the
response into exponential components for each of the real roots
and sinusoidal components for each pair of complex roots. However, in order to use this approach, the system equation must
be written in a factored form.   This is beyond the scope of this
chapter and will be discussed in Chapters 6 and 7.

Another approach uses the equal coefficient rule to estimate maximum values.[4] In the strictest sense, the equal coefficient rule is only applicable to linear, homogenous, stationary differential equations. However, it is often useful for equations with time-varying coefficients and nonlinearities. According to the rule, the maximum values of the dependent variable and its derivatives should be selected such that coefficients of the differential equation, written in normalized form, are equal. The method will be illustrated in the next section of this chapter.

4.3 EXAMPLES OF ESTIMATING MAXIMUM VALUES

In order to illustrate the material of the preceding section, consider the following example problems.

(a) **First-Order Linear Systems:** For this case, assume an equation of the form

$$\dot{x} + 4x = 10, \tag{4.3.1}$$

with $x(0) = x_o = 1.0$. Using the techniques of Section 4.2, $x_{ss} = 10/4 = 2.5$ and $x_o = 1.0$. Therefore, $x_m = 2.5$, $\dot{x}_m = -4(1)$ $+10 = 6.0$ and the time constant is $\tau = 1/4 = 0.25$ sec. The system will require from 1.0 to 1.25 sec to reach steady-state. As an additional example, consider the same system with the forcing function removed and a different initial condition. The system equation is

$$\dot{x} + 4x = 0, \tag{4.3.2}$$

with $x(0) = x_o = 2.0$. For this case, $x_{ss} = 0$ and $x_m = x_o = 2.0$. The maximum value of $\dot{x}$ occurs at t=0 and $\dot{x}_m = -4x_o = (-4)(2) =$ -8.0. For a negative forcing function, the system is described by

$$\dot{x} + 4x = -12, \tag{4.3.3}$$

with $x_o = 2.0$. For this input, $x_{ss} = -12/4 = -3$ and $x_m = |x_{ss}| =$ 3.0. The maximum derivative $\dot{x}_m = 4x_o - 12 = -4(2) - 12 = -20$.

(b) **Second-Order Linear System:** In order to illustrate the technique, consider the equation

$$\ddot{x} + 3\dot{x} + 9x = 18, \tag{4.3.4}$$

with $x_o = 0$ and $\dot{x}_o = 0$. At steady-state, $\ddot{x}$ and $\dot{x}$ go to zero and
$x_{ss} = 18/9 = 2.0$. Now, compare Equation (4.3.4) with the gener-
alized, linear, second-order system

$$\ddot{x} + 2\delta\omega_n\dot{x} + \omega_n^2 x = \omega_n^2 f(t). \tag{4.3.5}$$

Equating coefficients yields $\omega_n^2 = 9$, and therefore, $\omega_n = 3$. Also,
$2\delta\omega_n = 3$, and solving for δ yields, $\delta = 0.5$. Therefore, the system
is underdamped and will have an exponentially decaying sinusoidal
response. In this case, x starts at $x_o = 0$ and eventually settles
to $x_{ss} = 2.0$. If $\delta = 0$, the response would be a sinusoid with a
magnitude of $\| x_{ss}| - |x_o \|| = |2 - 0| = 2$. For the assumption of
zero damping, the maximum value of x would be, $x_m = 4$. However,
since $\delta = 0.5$, the system will not overshoot x_{ss} as much as for
$\delta = 0$. Thus, the value $x_m = 4$ is a conservative estimate of x_m.
From Equation (4.2.8), $\dot{x}_m = \omega_n x_m = (3)(4) = 12$. Since the
maximum expected values for both x_m and $\dot{x}_m$ were based on conservative approximations, the actual system variables should be
within the anticipated range.

As a second example, consider a system described by the
equation

$$\ddot{x} + 2.4\dot{x} + 9x = 0, \tag{4.3.6}$$

with $x_o = 5$ and $\dot{x}_o = 0$. In this case, $x_{ss} = 0$, and $\omega_n = \sqrt{9} = 3$.
Since $2\delta\omega_n = 2.4$, then $\delta = 2.4/2\omega_n = 0.4$. In order to provide
conservative estimates, assume $\delta = 0$. For the assumed zero damping,
the response is sinusoidal with an amplitude of 5. The maximum
positive excursion would be 5 and the maximum negative excursion
would be -5. Therefore, a conservative estimate is $x_m = 5$. By
Equation (4.2.8), $\dot{x}_m = \omega_n x_m = (3)(5) = 15$.

As a third example, consider a system described by the
equation

$$\ddot{x} + 4.8\dot{x} + 16x = 0, \tag{4.3.7}$$

where $x = 0$ and $\dot{x}_o = 10$. The steady-state value of the response
is $x_{ss} = 0$. In this case, $\dot{x}_m$ occurs at t=0 and $\dot{x}_m = 10$. The
undamped natural frequency is $\omega_n = \sqrt{16} = 4$. Since $2\delta\omega_n = 4.8$,
$\delta = 0.6$. However, for scaling assume $\delta = 0$. Equation (4.2.8) gives

$x_m = \dot{x}_m/\omega_n = 10/4 = 2.5$. The preceding examples were selected to consider the forcing function and initial conditions on x and $\dot{x}$ separately. When they occur in combinations, as they often do, consider them separately and attempt to estimate the composite effect. No simple rule can be given.

(c) **Higher-Order Linear Systems:** In order to illustrate the use of the equal coefficient rule, consider a fourth-order system described by the equation

$$\ddddot{x} + 5.4\dddot{x} + 18.2\ddot{x} + 31.8\dot{x} + 18x = 36 \qquad (4.3.8)$$

with $\dddot{x}(0) = \ddot{x}(0) = \dot{x}(0) = x(0) = 0$. Since the initial conditions on $\dddot{x}_o$, $\ddot{x}_o$, $\dot{x}_o$ and x_o are zero, the maximum value of $\dddot{x}$ occurs at t=o and from Equation (4.3.8) $\dddot{x}_m = 36/a_o = 36/1 = 36$. Also, $x_{ss} = 36/18 = 2$ and for zero damping, $x_m = 4$. In normalized form, the differential equation is written with each variable normalized to its maximum value. In this example, the normalized form is

$$\dddot{x}_m \left[\frac{\ddddot{x}}{\dddot{x}_m}\right] + 5.4\ddot{x}_m\left[\frac{\dddot{x}}{\ddot{x}_m}\right] + 18.2\dot{x}_m\left[\frac{\ddot{x}}{\dot{x}_m}\right] + 31.8\dot{x}_m\left[\frac{\dot{x}}{\dot{x}_m}\right] +$$

$$18x_m\left[\frac{x}{x_m}\right] = 36. \qquad (4.3.9)$$

Using know values, $\dddot{x}_m = 36$ and $x_m = 4$, gives

$$36\left[\frac{\ddddot{x}}{36}\right] + 5.4x_m\left[\frac{\dddot{x}}{\ddot{x}_m}\right] + 18.2\ddot{x}_m\left[\frac{\ddot{x}}{\dot{x}_m}\right] + 31.8\dot{x}_m\left[\frac{\dot{x}}{\dot{x}_m}\right] +$$

$$18(4)\left[\frac{x}{4}\right] = 36. \qquad (4.3.10)$$

Dividing by 36 yields

$$\left[\frac{\ddddot{x}}{36}\right] + .15\ddot{x}_m\left[\frac{\dddot{x}}{\ddot{x}_m}\right] + .505\ddot{x}_m\left[\frac{\ddot{x}}{\dot{x}_m}\right] + .884\dot{x}_m\left[\frac{\dot{x}}{\dot{x}_m}\right] + 2\left[\frac{x}{4}\right] = 1. \qquad (4.3.11)$$

In order to make the coefficients approximately one, $\dddot{x}_m = 6.64$, $\ddot{x}_m = 1.98$ and $\dot{x}_m = 1.13$. Therefore, choose $\dddot{x}_m = 36$, $\ddot{x}_m = 7$, $\ddot{x}_m = 2$, $\dot{x}_m = 1.2$ and $x_m = 4$. The normalized equation is

$$\left[\frac{\ddddot{x}}{36}\right] + 1.05\left[\frac{\dddot{x}}{7}\right] + 1.01\left[\frac{\ddot{x}}{2}\right] + 1.06\left[\frac{\dot{x}}{1.2}\right] + 2\left[\frac{x}{4}\right] = 1. \qquad (4.3.12)$$

The use of the equal coefficient rule will also be demonstrated in a later section.

4.4   SELECTING THE MAGNITUDE SCALE

Once the expected maximum values for the problem variables have been determined, suitable computing variables can be selected.   There are two approaches to selecting properly scaled computer variables.   One method bases the computing variable on the reference voltage or maximum linear excursion of the operational amplifiers.   The other method is unit scaling.   In the unit scale approach, the maximum excursion of the amplifier is taken as one unit and the computer variable selected on this basis.   On a 100-volt computer, 100 voltes = one unit, and on a 10-volt computer, 10 volts = one unit.   The appealing feature of unit scaling is the independence of scaling on the reference voltage of a particular computer.[3]   Thus, a program properly scaled by the unit method would work on either a 100-volt or a 10-volt computer.   Unit scaling has been widely adopted and will be used in this text.

For unit scaling, the computer variables are selected such that the maximum value of a particular variable corresponds to one unit or less.   For example, if the maximum value of a displacement, x_m, is estimated to be 17 meters, a conservative unit value would be 20 m.   Thus, 20 m = one unit and the computer variable would be $[x/20]$.   (Square brackets will be used to indicate computer variables).   If the maximum value of the displacement, x, was actually 17 m, the maximum unit value would be $[17/20] = 0.85$.   The maximum amplifier voltage would be $(0.85)(10) = 8.5$ volts on a 10-volt computer and 85.0 volts on a 100-volt computer.   A number of computers employ voltmeters and chart recorders calibrated for unit scaling.   Thus, at the maximum linear range of the amplifiers ($\pm 10v$ or $\pm 100v$) the read-out device indicates ± 1 unit.

As an additional example, consider a variable analogous to velocity, $\dot{x}$, which has an estimated maximum value, $\dot{x}_m$ = 135 m/sec.   A conservative unit value might be 140 or 150 m/sec. If the expected maximum value was determined from a number of "approximations", a more conservative scale of 200 m/sec = one

unit might be used initially. This would avoid exceeding the
linear range of the amplifier producing $\dot{x}$ and provide a
successful simulation on which to base improvements in the
scaling for subsequent computer runs. Since it is also important
to avoid extremely low voltage operation of the amplifiers, the
unit scale should be as large as convenient. In this case, assume
150 m/sec = one unit and use a computer variable $[\dot{x}/150]$. In
order to determine the velocity at a particular point in a
simulation run, it is necessary to convert from a unit value to
meters per second. Suppose the amplifier output is 7.25 volts
on a 10-volt computer. The unit value is (7.25)/10.0 = .725 units.
To determine the velocity, set the computer variable equal to the
unit value and solve for the original problem variable, $\dot{x}$,

$$\left[\frac{\dot{x}}{150}\right] = \frac{7.25 \text{ volts}}{10 \text{ volts}} = 0.725 \text{ units}, \qquad (4.4.1)$$

yielding

$$\dot{x} = (150)(0.725) = 108.75 \text{ m/sec}. \qquad (4.4.2)$$

The procedure will work for positive or negative values.
For example, assume that the amplifier producing $[\dot{x}/150]$ has an
output of -4.5 volts. To determine the velocity of the problem
variable, $\dot{x}$, set

$$\left[\frac{\dot{x}}{150}\right] = \frac{-4.5 \text{ volts}}{10 \text{ volts}} = -0.45 \text{ units} \qquad (4.4.3)$$

and

$$\dot{x} = (150)(-0.45) = -67.5 \text{ m/sec}, \qquad (4.4.4)$$

which is a negative velocity.

To convert from a particular velocity, like 110 m/sec into
units, substitute the problem velocity, $\dot{x}$ = 110 m/sec, into the
expression for computer variables in terms of units. In this
case,

$$\left[\frac{\dot{x}}{150}\right] = \frac{110}{150} = 0.733 \text{ units}. \qquad (4.4.5)$$

To determine the corresponding voltage on a 10-volt computer,
multiply by the reference voltage (10 volts) which gives

$$\text{Amplifier volts} = 0.733(10) = 7.33 \text{ volts.} \qquad (4.4.6)$$

On a 100-volt computer, the unit value is also multiplied by the reference voltage,

$$\text{Amplifier volts} = 0.733(100) = 73.3 \text{ volts.} \qquad (4.4.7)$$

Since simulation is carried out with computer variables, the output of a particular amplifier is recorded as a computer variable. In order to illustrate conversion from computer variables to problem variables, assume that the recording of Figure 4-4-1 is a pressure in Newtons per square meter represented by the computer variable [P/30]. The recording is in unit scaling with

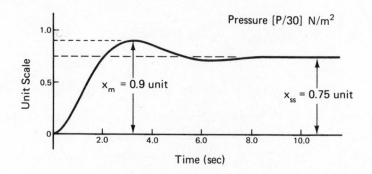

Figure 4-4-1.   Unit scale recording

a maximum of 0.90 units and a steady-state of 0.75 units. Converting the computer variables to the corresponding problem variables gives a maximum value of 27.0 N/m^2 and a steady-state of 22.50 N/m^2. It is often convenient to show <u>both</u> computer and problem values on the ordinate axis.

Thus, for the unit method of scaling, the computer variable will always be the problem variable divided by the expected maximum value of that variable or a convenient value larger than the expected maximum. In order to keep track of the scaling procedure, a scaling table should be prepared. It should include each problem variable and its units, the expected maximum value for each variable and the computer variable. Now that the scale factor has been discussed, an orderly magnitude scaling procedure can be presented.

4.5 MAGNITUDE SCALING PROCEDURE

Many magnitude scaling techniques have been developed for analog computer programming and all of them produce similar results. However, the procedure should be as straightforward as possible, and at the same time, reduce the likelihood of error. The method selected for presentation in this text is similar to a procedure that has been widely used and thoroughly tested.[3]

Before presenting the procedure, there are several conventions that should be noted:

* [ ] Square brackets will be used to enclose scaled computer variables.
* ( ) Parenthesis will be used to enclose potentiometer settings.
* Amplifier gains will not be enclosed.

These conventions are quite useful and help prevent scaling errors.

A step-by-step magnitude scaling procedure can be outlined as follows:

(1) Using the mathematical equations for the process to be simulated, prepare an unscaled computer diagram.

(2) Estimate the expected maximum value for each of the problem variables.

(3) Select a suitable computer variable for each problem variable and tabulate the results.

(4) Using the scaled variables, scale the equations for each amplifier.

(5) Draw a complete scaled diagram by connecting the amplifiers as scaled in step (4).

The only item of the procedure outlined in the preceding paragraph that has not been discussed is Item 4. To illustrate Step 4, consider the equation

$$\ddot{x} + 2\dot{x} + 4x = f(t). \tag{4.5.1}$$

This is the same equation used in the example problem of Section 3.3. However, the initial conditions have been changed to $\dot{x}(0) = 0$ and $x(0) = 20$. The initial condition on x makes mag-

nitude scaling a necessity on a 10-volt computer.   As   in
Section 3.3, consider f(t) = 0.   According to the magnitude
scaling procedure, the first step is to prepare an   unscaled
computer diagram.   This is shown in Figure 4-5-1.   To make the

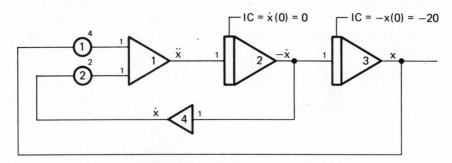

Figure 4-5-1.   Unscaled computer diagram

illustration more meaningful, assume that x is displacement,
measured in meters.   Thus, $\dot{x}$ is velocity in meters per second
and $\ddot{x}$ is acceleration in meters per second squared.

The next step of the procedure is to estimate the maximum
values of the problem variables.   For this equation, the undamped natural frequency, ω_n, is $\sqrt{4}$ = 2 radians per second.
As shown in Chapter 3, the maximum value of x (for the homogeneous case) is x_o, and from the initial condition, x_m = 20m.
The maximum value of $\dot{x}$ can be obtained from Equation (4.2.8)

$$\dot{x}_m = \omega_n^2 x_m = (2)(20) = 40 \text{ m/sec.} \qquad (4.5.2)$$

From Equation (4.2.9), the maximum value for $\ddot{x}$ is

$$\ddot{x}_m = \omega_n^2 x_m = (4)(20) = 80 \text{ m/sec}^2. \qquad (4.5.3)$$

The next step is the selection of computer variables.   For
unit scaling, the computer variable is the problem variable divided by its maximum expected value or a   convenient   larger
value.   Following the convention of enclosing computer variables
in square brackets, the computer variables are [x/30], [$\dot{x}$/40] and
[$\ddot{x}$/80].   With this information, the scaling table shown in Figure
4-5-2 can be prepared.   The even numbers selected for this example lead to "nice" scale factors.   In general,   the   expected

Problem Variable	Expected Maximum	Computer Variable
x	20	$\left[\dfrac{x}{20}\right]$
$\dot{x}$	40	$\left[\dfrac{\dot{x}}{40}\right]$
$\ddot{x}$	80	$\left[\dfrac{\ddot{x}}{80}\right]$

Figure 4-5-2. Scaling Table

maximum values are not even numbers and some adjustment is necessary. For example, an expected maximum value of 41.28 should be "rounded" to 50. Construction of the scaling table completes Step 3 of the procedure. Note that 25, 50 and 100 could have been selected as convenient unit values.

In Step 4, the scaled equation for each amplifier is developed. For the summing amplifier (amplifier 1), the unscaled equation is

$$\ddot{x} = -2\dot{x} - 4x. \tag{4.5.4}$$

To begin the scaling procedure, substitute the computer variables into Equation (4.5.4), using $80[\ddot{x}/80] = \ddot{x}$ and $20[x/20] = x$. Since each variable is multiplied and divided by the same number, substitution does not change the equation. Following substitution, the equation is

$$80\left[\frac{\ddot{x}}{80}\right] = -2\cdot40\left[\frac{\dot{x}}{40}\right] -4\cdot20\left[\frac{x}{20}\right]. \tag{4.5.5}$$

Dividing Equation (4.5.5) by 80 gives

$$\left[\frac{\ddot{x}}{80}\right] = -1\left[\frac{\dot{x}}{40}\right] -1\left[\frac{x}{20}\right] . \tag{4.5.6}$$

The scaled summing amplifier is shown in Figure 4-5-3. The minus signs of Equation (4.5.6) have been included to account for the

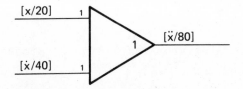

Figure 4-5-3. The scaled summing amplifier

inversion of the amplifier as discussed in Chapter 2.

To scale the integrators, a similar procedure   is   used.
Consider amplifier 2 which produces $-\dot{x}$ from $\ddot{x}$.   From Section
3.2, the unscaled equation for this integrator is

$$\dot{x} = -\int \ddot{x} \, dt \, .\tag{4.5.7}$$

Substitution of computer variables from the scaling table gives

$$-40 \left[\frac{-\dot{x}}{40}\right] = -\int 80\left[\frac{-\ddot{x}}{80}\right] dt \, ,\tag{4.5.8}$$

and dividing by -40 yields

$$\left[\frac{-\dot{x}}{40}\right] = \int 2\left[\frac{\ddot{x}}{80}\right] dt \, .\tag{4.5.9}$$

The negative sign on $[-\dot{x}/40]$ has been included to account for
the sign inversion of the integrator.   The coefficient of   2
on the right-hand side of Equation (4.5.9) can be separated
into an amplifier gain, a pot setting and a computer variable
as shown by the equation

$$\left[\frac{-\dot{x}}{40}\right] = \int 10(.2)\left[\frac{\ddot{x}}{80}\right] dt \, .\tag{4.5.10}$$

The scaled integrator for Equation (4.5.10) is shown in Figure
4-5-4.   Since the initial velocity is zero, no input   is   required for the initial condition terminal.   However, if $\dot{x}(0)\neq0$,

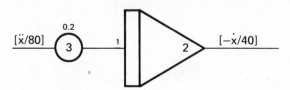

Figure 4-5-4.   The scaled integrator

then the IC input should be $[\dot{x}(0)/40]$.   Initial conditions
scaled in this manner will always produce convenient   pot
settings.

For the other integrator (amplifier 3) producing x,   the
unscaled equation is

$$x = -\int \dot{x} \, dt \, ,\tag{4.5.11}$$

and substitution of computer variables gives

$$20\left[\frac{x}{20}\right] = -\int -40\left[\frac{-\dot{x}}{40}\right] dt. \qquad (4.5.12)$$

Division by 20 and grouping terms for gain, pot setting and computer variable yields

$$\left[\frac{x}{20}\right] = \int 10(.2)\left[\frac{-\dot{x}}{40}\right] dt. \qquad (4.5.13)$$

The minus sign on $[-\dot{x}/40]$ is accounting for the inversion of the integrator. The scaled integrator is shown in Figure 4-5-5. Note

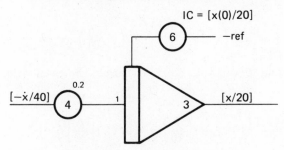

Figure 4-5-5. The scaled integrator

that the initial condition is scaled by the same factor as the output. Due to inversion, the initial condition potentiometer, 6, is connected to the negative reference.

Since all other amplifiers are properly scaled, it is not necessary to scale the inverter. The diagram can be completed as directed in Step 5 of the scaling procedure. This is shown in Figure 4-5-6. The scale factors selected should reflect the

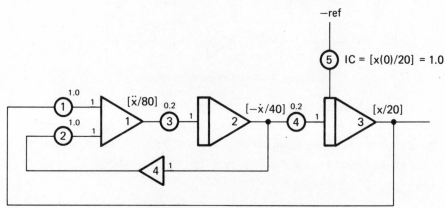

Figure 4-5-6. The scaled program

expected maximum values and be convenient to use. Therefore,
maximum expected values should be rounded upward to the nearest
convenient value such as 10, 25, 50, 100 or 0.1, 0.01, etc.

The equation for this example could have been programmed
using a summing integrator as discussed in Chapter 3. If the
summing integrator is used, it must be scaled accordingly. From
Section 3.4, the unscaled equation for the summing integrator is

$$\dot{x} = -\int (2\dot{x} + 4x)dt. \tag{4.5.14}$$

Substitution of the computer variables from the scaling table
gives

$$40\left[\frac{\dot{x}}{40}\right] = -\int\left(2\cdot 40\left[\frac{\dot{x}}{40}\right] + 4\cdot 20\left[\frac{x}{20}\right]\right)dt. \tag{4.5.15}$$

Division by 40 and grouping coefficients by gain and pot setting
yields

$$\left[\frac{\dot{x}}{40}\right] = -\int\left(10(.2)\left[\frac{\dot{x}}{40}\right] + 10(.2)\left[\frac{x}{20}\right]\right)dt. \tag{4.5.16}$$

The diagram for the complete program is shown in Figure 4-5-7.

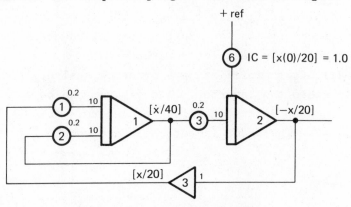

Figure 4-5-7.   The scaled program

If the problem had included a forcing function, f(t), it should
be scaled according to its maximum value, $[f(t)/f_m]$.

To illustrate the equal coefficient rule, the maximum values
for this example will be determined by that method. The unscaled
equation is

$$\ddot{x} + 2\dot{x} + 4x = f(t), \tag{4.5.17}$$

with $\dot{x}(0) = 0$, $x(0) = 20m$ and $f(t) = 0$. Equation (5.5.17) can be written in the normalized form

$$\ddot{x}_m \left[\frac{\ddot{x}}{\ddot{x}_m}\right] + 2 \, \dot{x}_m \left[\frac{\dot{x}}{\dot{x}_m}\right] + 4 \, x_m \left[\frac{x}{x_m}\right] = 0. \qquad (4.5.18)$$

Division by $\ddot{x}_m$ yields

$$\left[\frac{\ddot{x}}{\ddot{x}_m}\right] + 2 \, \frac{\dot{x}_m}{\ddot{x}_m} \left[\frac{\dot{x}}{\dot{x}_m}\right] + 4 \, \frac{x_m}{\ddot{x}_m} \left[\frac{x}{x_m}\right] = 0. \qquad (4.5.19)$$

The terms in square brackets could be used as computer variables. However, it may be desirable to select more convenient unit scale values.

According to the equal coefficient rule, the maximum values of the variables must satisfy the relation

$$1 = 2 \, \frac{\dot{x}_m}{\ddot{x}_m} = 4 \, \frac{x_m}{\ddot{x}_m} \, . \qquad (4.5.20)$$

From previous sections, $x_m = 20$ and Equation (4.5.20) yields, $\ddot{x}_m = 4 \, x_m = 80$ and $\dot{x}_m = \ddot{x}_m/2 = 40$. Thus, both methods yield the same maximum values for this example. Additional details on the equal coefficient method are presented in references (2,4).

In this example, magnitude scaling was required since the problem variables exceeded the range of the computer. Magnitude scaling is frequently employed for variables that are too small. As noted previously, error is introduced when amplifiers are operated at low levels. The magnitude scaling procedure will be illustrated with another example in Section 4.7.

4.6 TIME SCALING

Most of the reasons for time scaling have already been discussed. It was noted that the rate of change of computer variables must be within the range of the equipment used. Also, the time required for simulation must be reasonable. Thus, time scaling is essential if the analog computer is to be useful for a wide range of problems.

Several methods for time scaling have been introduced. Some require the determination of the time-scale factor at the beginning of the programming procedure.[4] In these approaches, the

differential equation describing the problem is time scaled to
yield an equation with a suitable solution rate. Another method
delays the selection of the time-scale factor until the problem
has been magnitude scaled.[3] The latter method will be used in
this text. The former method will be discussed briefly.

Before discussing the procedure for time scaling, certain
definitions are required. The time variable of the original,
unscaled equation will be called "problem time" or "real time."
The symbol for problem time will be t. The time variable of
the scaled equation will be called "computer time" or "scaled
time." The symbol for computer time will be T. The two time
variables will be related by the time-scale factor α,

$$T = \alpha t, \tag{4.6.1}$$

or

$$\alpha = \frac{T}{t} . \tag{4.6.2}$$

If $\alpha=1$, the computer solution proceeds at the same rate as the
original equation and the computer is operating in "real time."
If $\alpha>1$, the computer solution proceeds at a slower rate than the
original system. For $\alpha<1$, the computer time is faster than real
or problem time.

Since the integrators on the computer integrate with respect
to computer time, T, and not problem time, t, the time-scale
factor can be changed by controlling the integration rate of the
integrators. The integration rate is proportional to the gain of
the integrator. Thus, an analog computer program can be time
scaled by changing the gain of all integrators by the same amount.
No other changes are required. To increase the computer solution
rate, increase the gain of all integrators by the ratio of the
desired change in time. Decreasing the gain of the integrators
will reduce the rate of the computer solution. Changing all
integrator gains, and only the integrator gains, by the same ratio
and carefully keeping track of the relationship between real time
and computer time, is all that is necessary to time scale. The
term "integrator gain" as used here implies the product of the
potentiometer setting and the input/output gain of the integrator.

Thus, an integrator can be time scaled by changing a pot setting, the value of an input resistor and/or the size of the feedback capacitor.

In order to change real-time derivatives to computer-time derivatives, differentiate Equation (4.6.1) with respect to time

$$\frac{dT}{dt} = \alpha \qquad (4.6.3)$$

and solve for dt

$$dt = \frac{1}{\alpha} dT. \qquad (4.6.4)$$

By substitution, the basic derivative can now be written

$$\frac{dx}{dT} = \frac{1}{\alpha} \frac{dx}{dt} = \frac{1}{\alpha} \dot{x}. \qquad (4.6.5)$$

Equation (4.6.5) can be used to convert derivatives with respect to computer time into derivatives with respect to problem time.

To illustrate the procedure for time scaling, consider the example problem of Section 4.5. The unscaled equation is

$$\ddot{x} + 2\dot{x} + 4x = 0, \qquad (4.6.6)$$

with $\dot{x}(0) = 0$ and $x(0) = 20m$. The unscaled computer diagram is shown in Figure 4-5-1 and repeated in Figure 4-6-1 for convenience.

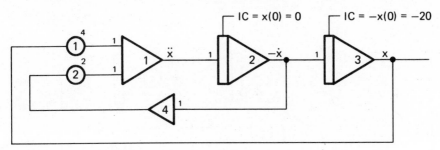

Figure 4-6-1. Unscaled computer program

Since time scaling does not affect the summing amplifier, Equation (4.5.6) and Figure 4-5-3 are correct and do not need changing. However, as stated previously, time scaling will affect the gain of the integrators.

In order to see the effect of time scaling on the integrators, consider the integrator producing $-\dot{x}$ from $\ddot{x}$ (amplifier 2). The unscaled equation is

$$\dot{x} = -\int \ddot{x}\, dt, \tag{4.6.7}$$

and substitution of Equation (4.6.4) for dt yields

$$\dot{x} = -\int \frac{\ddot{x}}{\alpha}\, dT. \tag{4.6.8}$$

Equation (4.6.8) illustrates the effect of time scaling on the gain of an integrator. Substitution of computer variables from the scaling table gives

$$-40\left[\frac{-\dot{x}}{40}\right] = -\int \frac{80}{\alpha}\left[\frac{\ddot{x}}{80}\right] dT, \tag{4.6.9}$$

which can be divided by -40 to yield

$$\left[\frac{-\dot{x}}{40}\right] = \int \frac{2}{\alpha}\left[\frac{\ddot{x}}{80}\right] dT. \tag{4.6.10}$$

The inversion of the integrator is accounted for by the minus sign on $[-\dot{x}/40]$. Similar manipulation of the equation for the integrator producing x from $-\dot{x}$ (amplifier 3) gives the scaled equation

$$\left[\frac{x}{20}\right] = \int \frac{2}{\alpha}\left[\frac{-\dot{x}}{40}\right] dT. \tag{4.6.11}$$

Again, note the minus sign to account for the inversion of the integrator. The scaled computer diagram is shown in Figure 4-6-2.

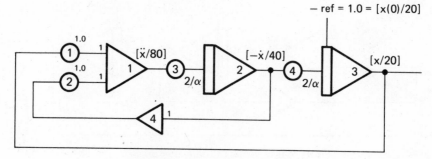

Figure 4-6-2. Scaled program

If $\alpha=1$, (computer time = real time) the problem is not time scaled and the computer diagram is identical to the program of Figure 4-5-6. If $\alpha=10$, the solution rate is reduced by a factor of 10,

and the integrator gains (amplifiers 2 and 3) of Figure 4-6-2 are
both 1 instead of 10. It would take 10 sec for the response of
the computer solution to duplicate the action of the original
system in 1 sec.

The solution rate of this problem could be increased by a
factor of 5 by changing the pot settings on both integrators to
1.0 (i.e., removing the pots) with integrator gains of 10. This
corresponds to $\alpha=0.2$. With this gain setting, an event that
required 1 sec in the original system will need only 0.2 sec in
the time-scaled system.

The example problem of the preceding discussion did not
require time scaling in order to be solved on an analog computer.
Obviously, some equations will need time scaling and others will
not. For second-order systems, an indication of the need for
time scaling can be determined from the undamped natural frequency, ω_n. It has been found that equations with ω_n in the
range, $0.1 < \omega_n < 10$, usually have solution rates suitable for
recording on strip chart and x-y recorders. For systems with
ω_n out of this range, the time-scale factor, α, should be selected such that

$$0.1 < \frac{\omega_n}{\alpha} < 10.0. \tag{4.6.12}$$

The reasoning behind this relationship will be developed in
Section 4.8. Actually, the computer amplifiers are capable of
much faster operation and problems are often run 500 times
faster for cathode ray tube (CRT) display of the results. If the
method of time scaling suggested here is used, it is not necessary
to select α in advance. However, it is helpful to know that time
scaling will be needed and have some idea of the expected range.
This will be illustrated by the example in the next section.

4.7 ILLUSTRATION: TIME AND MAGNITUDE SCALING

In order to illustrate both time and magnitude scaling procedures, consider the equation

$$\ddot{x} + 100\dot{x} + 10,000x = 10,000f(t), \tag{4.7.1}$$

where $\dot{x}(0) = 0$ and $x(0) = 0$. Comparing the terms of Equation
(4.7.1) with the generalized, linear, second-order equation

gives, ω_n^2 = 10,000 and $2\delta\omega_n$ = 100. Solving these equations yields
a damping ratio, δ=0.5, and an undamped natural frequency, ω_n=100.
The final value of the system response for f(t) = 1.0 (a unit
step) is x(t=∞) = 1.0. If the damping ratio were zero, the response would oscillate sinusoidally with a maximum value of 2.0
(see Section 3.6). Since the maximum value for the damped response is between 1.0 and 2.0, assume the maximum value, x_m=2.0.
This is a convenient scale to work with and will yield computer
variables which use most of the dynamic range of the amplifiers.
The corresponding maximum value of $\dot{x}$ is therefore

$$\dot{x}_m = \omega_n x_m = (100)(2) = 200. \tag{4.7.2}$$

The maximum value of x, can be determined from

$$\ddot{x}_m = \omega_n^2 x_m = (100)^2(2) = 20,000. \tag{4.7.3}$$

From the maximum values of x, $\dot{x}$, and $\ddot{x}$, it is obvious that
magnitude scaling will be necessary. If an x-y recorder is to
be used for plotting the solution, time scaling will be necessary
since ω_n is considerably larger than the suggested maximum value
of 10.0. If the output is to be displayed on a CRT, the solution
rate is adequate.

Following the suggested procedure, the first task is to
prepare an unscaled computer diagram. This is shown in Figure
4-7-1. The next step of the procedure is the preparation of a
scaling table. This is shown in Figure 4-7-2. The computer

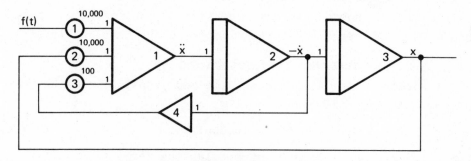

Figure 4-7-1. Unscaled program

Variable	Maximum Value	Computer Variable
x	2.0	$\left[\dfrac{x}{2}\right]$
$\dot{x}$	200.0	$\left[\dfrac{\dot{x}}{200}\right]$
$\ddot{x}$	20,000.0	$\left[\dfrac{\ddot{x}}{20,000}\right]$
f(t)	1.0	$\left[\dfrac{f(t)}{1.0}\right]$

Figure 4-7-2.   Scaling table

variables of the scaling table can now be used to scale the equation for each component of the unscaled program.   Since   the
expected values were based on zero damping, the actual maximum
values will be less than the values of Figure 4-7-2.   Thus, all
amplifiers will operate within their linear range.

For the summing amplifier, the equation is

$$\ddot{x} = -100\dot{x} - 10,000x + 10,000f(t). \tag{4.7.4}$$

Substituting computer variables and solving for the computer
variable for $\ddot{x}$, gives the scaled equation

$$\left[\frac{\ddot{x}}{20,000}\right] = -\left[\frac{\dot{x}}{200}\right] - \left[\frac{x}{2}\right] + \frac{1}{2}\left[\frac{f(t)}{1}\right]. \tag{4.7.5}$$

This completes the scaling for the summing amplifier.

For the integrator producing $-\dot{x}$ (amplifier 2) the unscaled
equation is

$$\dot{x} = -\int \ddot{x}\, dt. \tag{4.7.6}$$

Substituting computer variables and dividing by −200 yields

$$\left[\frac{-\dot{x}}{200}\right] = \int 100\left[\frac{\ddot{x}}{20,000}\right] dt, \tag{4.7.7}$$

which is the magnitude scaled equation for integrator two.   The
usual procedure at this point is to divide the coefficient   of
the right-hand side of Equation (4.7.7) into a reasonable   pot
setting (.05 to .95) and an integrator gain (1 or 10).   However,
the coefficient in this case is 100, which is out of the normal
range and an indication that time scaling will be required.   If

the need for time scaling had not been indicated previously by $\omega_n > 10$, the large integrator gain of Equation (4.7.7) would point out the need for time scaling. If the ω_n of the problem had been relatively small ($\omega_n < .1$), the coefficient of Equation (4.7.7) would have also been small. Thus, the need for time scaling is indicated by integrator gains that are either too small or too large.

Scaling the equation for the integrator producing x from $\dot{x}$ (amplifier 3) gives

$$\left[\frac{x}{2}\right] = \int 100\left[\frac{-\dot{x}}{200}\right]dt, \qquad\qquad (4.7.8)$$

where inversion is accounted for by the minus sign.

To see how time scaling can be used to provide more reasonable integrator gains, make the time-scale substitution as indicated in Equation (4.6.4). Equation (4.7.7) now becomes

$$\left[\frac{-\dot{x}}{200}\right] = \int \frac{100}{\alpha}\left[\frac{\ddot{x}}{20,000}\right]dT, \qquad\qquad (4.7.9)$$

and Equation (4.7.8) becomes

$$\left[\frac{x}{2}\right] = \int \frac{100}{\alpha}\left[\frac{-\dot{x}}{200}\right]dT. \qquad\qquad (4.7.10)$$

The complete scaled program can be drawn using Equations (4.7.5), (4.7.9) and (4.7.10). This is shown in Figure 4-7-3. The gains

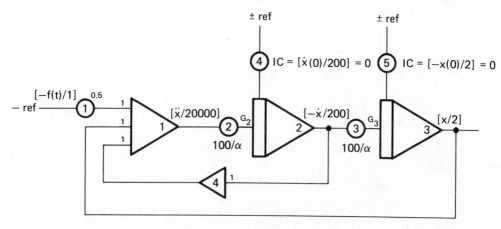

Figure 4-7-3. The scaled program

for integrators 2 and 3 and settings for pots 2 and 3 have not been assigned since the product of the pot setting and integrator gain (P_2G_2 and P_3G_3) must be equal to $100/\alpha$.

The only remaining task is the selection of the time-scale factor α. If $\alpha=100$, the $P_2G_2 = 1.0$ and $P_3G_3 = 1.0$. These gain values can be obtained with integrator gains of 1.0 and no potentiometers. In this case, the solution rate will be decreased (slowed) by a factor of 100. If $\alpha=10$, $P_2G_2 = 10$ and $P_3G_3 = 10$. This solution rate can be achieved with integrator gains of 10.0 without potentiometers. For $\alpha=50$, the requirements, $P_2G_2 = 2$ and $P_3G_3 = 2$, can be obtained with pot settings of 0.2 and integrator gains of 10.0. The time-scale factor, α, *must* be the *same* for both integrators. Also, note that the time scaling affects only the gain of the integrators.

If a summing integrator is used in place of the summing amplifier, the scaling procedure is slightly different. In order to illustrate the procedure, note that the unscaled equation of the summing integrator is

$$\dot{x} = -\int \ddot{x}\ dt = -\int [-100\dot{x} - 10{,}000x + 10{,}000f(t)]dt.$$

$$(4.7.11)$$

Substituting computer variables and dividing by -200 gives a scaled equation

$$\left[\frac{-\dot{x}}{200}\right] = \int \left(100\left[\frac{-\dot{x}}{200}\right] + 100\left[\frac{-x}{2}\right] + 50\left[\frac{f(t)}{1}\right]\right)dt. \qquad (4.7.12)$$

The inversion of the summing integrator is accounted for by the minus sign on the computer variable $[-\dot{x}/200]$. Time scaling by α gives the time-scaled equation

$$\left[\frac{-\dot{x}}{200}\right] = \int \left(\frac{100}{\alpha}\left[\frac{-\dot{x}}{200}\right] + \frac{100}{\alpha}\left[\frac{-x}{2}\right] + \frac{50}{\alpha}\left[\frac{f(T)}{1}\right]\right)dT. \qquad (4.7.13)$$

The computer program for this equation and the additional integrator required, Equation (4.7.10), is shown in Figure 4-7-4.

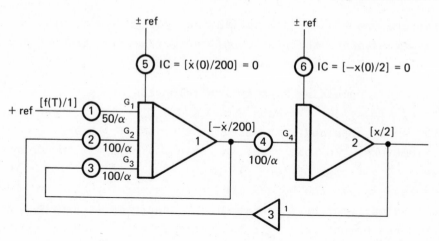

Figure 4-7-4.   Scaled program for $\ddot{x} + 100\dot{x} + 10{,}000x = 10{,}000f(t)$

The pot settings and integrator gains are determined from the
relations: $P_1G_1 = 50/\alpha$, $P_2G_2 = 100/\alpha$, $P_3G_3 = 100/\alpha$ and $P_4G_4 = 100/\alpha$.
Since pot settings should be in the range, $0.05<P<.95$, and the
available integrator gains are usually 1.0 and 10, the time-scale
factor for this problem must be in the range, $10<\alpha<2000$. However,
the recording instrument may dictate a smaller range.   For example, if $\alpha=2000$, each second of problem time will require 2000
sec of computer time.   This solution rate may be too slow.   It
is important to note that the forcing function, $f(t)$, must also
be time scaled to become $f'(T)$.   In this example $f(t)$ was a unit
step input and did not have to be changed.   However, sinusoidal,
ramp, and other time dependent forcing function must be scaled.

   The time-scale factor can be determined from the scaled
computer diagram by examining the computer variables at the
input and output of an integrator and comparing them with the
integrator gain.   For example, if the program of Figure 4-7-4
is time scaled by $\alpha=100$, then the gain of integrator 2 is 1.0.
However, $[-\dot{x}/200]$ is fed to the integrator and $[x/2]$ is produced.
This implies that the input variable is inverted, integrated and
multiplied by 100.   Since the actual gain is only 1.0, the program has been scaled by a factor of 100.   The reduction in gain
causes the computer solution to proceed at a slower rate than the
original problem.

Since the need to time scale is indicated by relatively large or small integrator gains, time scaling can be deferred until the magnitude scale is completed. It is then a matter of selecting a value for α to give reasonable integrator gains and convenient recording rates. However, in order to return to problem or real time, the time axis of the recordings must be relabeled. Therefore, α is usually selected to provide convenient conversion ratios. The response for the system of Figure 4-7-4 is shown in Figure 4-7-5. Note the dual labels on both

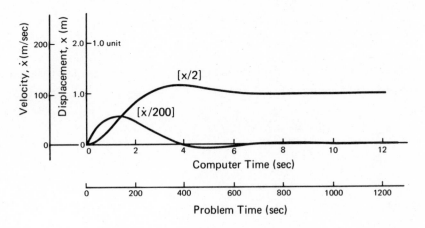

Figure 4-7-5. Response for scaled program

the absissa and ordinate. In addition, the value for α and the scale factor for x also are shown. The use of $\dot{x}$ and $\ddot{x}$ in time-scaled equations should be handled with care. Although $\dot{x}$ was defined, $\dot{x} = dx/dt$, after time scaling, all variables are recorded in computer time, T. However, as long as the relationship is understood, the convenience of the dot notation will be used.

4.8   ANOTHER APPROACH TO TIME SCALING

As noted previously, several approaches to time scaling have been developed, and each method has merit.[3,4] Another approach will be discussed briefly in order to give additional insight into the time-scaling process. For readers interested in the details, a couple of references have been cited and many others are available.

In this approach, the basic scaling relationship $(T=\alpha t)$ is developed for all derivatives as follows:

$$\frac{dx}{dt} = \alpha \frac{dx}{dT} ,$$

$$\frac{d^2x}{dt^2} = \alpha^2 \frac{d^2x}{dT^2} ,$$

$$\vdots \qquad \vdots$$

$$\frac{d^nx}{dt^n} = \alpha^n \frac{d^nx}{dT^n} . \qquad\qquad (4.8.1)$$

These relationships are then substituted for the derivatives of the unscaled differential equation. For example, the equation

$$a_o \frac{d^nx}{dt^n} + a_1 \frac{d^{n-1}x}{dt^{n-1}} + \ldots + a_n x = b_o f(t), \qquad (4.8.2)$$

becomes

$$\alpha^n a_o \frac{d^nx}{dT^n} + \alpha^{n-1} a_1 \frac{d^{n-1}x}{dT^{n-1}} + \ldots + a_n x = b_o f'(t). \qquad (4.8.3)$$

In comparing the scaled Equation (4.8.3) with the unscaled Equation (4.8.2), note that the derivatives are with respect to computer time and the coefficients are different. In addition, the forcing function is now a function of computer time, $f'(T)$.

Considerable insight can be gained by considering the effect of this approach to scaling on the generalized form of the linear, second-order differential equation. The unscaled equation is

$$\frac{d^2x}{dt^2} + 2\delta\omega_n \frac{dx}{dt} + \omega_n^2 x = \omega_n^2 f(t). \qquad (4.8.4)$$

Substituting the scaling relations of Equation (4.8.1) gives

$$\alpha^2 \frac{d^2x}{dT^2} + 2\delta\omega_n \alpha\frac{dx}{dT} + \omega_n^2 x = \omega_n^2 f'(T), \qquad (4.8.5)$$

and dividing by α^2 yields

$$\frac{d^2x}{dT^2} + \frac{2\delta\omega_n}{\alpha} \frac{dx}{dT} + \frac{\omega_n^2}{\alpha^2} x = \frac{\omega_n^2}{\alpha^2} f'(T). \qquad (4.8.6)$$

Associate α with ω_n and definite

$$\omega_n' = \frac{\omega_n}{\alpha} , \qquad\qquad (4.8.7)$$

where ω_n' is the undamped natural frequency of the scaled equation. Substituting Equation (4.8.7) into Equation (4.8.6) gives

$$\frac{d^2x}{dT^2} + 2\delta\omega_n' \frac{dx}{dT} + (\omega_n')^2 x = (\omega_n')^2 f'(T). \qquad (4.8.8)$$

Equation (4.8.8) describes a system with the same damping ratio, δ, as Equation (4.8.4). However, the independent variable and the undamped natural frequency have been scaled by the time-scale factor, α. Thus, the effect of time scaling is a change in the undamped natural frequency. Values of $\alpha>1$ yield $\omega_n'<\omega_n$ and result in a reduced solution rate. If $\alpha<1$, $\omega_n'>\omega_n$ and the computer simulation proceeds at a faster rate than the original problem.

Since the time-scaled equation has the same δ and the same initial conditions, the magnitude of the response is the same for both equations. One system responds at a different time rate. Extending the concept to the general system represented by Equation (4.8.2) indicates that time scaling changes the time of response but does not change the magnitude at corresponding points in time.

In order to illustrate the technique, consider the example problem of the previous section. The unscaled equation is

$$\frac{d^2x}{dt^2} + 100 \frac{dx}{dt} + 10,000x = 10,000f(t), \qquad (4.8.9)$$

where $x(0) = \dot{x}(0) = 0$ and $x_{ss} = 1.0$. As noted previously, $\omega_n = 100$ and time scaling will be necessary if an x-y recorder is to be used for recording the response. Substituting the relations of Equation (4.8.1) gives

$$\alpha^2 \frac{d^2x}{dT^2} + 100\alpha \frac{dx}{dt} + 10,000x = 10,000f'(T), \qquad (4.8.10)$$

and dividing by α^2 yields

$$\frac{d^2x}{dT^2} + \frac{100}{\alpha}\frac{dx}{dT} + \frac{10,000}{\alpha^2}x = \frac{10,000}{\alpha^2}f(T). \qquad (4.8.11)$$

Since the desirable range for ω_n' is $.1<\omega_n'<10$, select $\alpha=100$. Substituting $\alpha=100$ into Equation (4.8.11) gives

$$\frac{d^2x}{dT^2} + \frac{dx}{dT} + x = f'(T), \qquad (4.8.12)$$

with zero initial conditions. Since $\omega_n' = 1$ and $2\delta\omega_n' = 1$, the damping ratio of the scaled equation is, $\delta=0.5$. Thus, time scaling does not affect the damping ratio. Also, since $x_{ss} = 1.0$ and the maximum value of the overshoot on x will be between 1.0 and 2.0, choose $x_m = 2.0$.

The maximum value of dx/dT is $(dx/dT_m) = \omega_n'x_m = (1)(2) = 2$. Therefore, convenient computer variables are [x/2] and [dx/2dT]. The time scaled equation is now ready to be magnitude scaled.

Equation (4.8.12) can be scaled for a summing integrator by using the equation

$$\frac{dx}{dT} = -\int\frac{d^2x}{dT^2}\,dT = -\int\left(\frac{-dx}{dT} - x + f'(T)\right)dT. \qquad (4.8.13)$$

Substituting computer variables and dividing by -2 gives

$$\left[\frac{-dx}{2dT}\right] = \int\left(\left[\frac{-dx}{2dT}\right] + \left[\frac{-x}{2}\right] + \frac{1}{2}\left[\frac{f'(T)}{1}\right]\right)dT. \qquad (4.8.14)$$

The integrator producing [x/2] from [-dx/2dT] obviously requires a gain of one. The resulting program is shown in Figure 4-8-1.

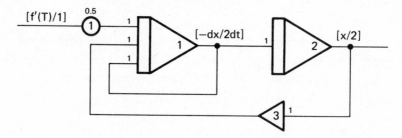

Figure 4-8-1. Scaled program for $\ddot{x} + 100\dot{x} + 10,000x = 10,000f(t)$

The program of Figure 4-8-1 has the same values as the program of
Figure 4-7-4 for α=100. Thus, both time scaling methods yield
the same computer program. However, note the different scale on
the derivative terms. In the first approach, time scaling is
done after magnitude scaling and the derivative is scaled $[-\dot{x}/200]$.
In the latter approach, time scaling is carried out first and the
derivative is scaled $[-dx/2dT]$. In the latter case the derivative
is with respect to T. To convert the derivatives with respect
to computer time, T, to derivatives with respect to real time, t,
use the following relations

$$\left[\frac{-dx}{2dT}\right] = \left[\frac{-dx}{2\alpha dt}\right] = \left[\frac{-dx}{2(100)dt}\right] = \left[\frac{-\dot{x}}{200}\right]. \qquad (4.8.15)$$

Thus, both approaches yield identical results. The difficulties
involved with converting derivatives with respect to computer
time to problem time is the reason the approach of Section 4.7
is preferred. However, understanding both approaches certainly
provides additional insight.

4.9 STATIC CHECKING

At the end of Chapter 3, Section 3.11 introduced static
checking. It was noted that the procedure checked for errors
in program development, component interconnection and most
equipment malfunctions. However, the discussions of time and
magnitude scaling in this chapter make it necessary to discuss
static testing in more detail. In particular, the procedure
should include a check of the scaling and the resulting program.

The first step of the procedure is identical to the method
discussed earlier. Initial conditions are substituted into the
original equation describing the system and a value for the
highest-order derivative determined. As before, "dummy" initial
conditions are assumed and used in place of terms having zero
initial conditions. The values from this step are used to check
programming, scaling, patching and computer components.

In order to check programming and scaling, substitute the
initial conditions used in the previous step into the scaled
computer variables at the output of the amplifiers. These values
can be used to calculate the output of every pot, and as a check,

the highest-order derivative. The converted variables and computed values should agree at every point on the program.

As pointed out in Chapter 3, summing integrators present a
problem since during a static check their output is a function
of the initial condition and not the sum of the inputs. This
problem can be avoided by checking the unit-scale value at the
summing junction. This variable is called the derivative of the
output of the integrator, i.e., it is the variable prior to
integration. If the problem has been time scaled so that the
computer operates at a different rate than the original problem,
it is necessary to convert the problem derivative into the computer derivative to complete the checking procedure. This
conversion is based on Equation (4.6.4), $dT = \alpha dt$. For example,
if the output of an integrator in unit scale is $[\dot{x}/\dot{x}_m]$, then the
unit-scale derivative is

$$\frac{d}{dT}\left[\frac{\dot{x}}{\dot{x}_m}\right] = \frac{d}{\alpha dt}\left[\frac{\dot{x}}{\dot{x}_m}\right] = \frac{d}{dt}\left[\frac{\dot{x}}{\alpha \dot{x}_m}\right] = \left[\frac{\ddot{x}}{\alpha \dot{x}_m}\right] . \qquad (4.9.1)$$

Thus, the derivative of an integrator is the derivative of the
output divided by the time-scale factor, α. Also, every term of
the original equation can be checked with its corresponding
computer variable. Equation (4.9.1) does not include the change
in sign due to amplifier inversion. It should be noted that the
programming and scaling can be checked "off line" prior to patching the problem on the computer. A number of digital computer
programs have been developed to scale and check analog computer
programs. These are discussed in Chapter 14.

The last phase of the static check, verification of patching
and computer components, is based on the previous calculations.
It is a matter of converting the unit-scale variables into voltages
and checking the values at corresponding points in the program.
As noted earlier, it usually is not necessary to check every point,
since a single check will often verify several other values.

To illustrate the procedure, consider the example of Section
4.7. The equation to be simulated is

$$\ddot{x} + 100\dot{x} + 10,000x = 10,000f(t), \qquad (4.9.2)$$

with $\dot{x}(0) = 0$ and $x(0) = 0$. In Section 4.7, two scaled programs were developed for the equation. The first, utilizing a summing amplifier to produce $\ddot{x}$, is shown in Figure 4-7-3. The second, uses a summing integrator and is shown in Figure 4-7-4. Neither program specifies α, the time-scale factor, and both have zero initial conditions. In order to illustrate the static test procedure, assume an α of 50 and "dummy" initial conditions of $x(0) = 1.5$ meters and $\dot{x}(0) = -175$ meters/sec. The resulting computer diagram, with $\ddot{x}$ explicit, is shown in Figure 4-9-1. The computer diagram for the summing integrator approach is shown in Figure 4-9-2.

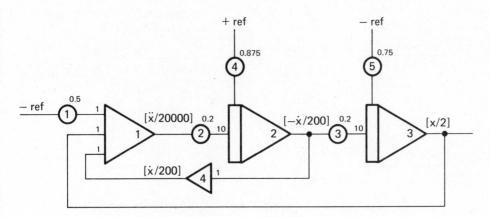

Figure 4-9-1. Scaled diagram for $\ddot{x} + 100\dot{x} + 10{,}000x = 10{,}000f(t)$

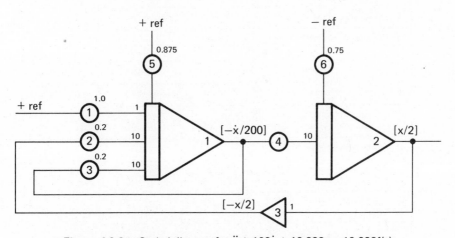

Figure 4-9-2. Scaled diagram for $\ddot{x} + 100\dot{x} + 10{,}000x = 10{,}000f(t)$

To begin the check procedure, plug the "dummy" initial conditions into Equation (4.9.2) and determine the corresponding value of $\ddot{x}$. In this case it is

$\ddot{x}(0) = 100\,(-175) - 10{,}000\,(1.5) + 10{,}000(1)$

$\ddot{x}(0) = 17{,}500 - 15{,}000 + 10{,}000$

$\ddot{x}(0) = 12{,}500.$ (4.9.3)

From this value and the corresponding initial conditions, a table for amplifier output values can be constructed as shown in Figure 4-9-3. A similar table for the potentiometers is shown in Figure 4-9-4. From Equation (4.9.1), the derivatives for the amplifiers used for integration can be calculated. The derivatives are shown in Figure 4-9-5. Using the computer diagram of Figure 4-9-1 and the tables of Figure 4-9-3, 4 and 5, note that the output values of

Amplifier	Scaled Output	Per Unit Output	Problem Value
1	$\left[\dfrac{\ddot{x}}{20{,}000}\right]$	$\dfrac{12{,}500}{20{,}000} = 0.625$	12,500 m/sec
2	$\left[-\dfrac{\dot{x}}{200}\right]$	$-\dfrac{175}{200} = 0.875$	-175 m/sec
3	$\left[\dfrac{x}{2}\right]$	$\dfrac{1.5}{2} = 0.75$	1.5 m
4	$\left[\dfrac{x}{200}\right]$	$\dfrac{-175}{200} = -0.875$	-175 m

Figure 4-9-3.   Amplifier static check data

	Pot	1	2	3
a	Representative value	$\dfrac{f(t)}{20{,}000}$	$\dfrac{100}{\alpha}$	$\dfrac{100}{\alpha}$
b	Pot setting	0.5	0.2	0.2
c	Computer variable input	$\left[\dfrac{-f(t)}{10{,}000}\right]$	$\left[\dfrac{\ddot{x}}{20{,}000}\right]$	$\left[\dfrac{-x}{200}\right]$
d	Per unit input	-1.0	0.625	0.875
e	Per unit output	-0.5	0.125	0.175
f	Computer variable output	$\left[\dfrac{-f(t)}{20{,}000}\right]$	$\left[\dfrac{\ddot{x}}{100{,}000}\right]$	$\left[\dfrac{-\dot{x}}{1{,}000}\right]$
g	Amplifier gain	1	10	10
h	Amplified computer variable	$\left[\dfrac{f(t)}{20{,}000}\right]$	$\left[\dfrac{\ddot{x}}{10{,}000}\right]$	$\left[\dfrac{-x}{100}\right]$
i	Amplified per unit value	-0.5	1.25	1.75

Figure 4-9-4.   Potentiometer static check table

Amplifier	Computer Variable Output	Derivative	Unit Scale Derivative
2	$\left[\dfrac{-\dot{x}}{200}\right]$	$\left[-\dfrac{-\ddot{x}}{(50)(200)}\right]=\left[\dfrac{\ddot{x}}{10,000}\right]$	$\left[\dfrac{12,500}{10,000}\right]=\left[1.25\right]$
3	$\left[\dfrac{x}{2}\right]$	$\left[-\dfrac{\dot{x}}{(50)(2)}\right]=\left[\dfrac{-\dot{x}}{100}\right]$	$\left[\dfrac{-(-175)}{100}\right]=\left[1.75\right]$

Figure 4-9-5. Derivative static check data

pots 2 and 3 (row i of Figure 4-9-4) must agree with the derivatives of Figure 4-9-5. Also, the output of amplifier 1
(Figure 4-9-3) must agree with the negative of the sum of the output of pot 1 (Figure 4-9-4) and amplifiers 3 and 4 (Figure 4-9-3).

From the tables, -(-0.5 - 0.875 + 0.75) = +0.625, which
agrees with the 0.625 entry for the amplifier 1 in Figure 4-9-3.
This check could have been carried out in the original problem
variables. It is a very important check and attention should be
given to algebraic sign and magnitude. If the check is invalid,
the errors can be traced by working backwards through the diagram.

Obviously, all of the information presented in Figure 4-9-3,
4 and 5 is not necessary. The extra details were included here
for their instructional value and are not normally tabulated.

As an additional example, amplifier, potentiometer and derivative data for the program of Figure 4-9-2 are presented in
Figures 4-9-6, 7 and 8.
As noted previously, agreement of the static test at certain key
points in the program is usually adequate. In the examples
presented here, amplifiers 1 and 5 are the most important points.

Amplifier	Scaled Output	Per Unit Output	Problem Value
5	$-\left\lfloor\dfrac{\dot{x}}{200}\right\rfloor$	$-\left\lfloor\dfrac{-175}{200}\right\rfloor = .875$	-175 m/sec
6	$\left\lfloor\dfrac{x}{2}\right\rfloor$	$\left\lfloor\dfrac{1.5}{2}\right\rfloor = .75$	1.5 m
7	$-\left\lfloor\dfrac{x}{2}\right\rfloor$	$-\left\lfloor\dfrac{1.5}{2}\right\rfloor = .75$	-1.5 m

Figure 4-9-6. Amplifier static check data

Pot	Representative Value	Static Check Setting	Per Unit Input	Per Unit Output	Amplified Output
8	$50/\alpha$	1.0	1.0	1.0	1.0
9	$100/\alpha$	0.2	0.75	0.15	-1.5
10	$100/\alpha$	0.2	0.875	0.175	1.75
11	$100/\alpha$	0.2	0.875	0.175	1.75

Figure 4-9-7. Potentiometer static check data

Amplifier	Computer Variable Output	Derivative	Per Unit Derivative
5	$-\left[\frac{\dot{x}}{200}\right]$	$+\left[\frac{\ddot{x}}{1000}\right]$	1.25
6	$\left[\frac{x}{2}\right]$	$-\left[\frac{x}{100}\right]$	1.75

Figure 4-9-8. Derivative static check data

The portion of the static check discussed so far is a check of programming and scaling and can be done off line. The remaining checks will uncover patching errors and most equipment malfunctions. Basically, the remaining check is carried out by patching the program, putting the computer in the static test or initial condition mode, and measuring the output of the key pots and amplifiers. Suggested static-check forms are shown in Figure 4-9-9.[3]

Title ________ Amplifier Sheet
Date ________ #____
Problem ________
Static Test

Amp No.	Mode	Output	Calculated Derivative Output	Measured Derivative Output	Notes

Title ________ Pot Sheet
Date ________ #____
Problem ________

Pot No.	Function	Static Check Setting	Output	Notes

Figure 4-9-9. Suggested static check sheets

4.10 ADDITIONAL COMMENT ON TIME AND MAGNITUDE SCALING

Magnitude scaling is required to enable each amplifier to
operate over its linear range. Serious errors are introduced
if an amplifier operates at very low levels or exceeds the maximum
linear range of operation. At low levels, electrical noise and
amplifier drift are the chief sources of error. At levels
exceeding the stated range of operation, the summing junction is
quite likely operating at a level which makes the assumption of
"virtual ground" inaccurate.

Magnitude scaling <u>does</u> <u>not</u> affect the net gain around any
program loop. That is, the product of all pot and amplifier
gains around a given loop should not be affected by magnitude
scaling. Note that a change in the magnitude scale will affect
a particular element but there must always be an offsetting
change at another point in the loop. Since the initial estimates of maximum values were based on approximations, it is
frequently necessary to adjust certain variables. For example,
if the output of amplifier 4 in Figure 4-10-1 is below desired
levels, its operating range could be raised by increasing the

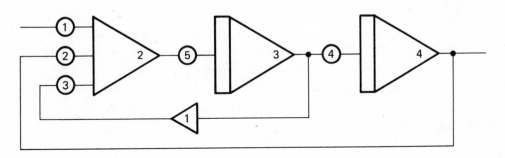

Figure 4-10-1. Magnitude scaling example

gain of pot 4 and/or the integrator input gain. However, a
corresponding decrease in the gain of pot 2 and/or the amplifier
input gain on amplifier 2 must be made to maintain the proper
loop gain.

If it is desired to reduce the level at the output of
amplifier 3, this can be accomplished by reducing the gain of
pot 5 and/or the input gain on the integrator. However, com-

pensating changes must be made in both the inner and the outer loops. These are made on pot 3, pot 4 or pot 2. Thus, the levels at any point in a program can be adjusted to improve scaling. This is an important aspect of programming and is used as a "fine tune" on the simulation.

In contrast to magnitude scaling, time scaling does change loop gains. Program loops with one integrator experience a gain change proportional to $1/\alpha$. The gain of program loops having two integrators will change by a factor of $1/\alpha^2$. In general, the gain of a loop containing n integrators will change by $1/\alpha^n$.

The coefficients of the examples presented in this chapter were selected to require uniform time scaling. Occasionally, systems will have diverse terms that make time scaling extremely difficult. In Section 4.7, it was stated that the need for time scaling can be identified by the requirement for either large or small integrator gains. In most cases, this is true since all of the system rate relationships are of the same general range. However, certain physical systems (e.g., the nuclear reactor) require the inclusion of terms that make time scaling difficult. A suitable scale for one term is either too fast or too slow for others. Problems of this type will require considerable effort before a suitable time scale is achieved. The same effect occurs occasionally in magnitude scaling. However, it is easier to handle.

A more general approach to time scaling has been developed.[5] However, it requires a knowledge of state variables and will be discussed in Chapter 7.

4.11 PROBLEMS

Problems covering the material for this chapter are identified by the appropriate section.

4.3.1 Determine the maximum expected value for the variables of the equation

$$\dot{x} + 6x = 4, \qquad\qquad\qquad (4.11.1)$$

with $x(0) = 0$.

4.3.2 Repeat Problem 4.3.1 with $x(0) = 10$.

4.3.3   Repeat Problem 4.3.1 with x(0) = -5.

4.3.4   How long does it take for the system described
        by Equation 4.10.1 to reach steady state?

4.3.5   Given the differential equation

$$2\ddot{x} + 160\dot{x} + 80{,}000x = 100{,}000, \qquad (4.11.2)$$

with $\dot{x}(0) = x(0) = 0$. Use the second-order
generalized response to estimate the maximum
expected values of x, $\dot{x}$, and $\ddot{x}$.

4.3.6   Repeat Problem 4.3.5 with $\dot{x}(0)$ = 0 and x(0) = 5.

4.3.7   Repeat Problem 4.3.5 with $\dot{x}(0)$ = 4 and x(0) = 0.

4.3.8   Repeat Problem 4.3.5 with $\dot{x}(0)$ = 5 and x(0) = 5.

4.3.9   Use the equal coefficient rule to determine the
        maximum expected value for the variables of
        Problem 4.3.5.

4.3.10 Given the differential equation

$$6\dddot{x} + 36\ddot{x} + 30\dot{x} + 36x = 72, \qquad (4.11.3)$$

where $\ddot{x}(0) = \dot{x}(0) = x(0) = 0$. Determine the
maximum expected values for the problem
variables.

4.3.11 Repeat Problem 4.3.10 with $\ddot{x}(0) = \dot{x}(0) = 0$ and
        x(0) = -2.

4.3.12 Repeat Problem 4.3.10 with $\ddot{x}(0)$ = 0, $\dot{x}(0)$ = 6
        and x(0) = 0.

4.3.13 Given the differential equation

$$\ddddot{x} + 10\dddot{x} + 29\ddot{x} + 26\dot{x} + 24x = -40, \qquad (4.11.4)$$

with $\dddot{x}(0) = \ddot{x}(0) = \dot{x}(0) = 0$. Determine the
maximum expected values.

4.3.14 Repeat Problem 4.3.13 with $\ddot{x}(0) = \ddot{x}(0) = 0$, $\dot{x}(0) = 4$ and $x(0) = 0$.

4.5.1 Develop a scaled program (with $\dot{x}$ explicit) for Equation 4.11.1.

4.5.2 Repeat Problem 4.5.1 with a summing integrator.

4.5.3 Develop a scaled program (with $\ddot{x}$ explicit) for Equation 4.11.2.

4.5.4 Repeat Problem 4.5.3 with a summing integrator.

4.5.5 Develop a scaled program (with $\dddot{x}$ explicit) for Equation 4.11.3.

4.5.6 Repeat Problem 4.5.5 with a summing integrator.

4.5.7 Develop a scaled program (with $\ddddot{x}$ explicit) for Equation 4.11.4.

4.5.8 Repeat Problem 4.5.7 with a summing integrator.

4.7.1 Discuss any time scaling that might be required for Problem 4.3.1.

4.7.2 Determine the range of suitable values for the time scale factor, α, of Problem 4.3.5.

4.7.3 Determine the range of suitable values for the time scale factor, α, of Problem 4.3.10.

4.7.4 Determine the range of suitable values for the time scale factor, α, of Problem 4.3.13.

4.7.5 Given the differential equation

$$\dddot{x} + 15\ddot{x} + 30\dot{x} + 60x = 90 , \qquad (4.11.5)$$

with $\ddot{x}(0) = \dot{x}(0) = 0$.

a) Determine expected maximum values.

b) Determine the range for the time scale factor α.

c) Develop a program to solve the equation.

4.7.6 Given the equation

$$\ddot{x} + 0.008\dot{x} + 0.001x = 0. \qquad (4.11.6)$$

a) Determine the expected maximum value.

b) Determine the range of α.

c) Develop a program to solve the equation.

4.7.7 To decrease the solution rate of a computer program, (increase, decrease) all integrator gains by the same amount. Circle the correct answer and give a physical reason for your answer.

4.7.8 Given the portion of the program shown
   a) Determine α.
   b) Determine the pot setting and gain to make the problem run twice as fast. (i.e., decrease α).
   c) Determine the pot setting and gain to reduce the solution rate of the problem by a factor of 3. (i.e., increase α).
   d) Change the problem to make α = 6.

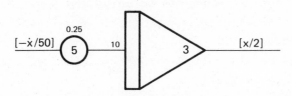

Figure 4-11-1.

4.7.9 Given the portion of the program shown
   a) Determine α.
   b) Determine the pot setting and integrator gain to reduce the solution rate by a factor of 3.
   c) Change the problem to make α = 10.

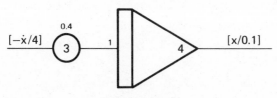

Figure 4-11-2.

4.7.10   Determine α for the program segment shown.

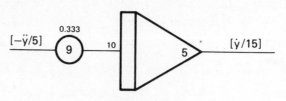

Figure 4-11-3.

4.7.11   Given the equations

$$\ddot{x} + 0.05\dot{y} + 0.05\dot{x} + 0.002x = 0.01, \qquad (4.11.7)$$

$$\ddot{y} + 0.05\dot{x} + 0.1\dot{y} + 0.001y = 0, \qquad (4.11.8)$$

where all initial conditions are zero.
a) Determine the equated main value.
b) Determine a suitable range for α.
c) Develop a program to solve the equations.

4.8.1   Use the alternate approach to time scaling on Problem 4.7.6.

4.8.2   Use the alternate approach to time scaling on Problem 4.7.5.

4.9.1   Perform static test calculations for Problem 4.3.1.

4.9.2   Perform static test calculations for Problem 4.3.5.

4.9.3   Perform static test calculations for Problem 4.3.10.

4.9.4   Perform static test calculations for Problem 4.3.13.

4.9.5   Perform static test calculations for Problem 4.7.5.

4.9.6   Perform static test calculations for Problem 4.7.6.

4.9.7   Patch Problem 4.3.1, perform static test check and record x.

4.9.8   Patch Problem 4.3.5, perform static test check and record x and $\dot{x}$.

4.9.9   Patch Problem 4.3.10, perform static test check and record x, $\dot{x}$ and $\ddot{x}$.

4.9.10 Patch Problem 4.3.13, perform static test check and record x, $\dot{x}$ and $\ddot{x}$.

4.9.11 Patch Problem 4.7.5, perform static test check and record x, and $\dot{x}$.

4.9.12 Patch Problem 4.7.6, perform static test check and record x and $\dot{x}$.

4.10.1 Develop a program to solve the equation

$$\ddot{x} + 10{,}001\dot{x} + .01x = .01, \qquad\qquad (4.11.9)$$

when $\dot{x}(0) = x(0) = 0$. Discuss any difficulty encountered.

4.10.2 Rescale the program of Figure 4-5-6 to reduce the output of integrator 2 by a factor of 2. (i.e., make it one-half of its present value).

4.10.3 Rescale the program of Figure 4-5-7 to reduce the output of integrator 1 to 80% of its present value.

4.10.4 Rescale the problem of Figure 3-8-1 to increase the output of amplifier 5 by a factor of 2.

4.10.5 Rescale the problem of Figure 3-9-1 to reduce the output of integrator 9 by a factor of 2.

4.12 REFERENCES FOR CHAPTER 4

(1) Johnson, C. L.: Analog Computer Techniques, McGraw-Hill Book Company, Inc., 1956.

(2) Rekoff, M. G., Jr.: Analog Computer Programming, Charles E. Merrill Books, Inc., Columbus, Ohio 1967.

(3) Carlson, A.; Hannauer, G.; Carey, T.; and Holsbery, P.: Handbook of Analog Computation, Electronic Associates, Inc., Princeton, N.J., 1965.

(4) Jackson, A. S.: Analog Computation, McGraw-Hill Book Company, Inc., New York, 1960.

(5) Cannon, Michael R.: "Magnitude and Time-Scaling of State-Variable Equation for Analog/Hybrid Computation," Simulation, Vol. 21, No. 1, pp. 23-28, July, 1973.

5

Simulation of Nonlinear Systems

5.1 INTRODUCTION

The solution of nonlinear differential equations is of great interest to engineers and scientists. Unfortunately, no general approach has been developed for solving nonlinear equations. For this reason, computer simulation is of greater assistance here than in the solution of linear differential equations.

Many types of nonlinearities are frequently encountered in the analysis of systems. One of the more common forms involves multiplication as exhibited by the equation

$$\ddot{x} + ax\dot{x} + bx = f(t). \tag{5.1.1}$$

Another form involves powers of the dependent variable and/or its derivatives such as

$$\ddot{x} + a\dot{x}^2 + bx = f(t). \tag{5.1.2}$$

The absolute value and other functional relationships are also encountered as illustrated by the equation

$$\ddot{x} + a|\dot{x}| + b \sin x = f(t). \hspace{3cm} (5.1.3)$$

In addition, some physical systems display characteristics that require the generation of special functions of the dependent variable.

In this chapter, the analog computer components needed for nonlinear system simulation will be presented along with appropriate programming methods.

The basic nonlinear computing elements are the diode, the function multiplier and the function generator. In the following sections, each of these elements will be discussed and its application illustrated with an example problem.

5.2 THE DIODE AS A NONLINEAR COMPUTING ELEMENT

The most widely used nonlinear computing element is the diode. There are several types of diodes and a number of symbols have been used. Figure 5-2-1(a) illustrates a popular symbol for the vacuum diode and the accepted symbol for the semiconductor diode is shown in Figure 5-2-1(b). The diode is a unidirectional conductor of electric current. The volt-amp characteristic curve for a diode is illustrated in Figure 5-2-2.

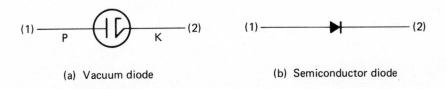

(a) Vacuum diode   (b) Semiconductor diode

Figure 5-2-1.   Diode symbols

If terminal (1) of the diode is electrically more positive than terminal (2), the diode is "forward-biased" and conducts current readily. The operation of a forward-biased diode is represented by the right-hand side of the curve in Figure 5-2-2(a). It is characterized by a large increase in current (i) for a very

small increase in the forward voltage (v). Typically, the forward voltage drop is in the range 0.2 to 0.5 volts for semiconductor diodes.

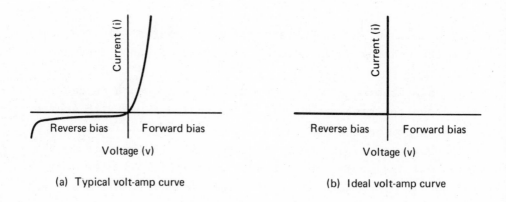

(a) Typical volt-amp curve   (b) Ideal volt-amp curve

Figure 5-2-2.   Diode characteristics

If terminal (2) is more positive than terminal (1), the
diode is reversed biased and conducts very little current (i).
This is illustrated by the left portion of the curve in Figure
5-2-2(a). This reverse "leakage" current is usually less than
5 µamps for semiconductor diodes and can be neglected in most
instances. Ignoring the low forward voltage drop and the small
reverse current, lead to the "ideal" diode characteristic of
Figure 5-2-2(b). The ideal diode conducts current when under
positive bias voltage. Note that the direction of the current
is in accord with the arrowhead of the symbol in Figure 5-2-1
(b). The ideal diode does not conduct current when the bias
voltage is reversed.

Based on the preceding discussion, the ideal diode can be
thought of as a switch that is open when terminal (2) is more
positive than terminal (1) (Figure 5-2-1). Under forward bias,
terminal(1) is more positivethan terminal (2), and the switch
can be considered closed.

A diode circuit used frequently in nonlinear simulation
utilizes the "limiting" function of diodes in the feedback
circuit.[1] The computer patching is shown in Figure 5-2-3.

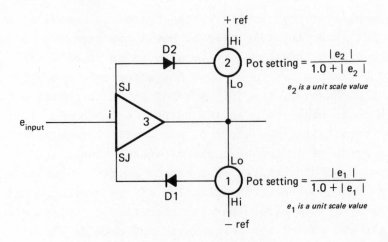

Figure 5-2-3. Diode limiter circuit

Note that the diodes are connected between the wiper arm of an ungrounded potentiometer and the summing junction of the amplifier, which is a virtual ground (provided the amplifier is operating in the linear range). Since this is the first encounter with the connection of additional elements to the summing junction, it might be advisable to review the circuit diagram of the summing amplifier of Figure 2-3-1. In effect, the diodes of Figure 5-2-3 are connected in parallel with the feedback resistor, R_f, of Figure 2-3-1. The operation of the circuit can be explained with the aid of the input-output characteristic of the limiter illustrated in Figure 5-2-4. If the

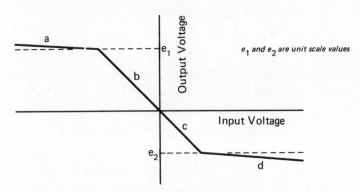

Figure 5-2-4. Input-output curve for diode limiter

input to amplifier 3 is positive, the output is negative and
both the "Hi" and "Lo" terminals of pot 1 are negative. Diode
D1 is back-biased and therefore behaves as an open switch.
Under these circumstances, D1 does not affect the operation of
the circuit. However, the "Hi" side of pot 2 is positive and
the low side is negative. As the output, e_o, becomes more
negative, eventually, the wiper of pot 2 will become negative
and cause diode D2 to become forward-biased. Under the circumstances, diode D2 behaves as a closed switch or "short
circuit." In explaining the operation of the summing amplifier
in Chapter 2, it was noted that the operational amplifier acts
to maintain the sum of the currents at the summing junction
equal to zero. An increase in the input voltage causes the
current in the summing junction to increase. In order to
maintain the sum of currents at the summing junction equal to
zero, there must be a corresponding decrease in the current
through the feedback resistor. This is achieved by a decrease
in the output voltage, e_o. However, the presence of diode D2,
operating as a closed switch, provides a path for any additional
current from the input. The operational amplifier is not
required to decrease the output voltage, e_o, in order to maintain the sum of currents at the summing junction equal to zero.
This operation is illustrated by segments (c) and (d) of the
curve in Figure 5-2-4. Until the output becomes more negative
than e_2^* (unit scaling) volts, both diodes are back-biased and
the gain (the slope of segment c) is determined by the ratio
of the feedback resistor to the input resistor.

     For negative inputs, the output is positive and diode D1
will be forward-biased if the output becomes more positive
than e_1^* (unit scaling) volts. Thus, the diodes do not affect
the operation of the amplifier until the output exceeds the
limits e_1 and e_2 as determined by the pot settings. Since the
actual diode is not ideal, the effective resistance during
forward-bias is not zero. Therefore, segments (a) and (d) of
Figure 5-2-4 do not have a slope of zero. Also, the corners
between segment (a) and (b) and between (c) and (d) are not
sharp but are rounded by the gradual "turn-on" of the diodes.
If a more precise limit is desired, additional elements are

required.[6,7] As noted previously, the slope of segments (b)
and (c) is determined by the input gain selected on the amplifier. Note that the circuit can be utilized with one diode if
limiting is desired in one direction only.

The equations for setting the limits on pots 1 and 2 of
Figure 5-2-3 are approximate. The easiest way to set the limits
is by direct observation. Use a large input and adjust the pot
until the desired limit is reached. Fortunately, it is not
necessary to understand the circuit details in order to use
limiters. Small plug-in units containing the diodes and pots
are available commercially.

A convenient scheme for setting the limiting values is shown
in Figure 5-2-5. The input sinusoid is adjusted to cause the output to exceed the desired limits. The limiting pots are adjusted
by observing the output on an x-y plotter or CRT.

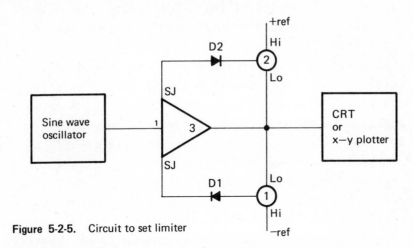

Figure 5-2-5. Circuit to set limiter

The diode limiting process can also be used to cut off the
entire positive or negative excursion of the output of an
amplifier. For example, the circuit of Figure 5-2-6 will not

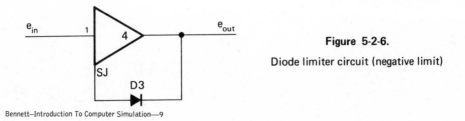

Figure 5-2-6.

Diode limiter circuit (negative limit)

permit the output to go negative. In order to understand the operation of this circuit, first note that as long as amplifier 4 is operating in the linear range, the summing junction is a virtual ground. For negative inputs, the output of amplifier 4 is positive and diode D3 is back-biased. Therefore, the diode does not conduct and has little or no affect on the operation of the amplifier. Under these circumstances, the gain of the amplifier is determined by the ratio of the feed-back resistance to the input resistance (1 in Figure 5-2-6). However, diode D3 is forward-biased for negative output values (positive input) and appears as a closed switch or short cir-cuit in parallel with the feedback resistor. As a result, the effective feedback resistance is zero. Therefore, the gain ratio, R_f/R_1, is also zero. With a gain of zero for positive input values, the amplifier output will not go negative. Ac-tually, the non-ideal nature of the diode permits the output voltage to reach the diode drop (0.3 to 0.5 volts) in the negative direction.

The operation of this circuit can be explained from another point of view. For negative inputs, the diode is back-biased (i.e., an open circuit) and the amplifier output must go positive in order to produce feedback current to cancel the input current. However, for positive inputs, the diode is forward-biased and enables a current to flow which balances the current due to the input. Therefore, the output of the amplifier does not go negative.   The input/output characteristic of the limiter circuit of Figure 5-2-6 is shown in Figure 5-2-7. If the diode is reversed, the positive output is limited.

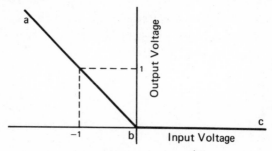

Figure 5-2-7. Diode limiter

In the analysis of physical systems, a discontinuity frequently encountered is "dead-space." Devices with dead-space have no response at the output until the input exceeds certain threshold levels. This characteristic is illustrated in Figure 5-2-8. A positive input must exceed the threshold (c) before an output is produced. In a similar manner, the

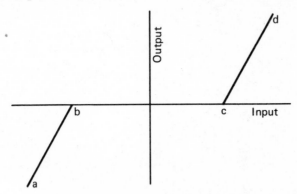

Figure 5-2-8. Characteristic of dead space

output is zero until the negative threshold (b) is exceeded. The threshold levels (b) and (c) may or may not be equal. Also, the gain (i.e., the slope of segments (a)-(b) and (c)-(d) may vary. A circuit to simulate dead-space is presented in Figure 5-2-9. As with the previous circuits, the corners

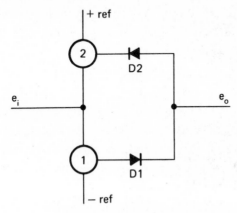

Figure 5-2-9. Dead-space circuit

at (b) and (c) are not sharp due to the non-ideal characteristics of the diodes. Note that pots 1 and 2 are of the ungrounded type. The positive turn-on level is determined by

the setting of pot 1 and the negative level is set by pot 2.
Trial and error is the best procedure for setting the pots.
A more precise circuit for dead-space is shown in reference
(8).

   To illustrate another use of diodes, consider the circuit
of Figure 5-2-10. In order to understand the operation of the

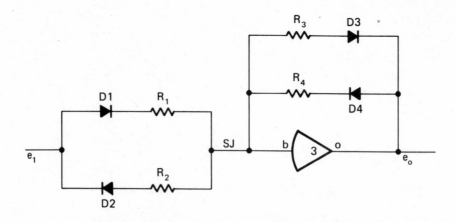

Figure 5-2-10.   Diode input/feedback circuit

circuit, note that the summing junction is a virtual ground
under normal limits of operation. If the summing junction is
at ground potential, diode D1 is forward-biased for positive
input voltages and diode D2 is reversed-biased. Thus, resistor
R_1 is the effective input resistor for positive inputs. Conversely, resistor R_2 is the effective input resistor for
negative inputs.

   In the feedback loop, diode D3 is forward-biased for
negative outputs, and due to inversion, is conducting for
positive input levels. In a similar manner, diode D4 is
forward-biased and conducts for positive outputs corresponding
to negative inputs. Thus, referring to Equation (2.3.9), the
equation for the amplifier of Figure 5-2-10 (for positive inputs) is

$$e_o = - \frac{R_3}{R_1} e_1,$$

(5.2.1)

where $e_1 > o$. In a similar manner, the equation for negative inputs is

$$e_o = - \frac{R_4}{R_2} e_1,$$

(5.2.2)

where $e_1 < o$. Figure 5-2-11 illustrates the characteristics of the amplifier connected as shown in Figure 5-2-10.

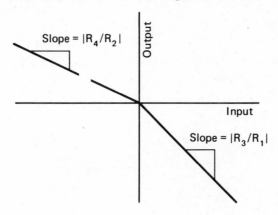

Figure 5-2-11. Input/output characteristic of the circuit of Figure 5-2-10

Another type of nonlinearity is produced by the "absolute value" circuit of Figure 5-2-12. The nonlinear circuits presented in this section illustrate the use of diodes to simulate

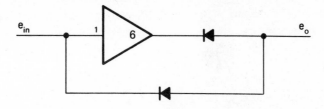

Figure 5-2-12. Absolute value circuit

various characteristics of physical systems. All of these circuits suffer from the affects of the non-ideal diodes. More accurate results can be obtained but they usually require more computing elements. Precision nonlinear circuits will not be presented here and the interested reader is referred to the books and technical journals listed as references for this chapter.

The discussion would not be complete without mentioning
Zener diodes. As the reverse-bias voltage is increased, there
is no appreciable increase in current until a certain voltage
is reached. At that point, the diode "breaks down" and conducts current while maintaining a constant voltage across the
diode. These diodes are available with a variety of Zener
voltages and can be used to establish limits and set levels.

5.3 EXAMPLE PROBLEM

To illustrate the use of diodes in simulation, consider
the system shown in Figure 5-3-1. The mass is subject to an
applied force, F, a spring force, K, and velocity dependent
friction, B. This is the same system used in section 3.7.

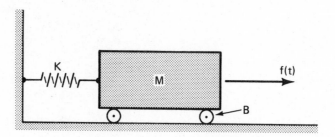

Figure 5-3-1. Spring-mass-damper system

However, in this case, the velocity dependent friction is a
function of the direction of travel. For positive velocities,
the friction coefficient, B = 2.0 Nt-sec/m and for negative
velocities, B = 1.5 Nt-sec/m. The other parameters are:
M = 5 Kg., K = 1.25 Nt/M and F = 2 Nt. The equation of motion is

$$M\ddot{x} + B\dot{x} + Kx = f(t). \tag{5.3.1}$$

Substituting the parameters for positive velocities gives

$$\ddot{x} + 0.4\dot{x} + 0.25x = 0.4, \tag{5.3.2}$$

where $\dot{x}>0$, $\dot{x}(0)=0$ and $x(0)=0$. For negative velocities

$$\ddot{x} + 0.3\dot{x} + 0.25x = 0.4, \tag{5.3.3}$$

where $\dot{x}<0$, $\dot{x}(0)=0$ and $x(0)=0$.

An unscaled program for this system is shown in Figure
5-3-2. The diodes permit the simulation of the different

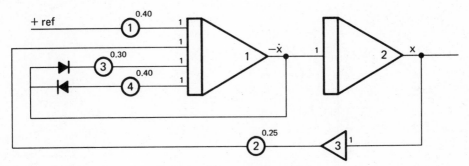

Figure 5-3-2. Unscaled program

friction coefficients for positive and negative velocities. When $\dot{x}$ is positive, $-\dot{x}$ is negative. For this condition, diode D1 is back-biased and diode D2 is forward-biased. Thus, D1 behaves as an open switch and D2 acts as a closed switch. Therefore, for positive velocities, the integrator receives the velocity input through pot 4, set at 0.4. For negative velocities, $-\dot{x}$ is positive and diode D1 is forward-biased. Diode D2 is back-biased and appears as an open circuit. Thus, for negative velocities, the velocity signal is fed through pot 3, set at 0.3.

Scaling is very important in this problem. The operating level of $\dot{x}$ should be scaled as high as possible to prevent the diode voltage drops from introducing excessive error. Based on the magnitudes of section 3.7, x is scaled for $[x/2.5]$, $\dot{x}$ is scaled for $[\dot{x}/1.0]$ and f(t) is scaled $[F/2]$. Since ω_n is 0.5, time scaling is not required. A scaled program is shown in Figure 5-3-3. The response of the system is shown in Figure 5-3-4.

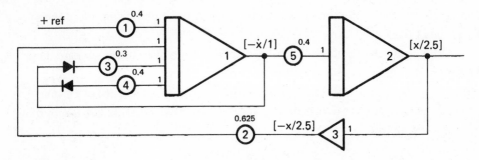

Figure 5-3-3. Scaled program

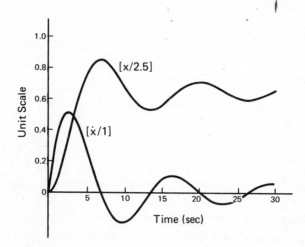

Figure 5-3-4. Response for velocity dependent damping

5.4 FUNCTION MULTIPLIERS

In the introduction to this chapter, the function multiplier was included as a basic computing element used in
nonlinear system simulation. The function multiplier should
be distinguished from the utilization of a pot to multiply by
a constant. The function multiplier can multiply a variable
function by a second variable function. In this section,
function multipliers will be introduced and their use for
multiplication, division and square root—operations illustrated.

The most popular function multiplier currently used on
analog computers is the quarter-square electronic multiplier.
Typically, these multipliers are capable of accuracies better
than 0.5 percent of full scale for frequencies less than
1000 Hertz (cycles per second). In earlier work, the servo-
multiplier was used. Unfortunately, the servo-multiplier is
limited to frequencies less than 10 Hertz and often requires
time scaling.

The quarter-square multiplier derives its name from the
functional relationship used to achieve multiplication. Assume
that two variable functions (x) and (y) are available in the
proper range for the computer. Combine the variables according
to the equation

$$z = \frac{1}{4} \ [(x+y)^2 - (x-y)^2].$$

(5.4.1)

Expanding the left side of Equation (5.4.1) yields

$$z = \frac{1}{4} [x^2 + 2xy + y^2 + 2xy - y^2 - x^2],$$ (5.4.2)

which can be reduced to

$$z = xy.$$ (5.4.3)

Thus, one <u>quarter</u> of the difference of the <u>square</u> of the terms (x+y) and (x-y) produces a "quarter-square multiplier."

The production of (x+y) and (x-y) can be achieved with summing amplifiers. A method for producing the square of each term will be covered in Section 5.7. There is one remaining problem. If (x) and (y) are properly scaled, then the product xy is likely to exceed the linear range of the computer. To avoid this problem, multipliers include an automatic scale factor equal to the reference voltage. Thus, on a ten-volt computer, the multiplier product is divided by ten to yield,

$$z = \frac{xy}{10}.$$ (5.4.4)

On a one hundred volt computer, the product is divided by one hundred. This is shown in Equation (5.4.5).

$$z = -\frac{xy}{100}.$$ (5.4.5)

Since the multipliers on most machines include inversion, Equation (5.4.4) and (5.4.5) have minus signs. The standard symbol for a multiplier is shown in Figure 5-4-1. As with

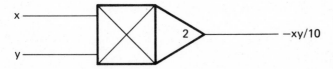

Figure 5-4-1. Multiplier symbol

amplifiers, the number at the apex of the figure identifies the particular multiplier.

On many machines, the multiplier networks provided on the patch panel do not include the required operational amplifiers and they must be patched by the programmer. Also, multiplier networks frequently require both +x and -x as well as +y and

−y. The operating manual for the particular machine should be consulted for multiplier patching. Most multipliers have variable input impedances and should be driven from amplifiers and not potentiometers.

A function multiplier can be utilized for division. In order to understand the principles involved, consider   the circuit of Figure 5-4-2. From earlier work, the sum   of the

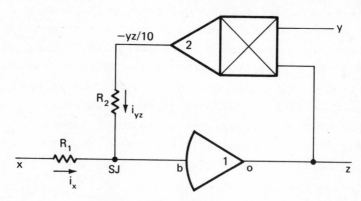

Figure 5-4-2. A division circuit

currents into the summing junction must be approximately zero. Therefore, for the circuit of Figure 5.4.2.

$$i_x + i_{yz} \cong 0,   \tag{5.4.6}$$

and by substitution, the equation becomes

$$\frac{x}{R_1} - \frac{yz}{10R_2} \cong 0.   \tag{5.4.7}$$

Solving for z yields a division expression

$$z = \frac{10R_2 x}{R_1 y} .   \tag{5.4.8}$$

If $R_1 = R_2$, the result is

$$z = 10 \frac{x}{y} ,   \tag{5.4.9}$$

and the circuit is dividing the variable (x) by the variable (y).

In using the division circuit, special consideration must be given to stability. The output of the amplifier is   fed back to the input, and as a result, there are problems.   The circuit of Figure 5-4-2 will operate in only two quadrants and (y) must be negative and (x) may be either positive   or negative.   Usually, the multiplier networks supplied on   a given computer will include patching instructions for   all combinations of division.   Therefore, consult the instruction manual for the best circuit for a particular computer.

Since the accuracy of a multiplier is best at mid-range inputs, scaling is very important.   Excessively small   input values should be avoided.   The programming symbol used   for division is shown in Figure 5-4-3.   As in the case   of   the

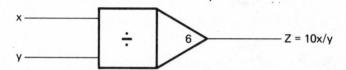

Figure 5-4-3.   Division programming symbol

multiplier, the number in the apex identifies the network used and the actual circuit patched may involve one or more operational amplifiers.

The multiplier can be used to take the square root of a variable.   Analysis of the circuit of Figure 5-4-4 yields an expression for the output of the form

$$z = - \sqrt{10 \frac{R_2 x}{R_1}} .$$

(5.4.10)

If $R_1 = R_2$, then the output is

$$z = -\sqrt{\frac{10x}{y}} .$$

(5.4.11)

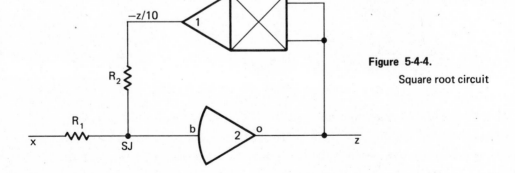

Figure 5-4-4.

Square root circuit

Due to the stability problems discussed earlier, the circuit of Figure 5-4-4 is restricted to positive values of x. There are methods to avoid this difficulty and the instruction manual for a particular computer should be consulted for suitable circuits. The programming symbol for the square root operation is shown in Figure 5-4-5. Repeated use of a multiplier can yield higher-

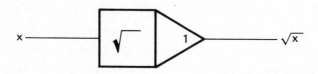

Figure 5-4-5.   Square root programming symbol

order roots, powers and other special functions.[6] The use of two multipliers to produce x^3 is illustrated in the next section.

5.5   EXAMPLE PROBLEM

To illustrate the programming of nonlinear differential equations, consider Rayleigh's equation,

$$\ddot{x} - \epsilon(1 - \frac{\dot{x}^2}{3})\dot{x} + x = 0. \qquad (5.5.1)$$

This equation has been the subject of numerous studies and the details of the nonlinear analysis will not be presented here. For further information, see references (6) and (7).

To program Equation (5.5.1), solve for $\ddot{x}$ and use repeated integration to produce $\dot{x}$ and x,

$$\ddot{x} = \epsilon\dot{x} - \epsilon\frac{\dot{x}^3}{3} - x. \qquad (5.5.2)$$

The nonlinear terms can be generated and fed back to a summing amplifier to produce $\ddot{x}$. If $\ddot{x}$ is not needed, a summing integrator can be used. The resulting program is shown in Figure 5-5-1.

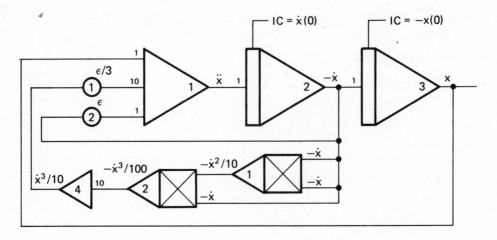

Figure 5-5-1. Program for Rayleigh's equation

The scaling principles introduced earlier are applicable here. However, the problem of determining maximum values is much more difficult for nonlinear equations. There are no general techniques, although linearization often yields some helpful guidelines for selecting maximum values. The method of equal coefficients presented in Chapter 4 is also useful.

The response of the circuit in Figure 5-5-1 is shown in Figure 5-5-2, with $\epsilon=2$, $\dot{x}(0) = 0$ and $x(0) = 3.0$. The initial

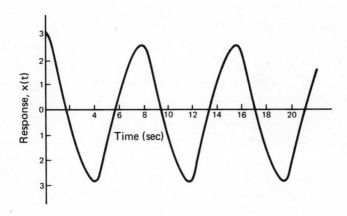

Figure 5-5-2. Response, $x(t)$, for Rayleigh's equation, $\epsilon = 2$

scaling was based on the equal coefficient rule. If $\dot{x}(0) = 0$
and $x(0) = 3.0$ then $\ddot{x}(0) = 3$.   Assuming $x_m = 3$ and $\ddot{x}_m = 3$,
scaling Equation 5.5.1 yields

$$3\left[\frac{\ddot{x}}{3}\right] - 2\ \dot{x}_m\left[\frac{\dot{x}}{\dot{x}_m}\right] + \frac{2}{3}\ \dot{x}_m^3\left[\frac{\dot{x}}{\dot{x}_m}\right]^3 + 3\left[\frac{x}{3}\right] = 0. \qquad (5.5.3)$$

Dividing by 3 and equating coefficients yields

$$\dot{x}_m = \frac{3}{2} = 1.5 \qquad\qquad (5.5.4)$$

and

$$\dot{x}_m = (\frac{9}{2})^{\frac{1}{3}} = (4.5)^{\frac{1}{3}} = 1.65. \qquad\qquad (5.5.5)$$

Initially, $\dot{x}_m$ was assumed to be 2.0. The scaling could have
included ϵ, and if the system is going to be simulated for a
number of values of ϵ, this would be worthwhile[6].
      In reading literature on the solution of nonlinear equa-
tions, one frequently encounters the phase plane. The next
section will discuss phase—plane techniques briefly.

5.6   PHASE-PLANE TECHNIQUES

      As noted previously, there is no general technique for
solving nonlinear equations. However, a number of methods
have been developed to assist with the analysis of nonlinear
systems. One of the more popular methods, the phase plane,
can be plotted directly during simulation on the analog computer. The phase plane is a plot of $\dot{x}$ versus x or $\ddot{x}$ versus
$\dot{x}$. For higher-order equations, other variables would be
plotted. In order to illustrate the technique, the phase—
plane plot for a linear, second-order system is shown in
Figure 5-6-1. The arrows along the trajectory indicate the

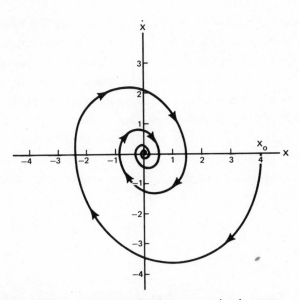

Figure 5-6-1. Phase plane for linear, second-order system

direction of increasing time. The trajectory illustrated is
the homogeneous case with $x(0) = x_o$, $\dot{x}(0) = 0$ and the final
value $x_{ss} = 0$.

In order to provide additional understanding, Figure 5-6-2
contains the phase-plane plot for the step response of the

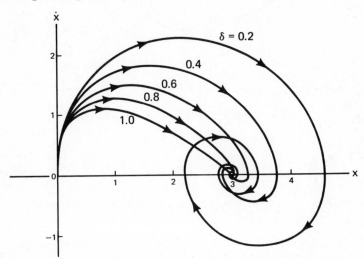

Figure 5-6-2. Step response of linear, second-order system

general, linear second-order system discussed in Section 3.6.
In this instance, the trajectory starts at the origin (i.e.,
$x(0) = \dot{x}(0) = 0$) and spirals to the steady-state conditions:
$x_{ss} = 1$ and $\dot{x}_{ss} = 0$. The figure includes trajectories for
several values of damping ratio, δ, and illustrates the effect
of the damping ratio on the response.

A phase-plane plot for a nonlinear system is shown in
Figure 5-6-3. This phase plane illustrates a common characteristic of nonlinear systems. For trajectories starting at

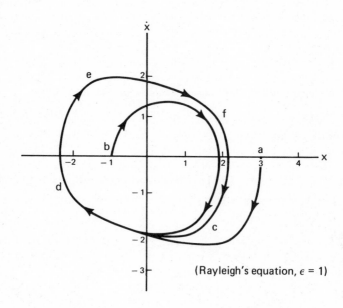

Figure 5-6-3.   Nonlinear system phase plane

initial values specified by (a) and (b), the system always
spirals into the closed path c-d-e-f. This is an oscillatory
condition called a "limit cycle." As stated previously, x
and $\dot{x}$ are available simultaneously from the analog computer
and an x-y plotter can be used to obtain phase-plane plots
directly during simulation. A phase-plane plot for the
solution to Rayleigh's equation in Section 5.5 is shown in
Figure 5-6-4. The oscillation of Figure 5-5-2 are displayed

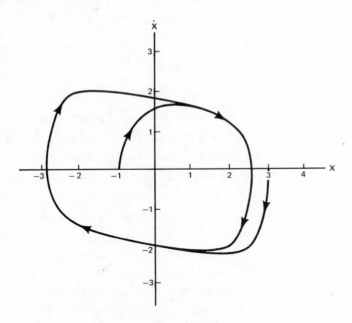

Figure 5-6-4. Phase plane for Rayleigh's equation, $\epsilon = 2.0$

as a limit cycle on the trajectory of Figure 5-6-4.

This brief discussion of phase-plane plots has been included to introduce the concept and help relate simulation techniques to nonlinear system analysis. Readers interested in additional material will find a number of books on the subject.[9]

5.7 NONLINEAR FUNCTION GENERATION

In many instances, the primary sources of nonlinearities in physical systems are devices with nonlinear input/output relationships. In fact, most "linear" systems incorporate nonlinear devices which are linearized by straight-line approximations of their characteristics. Usually, this requires a limit on their operating range (i.e., a "small" signal analysis). However, there are many systems that cannot be accurately simulated with linear models. In these instances, some means of generating the nonlinear characteristics is required. The computing element that produces these functions is called a nonlinear function generator. A programming symbol is shown in Figure 5-7-1.

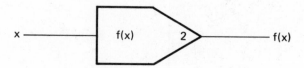

Figure 5-7-1. Programming symbol for function generator

Although it is not necessary to understand the electric circuits required to produce a nonlinear function, it is helpful to know some of the fundamentals involved. Most function generators utilize a series of diodes to alter the gain of an amplifier as a function of the input voltage. For example, the circuit of Figure 5-2-10 utilizes diodes to provide different gains for positive and negative inputs. A general purpose function generator may use as many as 10 diodes to provide 10 different values of gain. The input level at which each gain change occurs is determined by the setting on a potentiometer. A much simplified version of a variable gain function generator is shown in Figure 5-7-2. In order to understand the operation

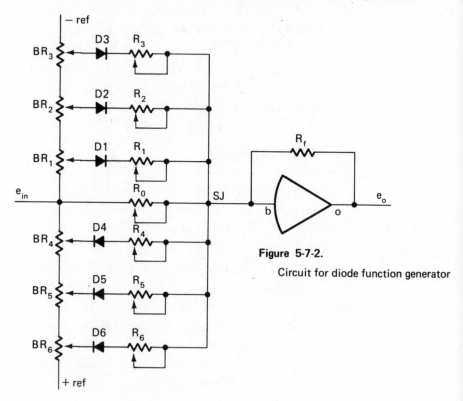

Figure 5-7-2.

Circuit for diode function generator

of the circuit, assume that the break-point potentiometers
(BR_1, BR_2,...,BR_6) are set to their maximum voltage levels
(i.e., the wiper arm is on the end of the potentiometer nearest
the reference supply). For low-level input voltages, all diodes
are back-biased (open switches) by the reference voltages and
the only input resistance is R_o. This gives an amplifier gain,
$G = -R_f/R_o$, which can be varied by changing the setting on the
gain resistor pot, R_o.

By moving the wiper arm of pot BR_1, the operator can vary
the level at which a positive input voltage overcomes the effect
of the negative reference on diode D1. For input voltages in
excess of the selected level, diode D1 is forward-biased (a
closed switch) and pot R_1 is an extra input resistor. For
input voltages in this range, the output of the amplifier is

$$e_o = - \frac{R_f}{R_o} e_{in} - \frac{R_f}{R_1} e_{in} = - e_{in} R_f(\frac{1}{R_o} + \frac{1}{R_1}), \qquad (5.7.1)$$

which can be written in the form,

$$e_o = - e_{in} R_f(\frac{R_o R_1}{R_o + R_1}). \qquad (5.7.2)$$

Since $R_o R_1/(R_o + R_1)$ is the parallel combination of R_o and R_1, the
effective gain is increased. The gain for input voltages in
this range can be varied by changing the setting of pot R_1.

In a similar manner, the level at which a positive input
overcomes the reverse-bias on diode D2 can be selected with
pot BR_2. For inputs in excess of this level, there are 3
input resistors (R_o, R_1 and R_2) and the gain is increased. The
effective gain for this level can be varied by adjusting pot
R_2. Pot BR_3 sets the level for "cutting-in" resistor R_3. Additional levels could be added if needed.

For negative input voltages, pot BR_4 determines the level
at which diode D4 begins to conduct and cut-in resistor R_4.
The remaining pots can be used to adjust the level and gain
for negative input voltages. If needed, additional pots could
be added. The non-ideal characteristics of the diodes cause
a slight "rounding" of each break-point and actually improve
the performance of the function generator.

The circuit of Figure 5-7-2 has a very limited range for general purpose function generation. However, it should provide a basic understanding of diode function generators and the adjustment procedures.

In order to understand the process of adjusting the function generator to produce a particular nonlinear function, consider the curve of Figure 5-7-3. The nonlinear curve to be

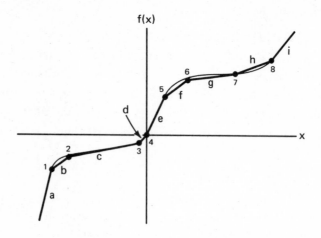

Figure 5-7-3. Straight-line approximation

generated is approximated by a series of straight-line segments (e.g., a, b,...,h, i). The connecting points at which the slopes change are called "break-points" (e.g., 1, 2,...,7, 8). The potentiometers (BR_1, BR_2,....,BR_6) determine the break-points for the simple function generator of Figure 5-7-2. Thus, the generation of a particular function is a matter of adjusting the break-points of the function generator to the required values and adjusting the gain at each level to match the slope of the straight-line approximation. To generate the curve of Figure 5-7-2, the positive portion of the curve is simulated first by adjusting the gain of segment (e) and break-point (5). Next, the gain of segment (f) is adjusted, followed by the break-point at (6). The procedure is continued for the remainder of the positive portion of the curve. The curve for negative values of (x) must be adjusted starting at x = 0 by setting slope (d) and then adjusting break-point (3). Next, the adjustments are

made for slope (c) and break-point (2). The procedure is
repeated for the remainder of the curve.

Commercially available function generators have from 5
to 12 segments for each portion (plus and minus) of the function
to be generated. Some function generators space the break-points
at regular intervals and do not permit adjustments. These
"fixed point" generators are not very versatile. Also, some function generators are not able to produce negative slopes and are
restricted to monotonically increasing functions. None of the
diode function generators are capable of generating multi-valued
functions.

The performance of a function generator deteriorates as the
frequency is increased but most units are capable of operating
up to 500 Hertz. This limitation may necessitate time scaling
in some instances. Function generators frequently require the
interconnection of an external operational amplifier. Since
patching instructions vary, the instruction manual should be
consulted for specific operating instructions.

Most manuals have <u>detailed</u> instructions for adjusting
function generators. One convenient method utilizes a sine or
triangular wave generator to provide the input, x, to the
function generator. The output, f(x), is observed on an oscilloscope while making the necessary slope and break-point adjustments. A diagram for the suggested approach is shown in Figure
5-7-4. As a rule, either a CRT or x-y plotter is used. If the

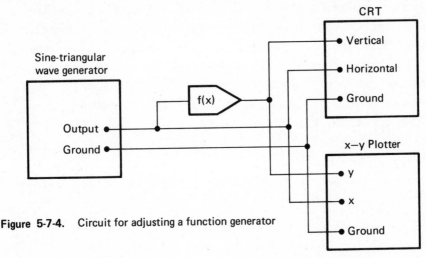

Figure 5-7-4. Circuit for adjusting a function generator

CRT is used, the frequency setting on the sine/triangular wave
generator must be high enough to avoid flicker of the trace.
By superimposing the desired curve on the CRT or plotter, the
adjustments can be made quickly. In setting a particular slope
and break-point, it is best to have all break-points of greater
value set at their maximum levels. Thus, any adjustments made
will affect only the particular slope and break-point. On most
function generators, any adjustment of a lower level break-point
or slope will change all higher values. Therefore, the adjustment
process should start with the lowest values and work toward the
higher level break-points and slopes.

For functions used frequently, such as logarithmetic and
trigonometric functions, fixed (i.e., non-adjustable) diode function generators are available. Also, the square - law function,
such as the one necessary for the quarter-square multiplier of
Section 5.4 can also be realized with a fixed diode function
generator.

A number of other devices have been used to generate functions. There are x-y plotters with special   curve - following
attachments which are capable of tracking a curve and providing
a proportional signal. Also, a whole series of electronic-and
servo-resolvers have been developed for coordinate transformations and function generation. Reference (7) presents a number
of these special purpose techniques.

Before completing the discussion of function generation,
the analog approximation of "transport" or "time—lag" should be
mentioned. One approach is a "loop" tape recorder with separate
"write" and "read" heads. Space and tape speed are set to give
the time lag desired. Another approach, utilizing only analog
computer components is based on the Padé approximation.   For
additional material, see reference (8).

Another important technique involves the use of a digital
computer to generate functions. This has several   advantages.
The functions can be pre-computed and stored or calculated on
line. This enables the generation of functions of more than

one variable and dynamic function alteration.   However,   the
necessary analog-to-digital and digital-to-analog conversion,
coupled with the compute or search time, may present   serious
problems.   Digital function generation will be discussed   in
Chapter 12.

5.8   PROBLEMS FOR CHAPTER 5

Problems covering the material of this chapter are identified by section.

5.2.1   In the circuit shown, which diode is back-biased?
Which one is forward-biased?

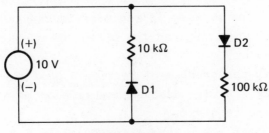

Figure 5-8-1.

5.2.2   Using the circuit of Problem 5.2.1, draw directional
arrors on the currents, if any, in the circuit elements.

5.2.3   Using the circuit equivalent of each component,
draw a complete electric diagram for Figure 5-2-3.

5.2.4   Give a physical reason for the limiting action
of the circuit of Figure 5-2-5.

5.2.5   Draw a complete electric diagram for the circuit
of Figure 5-2-6.   What is the effective feedback
resistance for positive inputs? For negative inputs?

5.2.6   For the input wave—form shown, sketch the
output for the circuit of Figure 5-2-6.

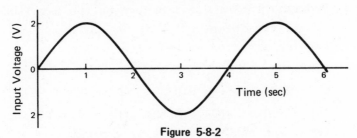

Figure 5-8-2

5.2.7   Show the effect of non-ideal diode characteristics
        in Problem 5.2.6.

5.2.8   Draw the complete electric diagram of the circuit
        of Figure 5-2-12.

5.2.9   Discuss the operation of the circuit of Problem
        5.2.8.

5.3.1   Develop a program to simulate the spring-mass-
        damper problem of Section 5.3 if the spring
        constant, K, is 0.9 Nt/M for positive deflections
        and 1.5 Nt/M for negative deflections   (i.e.,
        K = 0.9 Nt/M for x>0 and K = 1.5 Nt/M for x<0).

5.3.2   Solve the problem if the mass is changed to 100 Kg.
        Discuss scaling and the effect of operating levels
        on error.

5.3.3   Repeat the problem of Section 5.3 if the mass is
        0.5 Kg.   Again, discuss any time or magnitude
        scaling required.

5.3.4   Calculate the ω_n and δ for Problems 5.3.2 and
        5.3.3.

5.4.1   Develop a program to take the cube root of a
        function x.

5.4.2   Use the manuals for an available analog computer
        to determine the stated accuracy of the function
        multipliers.   What is the usable frequency range
        for the multiplier?

5.4.3   Discuss the time and magnitude scaling required
        for problems involving the multipliers of
        Problem 5.4.2.

5.5.1   Develop a scaled program for Rayleigh's equation
        if $\dot{x}(0)$ = 3, x(0) = 5 and ε = 5.

5.5.2   Program Problem 5.5.1 and check the magnitudes
        of all variables.

5.5.3   Develop a scaled program for Van der Pol's
        equation

$$\ddot{x} - \varepsilon\dot{x} + \varepsilon x^2\dot{x} + x = 0,$$

        for ε = 0.5, x(0) = 1 and $\dot{x}(0)$ = 0.

        Patch and run the resulting program.

5.5.4   Repeat Problem 5.5.3 with $\varepsilon = 1.0$, $x(0) = 5$ and $\dot{x}(0) = 1$.

5.5.5   Develop a program to produce the signal given by the expression

$$x(t) = A[1 + Mx(t)] \cos \omega_c t$$

where $x(t) > 1$ and $0 < M < 1$. What type of system is this?

5.6.1   Use the computer to plot the phase-plane trajectory for the system of Problem 5.5.2.

5.6.2   Use the computer to plot the phase-plane trajectory for the system of Problem 5.5.3.

5.6.3   Sketch the phase plane for a linear, second-order system with $\delta = .5$, $\omega_n = 1$, $x(0) = 5$ and $\dot{x}(0) = 0$.

5.6.4   Sketch a phase-plane plot for a linear second-order system for a unit step input and $\delta = 1.0$, $\omega_n = 1$, $x(0) = -1$ and $\dot{x}(0) = 0$.

5.6.5.   Repeat Problem 5.6.4 with $\delta = 1.0$, $\omega_n = 1$, $x(0) = 0$ and $\dot{x}(0) = 2$.

5.9   REFERENCES FOR CHAPTER 5

(1) Rogers, A. E., and T. W. Connally: <u>Analog Computation in Engineering Design</u>, McGraw-Hill Book Company, Inc., New York, 1960.

(2) James, M. L., G. M. Smith, and J. C. Wolford: <u>Analog and Digital Computer Methods in Engineering Analysis</u>, International Textbook Company, Scranton, Pa. 1965.

(3) Blum, J. J.: <u>Introduction to Analog Computation</u>, Harcourt, Brace and World, Inc., New York, 1969.

(4) "Transactions of CoED", Computers in Education Division, ASEE, P. O. Box 308, West Long Branch, New Jersey.

(5) "Simulation", Simulation Councils, Inc., P. O. Box 2228, LaJolla, California 92037.

(6) Jackson, A. S.: <u>Analog Computation</u>, McGraw-Hill Book Company, Inc., New York, 1960.

(7) "Handbook of Analog Computation"; Electronic Associates, Inc., West Long Branch, New Jersey, 1967.

(8) Johnson, C. L.: <u>Analog Computer Techniques</u>, McGraw-Hill Book Company, Inc., New York, 1956.

(9) Graham, D. and D. McRuer: <u>Analysis of Nonlinear Control Systems</u>, John Wiley & Sons, Inc., 1961.

6

Transfer Function Simulation

6.1 INTRODUCTION

In the study of physical systems, one of the first tasks is to develop a mathematical model of the system. Next, mathematical expressions describing the action of the system are written for the model. In most cases, the nonlinearities of the system are approximated with linear relationships. The solution to the system equation can then be determined by classical or operational methods.

The operational method for the solution of linear system equations led to the transfer function, which characterizes the input/output relationship of a system. Transfer functions have been widely used in the analysis and synthesis of control systems. Some of the techniques have been utilized in a number of other fields. Since transfer functions have many useful applications, it is important to develop methods for simulating systems expressed in transfer function form.

This chapter contains a brief introduction to the Laplace transform to provide background for transfer function representation of linear systems. Block diagram concepts are presented and used in the development of programming techniques for system simulation. The techniques are illustrated with several examples.

6.2 THE LAPLACE TRANSFORM

As noted in the previous section, the Laplace transform is basic to the discussion of transfer functions. The Laplace transform is defined by

$$\mathscr{L}[f(t)] = \int_{0}^{\infty} f(t)e^{-st}dt = F(s). \tag{6.2.1}$$

Equation (6.2.1) enables functions in the time domain, $f(t)$, to be transformed into the complex frequency domain, $F(s)$. The Laplace inversion integral

$$f(t) = \frac{1}{2\pi j} \int_{\sigma-j\infty}^{\sigma+j\infty} F(s)e^{st}ds, \tag{6.2.2}$$

can be used to convert functions of complex frequency, $F(s)$, back to the time domain. There are a number of restrictions on the process and additional details can be found in references (1) and (2). Tables of transforms and inverse transforms for most functions encountered in linear systems have been prepared, and it is seldom necessary to make the transformations of Equations (6.2.1) and (6.2.2). For the examples of this chapter, the only transforms that will be required are the transforms of a unit step function, $f(t) = 1$, and the exponential function, $f(t) = \exp(-\gamma t)$. The Laplace transforms are:

$$f(t) = 1 \rightarrow F(s) = \frac{1}{s} \tag{6.2.3}$$

and

$$f(t) = e^{-\gamma t} \rightarrow F(s) = \frac{1}{s+\gamma} . \tag{6.2.4}$$

In addition to the relationships of Equations (6.2.3) and (6.2.4), two properties of the Laplace transform will be useful. Given that $F(s)$ is the Laplace transform of the function of time $f(t)$, then the Laplace transform of df/dt is $sF(s) - f(0+)$, where $f(0+)$ is the initial condition on $f(t)$ in the time domain. This relationship can be extended to show that the Laplace transform of df^2/dt^2 is $s^2F(s) - sf(0+) - \dot{f}(0+)$. In working with transfer functions, initial conditions are assumed to be zero. Therefore,

$$\frac{df}{dt} \rightarrow sF(s),$$

$$\frac{d^2f}{dt^2} \rightarrow s^2F(s),$$

$$\vdots \qquad \vdots$$

$$\frac{d^nf}{dt^n} \rightarrow s^nF(s), \tag{6.2.5}$$

where $x(0) = \dot{x}(0) \ldots \overset{n}{x}(0) = 0$. If initial conditions are zero, the integral of a function is transformed to give

$$\int f(t)\,dt \rightarrow \frac{F(s)}{s}. \tag{6.2.6}$$

The relationships of (6.2.5) and (6.2.6) are derived in a number of books and the results will be used here without proof. For additional details see reference (1).

Although the objective of this chapter is the development of simulation techniques for systems expressed in transfer function form, it would be informative to see the complete solution of an equation by means of the Laplace transform. In order to illustrate the application of the Laplace transform, consider the linear, first-order differential equation,

$$\dot{x} + ax = f(t), \tag{6.2.7}$$

with $x(0) = 0$. Applying the Laplace transforms $\dot{x} \rightarrow sF(s)$ and $x(t) \rightarrow F(s)$ to Equation (6.2.7) yields

$$[s + a]X(s) = F(s). \tag{6.2.8}$$

To solve for the response, $X(s)$, for a particular input, $F(s)$, write Equation (6.2.8) in the form

$$X(s) = \frac{F(s)}{s + a}. \tag{6.2.9}$$

If the input is a unit step, Equation (6.2.3) gives the transform
F(s) = 1/s. Substituting into Equation (6.2.9) gives

$$X(s) = \frac{1}{s(s + a)}. \qquad (6.2.10)$$

A partial fraction expansion[1] of Equation (6.2.10) yields

$$X(s) = \frac{A}{s} + \frac{B}{s + a}, \qquad (6.2.11)$$

where
$$A = \frac{1}{s+a}\Big|_{s\to 0} = \frac{1}{a}, \qquad (6.2.12)$$

and
$$B = \frac{1}{s}\Big|_{s\to -a} = -\frac{1}{a}. \qquad (6.2.13)$$

Thus, Equation (6.2.11) can be written
$$(s) = \frac{1/a}{s} - \frac{1/a}{s + a}. \qquad (6.2.14)$$

The transforms given in (6.2.3) and (6.2.4) can be used to
determine the equivalent time function,

$$f(t) = \frac{1}{a} - \frac{1}{a}(e^{-at}) = \frac{1}{a}(1 - e^{-at}), \qquad (6.2.15)$$

which is the step response of the first-order system of Equation
(6.2.8).

As stated previously, this chapter will be devoted to the
development of simulation techniques for transfer functions. The
example of this section was included to illustrate the relationship
of the Laplace transform to classical methods for solving differential equations. Also, the example should provide a background for
introducing the transfer function.

6.3 TRANSFER FUNCTIONS

The transfer function is defined as the ratio of the Laplace
transform of the response, X(s), to the forcing function, F(s).
This can be written

$$G(s) = \frac{X(s)}{F(s)}. \qquad (6.3.1)$$

Knowledge of the transfer function, G(s), for a system enables the
expression of the response,

$$X(s) = F(s)G(s), \qquad (6.3.2)$$

where F(s) is the transform of the input forcing function. Thus, a system can be characterized by its transfer function, G(s). For example, the first-order system of Section 6.2 can be characterized by the transfer function

$$G(s) = \frac{X(s)}{R(s)} = \frac{1}{s + a}. \qquad\qquad (6.3.3)$$

The transfer function can be considered as the relationship of the output of a system to the input. Thus, the transfer function represents the "transfer" of signals from the input to the output. Therefore, the term transfer function is appropriate.

6.4 BLOCK DIAGRAMS

The input/output relationship of the transfer function, G(s), can be represented by the block of Figure 6.4.1. In this manner,

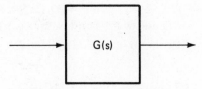

Figure 6-4-1.   Block diagram for G(s)

the transfer function enables the representation of a dynamic system by a block with a specified input/output relationship. The inclusion of a summing junction, as shown in Figure 6.4.2, permits the interconnection of blocks to represent complex systems. The summing junction can have any number of inputs and outputs. However, like the block, the direction of signal flow is given by the arrows. A number of techniques for manipulating block diagrams have been presented.[2,3] In addition, a related technique, signal flow graph analysis, has been developed.[4]

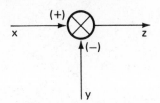

Figure 6-4-2.   Summing junction

The real power of the transfer function approach becomes evident when some of the block diagram manipulations are considered.

For example, if elements are cascaded, as in Figure 6-4-3, the over-
all transfer function is the product of the transfer functions of
the cascaded elements. The identity of Figure 6-4-3 makes it possi-

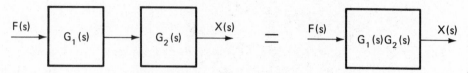

Figure 6-4-3. Cascaded transfer functions

ble to combine a number of transfer functions into a single expression. It can also be used to factor a complex function into several
simpler terms.

While many block diagram identities have been developed, only
a couple of the more important results will be presented here. The
most useful result is called the "fundamental block diagram identity" and is shown in Figure 6-4-4. In order to understand the
identity, note that

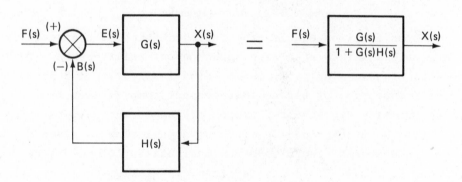

Figure 6-4-4. The fundamental block diagram identity

$$E(s) = F(s) - B(s), \tag{6.4.1}$$

$$B(s) = X(s)H(s), \tag{6.4.2}$$

and

$$X(s) = E(s)G(s). \tag{6.4.3}$$

Solving Equation (6.4.3) for $E(s)$ yields

$$E(s) = \frac{X(s)}{G(s)}. \tag{6.4.4}$$

Substitution of Equations (6.4.4) and (6.4.2) into Equation (6.4.1) yields

$$\frac{X(s)}{G(s)} = F(s) - X(s)H(s). \qquad (6.4.5)$$

Now, solving Equation (6.4.5) for X(s) gives

$$X(s) = \frac{G(s)F(s)}{1 + G(s)H(s)}. \qquad (6.4.6)$$

In order to determine the equivalent transfer function X(s)/F(s), divide Equation (6.4.6) by F(s). This gives the fundamental block-diagram identity,

$$\frac{X(s)}{F(s)} = \frac{G(s)}{1 + G(s)H(s)}. \qquad (6.4.7)$$

Thus, the system with "feedback" (left-hand side of Figure 6-4-4) can be reduced to a single block (right-hand side of Figure 6-4-4) by applying the identity. This derivation should also illustrate the use of block diagrams to indicate the inter-relationships of a system.

One other block diagram identity will be given without development. The identity, illustrated in Figure 6-4-5, can be simply stated, "elements in parallel add algebraically."

It should be noted that the block diagram of Figure 6-4-5 further reduces to the single block with a transfer function

$$\frac{X(s)}{F(s)} = \frac{G(s)}{1 + G(s)[H_1(s) + H_2(s)]}. \qquad (6.4.8)$$

Before developing methods for simulating transfer functions, it is important to note that the methods apply only for <u>linear</u> systems and that in taking the Laplace transform, initial conditions have been assumed to be zero.

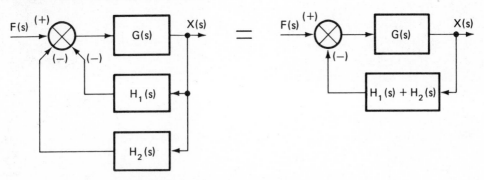

Figure 6-4-5. Block diagram with parallel blocks

6.5   SIMULATION OF SIMPLE TRANSFER FUNCTIONS

One approach to developing techniques for simulating transfer functions is to return to the original differential equation and use the methods of Chapter 3. For example, consider the transfer function for the first-order system of Equation (6.3.3). The transfer function is repeated here for convenience

$$G(s) = \frac{X(s)}{F(s)} = \frac{1}{s + a}.$$ (6.5.1)

Cross-multiplying gives

$$[s + a]X(s) = F(s),$$ (6.5.2)

which can be written in the form

$$sX(s) + aX(s) = F(s).$$ (6.5.3)

Transforming to the time domain yields

$$\dot{x} + ax = f(t),$$ (6.5.4)

which is the original differential equation. A program for Equation (6.5.4) is shown in Figure 6-5-1. Thus, with the exception of the inversion, the transfer function of Equation (6.3.3) can be simulated by the program of Figure 6-5-1.

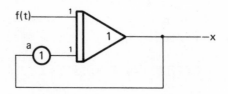

Figure 6-5-1.   Program for $\dfrac{1}{s + a}$

As a second illustration, consider a block with the transfer function

$$G(s) = \frac{X(s)}{F(s)} = \frac{1}{s}.$$ (6.5.5)

The original equation is

$$\dot{x} = f(t),$$ (6.5.6)

and the program is shown in Figure 6-5-2. The results of Figure

Figure 6-5-2.   The transfer function of an integrator

6-5-2 could be summarized by stating "the transfer function of a single integrator is $G(s) = \dfrac{-1}{s}$."

To further illustrate the method, consider the block diagram of Figure 6-5-3. By dividing the single block of the forward path of Figure 6-5-3, the block diagram can be redrawn as shown in Figure 6-5-4. The results of the two previous examples can be

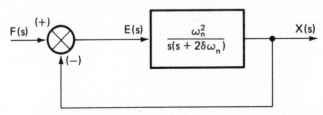

Figure 6-5-3. Block diagram for a second-order system

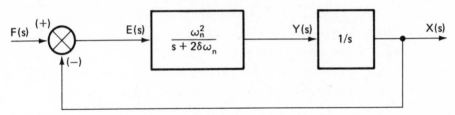

Figure 6-5-4. Block diagram for a second-order system

used to simulate the two inner blocks as shown in Figure 6-5-5(a). In order to complete the system, the action of the summing junction must be programmed to simulate the equation

$$E(s) = F(s) - X(s). \tag{6.5.7}$$

This expression can be represented by a summing amplifier as shown in Figure 6-5-5(b). The programs of Figure 6-5-5(a) and (b) can

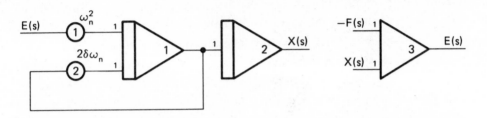

a) Forward path program   b) Summing junction

Figure 6-5-5. Program for system components

be combined as shown in Figure 6-5-6. Thus, transfer function
methods have been used to develop a program to simulate the block
diagram of Figure 6-5-3. It is important to notice that the posi-

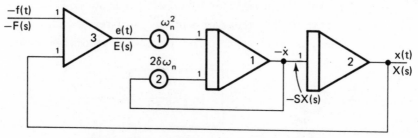

Figure 6-5-6. Program for second-order system

tion of amplifiers 1 and 2 could be reversed without affecting the
output, $x(t)$. However, if they are reversed as shown in Figure
6-5-7, the signal representing the derivative $\dot{x}(t)$, $[sX(s)]$, is no
longer available. Thus, the arrangement of blocks is often very
important. Strictly speaking, the dual labeling on Figure 6-5-6
is not correct. The actual signals available are the functions of
time $f(t)$, $x(t)$, $\dot{x}(t)$, etc. The frequency domain labels $F(s)$, $X(s)$,
$sX(s)$, etc., are included for convenience. Before leaving this

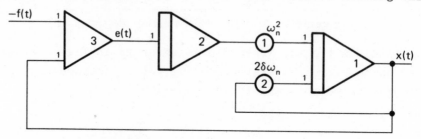

Figure 6-5-7. Program for a second-order system

example, it should be emphasized that zero initial conditions have
been assumed. Also, it is interesting to compare the program of
Figure 6-5-7 with the program of Figure 3-6-2 which was also developed for the generalized, linear second-order equation.

The system of Figure 6-5-3 could be simulated without sepa-
rating the terms of the block in the forward path as shown in
Figure 6-5-4. In this approach, the block in the forward path is
simulated directly from its transfer function,

$$\frac{X(s)}{E(s)} = \frac{\omega_n^2}{s^2 + 2\delta\omega_n s} . \qquad (6.5.8)$$

Equation (6.5.8) is cross-multiplied to yield

$$s^2 X(s) + 2\delta\omega_n sX(s) = \omega_n^2 E(s). \tag{6.5.9}$$

Transforming back to the time domain yields the differential equation

$$\ddot{x} + 2\delta\omega_n \dot{x} = \omega_n^2 e(t). \tag{6.5.10}$$

Programming this equation by the methods introduced in Chapter 3 results in the diagram of Figure 6-5-8. This program, when com-

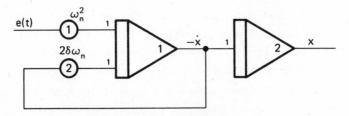

Figure 6-5-8. Program for $\dfrac{X(s)}{E(s)} = \dfrac{\omega_n^2}{s^2 + 2\delta\omega_n s}$.

bined with a summing amplifier to simulate the summing junction, is identical to the program of Figure 6-5-6.

Another approach to this problem is to apply the fundamental block diagram identity and reduce the block diagram of Figure 6-5-3 to a single block. Comparing the diagram of Figure 6-5-3 to the diagram of Figure 6-4-4 indicates that $G(s) = \omega_n^2/(s^2+2\delta\omega_n s)$ and $H(s) = 1$. Substituting these terms into Equation (6.4.7) yields

$$\frac{X(s)}{F(s)} = \frac{\dfrac{\omega_n^2}{s(s + 2\delta\omega_n)}}{1 + \left(\dfrac{\omega_n^2}{s(s + 2\delta\omega_n)}\right)(1)}, \tag{6.5.11}$$

which simplifies to,

$$\frac{X(s)}{F(s)} = \frac{\omega_n^2}{s^2 + 2\delta\omega_n s + \omega_n^2}. \tag{6.5.12}$$

Now, cross-multiplying yields

$$s^2 X(s) + 2\delta\omega_n sX(s) + \omega_n^2 X(s) = \omega_n^2 F(s). \tag{6.5.13}$$

Transforming back to the time domain results in the familiar, generalized, second-order differential equation

$$\ddot{x} + 2\delta\omega_n\dot{x} + \omega_n^2 x = \omega_n^2 f(t).$$

$$(6.5.14)$$

This equation has been programmed in Chapters 3 and 4. The programs are shown in Figures 3-6-1 and 3-6-2. Thus, there are a number of methods for developing a program for a given system.

The simulation of a system block diagram can be approached by
developing a program for each block and then interconnecting the
block programs in the same manner as the system. Another approach
reduces the block diagram to a single block represented by one
transfer function. The individual block approach offers two advantages. Since each block usually represents a component of the
system, simulation by block conserves the component relationships
and each component can be studied if desired. Also, the program
can be built and checked in parts, which is easier than "debugging"
a large interconnected program. On the other hand, simulating the
system from a single transfer function usually requires fewer
amplifiers. If the functioning of individual components is of no
interest, the single block representation is just as good as the
individual block approach.

6.6   SIMULATION OF HIGHER-ORDER TRANSFER FUNCTIONS

When a block diagram is reduced to a single block, the resulting transfer function is generally the ratio of two polynomials in
s. In order to investigate the programming of systems in this
form, consider the transfer function

$$G(s) = \frac{X(s)}{F(s)} = \frac{as^3 + bs^2 + cs + d}{s^4 + es^3 + gs^2 + hs + i}.$$

$$(6.6.1)$$

Cross-multiplying gives

$$[s^4 + es^3 + gs^2 + hs + i]X(s)$$

$$= [as^3 + bs^2 + cs + d]F(s).$$

$$(6.6.2)$$

When the equation is expressed in this form, derivatives of the
forcing function F(s) are required. (In this case, $\dddot{f}$, $\ddot{f}$ and $\dot{f}$ are
needed, and in most cases, not available). This problem can be

avoided by dividing by the highest order of s in the numerator.
In this case, dividing by s^3 gives

$$[s + e + \frac{g}{s} + \frac{h}{s^2} + \frac{i}{s^3}]X(s) = [a + \frac{b}{s} + \frac{c}{s^2} + \frac{d}{s^3}]F(s). \quad (6.6.3)$$

Unfortunately, a problem still exists. ·If the forcing function is
fed through the string of integrators as indicated by the right-
hand side of Equation (6.6.3), saturation is likely to occur for
most inputs. This difficulty can be avoided by grouping the terms
from the right-hand side of the equation with the terms of the
left-hand side having the same power of s. Thus, Equation (6.6.3)
becomes

$$sX(s) = -[eX(s) - aF(s)] - [gX(s) - bF(s)]\frac{1}{s}$$
$$- [hX(s) - cF(s)]\frac{1}{s^2} - [iX(s) - dF(s)]\frac{1}{s^3}. \quad (6.6.4)$$

This equation can be programmed as shown in Figure 6-6-1. To
understand the procedure for programming the equation, consider
summing integrator number one of Figure 6-6-1. Assume that the
desired output X(s) is known and available. By multiplying X(s)
by i(pot 1), adding -F(s)d (pot 2) and integrating, the output of
amplifier one is $-[iX(s) - dF(s)]\frac{1}{s}$. At summing integrator two, a
term -X(s)h is added to F(s)c and all three inputs are integrated.
The output of amplifier two is $[iX(s) - dF(s)]\frac{1}{s^2} + [hX(s)]-cF(s)]\frac{1}{s}$.
Note the accounting for amplifier inversion and the multiplication
of the input by $\frac{1}{s}$ in passing through an integrator.

Continuing around the loop, the output of summing amplifier 4
would be $[eX(s) - aF(s)] + [gX(s)-bF(s)]\frac{1}{s} + [hX(s)-cF(s)]\frac{1}{s^2}$
$+ [iX(s)-dF(s)]\frac{1}{s^3}$. According to Equation (6.6.4), this expression
is equal to $-sX(s)$. Integrating this term in integrator 5 yields
-X(s) which is the desired output. X(s) is fed back to the inputs
as needed. Notice that the summing and integration of amplifiers
4 and 5 could be combined. It is drawn in this manner to simplify
the discussion. To complete the process, the forcing function F(s)
is connected to the inputs as needed.

As noted previously, the use of F(s) and X(s), functions of
complex frequency, on the computer diagram of Figure 6-6-1 may be
misleading. The actual variables are functions of time, f(t) and

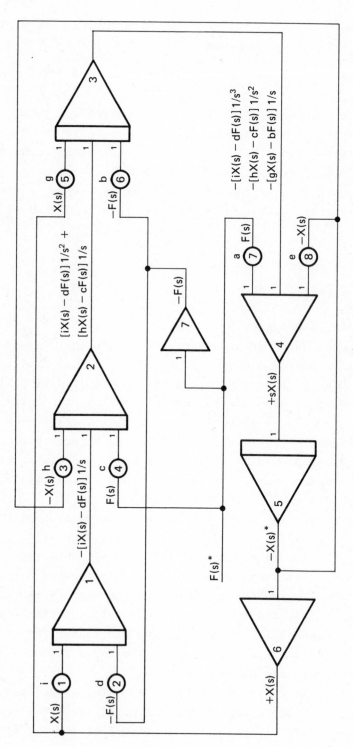

Figure 6-6-1. Program for general transfer function

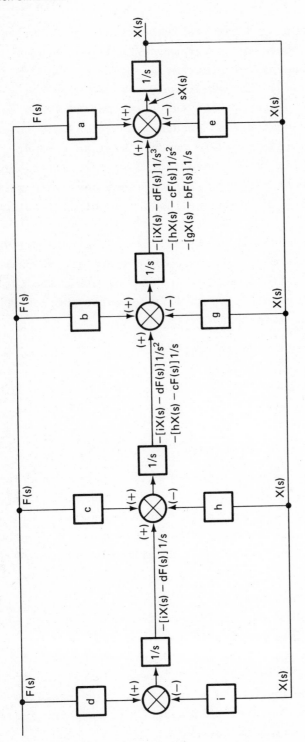

Figure 6-6-2. Block diagram for programming a general transfer function

x(t). Their frequency domain equivalents are shown on the diagram
to simplify the process of programming Equation (6.6.4).

The basic concept for programming Equation (6.6.4) can be
illustrated in a very straightforward manner by a block diagram.
Referring to Figure 6-6-2, note that F(s) and X(s) are combined
and integrated, repeatedly to produce an equivalence to sX(s).
This term is then integrated to produce X(s) as needed.

This method can be extended to transfer functions of any
order. Note that if the numerator does not contain powers of s,
it is not necessary to group the input and output functions as
shown here.

It should be noted that in the preceeding work all initial
conditions were assumed to be zero. If there are non-zero initial
conditions, their effect can be included by using the Laplace
transform for a variable with an initial value and keeping all of
the terms. The Laplace transfer to use is

$$\mathscr{L}\left[\frac{dx(t)}{dt}\right] = sX(x) - x(0^+),\tag{6.6.5}$$

or in the general case

$$\mathscr{L}\left[\frac{d^n x(t)}{dt^n}\right] = S^n X(s) - s^{n-1}x(0^+)$$
$$- s^{n-2}\dot{x}(0^+) - \ldots - \overset{(n-1)}{x}(0^+),\tag{6.6.6}$$

where $x(0^+)$ is the initial value of $x(t)$, $\dot{x}(0^+)$ is the initial
value of $\dot{x}(t)$ and $\overset{(n-1)}{x}(0^+)$ is the initial value of the $[n^{th}-1]$ derivative of $x(t)$. For more information on the inclusion of initial
conditions, see reference (5). This section has presented only
basic techniques. For additional details see references (2), (5)
and (6).

6.7 MAGNITUDE AND TIME SCALING

In the preceding discussions on transfer function simulation,
nothing has been said about magnitude and time scaling. Since the
transfer function states the relationship of the output to the
input, magnitude scaling cannot be developed from the transfer
function alone. However, the transfer function contains information on damping and natural frequencies, and once the input levels
are determined, scaling can proceed.

Magnitude scaling can be accomplished in the manner discussed in Section 4.5. However, it is frequently advantageous to scale directly on the diagram as discussed in Section 4.10. This heuristic approach is based on increasing or decreasing the operating levels at a point in the program at which the signals are too low or too high. Reciprocal changes must be made at other points in the program to balance the initial gain adjustments. For example, if the output of a given amplifier is too low, the gain of that amplifier is increased to raise the output signal level. Note that the gain of the following stage must be reduced by a corresponding amount. When using this method of scaling, the gain around every loop of the program must be held constant. This method of scaling has been called the "double-and-half" rule.[6] While the adjustment may not always be a factor of two, the corresponding change <u>must</u> <u>maintain</u> <u>the</u> <u>same</u> <u>loop</u> <u>gain</u>. This technique will be illustrated in a later section with an example problem.

As discussed in Section 4.6, time scaling is a matter of changing all integrator gains by the same amount. As a result, time scaling directly affects the gain of every loop in a program. If a loop contains one integrator, the change in loop gain is proportional to $1/a$, where a is the time-scale factor. If a loop contains two integrators, the gain change is proportional to $1/a^2$. Note that $a > 1$ reduces the computer solution rate.

Before completing the discussion of time scaling, it should be noted that the need for time scaling a transfer function can frequently be determined from the expression of the transfer function. The transfer function of all blocks should be time scaled by the same factor. Also, changes in the time scale must be applied to the forcing functions.

6.8 HIGHER-ORDER TRANSFER FUNCTIONS IN FACTORED FORM

In Section 6.6, the direct simulation of higher-order transfer functions led to a rather complicated program. This problem can be avoided if the polynomials of the numerator <u>and</u> denominator can be factored. For example, assume that the transfer function of Equation (6.6.1) could be factored into the form

$$G(s) = \frac{X(s)}{F(s)} = \frac{K(s+Z_1)(s+Z_2)(s+Z_3)}{(s+P_1)(s+P_2)(s+P_3)(s+P_4)} . \tag{6.8.1}$$

The factored transfer function can be separated into four transfer functions as shown,

$$G_1(s) = \frac{(s+Z_1)}{(s+P_1)} , \tag{6.8.2}$$

$$G_2(s) = \frac{(s+Z_2)}{(s+P_2)} , \tag{6.8.3}$$

$$G_3(s) = \frac{(s+Z_3)}{(s+P_3)} , \tag{6.8.4}$$

and

$$G_4(s) = \frac{K}{s+P_4} . \tag{6.8.5}$$

Since $G(s) = G_1(s)G_2(s)G_3(s)G_4(s)$, the transfer function can be simulated by cascading the individual terms.

The individual terms can be realized in a very straightforward manner. To illustrate the procedure set $G_1(s)=X_1(s)/F_1(s)$ and cross multiply Equation (6.8.2). This gives

$$(s + P_1)X_1(s) = (s + Z_1)F_1(s). \tag{6.8.6}$$

Dividing by s (to avoid the need for a derivative of the forcing function) yields

$$X_1(s) + P_1\frac{X_1(s)}{s} = F(s) + Z_1\frac{F(s)}{s} , \tag{6.8.7}$$

which can be programmed as shown in Figure 6-8-1. Once all of the

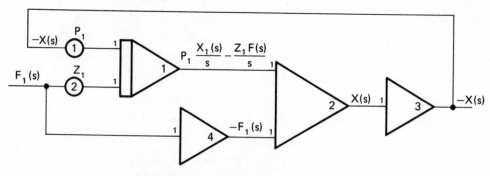

Figure 6-8-1. Program for $[s + P_1]/(s + Z_1)$

terms have been programmed, they can be connected together to form the complete function. This approach <u>does</u> <u>not</u> make efficient use of amplifiers.

In order to improve amplifier economy, considerable effort has been devoted to complex input and feedback networks for operational amplifiers. To understand the method, consider the diagram of Figure 6-8-2. In Section 2.3, it was shown that the sum of the

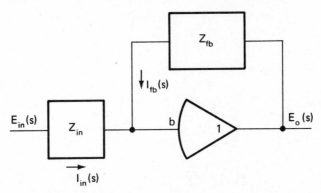

Figure 6-8-2. Complex input/feedback networks

currents at the summing junction is approximately zero. Therefore, the equation for the summing junction of Figure 6-8-2 is

$$I_{in}(s) + I_{fb}(s) \simeq 0. \tag{6.8.8}$$

Substituting for the currents of Equation (6.8.8) leads to

$$\frac{E_{in}(s)}{Z_{in}(s)} + \frac{E_{o}(s)}{Z_{fb}(s)} \simeq 0. \tag{6.8.9}$$

Now, solving for the ratio $E_{o}(s)/E_{in}(s)$ gives the transfer function,

$$G(s) = \frac{E_{o}(s)}{E_{in}(s)} = -\frac{Z_{fb}}{Z_{in}}. \tag{6.8.10}$$

This derivation can be summarized as follows: "the transfer function of an operational amplifier is the ratio of the feedback impedance to the input impedance." Thus, a single amplifier can be used to simulate a variety of transfer functions by properly configuring the input and feedback impedance.

To illustrate the procedure, consider a circuit of Figure 6-8-3.

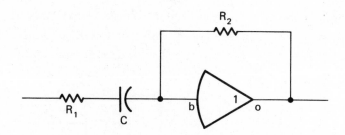

Figure 6-8-3. Complex input impedance network

For this network, $Z_{in} = R_1 + \dfrac{1}{sC_1}$ and $Z_{fb} = R_2$. Therefore, the transfer function is

$$G(s) = -\frac{Z_{fb}(s)}{Z_{in}(s)} = -\frac{R_2}{R_1 + \dfrac{1}{sC_1}} . \qquad (6.8.11)$$

Equation (6.8.11) can be written in the form

$$G(s) = -\frac{R_2 C_1 s}{R_1 C_1 s + 1} = -\frac{\tau_2 s}{1 + \tau_1 s} , \qquad (6.8.12)$$

where $\tau_2 = R_2 C_1$ and $\tau_1 = R_1 C_1$. The symbol τ is often used for the "time constant" of a complex network.

A network to simulate the transfer function of the form of Equation (6.8.2) is shown in Figure 6-8-4. The transfer function

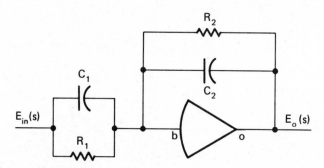

Figure 6-8-4. Complex circuit for transfer function

is

$$G(s) = \frac{E_o(s)}{E_{in}(s)} = -\frac{Z_{fb}(s)}{Z_{in}(s)} = -\frac{C_1}{C_2} \frac{\left(s + \dfrac{1}{R_1 C_1}\right)}{\left(s + \dfrac{1}{R_2 C_2}\right)} , \qquad (6.8.13)$$

which is expressed in the form of Equations (6.8.2) thru (6.8.4).
The remaining problem is the selection of appropriate values of
resistance and capacitance to give the desired parameters. This
concept can be extended to even more complicated networks. Additional networks and their impedance expressions are presented in
reference (6). Most general purpose computers are not designed to
accommodate the special networks, and as a result, this method is
used more frequently in special applications.

6.9 EXAMPLE PROBLEM

To illustrate the techniques presented in this chapter the
following example problem will be analyzed by several methods and
simulated by both individual blocks and a single transfer function.
The discussion will assume a knowledge of control theory and may
be beyond the scope of some students. The dynamic relationships
of the system are represented by the block diagram of Figure 6-9-1.

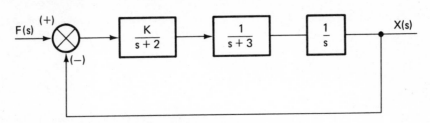

Figure 6-9-1. System block diagram

In this example, the purpose of the analysis and simulation will
be to determine the system response to a unit step input for a
variety of values of gain, K.

Before proceeding with this example, a few comments on contol system design might be helpful. For most contol systems,
increasing the gain of the forward path will cause a larger overshoot and an increase in settling time. Thus, a larger gain usually results in a less desirable transient response and a decrease
in the stability of the system. However, an increase in the forward gain will, in most cases, improve the steady-state error of
the system.

The most common problem encountered in control system design
is the determination of a value of gain to meet steady-state error
requirements, provide the desired degree of stability and an

acceptable transient response. With such diverse requirements, it
is apparent that the design procedure is a "trade-off" process in
which the gain is varied to determine the "best" value. Frequently, there is no single value of gain to meet all of the requirements. This situation leads to some of the more advanced problems
of control system design. Usually, compensating networks are
added to the system to enable the designer to achieve the specified characteristics.

From the preceding discussion, it appears that the example
problem, as stated, covers the first phase of the design procedure,
i.e., "the determination of the response for different values of
gain." From the block diagram, the transfer function of the forward path is

$$G(s) = \frac{K}{s(s+2)(s+3)} \cdot \qquad\qquad (6.9.1)$$

For the feedback path, $H(s) = 1$. The open loop transfer function
is

$$G(s)H(s) = \frac{K}{s(s+2)(s+3)} \cdot \qquad\qquad (6.9.2)$$

Using the fundamental block diagram identity to get the closed
loop transfer function gives

$$\frac{X(s)}{F(s)} = T(s) = \frac{K}{s(s+2)(s+3) + K} = \frac{K}{s^3 + 5s^2 + 6s + K} . \qquad (6.9.3)$$

Thus, the system of Figure 6-7-1 could be represented by a single
block as shown in Figure 6-9-2.

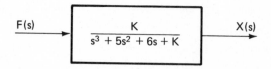

Figure 6-9-2. Single block representation of the system

To begin looking at the effect on the system of different
values of K, consider the Routh-Hurwitz array of Figure 6-9-3.[2]

	s^3	1	6	0
	s^2	5	K	0
Figure 6-9-3. Routh-Hurwitz array	s^1	$\dfrac{30 - K}{5}$	0	0
	s^0	K	0	0

In order for no roots of the characteristic equation to be in the right half of the s-plane, there must be no sign changes in the first column of the array. The last entry restricts K to values greater than zero. If K is negative, there will be one sign change indicating that one root of the characteristic equation is in the right half of the s-plane. The third term of column one will become negative for values of K greater than 30. Thus, for stable operation, 0 < K < 30.

The effect of K on system response can also be determined from a root locus as shown in Figure 6-9-4. From the root locus,

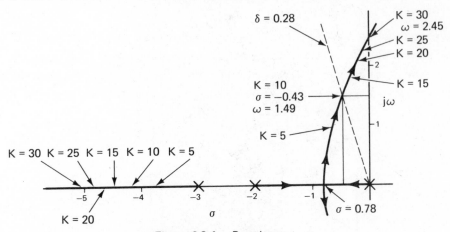

Figure 6-9-4. Root locus

the value of K that puts the roots on the j axis is K = 30. This verifies the value obtained from the Routh-Hurwitz array. Note that $j\omega = \sqrt{6} = 2.45$ radians for K = 30. This can also be determined from the auxiliary equation, $s^2 + 6 = 0$, on the Routh-Hurwitz array. The roots of the equation are $s = \pm j\sqrt{6}$, which agrees with the cross-over frequency of the root locus.

The system can also be studied with the aid of frequency response curves. Figure 6-9-5 contains a gain-phase (Bode) curve for K = 30. Note that the cross-over frequency, ω = 2.45 radians,

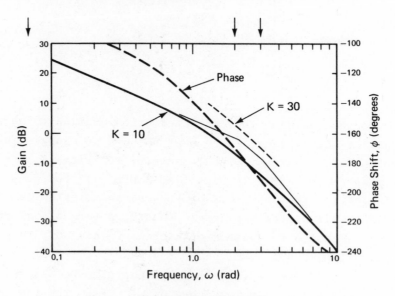

Figure 6-9-5. Bode plot

corresponds to the values from Routh–Hurwitz and root locus. Also, the phase shift is 180° indicating zero damping.

The system was simulated with the programs of Figures 6-9-6 and 6-9-7. Figure 6-9-6 is based on the simulation of each block

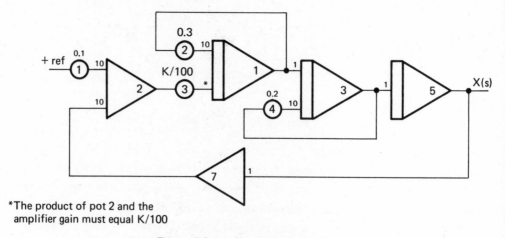

*The product of pot 2 and the amplifier gain must equal K/100

Figure 6-9-6. Simulation by blocks

and then interconnecting the blocks. Note that the 1/s term was placed next to the output. This enables direct recording of sX(s) or $\dot{x}(t)$, the derivative of the output. Figure 6-9-7 presents the program for simulating the single transfer function as shown in Figure 6-9-2. The signals analogous to internal points on the block diagram of Figure 6-9-1 are not available in Figure 6-9-7. However, sX(s), the derivative of the output, can be recorded directly.

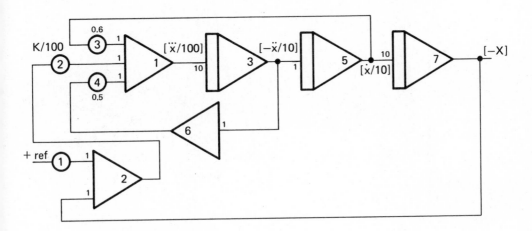

Figure 6-9-7.   Simulation of the transfer function

The response of the system to a unit step for several values of K is shown in Figure 6-9-8. To illustrate the relationship of the various methods of analysis and simulation, consider the response for K = 10. From the root locus, the damping ratio $\delta = 0.28$, $\sigma = \delta\omega_n = 0.43$, $\omega_d = 1.5$ and $\omega_n = 1.55$. Using the Bode plot, the phase margin ϕ_m is 34° and the gain margin G_m, is 4.0. An approximate relationship between damping ratio, δ, and phase margin, ϕ_m, is $\delta = \pi(\phi_m)/360$.[2] For this example, an approximate damping ratio from the Bode diagram is 0.297. For a damping ratio of 0.28, the corresponding overshoot is approximately 37%. The response for K = 10 in Figure 6-9-8 has an overshoot of 37%, which is better accuracy than expected from the approximate relations used.

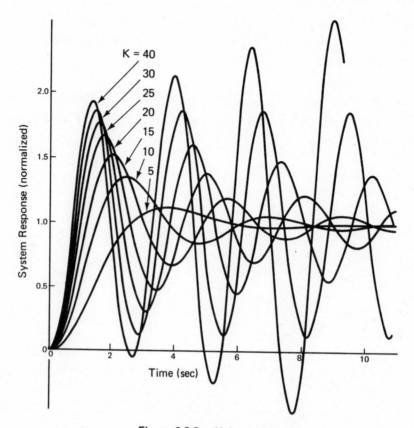

Figure 6-9-8. Unit step response

One other interesting relationship should be verified. By removing the connection between the output of amplifier 7 and the input of amplifier 2, the open—loop response of the system can be checked. Exciting the input with a one radian/sec sinusoid and measuring the corresponding output at amplifier 7 gives a gain of 1.4 and a phase shift of -139°. From the Bode plot of Figure 6-9-5, the curves for K = 10 indicate the gain should be 1.4 with a phase shift of -134° which is excellent agreement. Calculation of gain and phase analytically gives a gain of 1.414 and a phase shift of -135°. If necessary, the entire phase-gain curve could be checked.

As a final check of the experimental and analytical results, closed—loop frequency response was measured and compared with calculated values. At $\omega = 0.5$ radians, the closed—loop gain was measured to be 1.1 as compared to a calculated value of 1.09. The

phase shift measured was -20 degrees and the calculated value was
-18 degrees.   Using a Nichols chart, the closed-loop gain and
phase was 0.96 and -18 degrees.

   The comparison of analytical data with computer simulation
results could be discussed in much greater detail.   The studies
could be extended to include other types of forcing functions and
the resulting steady-state error.   Also, methods for system com-
pensation could be studied.   The example has illustrated the convenience of computer simulation and should serve as an introduction to control system simulation on the analog computer.

6.10   PROBLEMS FOR CHAPTER 6

   Problems covering the material of this chapter are identified
by section.

   6.2.1   Transform Equation (6.10.1) into the complex frequency
   domain

$$\dot{x} + 6x = 4f(t), \tag{6.10.1}$$

   with $x(0) = 0$.

   6.2.2   Transform Equation (6.10.2) into the complex frequency domain

$$\ddot{x} + 4\dot{x} + 4x = f(t), \tag{6.10.2}$$

   where $\dot{x}(0) = 0$ and $x(0) = 0$.

   6.2.3   Repeat problem 6.2.2 for the equation

$$\dddot{x} + 6\ddot{x} + 8\dot{x} + 6x = f(t), \tag{6.10.3}$$

   where the initial conditions are zero.

   6.2.4   Repeat problem 6.2.2 for the equation

$$\ddddot{x} + 8\dddot{x} + 12\ddot{x} + 16\dot{x} + 12x = f(t), \tag{6.10.4}$$

   with zero initial conditions.

   6.3.1   Develop a transfer function for the equation given in
   problem 6.2.1.

   6.3.2   Develop a transfer function for the equation given in
   problem 6.2.2.

   6.3.3   Develop a transfer function for the equation given in
   problem 6.2.3.

6.3.4   Develop a transfer function for the equation given in problem 6.2.4.

6.3.5   For the transfer function given determine the original differential equation.

$$\frac{X(s)}{F(s)} = \frac{6}{s + 2} \cdot$$

(6.10.5)

6.3.6   For the transfer function given determine the original differential equation.

$$\frac{X(s)}{F(s)} = \frac{12}{s^2 + 7s + 12} \cdot$$

(6.10.6)

6.3.7   For the transfer function given determine the original differential equation.

$$\frac{X(s)}{F(s)} = \frac{s + 1}{s^3 + 6s^2 + 8s + 6} \cdot$$

(6.10.7)

6.4.1   Reduce the block diagram shown to a single block.

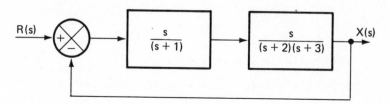

Figure 6-10-1

6.4.2   Reduce the block diagram shown to a single block.

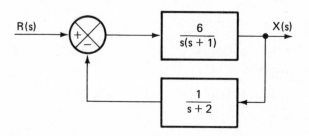

Figure 6-10-2

6.4.3   Reduce the block diagram shown to a single block.

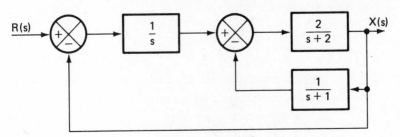

Figure 6-10-3

6.4.4   Reduce the block diagram given to a single block.

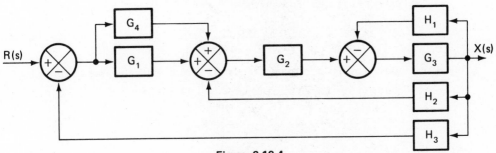

Figure 6-10-4

6.5.1   Develop a program to simulate the system of problem 6.2.1.

6.5.2   Develop a program to simulate the system of problem 6.2.2.

6.5.3   Develop a program to simulate the system of problem 6.2.3.

6.5.4   Develop a program to simulate the system of problem 6.3.5.

6.5.5   Develop a program to simulate the system of problem 6.3.6.

6.5.6   Develop a program to simulate the system of problem 6.4.1.

6.5.7   Develop a program to simulate the system of problem 6.4.2.

6.5.8   Develop a program to simulate the system of problem 6.4.3.

6.6.1   Develop a program to simulate a system described by the transfer function

$$\frac{X(s)}{G(s)} = \frac{s + 2}{s^2 + 3s + 2} .$$ (6.10.8)

6.6.2   Develop a program to simulate a system described by the transfer function

$$\frac{X(s)}{G(s)} = \frac{s^2 + 2s + 4}{s^3 + 3s^2 + 2s + 8} .$$ (6.10.9)

6.6.3   Develop a program to simulate a system described by the transfer function

$$\frac{X(s)}{G(s)} = \frac{s^3 + 3s^2 + 2s + 4}{s^4 + 3s^3 + 4s^2 + 5s + 8} .$$ (6.10.10)

6.8.1   Develop a program to simulate a system described by the transfer function

$$\frac{X(s)}{G(s)} = \frac{(s + 1)}{(s + 2)(s + 3)} .$$ (6.10.11)

6.8.2   Develop a program to simulate a system described by the transfer function

$$\frac{X(s)}{G(s)} = \frac{(s + 1)(s + 2)}{(s + 3)(s + 4)(s + 5)} .$$ (6.10.12)

6.8.3   Use complex input and feedback networks to simulate the transfer function $G(s)$ with a single amplifier

$$G(s) = \frac{s}{s + 1} .$$ (6.10.13)

6.8.4   Determine the transfer function of the network shown.

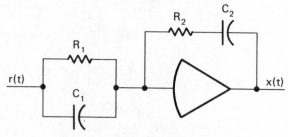

Figure 6-10-5

6.8.5   Discuss the high and low frequency equivalent networks for problem 6.8.4.

6.9.1　Carry out an analysis similar to Section 6.9 for this system.

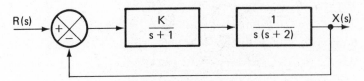

Figure 6-10-6

6.9.2　Carry out an analysis similar to Section 6.9 for this system.

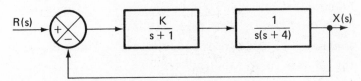

Figure 6-10-7

6.9.3　Carry out an analysis similar to Section 6.9 for this system.

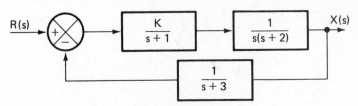

Figure 6-10-8

6.11   REFERENCES FOR CHAPTER 6

(1) Blackwell, W. A., Mathematical Modeling of Physical Networks, Macmillan, 1968.

(2) Gupta, S. C. and L. Hasdorff, Fundamentals of Automatic Control, John Wiley & Sons, Inc., New York, 1970.

(3) Dorf, R. C., Modern Control Systems, Addison-Wesley Publishing Co., Redding, Massachusetts, 1967.

(4) Robichaud, L. P. A., M. Boisvert and J. Robert, Signal Flow Graphs and Applications, Prentice-Hall, Inc., Englewood Cliffs, New Jersey, 1962.

(5) Johnson, C. L., Analog Computer Techniques, McGraw-Hill Book Co., Inc., New York, 1956.

(6) Jackson, A. S., Analog Computation, McGraw-Hill Book Co., Inc., New York, 1960.

(7) Blum, I. I., Introduction to Analog Computation, Harcourt, Brace & World, Inc., New York, 1969.

7

State Variable Simulation

7.1 INTRODUCTION

The transfer function techniques discussed in Chapter 6 were
based on the Laplace Transform and limited to linear, stationary
systems. Thus, they are applicable to systems in which the
nonlinearities are negligible and the parameters are essentially
constant. Methods for extending transfer function analysis to
nonlinear and time-varying systems have not been very successful.
In addition, the transfer function approach emphasizes a single-
input/single-output relationship and is not readily adaptable to
systems with multiple inputs and outputs. Despite these limitations, the frequency domain techniques are very useful and
are still quite popular.

In recent years, a great deal of attention has been given to
time domain analysis. This method utilizes state variables and is
applicable to nonlinear, time-varying and multivariable systems.
It is also useful in studying discrete-time and continuous-time

systems.   Instead of a differential equation of order n, the system is described by n, first-order differential equations.

The first section of this chapter is devoted to a brief dis-cussion of matrix-vector operations to provide background for state variable programming.   The concept of "state" is introduced along with techniques for writing the state equations for dynamic systems.   A procedure for developing programs to simulate systems in state variable form is presented and illustrated with several examples.   The chapter also contains material relating state variable simulation to the transfer function techniques of Chapter 6.

The material presented in this chapter is not a thorough treatment of state variable analysis.   Several books have been written on the subject and the interested reader is referred to the list of references at the end of this chapter.

7.2 MATRIX-VECTOR OPERATIONS

Since the state variable formulation is based on matrix-vector notation, a brief discussion of some basic operations will be presented in this section.   A "matrix" is a rectangular array containing n rows and m columns, written in the form

$$\underline{A} = \begin{bmatrix} a_{11} & a_{12} \cdot \cdot \cdot a_{1m} \\ a_{21} & a_{22} \cdot \cdot \cdot a_{2m} \\ \vdots & \vdots & \vdots \\ a_{n1} & a_{n2} & a_{nm} \end{bmatrix} \cdot \qquad (7.2.1)$$

Underlined, upper case letters will be used to denote matrices. A matrix with n rows and 1 column (n by 1) is   called   a   column "vector" and written as

$$\underline{x} = \begin{bmatrix} x_1 \\ x_2 \\ \vdots \\ x_n \end{bmatrix} , \qquad (7.2.2)$$

where underlined, lower case letters will be used to denote vectors.

If only the diagonal elements of a matrix are non-zero, the matrix is called a "diagonal" matrix and written in the form,

$$
\underline{A} = \begin{bmatrix} a_{11} & 0 & 0 & \cdots & 0 \\ 0 & a_{22} & 0 & \cdots & 0 \\ 0 & 0 & a_{33} & \cdots & 0 \\ \cdot & \cdot & \cdot & & \cdot \\ \cdot & \cdot & \cdot & & \cdot \\ \cdot & \cdot & \cdot & & \cdot \\ 0 & 0 & 0 & & a_{nm} \end{bmatrix} \cdot \qquad (7.2.3)
$$

If the diagonal elements are all equal to one and all other elements are zero, the matrix is an identity matrix and written in the form,

$$
\underline{I} = \begin{bmatrix} 1 & 0 & 0 & \cdots & 0 \\ 0 & 1 & 0 & \cdots & 0 \\ 0 & 0 & 1 & \cdots & 0 \\ \cdot & \cdot & \cdot & & \cdot \\ \cdot & \cdot & \cdot & & \cdot \\ \cdot & \cdot & \cdot & & \cdot \\ 0 & 0 & 0 & \cdots & 1 \end{bmatrix} \cdot \qquad (7.2.4)
$$

Arithmetic operations involving matrices are similar to scalar math with a few very important exceptions. In addition and subtraction ($\underline{C} = \underline{A} \pm \underline{B}$), the corresponding elements of $\underline{A}$ and $\underline{B}$ are added or subtracted. The elements of $\underline{C}$ are $c_{ij} = a_{ij} \pm b_{ij}$. Therefore, $\underline{A}$ and $\underline{B}$ must have the same dimensions. For example, let $\underline{A}$ and $\underline{B}$ be defined

$$
\underline{A} = \begin{bmatrix} 1 & 2 \\ 3 & 4 \\ 5 & 6 \end{bmatrix} \qquad (7.2.5)
$$

and

$$
\underline{B} = \begin{bmatrix} 7 & 8 \\ 9 & 10 \\ 11 & 12 \end{bmatrix} \cdot \qquad (7.2.6)
$$

The matrix, $\underline{C} = \underline{A} + \underline{B}$ is

$$
\underline{C} = \begin{bmatrix} 8 & 10 \\ 12 & 14 \\ 16 & 18 \end{bmatrix} \cdot \qquad (7.2.7)
$$

Matrix multiplication is more complex and requires the summation of the row-column products in order to determine the elements of the product. The elements of $\underline{C} = \underline{AB}$ are

$$c_{ij} = a_{i1}b_{1j} + a_{i2}b_{2j} + \ldots + a_{ik}b_{kj},$$

or

$$c_{ij} = \sum_{p=1}^{k} a_{ip}b_{pj}. \qquad (7.2.8)$$

Thus, matrix multiplication, $\underline{C} = \underline{AB}$, requires that the number of columns of $\underline{A}$ must equal the number of rows in $\underline{B}$. Also, the product $\underline{C}$ will have the same number of rows as $\underline{A}$ and the same number of columns as $\underline{B}$. Therefore, if $\underline{A}$ is an n-by-m matrix and $\underline{B}$ is an m-by-k matrix, the product will be of order n-by-k. For example, let

$$\underline{A} = \begin{bmatrix} 1 & 2 & 3 \\ 4 & 5 & 6 \end{bmatrix} \qquad (7.2.9)$$

and

$$\underline{B} = \begin{bmatrix} 1 & 2 \\ 3 & 4 \\ 5 & 6 \end{bmatrix}. \qquad (7.2.10)$$

The product $\underline{C} = \underline{AB}$ is

$$c_{11} = a_{11} \cdot b_{11} + a_{12} \cdot b_{21} + a_{13} \cdot b_{31},$$

or

$$c_{11} = (1)(1) + (2)(3) + (3)(5) = 22. \qquad (7.2.11)$$

The complete product matrix is

$$\underline{C} = \begin{bmatrix} 22 & 28 \\ 49 & 64 \end{bmatrix}. \qquad (7.2.12)$$

The product of a matrix of order n-by-m and a column vector of order m-by-1 is an n-by-1 column vector. This particular combination is frequently encountered in the solution of simultaneous algebraic equations. For example, the equations

$$1x_1 + 2x_2 + 3x_3 = y_1$$
$$4x_1 + 5x_2 + 6x_3 = y_2$$
$$7x_1 + 8x_2 + 9x_3 = y_3$$

can be written in the compact form,

$$\begin{bmatrix} 1 & 2 & 3 \\ 4 & 5 & 6 \\ 7 & 8 & 9 \end{bmatrix} \begin{bmatrix} x_1 \\ x_2 \\ x_3 \end{bmatrix} = \begin{bmatrix} y_1 \\ y_2 \\ y_3 \end{bmatrix}. \qquad (7.2.13)$$

The equation can be further simplified by using matrix-vector notation. Thus, Equation (7.2.13) can be written in the form

$$\underline{A}\underline{x} = \underline{y}, \qquad (7.2.14)$$

where $\underline{x}$ and $\underline{y}$ are 3 by 1 column vectors and the coefficient matrix is

$$\underline{A} = \begin{bmatrix} 1 & 2 & 3 \\ 4 & 5 & 6 \\ 7 & 8 & 9 \end{bmatrix}. \qquad (7.2.15)$$

The matrix-vector operations presented here are adequate for the initial discussion of state variables. Other operations will be presented later. However, a complete and thorough treatment is beyond the scope of this book. Additional details are available in books devoted to the subject.[5,6]

7.3 THE CONCEPT OF STATE

The "state" of a system is the smallest set of numbers which must be known at a point in time in order to predict the response of the system at some future time due to a set of inputs. Thus, the state of a system is the minimum set of numbers needed to define the behavior of the system. Variables describing the state are called "state variables."

The concept of state can be illustrated by a simple spring-mass-damper system. If the position and velocity of the mass are known at a given time, the second-order differential equation describing the motion of the mass can be solved. Thus, the state of the system is described by the potential and kinetic energies of the mass. An R-L-C circuit is the electrical analogy of the spring-mass-damper system. The behavior of an R-L-C circuit is also described by a second-order differential equation. In this case, the energy stored in the inductor and the capacitor are indicative of the state of the system. The state variables must relate to these energies and the obvious choice of state variables would be the voltage on the capacitor, v_C, and the current through the inductor, i_L. (Note that $W_C = \frac{1}{2}Cv_C^2$ and $W_L = \frac{1}{2}Li_L^2$.) Since it is known that $i_L = C(dv_C/dt)$, and for the series case, $i_C = i_L$, the state variables could be i_L and di_L/dt. In most cases, more than one set of state variables are possible. The set selected will depend upon the problem and the desired information.

The minimum set of state variables will always equal the order of the system. For example, the second-order systems discussed in preceding paragraphs required two state variables. In some instances, it is useful to define additional variables to provide specific information. However, this is a matter of convenience and the extra variables are redundant.

In order to take advantage of the convenience of matrix-vector notation, the state variables are considered as elements of the "state vector." Thus, the behavior of a dynamic system of order n is described by an n-dimensional state vector.

7.4   STATE VARIABLE PROGRAMMING: PHASE VARIABLES

As stated in an earlier section, state variable techniques utilize n first-order differential equations instead of one differential equation of order n. Thus, simulation of systems written in state variable form is a process of solving simultaneously, n first-order differential equations.

In order to illustrate the method, the generalized, linear second-order differential equation will be transformed into two first-order equations of state variable form. The basic equation is

$$\ddot{x} + 2\delta\omega_n\dot{x} + \omega_n^2 x = \omega_n^2 f(t), \qquad (7.4.1)$$

where $x(t=0) = x_o$, $\dot{x}(t=0) = \dot{x}_o$ and $f(t)$ is a forcing function, f. Let the dependent variable, x, be the first state variable, x_1 and the derivative of the dependent variable, $\dot{x}$, be the second state variable, x_2. These assumptions can be written in the form

$$x_1 = x, \qquad (7.4.2)$$

and

$$x_2 = \dot{x} = \dot{x}_1. \qquad (7.4.3)$$

One first-order differential equation involving the state variables is already available, since Equation (7.4.3) can be written in the form

$$\dot{x}_1 = x_2. \tag{7.4.4}$$

The other first-order differential equation can be derived from the original equation, i.e., Equation (7.4.1.), with the help of the following relationship

$$\ddot{x}_1 = \dot{x}_2 = \ddot{x}. \tag{7.4.5}$$

Equation (7.4.5) is obtained by differentiating Equation (7.4.4) and noting that: $x_1 = x$, $\dot{x}_1 = \dot{x}$ and $\ddot{x}_1 = \ddot{x}$. Solving Equation (7.4.1) for $\ddot{x}$ yields

$$\ddot{x} = -2\delta\omega_n\dot{x} - \omega_n^2 x + \omega_n^2 f. \tag{7.4.6}$$

Substituting state variables for the dependent variable and its derivatives in Equation (7.4.6) yields

$$\dot{x}_2 = 2\delta\omega_n x_2 - \omega_n^2 x_1 + \omega_n^2 f. \tag{7.4.7}$$

The two first-order state variable equations can be written in the form

$$\dot{x}_1 = x_2$$

$$\dot{x}_2 = -\omega_n^2 x_1 - 2\delta\omega_n x_2 + \omega_n^2 f. \tag{7.4.9}$$

Equation (7.4.8) can be written in matrix-vector form as

$$\begin{bmatrix} \dot{x}_1 \\ \dot{x}_2 \end{bmatrix} = \begin{bmatrix} 0 & 1 \\ -\omega_n^2 & -2\delta\omega_n \end{bmatrix} \begin{bmatrix} x_1 \\ x_2 \end{bmatrix} + \begin{bmatrix} 0 \\ \omega_n^2 \end{bmatrix} f. \tag{7.4.10}$$

Using matrix-vector notation gives

$$\underline{\dot{x}} = \underline{A}\underline{x} + \underline{b}f, \tag{7.4.11}$$

where

$$\underline{x} = \begin{bmatrix} x_1 \\ x_2 \end{bmatrix}, \quad \underline{A} = \begin{bmatrix} 0 & 1 \\ -\omega_n^2 & -2\delta\omega_n \end{bmatrix} \text{ and } \underline{b} = \begin{bmatrix} 0 \\ \omega_n^2 \end{bmatrix}.$$

Since the state variable form for this case is actually two first-order, simultaneous equations, a simulation program can be

developed using the method presented in Section 3.9. The resulting
simulation diagram is shown in Figure 7-4-1. Integrator 1 is
producing state variable x_1 and integrator 2 is producing state
variable x_2. The use of amplifiers 5 and 6 for inversion is
redundant. Eliminating these amplifiers and redrawing the diagram

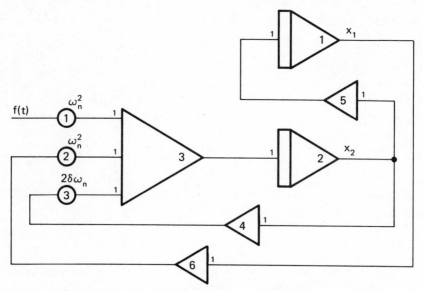

Figure 7-4-1. State variable program for $\ddot{x} + 2\delta\omega_n\dot{x} + \omega_n^2 x = \omega_n^2 f$

yields the program shown in Figure 7-4-2. The program shown in
Figure 7-4-2 is identical to the program developed in Section 3.6.
This is as it should be since both programs solve the same dif-
ferential equation.

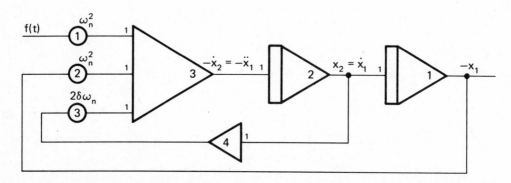

Figure 7-4-2. Revised state variable program

In studying systems described by state variables, it is often convenient to plot the state variables in "state space." A state space trajectory or plot for the example problem in Section 3.7 is shown in Figure 7-4-3. Note that the original problem variable

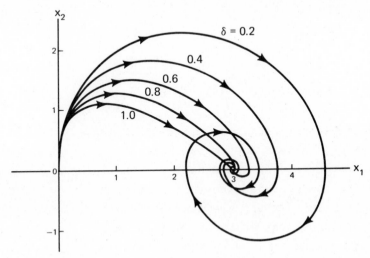

Figure 7-4-3. State space trajectory

x is now the state variable x_1 and the derivative of the dependent variable, $\dot{x} = \dot{x}_1 = x_2$. Since "phase variables" were used in this example, the diagram is identical to the phase-plane plots discussed in Section 5.6.

The procedure can be applied to systems of order n to produce n first-order differential equations of the form of Equation (7.4.11). If the general form for a system of order n [Equations (3.2.1 and 4.2.1)] is used

$$a_o \frac{d^n x}{dt^n} + a_1 \frac{d^{n-1}}{dt^{n-1}} + \ldots + a_n x = b_o f(t), \tag{7.4.12}$$

then

$$\underline{A} = \begin{bmatrix} 0 & 1 & 0 & 0 & \ldots & 0 \\ 0 & 0 & 1 & 0 & \ldots & 0 \\ 0 & 0 & 0 & 1 & \ldots & 0 \\ \cdot & & & & & \cdot \\ \cdot & & & & & \cdot \\ \cdot & & & & & \cdot \\ \dfrac{a_n}{a_o} & \dfrac{a_{n-1}}{a_o} & \dfrac{a_{n-2}}{a_o} & \dfrac{a_{n-3}}{a_o} & \ldots & \dfrac{a_1}{a_o} \end{bmatrix}, \tag{7.4.13}$$

and

$$\underline{b} = \begin{bmatrix} 0 \\ 0 \\ 0 \\ \cdot \\ \cdot \\ \cdot \\ 1 \end{bmatrix}.$$

(7.4.14)

Note that $\underline{x}$ is an n-vector, $\underline{A}$ is an n-by-n matrix and $\underline{b}$ is an n-vector.

This particular choice of state variables is often referred to as "phase variables" due to the integral relationship between each state variable. As noted earlier, this produces programs which are the same form as those of Chapter 3.

At this point, it appears that the state variable approach has done nothing except enable the use of matrix-vector notation. However, the systems that have been considered were single-input/single-output and only the phase variable form has been developed. The real power of the state variable approach is demonstrated when multivariable systems are studied and other choices of state variables are utilized.

7.5 STATE VARIABLE PROGRAMMING: MULTIVARIABLE SYSTEM

If more than one input or forcing function is to be considered, then the state equation is of the form

$$\dot{\underline{x}} = \underline{A}\underline{x} + \underline{B}\underline{u},$$

(7.5.1)

where $\underline{x}$ is an n-vector, $\underline{A}$ is an n-by-n matrix, $\underline{u}$ is an m-dimensional control vector and $\underline{B}$ is an n-by-m matrix. The elements of $\underline{B}$ indicate the effect of the control variables, u_1, u_2,...,u_m, on the state variables. In order to illustrate the programming of equations in this form, let n=3 and m=2. For this case, the state and control variables are

$$\underline{x} = \begin{bmatrix} x_1 \\ x_2 \\ x_3 \end{bmatrix} \quad \text{and} \quad \underline{u} = \begin{bmatrix} u_1 \\ u_2 \end{bmatrix}.$$

(7.5.2)

The matrices are

$$\underline{A} = \begin{bmatrix} a_{11} & a_{12} & a_{13} \\ a_{21} & a_{22} & a_{23} \\ a_{31} & a_{32} & a_{33} \end{bmatrix} \text{ and } \underline{B} = \begin{bmatrix} b_{11} & b_{12} \\ b_{21} & b_{22} \\ b_{31} & b_{32} \end{bmatrix}. \qquad (7.5.3)$$

For the system defined by Equation (7.5.2) and (7.5.3), a simulation diagram is developed in Figure 7-5-1. In most treatments

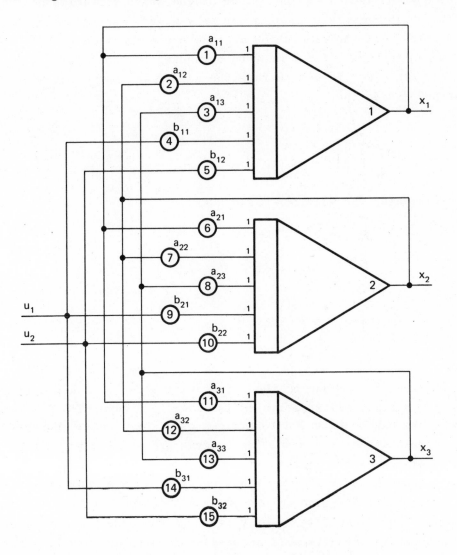

Figure 7-5-1. Program for $\underline{\dot{x}} = \underline{A}\underline{x} + \underline{B}\underline{u}$

of state variables, the state vector, $\underline{x}$, is not considered to be the output. Instead, the output vector, $\underline{y}$, is a linear combination of the state vector, $\underline{x}$, and the control vector $\underline{u}$. Thus, the multivariable output is expressed in the form

$$\underline{y} = \underline{C}\underline{x} + \underline{D}\underline{u}, \tag{7.5.4}$$

where $\underline{y}$ is a p-dimensional output vector, $\underline{C}$ is a matrix of order p-by-n which indicates the effect of the state variables on the output. The matrix $\underline{D}$ is of order p-by-m and couples the control variables. If the simulation is to include Equation (7.5.4), the elements in Figure 7-5-2 must be connected to those of Figure 7-5-1. In order to demonstrate the use of an "output" vector, let p=2 and define

$$\underline{y} = \begin{bmatrix} y_1 \\ y_2 \end{bmatrix}. \tag{7.5.5}$$

In this case, the matrices $\underline{C}$ and $\underline{D}$ are

$$\underline{C} = \begin{bmatrix} c_{11} & c_{12} & c_{13} \\ c_{21} & c_{22} & c_{23} \end{bmatrix} \tag{7.5.6}$$

and

$$\underline{D} = \begin{bmatrix} d_{11} & d_{12} \\ d_{21} & d_{22} \end{bmatrix}. \tag{7.5.7}$$

The program for producing the output variables, y_1 and y_2, from the control and state variables is shown in Figure 7-5-2. The procedure can be extended to systems of higher order. However, the complexity of the resulting program grows rapidly as the order of the system increases.

Although the result will not be used in this chapter, this is an appropriate point to present the solution of the state variable equations. In keeping with the introductory nature of this book, the results will be presented without proof. For further details, see references (1-4) at the end of this chapter.

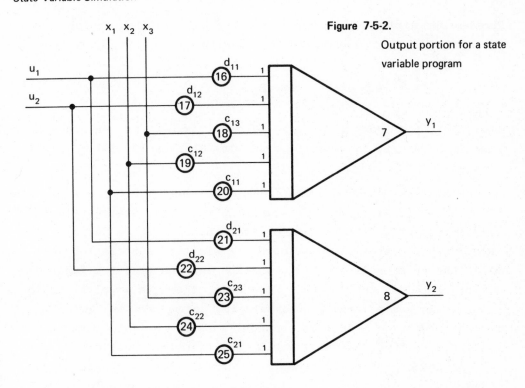

Figure 7-5-2.

Output portion for a state variable program

For state equations of this form

$$\dot{\underline{x}} = \underline{A}\underline{x} + \underline{b}u, \qquad\qquad (7.5.8)$$

the solution is

$$\underline{x}(t) = e^{\underline{A}t}\underline{x}(0) + \int_0^t e^{\underline{A}(t-\tau)}\, \underline{b}u(\tau)d\tau, \qquad\qquad (7.5.9)$$

where $\underline{x}(0)$ is the initial condition vector and τ is a variable of integration. If the state equation is of the form

$$\dot{\underline{x}} = \underline{A}\underline{x}, \qquad\qquad (7.5.10)$$

the solution simplifies to

$$\underline{x}(t) = e^{\underline{A}t}\underline{x}(0). \qquad\qquad (7.5.11)$$

The simplicity of the latter form is so appealing that the input, $\underline{u}(t)$, is often formulated as a state variable and the state vector $\underline{x}$ is adjoined to include the extra "states". This also requires an expansion of the $\underline{A}$ matrix. It is interesting to note the similarity of Equations (7.5.8) and (7.5.9) to the solution of a first-order differential equation. The analogy also holds for the term $e^{\underline{A}t}$, which can be evaluated with the series expansion

$$e^{\underline{A}t} = \underline{I} + \underline{A}t + \frac{\underline{A}^2t^2}{2!} + \frac{\underline{A}^3t^3}{3!} + \ldots + \frac{\underline{A}^nt^n}{n!} , \qquad (7.5.11)$$

where $\underline{I}$ is the identity matrix. The matrix $e^{\underline{A}t}$ is called the transition matrix and will be used in Chapter 13 for digital simulation.

7.6   RELATION TO TRANSFER FUNCTION REPRESENTATION

In Section 7.4, the relationship of the state-variable formulation to a differential equation describing a single input/output system was developed. A similar correlation between the system differential equation and the transfer function was presented in Chapter 6. Obviously, there is a relationship between the state-variable formulation of a system and its transfer function. In this section, a state-variable formulation will be developed for two forms of the transfer function.

As noted previously, the transfer function approach is primarily concerned with a relationship between a single input and a single output as shown in Figure 7-6-1.

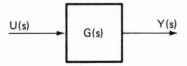

Figure 7-6-1.   Transfer function

The transfer function is usually the ratio of two polynomials in s of the form

$$G(s) = \frac{a_n s^n + a_{n-1} s^{n-1} + \ldots + a_1 s + a_o}{s^m + b_{m-1} s^{m-1} + \ldots + b_1 s + b_o} , \qquad (7.6.1)$$

or in factored form

$$G(s) = \frac{K(s + Z_1)(s + Z_2)(s + Z_3)\ldots(s + Z_n)}{(s + P_1)(s + P_2)(s + P_3)\ldots(s + P_m)} . \qquad (7.6.2)$$

In order to illustrate the relationship between state variables and transfer functions expressed in the form of Equation (7.6.1), consider the equation

$$G(s) = \frac{Y(s)}{U(s)} = \frac{as^3 + bs^2 + cs + d}{s^4 + es^3 + gs^2 + hs + i} \ . \qquad (7.6.3)$$

This is the same equation that was used in Section 6.6 to illustrate a programming technique for transfer functions. In order to develop the state-variable equations, divide the numerator and denominator by the highest power of s in the denominator. In this case, dividing by s^4 yields

$$G(s) = \frac{Y(s)}{U(s)} = \frac{as^{-1} + bs^{-2} + cs^{-3} + ds^{-4}}{1 + es^{-1} + gs^{-2} + hs^{-3} + is^{-4}} \ , \qquad (7.6.4)$$

where Y(s) represents the output and U(s) is the input. Now, define a new variable

$$E(s) = \frac{U(s)}{1 + es^{-1} + gs^{-2} + hs^{-3} + is^{-4}} \ , \qquad (7.6.5)$$

such that the output can be expressed as

$$Y(s) = G(s)U(s) = G(s)E(s)[1 + es^{-1} + gs^{-2} + hs^{-3} + is^{-4}]. \qquad (7.6.6)$$

By substituting Equation (7.6.4) for G(s), the output can be written in terms of E(s)

$$Y(s) = as^{-1}E(s) + bs^{-2}E(s) + cs^{-3}E(s) + ds^{-4}E(s). \qquad (7.6.7)$$

A simulation diagram for E(s) can be developed from Equation (7.6.5) written in the form

$$E(s) = U(s) - es^{-1}E(s) - gs^{-2}E(s) - hs^{-3}E(s) - is^{-4}E(s). \qquad (7.6.8)$$

The output, Y(s), can be generated from the terms of Equation (7.6.8) multiplied by appropriate constants. The diagram is shown in Figure 7-6-2. By assigning time domain state variables

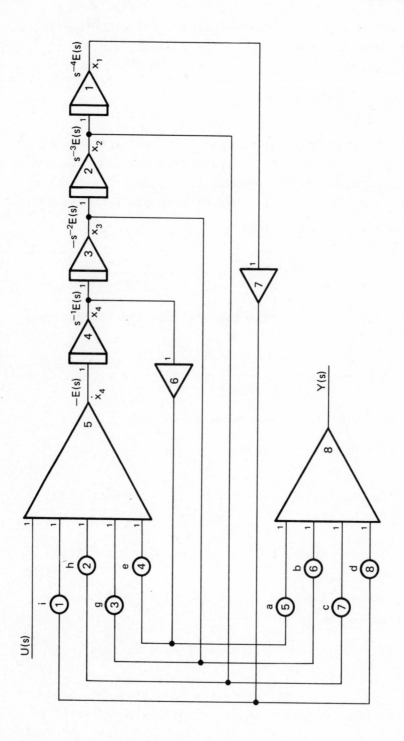

Figure 7-6-2. State variable simulation diagram

to the output of each integrator of Figure 7-6-2, the following
equations can be written

$$\dot{x}_1 = x_2,$$

$$\dot{x}_2 = x_3,$$

$$\dot{x}_3 = x_4,$$

$$\dot{x}_4 = E(s) = - i\ x_1 - h\ x_2 - g\ x_3 - e\ x_4 + u. \qquad (7.6.9)$$

These equations can be written in the form of the state and output
equations

$$\underline{\dot{x}} = \underline{A}\underline{x} + \underline{b}u \qquad (7.6.10)$$

and

$$\underline{y} = \underline{C}\underline{x} , \qquad (7.6.11)$$

where,

$$\underline{A} = \begin{bmatrix} 0 & 1 & 0 & 0 \\ 0 & 0 & 1 & 0 \\ 0 & 0 & 0 & 1 \\ -i & -h & -g & -e \end{bmatrix} , \quad \underline{b} = \begin{bmatrix} 0 \\ 0 \\ 0 \\ 1 \end{bmatrix} , \qquad (7.6.12)$$

and

$$\underline{C} = [d\ c\ b\ a]. \qquad (7.6.13)$$

This is the same basic form that was developed for the phase
variable case in an earlier section. However, instead of considering state variable x_1 as the output, the present example
uses a linear combination of the state variables as the output.

Additional understanding can be obtained by comparing the
simulation diagram of Figure 7-6-2 with the program developed
in Chapter 6 (Figure 6-6-1) for the same transfer function. If
state variables were assigned to the output of the integrators
in Figure 6-6-1, a different $\underline{A}$ matrix would result since that
state assignment is different from the state variables of Figure
7-6-2. Instead of the output, X(s), being a linear combination
of the assumed state variables, as in Figure 7-6-2, it is one of
the state variables. The method presented here is developed for

a general system of order n in reference (2) and a similar technique, based on flow graphs, is presented in reference (3).

If the transfer function is given in factored form as in
Equation (7.6.2), then a different approach can be utilized to
develop a state model from the transfer function. A partial
fraction expansion of Equation (7.6.2) yields

$$G(s) = \frac{K_1}{(s + P_1)} + \frac{K_2}{(s + P_2)} + \frac{K_n}{(s + P_n)} , \qquad (7.6.14)$$

where

$$K_n = (s + P_n) \, G(s)\big|_{s \to -P_n}.$$

If there are repeated roots (i.e., $P_i = P_j$) in Equation (7.6.2),
Equation (7.6.14) will have a different form.[7] For the case of
distinct real roots shown here, the response, $Y(s)$, is

$$Y(s) = U(s)G(s) = \frac{U(s)K_1}{(s + P_1)} + \frac{U(s)K_2}{(s + P_2)} + \cdots + \frac{U(s)K_n}{(s + P_n)}.$$

$$(7.6.15)$$

Thus, the output $Y(s)$, is the weighted sum of the responses of n
first-order terms. A simulation diagram for Equation (7.6.15) is
shown in Figure 7-6-3.

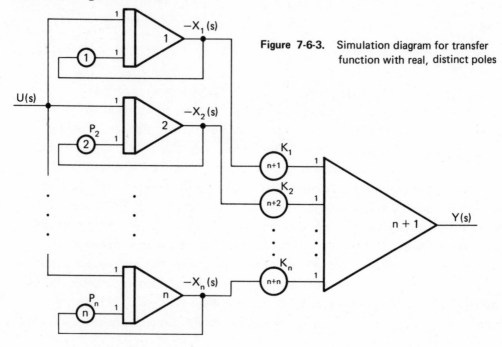

Figure 7-6-3. Simulation diagram for transfer
function with real, distinct poles

The differential equations for the state variables are:

$$\dot{x}_i = P_i x_i + u,$$ (7.6.16)

where $i = 1,2,\ldots,n$. The state variable equations can be written in the form

$$\underline{\dot{x}} = \underline{A}\underline{x} + \underline{b}u,$$ (7.6.17)

where

$$\underline{A} = \begin{bmatrix} -P_1 & 0 & 0 & \cdots & 0 \\ 0 & -P_2 & 0 & \cdots & 0 \\ 0 & 0 & -P_3 & \cdots & 0 \\ \cdot & \cdot & \cdot & & \cdot \\ \cdot & \cdot & \cdot & & \cdot \\ \cdot & \cdot & \cdot & & \cdot \\ 0 & 0 & 0 & \cdots & -P_n \end{bmatrix}$$ (7.6.18)

and

$$\underline{b} = \begin{bmatrix} 1 \\ 1 \\ 1 \\ \cdot \\ \cdot \\ \cdot \\ 1 \end{bmatrix}.$$ (7.6.19)

The output equation is of the form

$$y = \underline{C}\underline{x},$$ (7.6.20)

where $\underline{C} = [K_1, K_2, K_3, \ldots, K_n]$. The matrix $\underline{C}$ is a 1 by n matrix often referred to as a row vector. A row vector is the "transpose" of the column vector defined in Equation (7.2.2). The transpose operation is defined as the reversal or transpose of the row-column subscripts of a matrix. Thus, the element in the first row and third column of a matrix is transposed to the third row and first column position of the transposed matrix, (i.e., $C_{ij}^T = C_{ji}$, $i=1,\ldots,n$ and $j=1,\ldots,m$). The transpose notation could be used to write Equation (7.6.20) in the form

$$y = \underline{c}^T\underline{x} = [c_1 x_1 + c_2 x_2 + \cdots + c_n x_n],$$ (7.6.21)

where $\underline{c}$ and $\underline{c}^T$ are vectors

$$\underline{c} = \begin{bmatrix} K_1 \\ K_2 \\ \cdot \\ \cdot \\ \cdot \\ K_n \end{bmatrix} \quad \text{and} \quad \underline{c}^T = [K_1, \ K_2, \ \ldots, \ K_n]. \tag{7.6.22}$$

When the system is modeled in this form, the $\underline{A}$ matrix is a diagonal matrix and the off-diagonal terms are all zero. Thus, there is no "coupling" between states and the state equations do not have to be solved simultaneously unless the output is desired. This simplification of the computational requirements is most useful, and considerable effort is often devoted to manipulating the system equations into diagonal form.

It should be noted that there is no unique set of state variables for a given system. The ability to obtain different state variable formulations is one of the advantages of modern control theory and the interested reader is referred to the references at the end of this chapter.

7.7 EXAMPLE PROBLEM

In order to illustrate the methods presented in the previous section, consider the following transfer function

$$G(s) = \frac{Y(s)}{U(s)} = \frac{5(s+2)(s+4)}{(s+1)(s+3)(s+5)} , \tag{7.7.1}$$

which can also be written in the form

$$G(s) = \frac{5s^2 + 30s + 40}{s^3 + 9s^2 + 23s + 15} . \tag{7.7.2}$$

To use the first method, divide Equation (7.7.2) by s^3 to get an equation of the form

$$G(s) = \frac{5s^{-1} + 30s^{-2} + 40s^{-3}}{1 + 9s^{-1} + 23s^{-2} + 15s^{-3}} . \tag{7.7.3}$$

Define

$$E(s) = \frac{U(s)}{1 + 9s^{-1} + 23s^{-2} + 15s^{-3}} , \tag{7.7.4}$$

and write an expression for the output

$$Y(s) = G(s)U(s) = G(s)E(s) \; [1 + 9s^{-1} + 23s^{-2} + 15s^{-3}].$$

(7.7.5)

Equation (7.7.5) can be simplified to

$$Y(s) = 5s^{-1}E(s) + 30s^{-2}E(s) + 40s^{-3}E(s).$$

(7.7.6)

The previous equations can be programmed as shown in Figure 7-7-1.

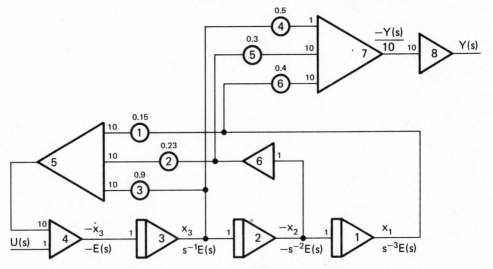

Figure 7-7-1. State variable simulation diagram

The simulation diagram of Figure 7-7-1 could be redrawn to conserve amplifiers. Also, the amplifier gains could be redistributed. However, these changes have not been made to avoid confusion. The state equations for the system shown in Figure 7-7-1 are

$$\begin{bmatrix} \dot{x}_1 \\ \dot{x}_2 \\ \dot{x}_3 \end{bmatrix} = \begin{bmatrix} 0 & 1 & 0 \\ 0 & 0 & 1 \\ -15 & -23 & -9 \end{bmatrix} \begin{bmatrix} x_1 \\ x_2 \\ x_3 \end{bmatrix} + \begin{bmatrix} 0 \\ 0 \\ 1 \end{bmatrix} u,$$

(7.7.7)

and

$$y = \begin{bmatrix} 40 & 30 & 5 \end{bmatrix} \begin{bmatrix} x_1 \\ x_2 \\ x_3 \end{bmatrix}.$$

(7.7.8)

The same transfer function can be written in state variable form using the second method presented in the previous section. In this case, the transfer function is expanded in factored form

$$G(s) = \frac{Y(s)}{U(s)} = \frac{K_1}{(s+1)} + \frac{K_2}{(s+3)} + \frac{K_3}{(s+5)} \, , \qquad (7.7.9)$$

where

$$K_1 = \frac{5(s+2)(s+4)}{(s+3)(s+5)} \bigg|_{s \to -1} = \frac{5(1)(3)}{(3)(4)} = \frac{15}{8} = 1.875,$$

$$K_2 = \frac{5(s+2)(s+4)}{(s+1)(s+5)} \bigg|_{s \to -3} = \frac{5(-1)(1)}{(-2)(2)} = \frac{-5}{-4} = 1.25,$$

and

$$K_3 = \frac{5(s+2)(s+4)}{(s+1)(s+3)} \bigg|_{s \to -5} = \frac{5(-3)(-1)}{(-4)(-2)} = \frac{15}{8} = 1.875.$$

Programming Equation (7.7.9) yields the diagram shown in Figure 7-7-2.

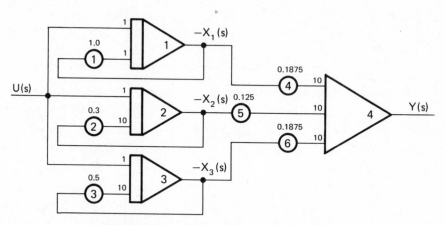

Figure 7-7-2. State variable simulation diagram

The resulting state equations are

$$\begin{bmatrix} \dot{x}_1 \\ \dot{x}_2 \\ \dot{x}_3 \end{bmatrix} = \begin{bmatrix} -1 & 0 & 0 \\ 0 & -3 & 0 \\ 0 & 0 & -5 \end{bmatrix} \begin{bmatrix} x_1 \\ x_2 \\ x_3 \end{bmatrix} + \begin{bmatrix} 1 \\ 1 \\ 1 \end{bmatrix} u. \qquad (7.7.10)$$

and

$$y = [1.875 \quad 1.25 \quad 1.875] \begin{bmatrix} x_1 \\ x_2 \\ x_3 \end{bmatrix} . \qquad (7.7.11)$$

As noted in Section (7.6) the $\underline{A}$ matrix is diagonal and the state equations are uncoupled. It should be emphasized that the two methods give identical results even though the state variables are different. Other sets of state variables could be used, and in some cases, a particular choice is advantageous.

7.8 MAGNITUDE AND TIME SCALING

The magnitude and time scaling of systems expressed in state variable form can be accomplished by a series of matrix – vector operations.[8] However they are beyond the scope of this book and the reader is referred to references (8) and (9) for additional information. The experience gained in scaling from previous chapters is very useful. Magnitude scaling can be achieved by adjusting gains to bring amplifier outputs to rea- sonable values as discussed in Section 4.10. Note that magnitude scaling should not change the net gain around any loop of a simulation diagram.

As noted in Chapter 4, a problem can be time scaled by changing the gain of all integrators (only integrators) by the same amount. Time scaling can also be achieved by substituting T/α for t, the independent variable. The need to time scale is usually indicated by unrealizable amplifier gains.

There is one special case that should be noted. When the $\underline{A}$ matrix is diagonal, the n first-order differential equations are uncoupled and scaling is considerably simplified. However, the time-scale factor, α, must be the same for each of the equations.

7.9 EXAMPLE PROBLEM

As an additional illustration of the techniques developed in this chapter, a state model for the example problem of Section 6.9 will be developed in this section. A block diagram of the system is shown in Figure 7-9-1.

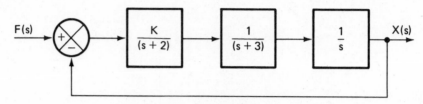

Figure 7-9-1. System block diagram

The transfer function for the system is

$$\frac{X(s)}{F(s)} = \frac{K}{s^3 + 5s^2 + 6s + K} .$$

(7.9.1)

The state equations are

$$\begin{bmatrix} \dot{x}_1 \\ \dot{x}_2 \\ \dot{x}_3 \end{bmatrix} = \begin{bmatrix} 0 & 1 & 0 \\ 0 & 0 & 1 \\ -K & -6 & -5 \end{bmatrix} \begin{bmatrix} x_1 \\ x_2 \\ x_3 \end{bmatrix} + \begin{bmatrix} 0 \\ 0 \\ 1 \end{bmatrix} f,$$

(7.9.2)

where state variable $x_1 = x$. The state equations are derived from Figure 7-9-2 which implements $E(s)$ as given by

$$E(s) = \frac{F(s)}{1 + 5s^{-1} + 6s^{-2} + Ks^{-3}} .$$

(7.9.3)

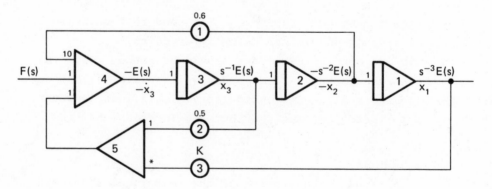

*Product of pot 3 and amplifier
gain must be equal to K

Figure 7-9-2. State variable simulation program

A careful check will identify the similarity of the simulation diagrams of Figure 7-9-2 and Figure 6-9-7. The output response, for various values of gain, K, is shown in Figure 6-9-8. This and other example problems will be used in later sections on digital simulation.

7.10 PROBLEMS FOR CHAPTER 7

Problems covering the material in this chapter are identified by section number for the convenience of the reader.

7.2.1 For the matrices and vectors given, carry out the specified matrix-vector operations:

$$\underline{A} = \begin{bmatrix} 0 & 1 & 2 \\ 4 & 3 & 5 \\ 2 & 0 & 1 \end{bmatrix} \quad \underline{B} = \begin{bmatrix} 1 & 3 \\ 5 & 7 \\ 0 & 2 \end{bmatrix} \quad \underline{c} = \begin{bmatrix} 3 & 2 & 4 \end{bmatrix}$$

$$\underline{d} = \begin{bmatrix} 1 \\ 5 \\ 7 \end{bmatrix} \quad \underline{E} = \begin{bmatrix} 1 & 5 & 7 \\ 2 & 4 & 1 \\ 3 & 2 & 0 \end{bmatrix} \quad \underline{I} = \begin{bmatrix} 1 & 0 & 0 \\ 0 & 1 & 0 \\ 0 & 0 & 1 \end{bmatrix}$$

a) $\underline{F} = \underline{A} + \underline{E}$
b) $\underline{G} = \underline{A} - \underline{E}$
c) Discuss $\underline{A} + \underline{B}$ and $\underline{c} + \underline{d}$.

7.2.2 For the matrices and vectors of 7.2.1 perform the following operation:
a) $\underline{H} = \underline{AE}$
b) $\underline{K} = \underline{EA}$
c) Compare the elements of $\underline{H}$ and $\underline{K}$ and discuss the results.

7.2.3 Using the matrices and vectors of 7.2.1, determine
a) $\underline{M} = \underline{cd}$
b) Attempt $\underline{dc}$ and comment on the result.

7.2.4 Using the matrices and vector of Problem 7.2.1, determine
a) $\underline{N} = \underline{IA}$
b) $\underline{P} = \underline{AI}$
c) $\underline{Q} = \underline{A}^2$

7.3.1 Given a parallel RLC circuit, discuss possible choices for state variables.

7.3.2   Given a series RLC circuit, discuss possible choices for state variables.

7.3.3   Discuss the assignment of redundant state variables and reasons why it might be desirable.

7.4.1   Given the differential equation shown, determine the state equations for a "phase" variable state assignment

$$\dddot{x} + 3\ddot{x} + 5\dot{x} + 8x = 16. \tag{7.10.1}$$

7.4.2   Given the differential equation shown, determine the state equation

$$\ddddot{x} + 3\dddot{x} + 5\ddot{x} + 8\dot{x} + 9x = 2\ddot{u} + 3\dot{u} + 4u. \tag{7.10.2}$$

7.4.3   For the state equations given, determine a third-order differential equation with $x = x_1 = [\text{the output}]$ and u as an input.

$$\begin{bmatrix} \dot{x}_1 \\ \dot{x}_2 \\ \dot{x}_3 \end{bmatrix} = \begin{bmatrix} 0 & 1 & 0 \\ 0 & 0 & 1 \\ -2 & -4 & -5 \end{bmatrix} \begin{bmatrix} x_1 \\ x_2 \\ x_3 \end{bmatrix} + \begin{bmatrix} 0 \\ 0 \\ 1 \end{bmatrix} u. \tag{7.10.3}$$

7.4.4   For the state equations given, determine a third-order differential equation with the output y.

$$\begin{bmatrix} \dot{x}_1 \\ \dot{x}_2 \\ \dot{x}_3 \end{bmatrix} = \begin{bmatrix} 0 & 1 & 0 \\ 0 & 0 & 1 \\ -5 & -7 & -8 \end{bmatrix} \begin{bmatrix} x_1 \\ x_2 \\ x_3 \end{bmatrix} + \begin{bmatrix} 0 \\ 0 \\ 1 \end{bmatrix} u. \tag{7.10.4}$$

$$y = \begin{bmatrix} -3 & -4 & 0 \end{bmatrix} \begin{bmatrix} x_1 \\ x_2 \\ x_3 \end{bmatrix}. \tag{7.10.5}$$

7.5.1   Develop a simulation diagram for the system of Problem 7.4.1.

7.5.2   Develop a simulation diagram for the system of Problem 7.4.2.

7.5.3   Develop a simulation diagram for the system of Problem 7.4.3.

7.5.4 Develop a simulation diagram for the system of Problem 7.4.4.

7.6.1 Given the transfer function shown, develop a state model and determine state equations using phase variable state assignment

$$G(s) = \frac{12\left[(s+2)(s+4)\right]}{s\left[(s+1)(s+3)\right]}.$$ (7.10.6)

7.6.2 Given the transfer function of Problem 7.6.1, develop a state model in which the $\underline{A}$ matrix is diagonal.

7.6.3 Determine a transfer function for the system described by Equation 7.10.3.

7.6.4 Determine a transfer function for the system described by Equations (7.10.4 and 7.10.5).

7.11 REFERENCES FOR CHAPTER 7

(1) Ogata, K., State Space Analysis of Control Systems, Prentice Hall, Inc., Englewood Cliffs, New Jersey, 1967.

(2) Gupta, S. and L. Hasdorff, Fundamentals of Automatic Control, John Wiley & Sons, Inc., New York, 1970.

(3) Dorf, R. C., Modern Control System, Addison-Wesley Publishing Company, Reading, Massachusetts, 1967.

(4) DeRusso, P. M., R. J. Roy, and C. M. Close, State Variables for Engineers, John Wiley & Sons, Inc., New York, 1965.

(5) Tropper, A. M., Matrix Theory for Electrical Engineers, Addison-Wesley Publishing Company, Reading, Massachusetts, 1962.

(6) Brace, R. M., Matrix Algebra for Electrical Engineers, Addison-Wesley Publishing Company, Reading, Massachusetts, 1962.

(7) Blackwell, W. A., Mathematical Modeling of Physical Networks, The Macmillan Company, 1968.

(8) Cannon, M. R., "Magnitude and Time Scaling of State-Variable Equations for Analog/Hybrid Computation," Simulation, Vol. 21, No. 2, pp. 23-28, July 1973.

(9) Baker, D. W., "Time Scaling Rule for a General Case," Simulation, Vol. 21, No. 5, pp. 144, November 1973.

*

B

HYBRID SIMULATION

8

Introduction to Hybrid Computers and Hybrid Computing Elements

8.1 INTRODUCTION

As its name indicates, the "Hybrid" computer is a combination of analog and digital computer technology. However, there is no universal configuration and the term is used to describe a wide variety of machines. In this chapter, the characteristics of both analog and digital computers will be summarized. With this background, the concept of a hybrid machine is introduced and several classifications of hybrid computers are discussed. Also, a brief history of hybrid computers is presented. The latter portion of the chapter is devoted to the presentation of hybrid computing elements and illustrations of their operation.

8.2 CHARACTERISTICS OF THE ANALOG COMPUTER

Before presenting the hybrid computer, it is important to discuss the characteristics of analog and digital computers. Considerable information on the analog computer has been provided in the first seven chapters of this book. As background for the discussion of hybrid computers, the characteristics of the analog computer will be summarized in this section.

The rapid growth of computer simulation was discussed in Chapter 1. Both analog and digital computers were mentioned without citing the advantages of either.

In Chapter 2, the operational amplifier was presented as the basic analog computing element. It was shown that the "op-amp" is capable of integration and algebraic summation of continuous variables. The direct integration of continuous signals is one of the primary advantages of the analog computer.

Another advantage is found in the manner in which the integrators and the components are utilized. As presented in Chapter 3, the analog computer is a parallel device operating simultaneously on all of the variables of a problem. The action of each variable on other problem variables is established directly by patching in the appropriate computing elements. As a result, the analog computer program has a unique relationship to the structure of the system being simulated. Thus, analog simulation is both "natural" and instructive.

In Chapter 4, techniques for estimating the maximum values of system variables were presented along with methods for scaling system equations. Also, the time scaling procedures provided a means for controlling the solution rate of the computer. Time scaling and mode control (operate, rest and hold) enabled the operator to control the "march-of-time" in a simulation.

Methods for direct simulation of certain classes of nonlinearities were presented in Chapter 5. The discussion also included analog multiplication, division and root finding.

Chapters 6 and 7 were devoted to the simulation of systems expressed in transfer function and state variable form. This enabled further development of the relationship of the analog program to system structure.

Thus, the salient features of the analog computer are: continuous variables, direct integration, parallel operation, and the unique problem/computer-time/user relationship. By means of direct integration and parallel operation, the analog computer is often able to operate in "real-time" or even faster. Therefore, speed must be added to the list of attributes of the analog computer.

As noted in the previous chapters, the analog computer has several limitations. It is generally limited to 3 or 4 place accuracy. Also, integration is with respect to time, and as a result, the handling of other independent variables requires special techniques. Another limitation of the analog computer is the difficulty of storing information. Finally, the scaling required for most simulations is time consuming and laborious. However, it often forces the system designer to acquire a better understanding of the system.

8.3   CHARACTERISTICS OF THE DIGITAL COMPUTER

Before discussing the characteristics of the digital computer, it is desirable to contrast analog and digital signals. In the previous chapters, the computing elements have been analog in nature. The output and input voltages are continuous functions of time and the circuits are designed to operate over the full range of values from the minus reference voltage to the positive reference voltage.

In contrast, digital circuits are designed to operate at only two levels or values. Although the output voltage of a digital circuit takes on values between the two levels, the transition from one level to the other is as fast as possible. Since digital signals are intended to be in one or the other state, only the two levels need be specified. Thus, digital signals are binary in nature. Usually, the higher voltage level is called the "one" state and the lower voltage level is called the "zero" state. Several other terms that have been used to describe the states are: true and false, set and reset, on and off and high and low.

The basic digital components can be divided into two categories: logic elements and storage elements. Both operate from and produce discrete signals which are restricted to two distinct levels. The logic circuits perform logical operations on binary signals. A number of digital signals can be grouped to represent many distinct levels of a single variable. The logic and storage elements can be combined to perform arithmetic operations on these variables such as counting, addition, subtraction, multiplication and division. For additional information, see Chapters 9 and 10 and references (1) and (2).

For economic reasons, the arithmetic portion of a digital computer is usually time-shared and the operations are carried out in a sequential fashion.[3] Thus, operations on the variables of a problem are performed one after the other. This scheme is quite different from the parallel operation of the analog computer.

From this brief description of the digital computer, several advantages can be identified. One of the most important attributes of the digital computer is accuracy. By increasing the number of binary signals used to represent a given variable, any level of accuracy can be achieved. Another important advantage is the ability to store information. Also, the logical decision capability is quite useful. Thus, the digital computer is able to perform a wide variety of arithmetic and logical functions.

By means of floating point operations, the digital computer can represent a wide range of variables, and as a result, the scaling required on the analog computer can be avoided.[4] In contrast to the analog computer, independent and dependent variables are handled in the same manner. Also, the digital computer is not capable of direct integration and numerical approximations must be used. Finally, the development of special purpose compilers has simplified programming and enabled the machine to switch from one type of problem to another with ease.

Some of the characteristics that are advantageous also create limitations. For example, discrete representation of variables increases the accuracy but complicates the process of interfacing a digital computer to a continuous process. Also, the simplified programming techniques occasionally conceal the relationships among system components. Since the digital computer operates on the problem variables in a sequential nature, it is often unable to function fast enough to achieve "real-time" operation on complex problems. Also, the numerical approximations used for integration and differentiation require careful consideration of the trade-off between solution time and accuracy.

8.4 HYBRID COMPUTER CLASSIFICATION

From the descriptions of analog and digital computers in the previous sections, it appears that a combination of the two machines would be advantageous. This is indeed true and a number of "hybrid" computers have been built. However, since any combination of analog and digital elements is a "hybrid" computer, some classification scheme is desirable. Hybrid computers range from an analog computer with a small amount of patchable digital logic to a digital computer with analog arithmetic elements, with many intermediate classifications.

For this discussion, consider four levels or classifications of hybrid computers. Type one is an analog computer with patchable digital logic elements. This configuration, discussed in detail in Chapter 9, enables the analog program to be supplemented with logical decisions that change the program parameters, simulate actual events, and provide limited optimization capability.

Since the rapid transition of digital signals can introduce electrical noise into the analog system, a separate patching area is usually provided for the digital elements. Some systems even provide a separate patch panel and special "trunk" lines to interconnect the two patch panels.

The second group, presented in Chapter 10, includes analog computers with patchable digital logic, a digital clock and several digital registers. The register elements provide limited digital storage, counting and shifting operations. This combination of analog and digital elements permits automatic parameter sweeps, program cycling and counting, simulation of continuous/discrete systems, small adaptive control studies, and serial or stage type simulations.

A third category of hybrid computers, discussed in Chapter 12, consists of analog computers having clocked logic and an interface for a small digital computer. The interface typically includes mode control and monitoring, one or more "slow" channels of analog-to-digital conversion (ADC), and provision for setting the pots on the analog computer from the digital computer. Also, the system may include a few digital-to-analog (DAC) conversion channels. This combination of equipment provides computer con-

trolled "set-up" and "check-out" of the problem programmed on the
analog computer.   Also, the digital computer can provide program
storage, arithmetic calculations, function storage and automatic
parameter modification.

The final classification, also discussed in Chapter 12, covers
the "full" or "balanced" hybrid computer.   The analog computer is
usually quite large and includes a full complement of patchable
digital logic, and possibly, electronic switching to facilitate
automatic program patching and alteration.   The interface provides
a number of high-speed ADC and DAC channels, mode control and
monitoring, as well as sense and interrupt lines.   The digital
computer is large enough to carry out a significant portion of the
calculations and can have complete control of the problem solution.
With two-way communication and control, the system is very flexible
and can handle a wide variety of problems such as data reduction,
optimal-adaptive studies, etc.

8.5   A BRIEF HISTORY OF HYBRID COMPUTERS

The first hybrid computers were constructed in 1958 at
Convair Astronautics in San Diego, California and Space Technology
Laboratories in Redondo Beach, California.[11]   Both computers were
used to simulate missiles and involved the interconnection of
large analog and digital computers.   Small-to-medium scale analog
computers with patchable digital logic were not available commercially until 1961.

By the mid 1960's, balanced hybrid systems were being employed
in a wide variety of applications.   Also, a full line of analog
computers featuring electronic mode control, patchable digital
logic and several digital registers were available.   Thus, hybrid
computer technology is relatively new and has been constantly
changing as new hardware developments and applications are found.

Chapters 9, 10 and 11 will concentrate on the application of
the first three categories of hybrid computers described in
Section 8.4.   Hybrid software and hybrid system configurations
will be presented in Chapter 12.   Hopefully, an appreciation for
the capabilities of the full hybrid system can be gained.   The
remainder of this chapter is devoted to a study of the hybrid
computing elements.

8.6   HYBRID COMPUTING ELEMENTS: THE ANALOG SWITCH

By definition, the hybrid computing elements   operate   on
and/or produce a combination of analog and digital signals. These
elements enable the interconnection (interfacing) of analog and
digital systems.   Since the hybrid computing elements involve
both analog and digital signals, some method will be needed   to
distinguish analog and digital signal lines.   Digital signal lines
will be indicated with a bar at each end as shown in Figure 8-6-1.

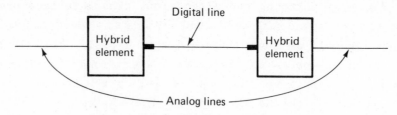

Figure 8-6-1.   Digital signal line identification

One of the most useful hybrid computing elements is the analog switch.   There are two basic types of analog switches available on most systems.   One type is electro-mechanical in nature
and the other utilizes solid-state electronic switching. Basically
the device enables the opening and closing of an analog   signal
path as a function of a digital logic level.   Usually,   a   digital

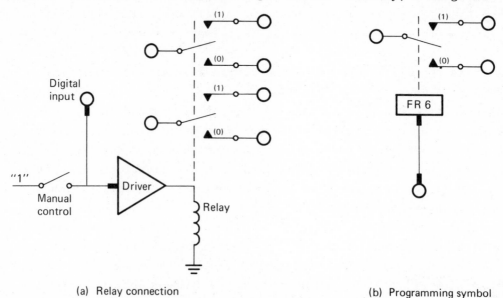

(a) Relay connection   (b) Programming symbol

Figure 8-6-2.   The function relay

signal at logic level "one" closes the switch and a logic "zero" opens the path. In most systems, the electro-mechanical unit is a double pole, double throw switch as shown in Figure 8-6-2(a). Figure 8-6-2(b) illustrates a programming symbol which includes a device number in the block. Note that the digital signal lines have been identified as specified in Figure 8-6-1.

The contacts of the relay are labeled to indicate the connection made for each input logic state. Also, a manual input is included in the circuit of Figure 8-6-2(a) and is provided on most computers. Thus, analog signals can be switched in response to a digital signal or a manual operation.

Since the relays used require approximately one millisecond to operate, switching time can be critical in systems operating at high solution rates. Also, the contacts of the relay can be damaged if excessive electric currents are switched. Therefore, care must be exercised to avoid switching a reference to ground or the positive reference supply to the negative reference. The current levels associated with a properly programmed problem will not damage the relay.

The need for faster switching time led to the development of the second type of analog switch which is electronic in nature. Utilizing the field-effect transistor (FET), the electronic switch operates in less than one microsecond. However, there are some restrictions on its use. The operational limitations are a result of the fact that the switch is actually a variable resistance. The device has a very high resistance (several megohms) in the open or off state and less than ten ohms in the on or closed state. Ideally, these values should be infinity and zero, respectively.

In order to minimize the effect of the non-ideal character- istics, the switch is connected to a resistor and the combination used as a switchable input resistor. The value of the resistor used with the switch is selected to yield an input gain ratio of ten when coupled with the resistance of the switch. A programming symbol for the electronic switch is shown in Figure 8-6-3. The device identification number is contained in the diamond and the digital signal lines are specified. The output terminal (SJ) must be connected to the summing junction of an amplifier. Thus,

the electronic switch is a gain-of-ten input to an amplifier that
can be turned on and off by a digital signal.

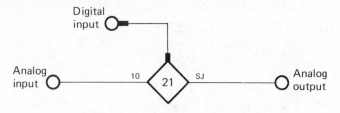

Figure 8-6-3.   Electronic switch programming symbol

In addition to the restrictions cited in previous paragraphs,
there are other traits that should be pointed out. If either type
of analog switch is to be driven from a potentiometer, care must
be exercised in setting the pot, since the output loading of the
pot may be a function of the state of the switch. Also, if the
output of the pot is connected to other devices, the effective
setting of the pot may be changed by the operation of the switch.
This problem is avoided on some computers by connecting the
output (SJ) side of the "gain-of-ten" switch to ground when it is
in the open state. Thus, the switch is either connected to the
"virtual" ground at the amplifier summing junction or to reference
ground through another switch. As a result, the effective resistance is always that of a gain-of-ten input.

Analog switches can be used to change the configuration of
a program, system parameters, input forcing functions, initial
conditions, etc. Some computer systems provide switches specifi-
cally for switching the plus and minus references and for static
testing. Since the switches can be controlled by a digital computer, they enable automatic program check-out, operation and
alteration. The use of analog switches will be illustrated in
the latter portion of this chapter.

8.7 HYBRID COMPUTING ELEMENTS: THE TRACK-STORE

In summarizing the characteristics of the analog computer
in Section 8.2, the lack of memory was cited. However, the Hold
mode of an integrator is a form of analog memory. A special unit
using the same principle has been developed and is called track-
store. The intent of the track-store is the provision of analog
memory.

The operation of a track-store unit can be summarized as follows: when the digital signal at the track terminal is a logic "one", the analog output follows or tracks the analog input; when the digital signal at the track terminal is changed to a logic "zero", the analog output holds the value that was at the analog input the instant the track terminal went from logic "one" to logic "zero". This operation is illustrated in Figure 8-7-1.

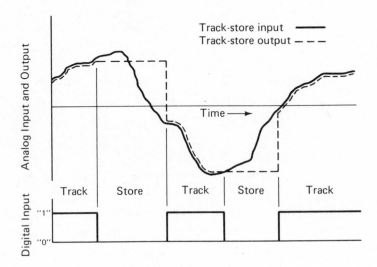

Figure 8-7-1. Track-store operation

Thus, the track-store operates in the same manner as a summing amplifier when the track terminal is a logic "one". It operates as an integrator in the Hold mode when the track terminal is a logic "zero".

A circuit to provide track-store capability is shown in Figure 8-7-2. Electronic switches #1 and #4 are closed for the Store (Hold) mode and open for tracking. Switches #2 and #3 are closed for tracking and open for holding or storing. This is an excellent example of the use of electronic switches. The track-store unit is similar to summing and integrating amplifiers and most computer manufacturers provide switching networks that couple to an integrator or a summing amplifier to make a track-store unit. Since these amplifiers already contain several input resistors and/or provisions for an initial condition, these features are also utilized in the track-store. Thus, the typical

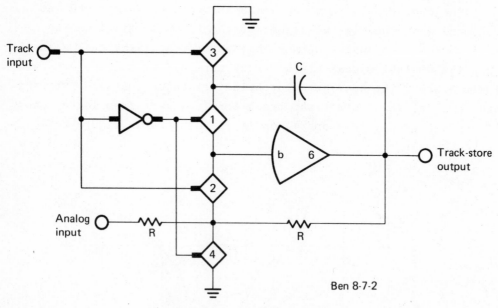

Ben 8-7-2

Figure 8-7-2.   Track-store circuit

track-store will track the sum of the analog inputs when in the
Track mode and hold the value of the input sum when switched to
the Store mode. When the initial condition control terminal is
switched to the logic "one" state, it overrides the Track mode
and the storage capacitor is charged to the analog value held at
the initial condition input. A programming symbol for the track-
store unit described here is shown in Figure 8-7-3(a). Note the

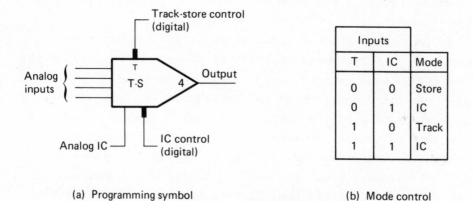

(a) Programming symbol   (b) Mode control

Figure 8-7-3. Track-store programming symbol and mode control

distinction made for digital signal lines. Figure 8-7-3(b) contains a mode control table indicating that the initial condition
mode is dominant. Since the track-store units on different computers may vary in their operation, the instruction manual for
the particular machine to be used should be read carefully.

A method frequently used to provide track-store operation
utilizes the integrating networks. The variable to be tracked,
is connected to the initial condition terminal of an integrator.
When the integrator is in the IC or Reset mode, the output tracks
the initial condition input. When the integrator is in the Hold
mode, the unit stores. The Operate mode is not used. This technique requires integrators with individual electronic mode
control. This approach has led to the track-store symbol shown
in Figure 8-7-4(a).[9] The addition of a capacitor and appropriate switches to a summing amplifier, as discussed earlier, led
to the symbol in Figure 8-7-4(b).[10] The symbol in Figure 8-7-3
(a) will be used in the remainder of this book.

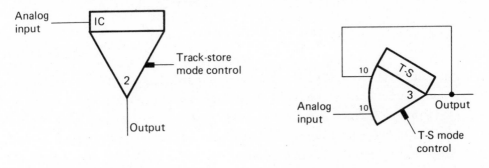

(a) Integrator track-store symbol   (b) Summer track-store symbol

Figure 8-7-4.   Other track-store programming symbols

Before presenting example problems, it is desirable to
discuss some practical considerations for the use of track-store
units. Since the analog value is stored on a capacitor, there
is a slight decay with time. However, the use of quality components and careful circuit design limit the decrease to less
than 0.001% of reference voltage per second. Thus, storage for
several seconds will not affect the anticipated accuracy of the
analog computer.

In switching from Store to Track, the output does not
follow the input instantaneously. Typically, the tracking time
constant is less than 0.2 microsec. In most practical situations,
this delay can be ignored. However, the programmer should be
aware of the possibility of a tracking error. Also, the bandwidth
of most track-store units is less than the bandwidth of the
computing amplifiers and should be given careful consideration.

8.8 EXAMPLE PROBLEMS

In order to illustrate the use of track-store units, the
following examples will discuss the operation of two track-store
units in tandem as shown in Figure 8-8-1. Assume that the units

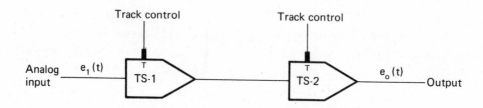

Figure 8-8-1.   Cascaded track-store units

are supplied with a logic signal that alternates between logic
"zero" and logic "one" so that TS-1 is in the Track mode when
TS-2 is in Store. In a similar manner, TS-1 is in Store when TS-2
is tracking. The required logic signals are shown in Figure 8-8-2.
Since TS-1 has a zero initial condition and starts in the Track
mode, TS-1 follows the input until T_1. Also, TS-2 has a zero
initial condition, and therefore, stores a zero value throughout
the first period. At T_1, TS-1 goes into the Store mode and holds
the value $e_1(t=T_1)$. However, TS-2 goes into the Track mode and
tracks the output of TS-1 which is $e_1(T_1)$ until T_2. At T_2, TS-1
goes back into Track and begins following the input $e_1(t)$. However, TS-2 goes into Store and holds the value of TS-1 until T_3
when the cycle repeats. The resulting waveforms for the tandem
track-store units are shown in Figure 8-8-2. This circuit is
frequently used to track sequential values of an analog function
and is sometimes referred to as a "bucket brigade".[8]

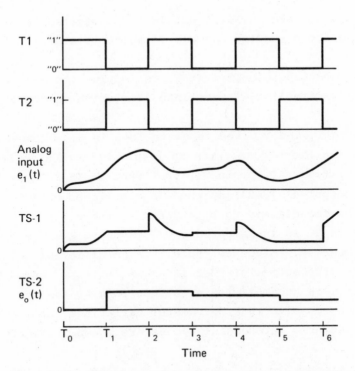

Figure 8-8-2. Operating waveforms for the tandem track-store units of Figure 8-8-1

Another popular variation of tandem track-store units utilizes a feedback path as shown in Figure 8-8-3. The input signals

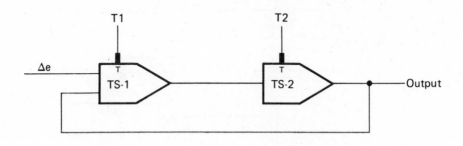

Figure 8-8-3. Track-stores connected to provide analog accumulation

for the track terminals are shown in Figure 8-8-4. If the input is an increment Δe, the output of TS-1 just prior to time T_1, will be zero since TS-1 is in the Store mode with a zero initial condition. Since TS-2 is tracking the output of TS-1, the output of TS-2 is also zero. (Note that TS-1 was started in Store in contrast to the preceding example in which it started off in the Track mode).

Since the input to TS-1 at T_1 is Δe plus the output of TS-2 (zero at this time), TS-1 goes into Track with an output equal to Δe.

Between T_1 and T_2, the input to TS-2 is Δe. However, TS-2 went into the Store mode with an input of zero and its output is zero for $T_1 < t < T_2$. Prior to T_3, the input to TS-1 is Δe (the input) plus Δe (output of TS-2) and when TS-1 switches back to Track, its output goes immediately to $E_0 = 2\Delta e$. As the cycle continues, the output of TS-2, is incremented by Δe each cycle and accumulates the increment Δe. Since Δe could take on different values for each cycle, the output of TS-2 is $\Delta e_1 + \Delta e_2 + \ldots + \Delta e_n$. This is quite useful in accumulating such functions as the sum of the error for successive runs, parameter variations, etc. The resulting waveforms for several cycles are shown in Figure 8-8-4.

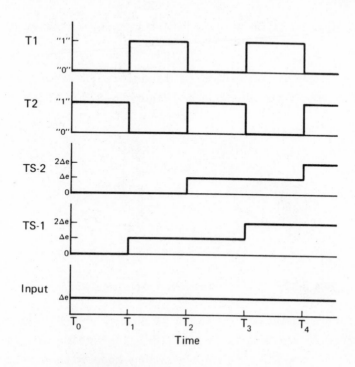

Figure 8-8-4. Waveforms for T–S accumulator

8.9 HYBRID COMPUTING ELEMENTS: THE COMPARATOR

The hybrid computing elements that have been discussed in previous sections enabled digital control of analog operations. In order to permit analog signals to interact with a digital system, a device that produces or changes a digital output in response to an analog input is needed. This is the role of the electronic comparator.

Basically, the comparator has an analog input and a digital output. The digital output is in the "one" state when the analog input is positive. The output goes to the "zero" state when the analog input goes negative. In most cases, the comparator will have two or more analog inputs and the digital output is "one" if the algebraic sum of the inputs is positive and "zero" if the sum is negative.

A comparator can be made by utilizing a high gain amplifier with the output clamped at the desired logic levels. In other words, a small positive signal at the input causes the amplifier to saturate at one logic level and a small negative input signal drives the amplifier to the other logic level. Based on the discussion of diodes in Chapter 5, the circuit of Figure 8-9-1 will operate as a comparator. If the sum of the inputs is negative, the output attempts to go to the positive reference, but

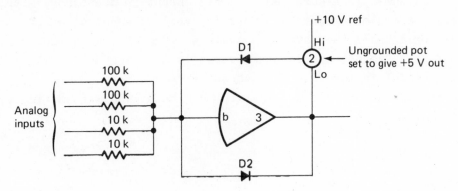

Figure 8-9-1.   Analog circuit for a comparator

is held at approximately +5 volts by the diode D1. If the algebraic sum of the inputs is positive, the output is held at or near zero volts by the diode D2. This circuit is the inverse of the previous definition of a comparator. However, the

inclusion of an inverter is all that is necessary to correct this
fault.

It is frequently desirable to override the action of the
comparator and prevent the output from changing state. This
function is provided by means of a "latch" terminal. A binary
"one" on the latch terminal locks the comparator in its present
state. A binary "zero" permits the comparator to operate in the
normal fashion. A programming symbol for the comparator is shown
in Figure 8-9-2. Note the distinction made on digital signal lines.

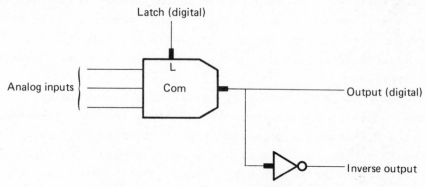

Figure 8-9-2. Comparator programming symbol

In addition to the normal output, most comparators have a second
output as shown in Figure 8-9-2. This output is the opposite or
inverse of the other output. That is, when the normal output
is at logic "one" the inverse output is a "zero". When the normal
output is a "zero", the inverse output is a logic "one". This is
a very useful feature and is used quite frequently.

The operation of the comparator can be stated mathematically
as follows:

$$\text{output} = \text{"1"} \text{ if } x + y > 0, \qquad\qquad (8.9.1)$$

and

$$\text{output} = \text{"0"} \text{ if } x + y < 0. \qquad\qquad (8.9.2)$$

Thus, the output is a logic "one" if $x + y > 0$ or $x > -y$. If
$y=0$, then the comparator will detect the algebraic sign of x
and change logic states each time x passes through zero. On
some comparators, it is not necessary to connect one terminal to

zero in order to detect the zero crossing of the other terminal (i.e., an unpatched terminal is equivalent to zero). However, this is an important detail that should be verified for the computer being used. Figure 8-9-3 illustrates the operation of a comparator for various input conditions.

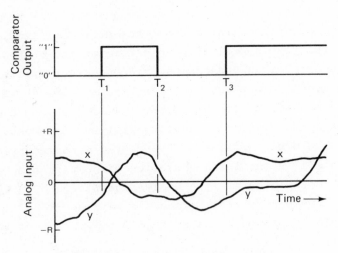

Figure 8-9-3. Comparator circuit operation

The discussion of the operation of a comparator was based on ideal characteristics. Before presenting an example problem, some of the practical aspects of comparator operation should be covered. In presenting the operating characteristics, it was implied that the output of the comparator switched logic states instantaneously. Actually, a finite amount of time is required, and for most units, switching time is less than one microsecond. In most instances this can be ignored.

Another important characteristic is the switching level. The equations of operation indicate that the output switches when the input is zero. Actually, a low threshold (usually less than 5 mV) is required to cause the unit to switch and the unit displays a hysteresis switching characteristic. When the input is decreasing from large positive values, it must go slightly negative before the comparator switches states. Going from negative to positive also requires a small positive threshold. At first, this hysteresis appears to be undesirable. However, the small range about zero in which the unit will not switch is

advantageous. The threshold prevents the unit from "chattering"
due to electrical noise when the input is near zero.

8.10 EXAMPLE PROBLEMS

The application of comparators and track-store units are
often involved in complex problems. However, for instructional
purposes, the problem presented here is quite simple and the
emphasis will be on comparator and track-store utilization.

Assume that it is desirable to determine the peak value of
the step response of an underdamped, second-order system.   The
underdamped second-order equation has been discussed in previous
chapters and equations for the peak value of the overshoot   are
available in a number of classical control system books.[11] Since
the reader should be familiar with the system characteristics,
the only problem is the interconnection of comparators and
track-store units to obtain the desired quantity.

When the response, $x(t)$, reaches a maximum slope (i.e., the
derivative of the response, $\dot{x}$) will go from a positive value to

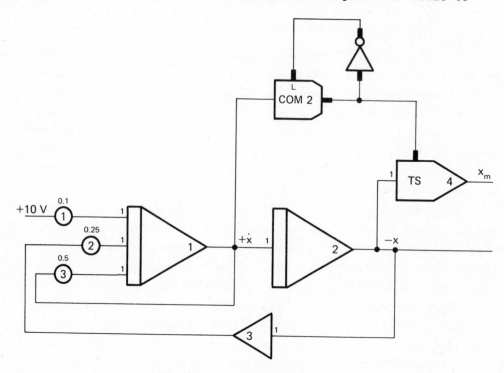

Figure 8-10-1. Peak-storing circuit

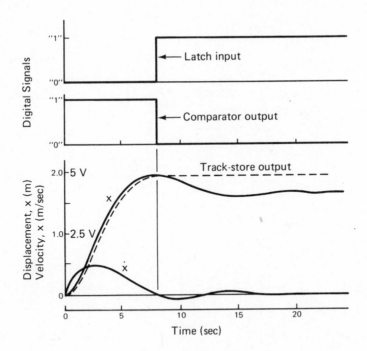

Figure 8-10-2. Peak-storing circuit response

a negative value. This can be detected by a comparator and the resulting change in logic level used to put a track-store unit into the Store mode. Since the derivative, $\dot{x}$, will go through zero at each maximum and minimum in the response, the comparator will continue to change logic levels and switch the track-store unit from Track to Store alternately. Therefore, some way of latching the circuit after the first maximum must be included. This can be accomplished with the "latch" terminal on the comparator. The circuit is shown in Figure 8-10-1 and the corresponding waveforms are shown in Figure 8-10-2. Note that all digital signal lines are identified at the input and output terminals. Since the comparator will latch on its own output, it will be necessary to reset it manually after each run.

As a second example, assume that the value of the minimum following the first maximum is desired. In order to see how this can be accomplished, consider the circuit of Figure 8-10-3. Comparator 1 monitors $\dot{x}$ and goes from logic 1 to logic 0 when

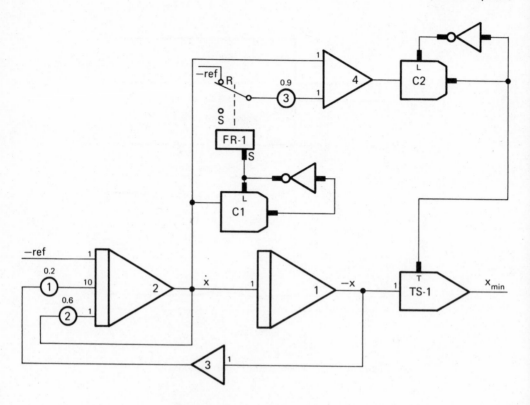

Figure 8-10-3. Minimum storing circuit

$\dot{x}$ goes negative. The output of comparator 1 sets function relay
1 to the set state and removes the minus reference when $\dot{x}$ goes
negative. When x reaches the minimum, $\dot{x}$ goes positive and comparator 2 switches from logic 1 to logic 0. The output of
comparator 2 puts track-store 1 in the Store mode holding the
value of the desired minimum. The corresponding waveforms are
shown in Figure 8-10-4. Further cycling of comparators 1 and 2
is prevented by utilizing the latching feature on both comparators.
Before leaving this example, note that the input to comparator 2
is open during the operation of the function relay. Electrical
noise could cause the comparator to switch states prematurely
and cause the track-store to store the wrong value. An alternate
approach uses comparator 1 to latch comparator 2 during the time
$\dot{x}$ is positive and unlatch comparator 2 after $\dot{x}$ goes negative.

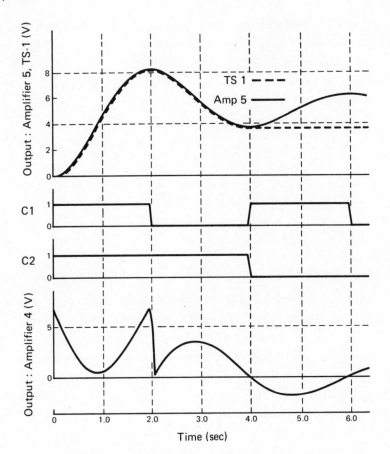

Figure 8-10-4. Waveforms for minimum storing circuit

8.11 MODE CONTROL

The simultaneous control of all integrators (Reset, Hold and
Operate) restricts utilization of the computer. Most computers
permit individual mode control of the integrators. Usually, the
mode is controlled by digital logic inputs on the integrator
networks. A mode control bus is also included so that all or any
group of integrators can be controlled simultaneously.

The inclusion of individual mode control enables generation
of special waveforms, evaluation of run functions, sequential use
of amplifiers for stage type simulations, etc. When coupled with
the interface elements of previous sections and the digital
circuitry of Chapters 9 and 10, individual mode control makes
possible a new approach to analog computation.

In order to control the three basic modes, a minimum of two inputs are required. The two terminals are usually labeled "Reset" and "Operate", "Hold" and "Operate" or "Hold" and "Reset". Figure 8-11-1 shows an integrator symbol with the additional inputs.

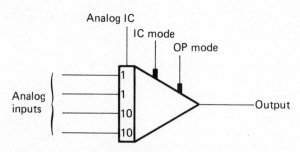

Figure 8-11-1. Integrator symbol with mode control inputs

The input labeled analog IC is the input for the analog value of the desired initial condition. The other terminal labeled IC on the sloping part of the integrator is the mode control input for the digital logic signal. The remaining mode control terminal (OP) is also shown on the sloping portion of the symbol. Note that the digital signal lines are properly identified. If the individual mode control is not used, the inputs are omitted and the integrator is assumed to operate from the mode control bus with other integrators. Therefore, the absence of mode control inputs on a computer diagram indicates the usual analog mode control.

With two inputs, there are four possible combinations and two of the combinations produce the same mode as shown in Figure 8-11-2. Since different computers may have other assignments

DIGITAL INPUT		
IC	OP	MODE
0	0	Hold
0	1	Operate
1	0	Reset
1	1	Reset

Figure 8-11-2. Mode control table

for the mode control states, the operator's manual should be read carefully before developing a program.

In addition to basic integrator mode selection by means of digital logic signals, many computers provide for the selection of the integrating capacitor. As many as six capacitors of different values are included. Typically, they range from 0.0001 microfarad to 10.0 microfarads. The capacitor selected is usually the result of two logic signals and the time-scale selector. The selection of one state out of six possible states requires a minimum of three binary signals. The ability to select the integrating capacitor permits digital control of the integrator gain, and therefore, automatic time scaling. Thus, digital signals can control the gain, mode and configuration of an analog program. As stated earlier, these features are handled differently on most machines and the instruction manual should be consulted.

Mode control could have been used to determine the maximum and minimum values in the examples of Section 8.10. If the remainder of the response is of no interest, the output of the comparators could have been used to put the integrating amplifiers into hold at the maximum or minimum values.

The increased capability of integrator mode control indicates a need for a more flexible mode control bus system. As a result, the manual and free-running repetitive operation controllers have been supplemented with additional manual modes available and a digitally controlled repetitive operation timer. For example, many machines include a "Set-Pot" mode which connects summing junctions to electrical ground and provides feedback for all amplifiers. Some machines also include a "Problem-Verify" mode which switches in preset conditions for static check purposes.

The automatic run timer or repetitive operation controller usually includes a digital input which enables the machine to respond to a change in a logical variable. Also, some computers provide repetitive operation controllers with three or four states instead of usual "Operate" and "Reset" cycles. The additional states can be used for initialization of stages in a sequential simulation, the evaluation of run variables and cost functions, and the calculation of new initial conditions.

The run timer or controller must have at least one logic output and a typical assignment might be "1" for operate and "0" for reset. The inclusion of two output variables makes four states possible. A repetitive operation controller incorporating some of the features that have been discussed is an important programming element and is quite useful. Figure 8-11-3 presents a typical programming symbol which includes identification of digital signal lines.

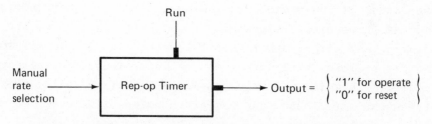

Figure 8-11-3. Repetitive operation controller programming symbol

For the rep-op timer illustrated in Figure 8-11-3, the length of time spent in the logic "1" state for Operate is determined by the manual input. This is usually a selector switch for a basic range of time and a potentiometer for variations in each range selected. In addition, some machines include a time scale selector which will change the time by a factor of 500. Thus, the Operate period is a function of the time scale selected [slow or fast], the time range selector, and the potentiometer setting. The Reset period is determined in a similar fashion. Therefore, the Operate period and Reset period are variable over a wide range. When the digital signal on the Run terminal is logic "1", the timer cycles. When the Run input is a logic "0", the timer stops cycling. This is illustrated in Figure 8-11-4. Note that the length of time in

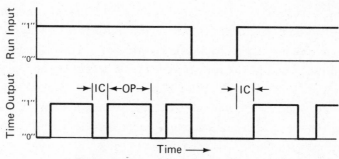

Figure 8-11-4. Rep-op timer operation

reset (IC) and operate (OP) are determined by manual inputs. Since all, or any portion of the integrators can be controlled by the rep-op timer, many interesting possibilities can be devised.

8.12 PROBLEMS FOR CHAPTER 8

Problems covering the material of this chapter are identified by section.

8.2.1 List 5 advantages of the analog computer.

8.2.2 Consider the analog computer as a portion of a hybrid computer and list the advantages cited in Problem 8.2.1 in order of decreasing importance.

8.3.1 List 5 terms used to identify the logic "1" state of a digital variable.

8.3.2 List 5 attributes of analog and digital computers in corresponding pairs.

8.3.3 Name the two types of components found in digital computers.

8.3.4 List 5 advantages of the digital computer.

8.6.1 Name the two types of analog switches.

8.6.2 Draw the complete electric circuit (show all resistors, etc.) for an electronic switch connected to a summing amplifier.

8.6.3 Discuss the use of function relays to implement static testing. What important advantage is offered?

8.6.4 Develop a program for a linear, second-order system with $\omega_n=2$ and $\delta=.2$ or $.4$ as selected by a function relay.

8.6.5 Use function relays to carry out the static test on Problem 8.6.4.

8.7.1 Connect an integrator to operate as a track-store. What connections are required on the mode control terminals?

8.7.2 Use an electronic multiplier and two track-store units to develop a program that will obtain the response of a linear, second-order system ($\omega_n=1.2$) for $\delta=0.2$, 0.4, 0.6 and 0.8 on successive run cycles.

8.7.3 Use a function relay or electronic switch to include a run with $\delta=0$ in Problem 8.7.2.

8.7.4   Put the track-store unit of Problem 8.7.1 in the Track mode. Monitor the output with an oscilloscope and connect a square-wave oscillator to the input. Comment on the results.

8.10.1 Use a summing amplifier to construct a comparator.

8.10.2 Sketch the input/output characteristics of a comparator. Be sure to include hysteresis.

8.10.3 Develop a program to track and store each maximum in the step response of a second-order system ($\delta=.2$ and $\omega_n=1.5$). The track-store should hold each maximum until the next one occurs.

8.10.4 Develop a program that will take two input signals and produce one output that is the larger of the two input signals.

8.10.5 Develop a program that will take two input signals and produce at the output the larger of the two input signals minus the difference of the two input signals.

8.10.6 Develop a precision absolute value circuit. The absolute value circuit of Figure 5-2-12 will have diode voltage drop errors. The circuit developed here should provide more precise operation.

8.10.7 Develop a precision dead-space circuit. See Figure 5-2-8 for information.

8.10.8 Use a comparator and analog switches to simulate the system in Section 5.3.

8.10.9 Sketch the output of the circuit shown for a sinusoidal input with a magnitude of 5 volts.

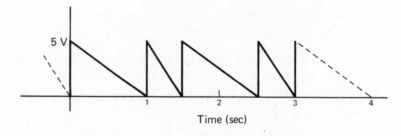

Time (sec)

Figure 8-12-1.

8.10.10 Sketch the output for the circuit shown for a sinusoidal input with a magnitude of 5 volts.

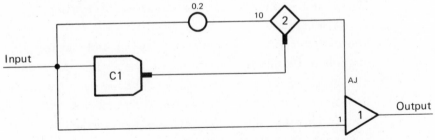

Figure 8-12-2.

8.11.1 Set up a second-order system ($\delta=0.2$ and $\omega_n=2$) to
display the step response on a CRT with repetitive
operation. Change ω_n to 20 and make the necessary
changes in the rep-op timer to display the response.

8.11.2 Use two integrators and the rep-op timer to produce
the wave-form shown.

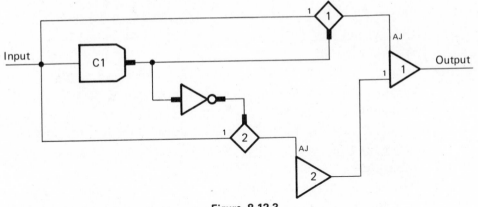

Figure 8-12-3.

8.11.3 Repeat Problem 8.11.2 using one integrator, electronic switches and the rep-op timer.

8.11.4 Repeat either 8.11.2 or 8.11.3 for the time axis
set for milliseconds instead of seconds.

8.11.5 Use a comparator to detect the occurrence of a
maximum in the step response of the second-order
system of Problem 8.9.3. Connect the output of
the comparator to put the computer in the Hold
mode at the first maximum of the response.

8.11.6 Use two comparators to put the computer into the Hold mode when the second-order system response ($\delta=.2$ and $\omega_n=3$) is at the minimum following the first maximum.

8.11.7 Use comparators, track-store units and analog switches to develop a program that will decrease the damping of a second-order system in steps of 0.1 from 1.0 until the percent overshoot for a step input exceeds a preset percentage setting on a potentiometer.

8.11.8 Develop a program that will compare the percent overshoot of a second-order system step response with a percentage setting on a potentiometer and either increase or decrease the damping until the system overshoot is within some ε of the value set on the pot.

8.13 REFERENCES FOR CHAPTER 8

(1) Hill, J. and G. R. Peterson, Introduction to Switching Theory and Logical Design, John Wiley & Sons, Inc., New York, 1968.

(2) Torng, H. C., Switching Circuits Theory and Logic Design, Addison-Wesley Publishing Company, Reading, Massachusetts, 1972.

(3) Hill, J. and G. R. Peterson, Digital Systems: Hardware Organization and Design, John Wiley & Sons, Inc., New York, 1973.

(4) Wegner, P., Programming Languages Information Structures and Machine Organization, McGraw-Hill Book Company, New York, 1968.

(5) Davis, J., and P. Rabinowitz, Numerical Integration, Blaisdell Publishing Company, Waltham, Massachusetts, 1967.

(6) Bekey, G. A. and W. J. Karplus, Hybrid Computation, John Wiley & Sons, Inc., New York, 1968.

(7) Hannauer, G., "A Classification of Hybrid Computers With Applications," Education and Training Memo No. 65-13, Electronic Associates, Inc., West Long Branch, New Jersey, March 1965.

(8) "Basics of Parallel Hybrid Computation," Electronic Associates, Inc., West Long Branch, New Jersey.

(9) Hausner, A., <u>Analog and Analog/Hybrid Computer Programming</u>, Prentice Hall, Englewood Cliffs, New Jersey, 1971.

(10) Gupta, S. and L. Hasdorff, <u>Fundamentals of Automatic Control</u>, John Wiley & Sons, Inc., New York, 1970.

(11) Vichnevetsky, R., "A Short History and Introduction to Hybrid Computation," ACES Meeting, Loyola University, Los Angeles, California, November 1967.

9

Combinational Digital Logic in System Simulation

9.1 INTRODUCTION

In the first seven chapters of this book, the computing elements are analog in nature. The output and input voltages are continuous functions of time, and the circuits are designed to operate over the full range of values from the minus reference voltage to the positive reference voltage.

In Chapter 8, hybrid circuits were introduced. The hybrid elements include both analog and digital circuits. It was noted that digital circuits are designed to operate at only two levels or values. The voltages of digital circuits take on values between the two levels, but the transition between levels is as fast as possible. Since digital signals are intended to be in one or the other state, only the two levels are specified. Thus, digital systems employ two level or binary variables. Usually, the higher voltage level is called the *one* (1) state and the lower voltage level is called the *zero* (0) state. This is by

definition a *positive* state assignment. The reverse assignment
is defined as *negative*. For example, if the 1 level is set for
minus two volts and the 0 level is minus six volts, the assignment
is *positive*. If the 1 level equals minus two volts and the 0
level equals plus four volts, the state assignment is *negative*.

The voltages for the high and low (1 and 0) levels are of
little importance to the user. At present, plus five volts and
zero volts are the most popular voltage levels for the 1 and 0
states. Several other terms that have been used to describe the
two states are: true and false, set and reset, on and off, and
high and low.

One obvious use of digital circuitry is the representation
of the status of discrete processes. For example, a single bit
can represent the state of a valve, switch, light, or other
similar physical device. If the device is *on* or *in use*, the
digital signal could be defined to be in the 1 state. If the
device is *off* or *not in use*, the digital signal is in the 0
state. Thus, digital circuitry can represent the status of a
discrete physical system in a very compact form.

Another important application of digital circuits is the
representation of logical variables. By equating the two discrete levels of digital circuits to the *yes-no*, or *true-false*
conditions of symbolic logic, a system capable of performing logical operations can be built. The following section is devoted
to a discussion of this application of digital circuits.

9.2 BASIC COMBINATIONAL LOGIC ELEMENTS

The term *combinational* is included in the title since the
output of logic elements of this type is a function of the present
combination of logic signals at the input. In other words, the
previous states do not influence the output. There is a class of
logic elements in which previous states can influence the output
at a given instant. Circuits of this type contain memory and their
output is a function of the present combination of input signals
and the preceding sequence of events. These devices are called
sequential logic circuits and are discussed in Chapter 10.

An investigation of combinational logic indicates that there
are eight distinct logical connectives that govern the combination of logical variables.[1] Fortunately, it is not necessary to

build a digital circuit for all eight connectives. Several sub-
sets of the eight possible connectives can be interconnected to
produce the other functions. The easiest logic circuits to use
are the AND, OR and INVERTER functions. Since this group is
functionally complete, all possible logical connectives can be
constructed from the OR and INVERTER or from the AND and INVERTER.

   To begin the discussion of combinational logic, consider
first the INVERTER. It performs the logical operation of nega-
tion or complementation and is often referred to as a NOT circuit.
If a logic signal called, a, is at the input, the complement of a,
written $\bar{a}$ or a', is at the output. The complement of logic 1 is
logic 0, and the complement of logic 0 is logic 1. The operation
of the INVERTER is shown in the truth table of Figure 9-2-1.

input, a	output, $\bar{a}$
0	1
1	0

Figure 9-2-1. Truth table for the INVERTER

Two of the most widely used programming symbols for the INVERTER
are shown in Figure 9-2-2. In discussing the output of a

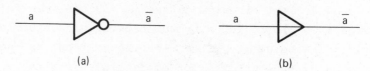

(a)   (b)

Figure 9-2-2. INVERTER symbol

comparator in Section 8.9, the availability of both the *true* output and its complement were discussed.

   The next combinational logic element to be presented is the
AND circuit. The output of the AND circuit is logic 1, if and
only if, all inputs are at the logic 1 level. A special form of
mathematics called Boolean Algebra has been applied to binary
operations. The logical AND function is equivalent to logical
multiplication as defined in Boolean Algebra. Thus, if the inputs
to an AND circuit are a and b, then the output of the circuit
is written a·b. A symbol for an AND circuit is shown in Figure
9-2-3.

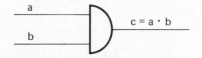

Figure 9-2-3. Symbol for AND circuit

The input/output combinations for an AND circuit are shown in the truth table in Figure 9-2-4. The definition of an AND circuit

AND	Circuit	
Input		Output
a	b	$a \cdot b = c$
0	0	0
0	1	0
1	0	0
1	1	1

Figure 9-2-4. Truth table for the AND circuit

can be extended to any number of inputs. The output is a logic 1 only when all inputs are at logic 1. The operation of an AND circuit can be stated in the following manner: "the output is at logic 1 only when input a <u>and</u> input b <u>and</u> ... <u>and</u> input z are at logic 1."

For the AND circuit of Figure 9-2-3, the output is $c = a \cdot b$. Referring to the truth table of Figure 9-2-4, note that if input to terminal b is held at a logic 1, the output, c, takes on the state of the logic signal at terminal a. This result can also be determined from the expression for the output since $c = a \cdot b = a \cdot 1 = a$. Conversely, if the signal at terminal b is held at logic 0, the output is also at logic 0. Thus, the AND circuit can be considered as a *gate*. If b equals logic 1, the logic signal at a is *gated* through to the output. If b is at logic 0, the signal at a is gated off and the output is held at logic 0. Therefore, the AND circuit is often called an AND *gate*. The term gate has been extended to other logic circuits and is used interchangeably with the terms circuit and element.

To complete the description of the basic logic elements, consider the OR circuit. The output of the OR circuit is a logic 1 when any of the inputs are in the logic 1 state. The equivalent

operation from Boolean Algebra is logical addition, $c = a + b$. [2]
Many symbols have been used to represent an OR circuit. Figure
9-2-5 contains two of the more popular symbols.

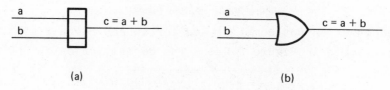

(a)   (b)

Figure 9-2-5. Symbols for the OR gate

A truth table describing the OR gate is presented in Figure
9-2-6. From the truth table, the operation of an OR gate can be
stated in the following manner: "the output of the OR circuit is
a logic 1 when input a, <u>or</u> input b,- <u>or</u> ... <u>or</u> input z is a logic
1." Note that the expression includes the condition for more than
one input at logic 1. A special variation of the OR gate is

OR		Circuit
Input		Output
a	b	c=a+b
0	0	0
0	1	1
1	0	1
1	1	1

Figure 9-2-6. Truth table for the OR gate

called the EXCLUSIVE OR. The action of this gate could be described as follows: "the output is a logic 1 when input a <u>or</u> b are
logic 1, but is a logic 0 when both a and b are logic 1."   This
gate *excludes* the condition in which both inputs are logic 1.

The fundamental operation of the OR gate can also be determined from Boolean Algebra. As stated earlier, the OR gate is
the equivalent to Boolean addition, $c = a + b$. For a and b both
equal to logic zero, the output is $c = 0 + 0 = 0$.   For a = 1 and
b = 0, $c = 1 + 0 = 1$, as predicted by the truth table.   Also,
a = 0 and b = 1 gives $c = 0 + 1 = 1$. The combination, a = 1 and
b = 1, yields $c = 1 + 1 = 1$. The logical addition, $1 + 1 = 1$, is
the only variation from ordinary addition. It should be emphasized

that a logic 1 plus a logic 1 is logic 1. Since 1 plus 0 is also 1, a logic 1 plus any logical variable reduces to logic 1. Thus, the expression x = (y + 1 + $\bar{z}$) would reduce to x = 1 regardless of the values of y and $\bar{z}$.

Before leaving the discussion on the basic logic elements, it should be noted that the, AND, OR, inverter element can be constructed from operational amplifiers. The nonlinear techniques of Chapter 5 are required to maintain the necessary voltage levels. Now that the basic logic gates have been introduced, techniques for interconnecting the gates to realize logical expressions can be presented. The next section will be devoted to combining logic gates.

9.3 LOGICAL EXPRESSIONS

In order to understand how logic gates can be interconnected to develop logical functions, consider the logic diagram or circuit of Figure 9-3-1. The output of AND gate number one is a·b.

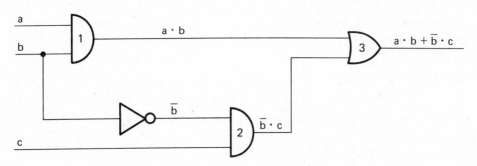

Figure 9-3-1.   Logic diagram

Gate number two is producing $\bar{b}$·c at its output, and the output of the OR circuit of gate number three is a·b + $\bar{b}$·c. The operation of the complete circuit can be expressed in the following manner: "the output will be a logical 1 only when a and b are both 1 or when b is a 0 ($\bar{b}$ is a 1) and c is 1."

A truth table for the logic circuit of Figure 9-3-1 can also be used to determine the operating characteristics of the circuit. The truth table shown in Figure 9-3-2 develops the output for each gate of the circuit. Note that the first three columns list all possible combinations of the three input variables. Since the

INPUTS			I	1	2	3
a	b	c	$\bar{b}$	a·b	$\bar{b}$·c	a·b + $\bar{b}$c
0	0	0	1	0	0	0
0	0	1	1	0	1	1
0	1	0	0	0	0	0
0	1	1	0	0	0	0
1	0	0	1	0	0	0
1	0	1	1	0	1	1
1	1	0	0	1	0	1
1	1	1	0	1	0	1

Figure 9-3-2.   Truth table for logic circuit

truth table includes every possible combination of the input
variables, it is often useful in proving the equality of two
logical expressions.   This method is called proof by *perfect
induction*.

While it is quite helpful to be able to analyze a logic
circuit and write an expression describing its operation, it is
even more beneficial to be able to develop the circuit from a
logical expression or its equivalent word description. To illustrate this procedure, consider the following situation.   A logic
circuit is to have a 1 at its output if the variable a is a 1
and either b is a 1 or c is not a 1 (i.e., c is a 0).   From this
word description, the logical function

$$f(a,b,c) = a \cdot (b + \bar{c}), \qquad (9.3.1)$$

can be written.   For convenience, the (·) used for logical multiplication (AND) is often omitted if the meaning is not lost. For
example, Equation (9.3.1) could also be written in the form

$$f(a,b,c) = a(b + \bar{c}). \qquad (9.3.2)$$

Since logical multiplication is commutative, associative and
distributive, logical expressions can often be manipulated into
more convenient forms.   The logical expression of Equation (9.3.2)
can also be written

$$f(a,b,c) = a \cdot b + a \cdot \bar{c} = ab + a\bar{c}. \qquad (9.3.3)$$

A word description for the logical expression of Equation (9.3.3) is as follows: "the function is a 1 when a and b are 1 or when a is a 1 and c is not 1." The ability to express a given function in several different forms is useful in any logical decision process and often leads to significant simplications.

Since Equations (9.3.2) and (9.3.3) have the same meaning, either form can be used to develop the circuit. The logic circuit of Figure 9-3-3 is based on Equation (9.3.2). The logic

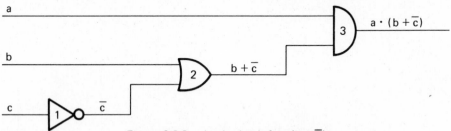

Figure 9-3-3. Logic circuit for $a(b + \bar{c})$

circuit of Figure 9-3-4 was developed from Equation (9.3.3). Notice that the circuit of Figure 9-3-3 requires one less logic gate. Gate economy is important and a number of techniques to

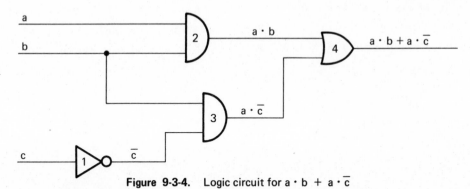

Figure 9-3-4. Logic circuit for $a \cdot b + a \cdot \bar{c}$

minimize the number of gates in an expression have been developed. None of these methods will be presented here and the interested reader is referred to the references at the end of this chapter.

The expression represented by Equation (9.3.2) and (9.3.3) is an excellent function to illustrate the use of perfect induction to prove logical equalities. The resulting truth table is shown in Figure 9-3-5. Column 6 represents every possible value of the function as expressed by Equation (9.3.3). Column 8

contains all combinations of the function expressed in the form
of Equation (9.3.2). Since columns 6 and 8 are identical for all
input combinations, the expressions are equivalent. Although the
example used to illustrate proof by perfect induction is quite
simple, the basic techniques are applicable to more complicated
functions.

1	2	3	4	5	6	7	8
a	b	c	a·b	a·c	a·b + a·c	b + $\bar{c}$	a·(b + $\bar{c}$)
0	0	0	0	0	0	1	0
0	0	1	0	0	0	0	0
0	1	0	0	0	0	1	0
0	1	1	0	0	0	1	0
1	0	0	0	1	1	1	1
1	0	1	0	0	0	0	0
1	1	0	1	1	1	1	1
1	1	1	1	0	1	1	1

Figure 9-3-5. Truth table—proof by perfect induction

As stated earlier, the minimization or reduction techniques
will not be discussed in this book. However, several theorems
from Boolean Algebra are listed since they are quite useful.

Theorem	Dual	
$0 \cdot X = 0$	$1 + X = 1$	(9.3.4)
$1 \cdot X = X$	$0 + X = X$	(9.3.5)
$XX = X$	$X + X = X$	(9.3.6)
$X\bar{X} = 0$	$X + \bar{X} = 1$	(9.3.7)
$XY = YX$	$X + Y = Y + X$	(9.3.8)
$XYZ = (XY)Z = X(YZ)$	$X + Y + Z = (X + Y) + Z$ $= X + (Y + Z)$	(9.3.9)
$\overline{XY...Z} = \bar{X} + \bar{Y} + ... + \bar{Z}$	$X + Y + ... + Z = \overline{\bar{X}\bar{Y}...\bar{Z}}$	(9.3.10)
$XY + XZ = X(Y + Z)$	$(X + Y)(X + Z) = X + YZ$	(9.3.11)
$XY + X\bar{Y} = X$	$(X + Y)(X + \bar{Y}) = X$	(9.3.12)
$X + XY = X$	$X(X + Y) = X$	(9.3.13)
$X + \bar{X}Y = X + Y$	$X(\bar{X} + Y) = X$	(9.3.14)

The theorems are expressed in pairs. The paired expressions are the *dual* of each other. The *dual* relationship is based on complementing the logical operations. For example, logical addition is changed to logical multiplication and logical multiplication replaces logical addition. While the dual relationship is an aid to remembering the theorems, its principal application is in the manipulation of logical expressions. If two Boolean functions are equal, then their dual expressions are also equal.

9.4 DEMORGAN'S THEOREM

The relation expressed in Equation (9.3.10) is known as DeMorgan's Theorem and is quite useful in working with digital logic. Since it is an important relationship, its application will be illustrated in this section. The theorem can be stated as follows: "the complement of a logical expression can be formed from the original expression by complementing each variable and each operation." Thus, symbolically, $a \rightarrow \bar{a}$, $\bar{a} \rightarrow a$, $+ \rightarrow \cdot$, and $\cdot \rightarrow +$.

In order to illustrate the application of DeMorgan's Theorem, consider the expression

$$f(a,b,c) = a(b + \bar{c}). \qquad (9.4.1)$$

The logical complement is

$$\overline{f(a,b,c)} = \overline{a(b + \bar{c})}. \qquad (9.4.2)$$

By DeMorgan's Theorem, Equation (9.4.2) can be written in the form

$$\overline{f(a,b,c)} = \bar{a} + \overline{(b + \bar{c})}. \qquad (9.4.3)$$

To determine a more straightforward expression, work inside of the parenthesis to get

$$\overline{(b + \bar{c})} = (\bar{b} \cdot c). \qquad (9.4.4)$$

Substituting Equation (9.4.4) into Equation (9.4.3) yields

$$\overline{f(a,b,c)} = \bar{a} + (\bar{b} \cdot c) = \bar{a} + \bar{b}c. \qquad (9.4.5)$$

This result can be verified by a truth table as shown in Figure 9-4-1. Notice that column 7 of Figure 9-4-1 is the complement of column 8 of Figure 9-3-4. This complement relationship verifies the inversion or complementation process.

1	2	3	4	5	6	7
a	b	c	$\bar{a}$	$\bar{b}$	$\bar{b}\cdot c$	$\bar{a} + \bar{b}\cdot c$
0	0	0	1	1	0	1
0	0	1	1	1	1	1
0	1	0	1	0	0	1
0	1	1	1	0	0	1
1	0	0	0	1	0	0
1	0	1	0	1	1	1
1	1	0	0	0	0	0
1	1	1	0	0	0	0

Figure 9-4-1.   Truth table for $\overline{f(a, b, c)} = \bar{a} + \overline{b}c$

A second example is included to further illustrate the use of DeMorgan's Theorem. Given the function

$$f(x,y,z) = x(\bar{y} + z) + y\bar{z}, \qquad\qquad (9.4.6)$$

the complement is

$$\overline{f(x,y,z)} = \overline{x(\bar{y} + z) + y\bar{z}}. \qquad\qquad (9.4.7)$$

Equation (9.4.7) can be written in the form

$$\overline{f(x,y,z)} = [\overline{x(\bar{y} + z)}][\overline{y\bar{z}}].$$

Applying DeMorgan's Theorem to the terms inside of the brackets yields

$$\overline{f(x,y,z)} = [\bar{x} + \overline{(\bar{y} + z)}][\bar{y} + z], \qquad\qquad (9.4.8)$$

and finally

$$\overline{f(x,y,z)} = [\bar{x} + y\bar{z}][\bar{y} + z]. \qquad\qquad (9.4.9)$$

In order to avoid mistakes, it is a good practice to add extra parenthesis before applying DeMorgan's Theorem. This simplifies the process and the extra parenthesis can be removed after the complementing operation is completed.

9.5   NAND AND NOR GATES

In the fabrication of electronic circuits to build logic gates, it is often more convenient to construct a gate with its output complemented. Thus, the complemented or negative AND gate is

called a NAND gate. Functionally, the NAND gate is an AND gate
followed by an INVERTER. Figure 9-5-1 illustrates two suitable
symbols for the NAND gate. The symbol in Figure 9-5-1(b) will be
used in this book. Notice that the logic signal ahead of the

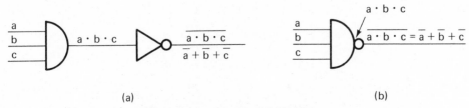

(a)   (b)

Figure 9-5-1. Symbols for NAND gates

INVERTER is $a \cdot b \cdot c$, and the complementation (DeMorgan's Theorem)
gives $\bar{a} + \bar{b} + \bar{c}$ at the output of the NAND gate. The small circle
in Figure 9-5-1(b) is used to indicate inversion. This simplifies
the symbol and reduces the complexity of logic diagrams. The
truth table for the NAND gates is shown in Figure 9-5-2.

a	b	c	$\bar{a} + \bar{b} + \bar{c}$
0	0	0	1
0	0	1	1
0	1	0	1
0	1	1	1
1	0	0	1
1	0	1	1
1	1	0	1
1	1	1	0

Figure 9-5-2. Truth table for NAND gate

The negative OR gate is called a NOR gate and is an OR gate
followed by an INVERTER or a NOT gate. Figure 9-5-3 presents two
widely used symbols for NOR gates. The symbol in Figure 9-5-3(b)

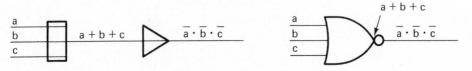

Figure 9-5-3. NOR gate symbols

will be used in this book. A truth table for the NOR gate is illustrated in Figure 9-5-4.

a	b	c	$\bar{a} \cdot \bar{b} \cdot \bar{c}$
0	0	0	1
0	0	1	0
0	1	0	0
0	1	1	0
1	0	0	0
1	0	1	0
1	1	0	0
1	1	1	0

Figure 9-5-4. Truth table for NOR gate

The operation of NOR and NAND gates is not as straightforward as that of AND or OR gates. However, a great deal of the commercially available logic is of the NOR/NAND type and it is important to be able to properly utilize them.

The operation of NOR and NAND gates is not as difficult to follow as it might appear. A knowledge of DeMorgan's Theorem and the basic OR and AND gates is adequate for most circuits. For example, consider the three gate circuit shown in Figure 9-5-5.

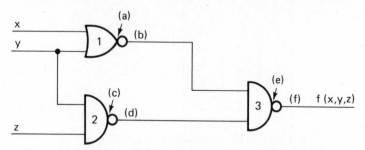

Figure 9-5-5. A logic circuit using NOR/NAND logic

At point (a), x and y have passed through an OR gate (gate one) and the signal at (a) is x + y. In going from point (a) to point (b), the signal is inverted or complemented to complete the NOR operation. Using DeMorgan's Theorem, the signal at point (b) is $\overline{x + y} = \bar{x} \cdot \bar{y}$. At point (c) of gate two, y and z have been combined by the AND to form y·z. From (c) to (d), inversion occurs and the signal at (d) is $\overline{y \cdot z} = \bar{y} + \bar{z}$. This completes the NAND operation of gate two.

The outputs from gates one and two are combined by the AND portion of gate three to give $\bar{x}\ \bar{y}(\bar{y} + \bar{z})$ at point (e). This expression is complemented to produce $\overline{\bar{x}\ \bar{y}(\bar{y} + \bar{z})} = z + y + yz$ at point (f). The output of the circuit can be expressed as $f(x,y,z) = x + y + yz$. By the theorem of Equation (9.3.13), the expression reduces to $f(x,y,z) = x + y$. This indicates that the status of the logic variable z has no bearing on the output of the circuit. Also, a single AND gate combining x and y will have the exact same output as the three gate circuit in Figure 9-5-5. Thus, the use of Boolean Theorems or other methods of logic minimization can often lead to significant reductions in the number of gates required to realize a particular logic expression.

9.6 AND AND OR FUNCTIONS FROM NAND AND NOR GATES

As stated in the previous section, most of the available logic circuitry is NAND and NOR. Since AND and OR functions are frequently required, it is important to be able to construct the AND and OR functions from NAND and NOR logic。

First, consider the problem of constructing the AND function from NAND gates. Two NAND gates can be connected to provide the AND function as shown in Figure 9-6-1。 To understand the circuit,

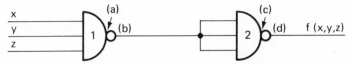

Figure 9-6-1. AND from NAND

note that the signal at (a) is $x \cdot y \cdot z$. Applying DeMorgan's Theorem to determine the signal at (b) gives, $\overline{x \cdot y \cdot z} = \bar{x} + \bar{y} + \bar{z}$. The second NAND gate acts as an inverter. The signal at (c) is $(\bar{x} + \bar{y} + \bar{z})(\bar{x} + \bar{y} + \bar{z})(\bar{x} + \bar{y} + \bar{z})$. By the theorem expressed in Equation (9.3.6), the signal at (c) reduces to $(\bar{x} + \bar{y} + \bar{z})$. After passing through the inversion portion of NAND gate two, the output at (d) is $(\overline{\bar{x} + \bar{y} + \bar{z}}) = x \cdot y \cdot z$, which is the desired AND function.

In much of the available NAND logic, an unconnected input to a gate is *high* or a binary 1. Since $x \cdot 1 \cdot 1$ reduces to x, it is not necessary to connect all of the inputs together to construct an inverter. However, this simplification should be verified before leaving inputs unconnected.

An OR gate can be constructed from NAND logic as shown in Figure 9-6-2. The logic signals are shown directly on the circuit and the operating details are left to the reader.

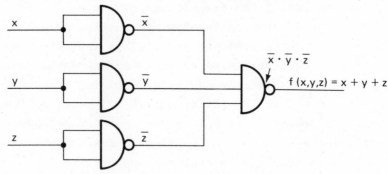

Figure 9-6-2.   OR gate from NAND gates

Figure 9-6-3 illustrates the construction of an AND gate from NOR logic. The signals are shown on the diagram and the operating details of the circuit are left to the reader. Note that the extra inputs on a NOR gate being used as an inverter must either be connected to the input signal or connected to logic 0.

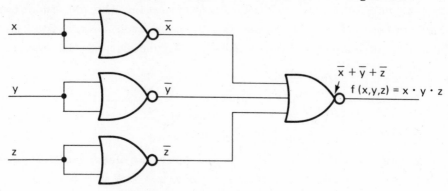

Figure 9-6-3.   AND function from NOR gates

To construct an OR gate from NOR gates, all that is necessary is the inversion of the output. Thus, the circuit of Figure 9-6-4 provides the OR function. As with the previous examples, the details of operation are left to the reader.

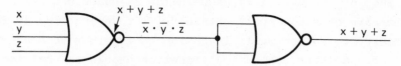

Figure 9-6-4.   OR function from NOR gates

It was stated earlier that all logic connectives could be constructed from AND, OR and NOT gates. Since all three of these functions can be constructed from either NAND or NOR logic, both NAND and NOR gates are functionally complete. This means that all possible logical connectives can be constructed from either NAND gates or NOR gates. Thus, in addition to being easier to build, the NAND and NOR gates are functionally complete and no other gates are required. However, having only one type of gate available is often inefficient.

It should be noted that the patchable digital logic available on parallel hybrid computers usually consists of AND gates with inverters to form NAND gates. Thus, all logical connectives can be constructed from this gate. A symbol for the gate is shown in Figure 9-6-5. Since the true output, d, and its complement,

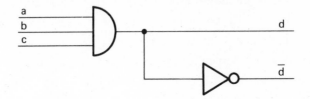

Figure 9-6-5. A universal AND/NAND gate

$\bar{d}$, are provided, the gate can be used as a NAND and/or an AND gate. It is important to realize that the inverter cannot be used separately by connecting an input to d and getting the complement at $\bar{d}$.

9.7 EXAMPLE PROBLEMS

The most obvious application of digital logic is the implementation of logical decisions. Another important application of digital logic is the simulation of systems involving discrete events. The on-off or open-closed status of motors, valves, etc., can be represented by a logical variable. However, the digital memory devices that will be discussed in Chapter 10 are more useful for this type of simulation. The emphasis of this chapter will be on interconnecting digital circuits to simulate logical operations.

The logical variables for simulation can come from a number of sources. The operator may input logic states into a circuit

by means of special digital switches. The state of continuous
signals can be reflected in a logic circuit by comparators. Also,
the IC/Hold/Operate modes generated by the rep-op timer are
digital signals and can be utilized in logic circuits. The digital signals can also control the mode of track-store units and
determine the Operate/IC mode on both the analog and the digital
portions of the computer. In addition, logic signals can be used
to drive the latch on comparators and operate analog relays and
switches. Thus, in addition to simulating discrete events, digital logic can be used to control the mode, cycling and configuration of an analog simulation.

Since it is often desirable to produce a specified binary
output as a function of input combinations, this section will
present a problem to illustrate a procedure for developing a
digital network to produce the desired logic states. The first
step of the process is to determine the desired input conditions
which produce a logic 1 at the output. For example, consider a
logical network with three input variables, a, b and c.   Assume
that an output state of logic 1 is desired for the following
input combinations: when a and b are 0 and c is 1, or when a is
0 and b and c are logic 1, or when a and b are 1 and c is 0.
Also, the output must be a 0 for all other input combinations.
The truth table for the above conditions is shown in Figure 9-7-1.

Row	Input	States		Output
Number	a	b	c	
0	0	0	0	0
1	0	0	1	1
2	0	1	0	0
3	0	1	1	1
4	1	0	0	0
5	1	0	1	0
6	1	1	0	1
7	1	1	1	0

Figure 9-7-1.   Truth table for example problem

Thus, the input combination of rows 1,3 and 6 have an output
state of 1. The input combinations of all other rows have an
output of 0.

The second step of the process is based on the statement of conditions for which the output is logic 1. Since this statement is logical in nature, it can be implemented directly. Each expression of input states requiring a logic 1 at the output combines the inputs with an AND function. For example, row 1 requires a 1 at the output when a=0 and b=0 and c=1. For row 3, an output of 1 is required when a=0 and b=1 and c=1. Row 6 requires a=1 and b=1 and c=0. The output should be a 1 when the first set of conditions (row 1) is met or when the second set of conditions (row 3) is present or when the third set of conditions (row 6) is obtained. Thus, the input variables are combined first in AND gates and the output of each AND gate is connected to an OR gate as shown in Figure 9-7-2.

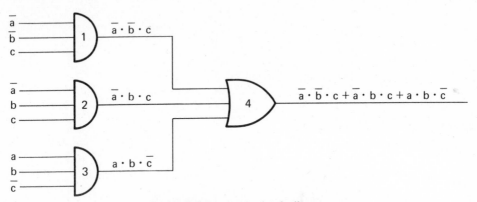

Figure 9-7-2. Logic circuit diagram

The input variables on each AND gate are labeled according to the row-column entry for the particular variable on the truth table. If the column contains a 1 in row 1, then the gate representing that row has the variable, a, connected to an input. If the corresponding entry of the truth table is a 0, then the complement of the variable, $\bar{a}$, is connected. For this particular problem, the inputs to AND gate number one (corresponding to row 1) are the variables $\bar{a}$, $\bar{b}$ and c as shown in Figure 9-7-2. Gate number two (representing row 3) has $\bar{a}$, b and c connected as inputs. Gate number three (row 6) has a, b and $\bar{c}$ as inputs.

In order to understand the operation of this circuit, note that the output of each AND gate will be a 1 for only one combination of inputs. The output of the AND gates will be a 0

for all other input combinations. By selecting either the true
variables (a, b and c) or the complements ($\bar{a}$, $\bar{b}$ and $\bar{c}$) as inputs
to the AND gates, an output of 1 for each specified combination
of inputs is assured. Thus, a logic circuit to produce the
desired output can be constructed in this manner. The desired
operation can be confirmed by constructing a truth table for the
circuit of Figure 9-7-2.

As a second illustration of the realization process, consider the truth table shown in Figure 9-3-2. Since the output
must be a 1 for rows 1, 5, 6 and 7, four AND gates and one OR
gate will be required. The resulting circuit is shown in
Figure 9-7-3.

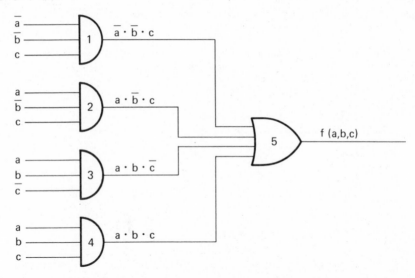

Figure 9-7-3. Gates connected for truth table of figure 9-3-2

Since the problem expressed by the truth table in Figure
9-3-2 has been implemented in Figure 9-3-3 and 9-3-4, it is interesting to compare these circuits with that of Figure 9-7-3.
The circuit of Figure 9-3-3 requires only two gates and an
inverter, and Figure 9-3-4, requires three gates and an inverter.
Note that Figure 9-7-3 requires five gates and three inverters.
Since the outputs are identical, the most economical way to
produce the required operation is shown in Figure 9-3-3. It is
obvious that the method for realizing functions presented in
this section is not minimal and the application of the Karnaugh

Map or other minimization techniques can often produce considerable savings.

There is an analogous process for designing digital circuits. The outputs of several OR gates are combined with a single AND gate to realize a function. An OR gate is used for each row containing a 0 in the output column. Also, the variable assignment is reversed, an uncomplemented variable is connected to the input of the OR gate for variables in the row which are logic 0. A complemented variable is connected to the input of the OR gate if a 1 appears in the particular row. This method will not be presented here.[2]

9.8   SOME SPECIAL CONSIDERATIONS

In previous sections of this chapter, ideal conditions were assumed. For example, it was assumed that the transition from one logic state to another occurred instantaneously. In fact, the switching time can run as high as 100 nanoseconds. As a result, logic circuits must be developed with care to avoid *race* problems that occur when the output of a circuit is dependent upon the transition of two or more variables. The switching delay is often called propagation delay and must be considered carefully. There are instances in which the propagation delay is advantageous. In other words, the logic circuit is used to produce a short time delay to avoid a race problem at some other point in a circuit. There is no standard delay time, and the manual describing the available equipment should be consulted. If a logic gate is used to produce a time delay, the symbol shown in Figure 9-8-1 is suggested. Note that the length of delay and gate number are written directly inside of the symbol.

Figure 9-8-1.   Programming symbol for digital delay

Another practical consideration is the ability of a logic circuit to drive other logic circuits. It was implied that a logic gate would drive as many inputs on other logic gates as desired. Unfortunately, the output of a logic element can only

drive a limited number of other gates. Most manufacturers
suggest that no more than eight or ten inputs be driven from a
single output. This is seldom a limiting factor in working
with patchable digital logic and should not constrain most programmers. However, the instruction manual should be checked
carefully.

Another problem encountered in learning to use logic is
the tendency to connect the outputs of gates together. In other
words, if two or more gates drive the same device, it seems
quite natural to connect the output of each gate to a single
input on that device. Most digital logic will not tolerate this
and damage to the gate can result. There are some gates that
can be *wire ORed* (i.e., outputs connected together in an *or*
function). Usually, the 0 state is dominate and the combined
output is 0 if one or more of the individual gates have an
output of 0. The outputs of all gates are pulled to the 0 state
even though their input conditions indicate the output should be
1. Since the *wire ORed* capability is not available on all gates
an OR gate must be used if the outputs of several gates are to
drive the same input. As before, the instruction manual for the
equipment should be checked for such details.

The expected voltage levels for 1 and 0 levels often leads
to problems in analog/hybrid programming. Since digital logic
is designed to tolerate considerable variations in the voltage
levels, a logic 1 may range from 3.5 to 6 volts. Also, a logic
0 may be as high as 1.5 volts. The acceptable levels of operation are established by the manufacturer. Thus, in combining
analog and digital signals, these variations should be considered.

The desire to interconnect the digital and analog portions
of the computer have led to the development of *trunk* lines. Most
computers provide trunk lines that interconnect the analog and
digital patching areas. This enables the separate handling of
patch panels and minimizes noise problems associated with mixing
the two types of signals.

Since most applications of patchable, digital logic in
simulation will require manual intervention, some means for
switch or push button input should be included. Usually, a

special digital switch or digital push button designed to eliminate switch bounce is provided. This is essential since any
attempt to operate digital logic directly from a switch or push
button may result in several changes of state with each operation
of the push button. In other words, in attempting to produce
one pulse, several pulses will be produced as a result of switch
bounce or noise. In some applications, switch bounce is not a
problem. However, many circuits are completely useless as a
result of switch bounce.

9.9 AN EXAMPLE PROBLEM

There are many examples that could be used to illustrate the
use of digital logic in simulation. The problem selected for
discussion in this section is an extension of a problem that has
been used several times. Assume that the physical system represented by a linear, second-order equation would be damaged if the
velocity ($\dot{x}$) exceeded a certain value when the position (x) is
more than a specified distance away from a desired value. The
basic analog program was used in Section 8.10 to illustrate the
use of comparators and track-store units. In this instance, the
setting on pot 3 will be decreased in order to decrease system
damping and produce more overshoot.

For this discussion, assume that the velocity limit is 0.2
meters per second and the displacement limit is 1.65 meters.
Since the two conditions must occur simultaneously, that is,
condition 1 <u>and</u> condition 2 are met, the existence of the undesirable condition can be detected with an AND gate. The only
remaining requirement is a comparator circuit to detect the
occurrence of each limiting condition. Since the velocity can
be in excess of 0.2 meters per second in either direction, an
absolute value circuit could be used to generate $|\dot{x}|$ from $\pm\dot{x}$.
An alternate approach would use two comparators, one to detect
velocity ($\dot{x}$) in excess of $+\dot{x}_L$ and another comparator to detect
velocity in excess of $-\dot{x}_L$.

Figure 9-9-1 contains the basic analog circuit with the
necessary hybrid and digital elements to detect the required
conditions. Comparator No. 3 is connected and biased so that

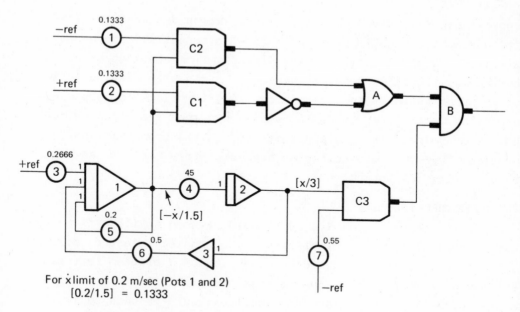

For ẋ limit of 0.2 m/sec (Pots 1 and 2)
[0.2/1.5] = 0.1333

For x limit of 1.65 m (Pot 7)
[1.65/3.0] = 0.55

Figure 9-9-1. Second order system with position and velocity detecting comparators

the output is 0 for x less than 1.65 (x < 1.65). If x is greater than 1.65 (x > 1.65), comparator No. 3 is in the 1 state. The integrator producing -ẋ is connected to comparators No. 1 and No. 2. Comparator No. 1 is in the 0 state when -ẋ > 0.2 meters/ sec. Comparator No. 2 is biased so that it is in the 1 state when ẋ > 0.2 meters/sec. It should be noted that the magnitude scaling is particularly important in this example. If a direct scale (1 computer volt = 1 meter per second) is used, the comparator will be working at a very low level and maximum accuracy cannot be achieved.

Figure 9-9-2 presents the waveforms for the computing elements of Figure 9-9-1. Comparator No. 3 goes to the binary 1 state on the first and second overshoots, but AND gate (B) does not go to the 1 state unless comparator No. 1 is a 0 or comparator No. 2 goes to the 1 state indicating a velocity in excess of 0.2 meters per second. Note that any point in the response of the circuit having a velocity greater than 0.2 meters per second, and simultaneously, a displacement greater than 1.65 meters is indicated by a binary 1 at the output of the AND gate.

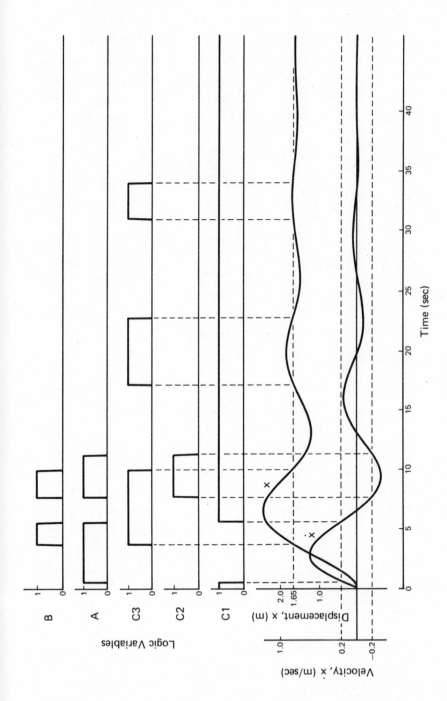

Response Curves For Example Problem

Figure 9-9-2. Response curves for example problem

This illustration can be extended by adding an additional condition. Suppose the system would be damaged if the velocity exceeds 0.2 meters per second when displacement is greater than 1.65 meters or if the displacement exceeds 1.85 meters. The first condition is the same as stated earlier. The second level of displacement can be detected by a comparator and combined with the first condition with an OR gate, as shown in Figure 9-9-3.

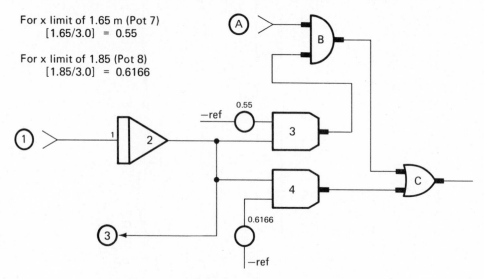

For x limit of 1.65 m (Pot 7)
    [1.65/3.0] = 0.55

For x limit of 1.85 (Pot 8)
    [1.85/3.0] = 0.6166

Figure 9-9-3.   Combining several output specifications with
AND and OR gates

The resulting curve for the circuit with the extra OR gate could be added to Figure 9-9-2.

This example has not shown the full power of combining digital logic with analog computing elements. Hopefully, it has illustrated some basic techniques that can be extended to other systems.

9.10 PROBLEMS

Problems covering the material of this chapter are identified by the appropriate section.

9.2.1   Use diode limiting circuits to construct a logic
        INVERTER from an operational amplifier.

9.2.2   Use diode limiting circuits to construct a two input
        AND gate from an operational amplifier.

9.2.3   Use diode limiting circuits to construct a two input
OR gate from an operational amplifier.

9.2.4   Construct the truth table for an exclusive OR gate.

9.2.5   Construct the truth table for a four input AND gate.

9.2.6   Write a Boolean expression for a three input AND
gate with a, $\bar{b}$ and c at the inputs.

9.2.7   Write a Boolean expression for the output of a four
input OR gate with x, $\bar{y}$, z and w as inputs.

9.2.8   Complement (0→1 and 1→0) all terms of the truth
table of Figure 9-2-4. What type of logic element
is produced?

9.3.1   Write a Boolean expression for the output of the
logic circuit shown below,

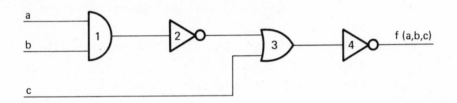

Figure 9-10-1.

9.3.2   Write a Boolean expression for the output of the
logic circuit shown below,

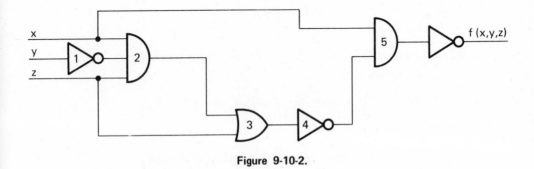

Figure 9-10-2.

9.3.3   Write a Boolean expression for the logic circuit
shown below,

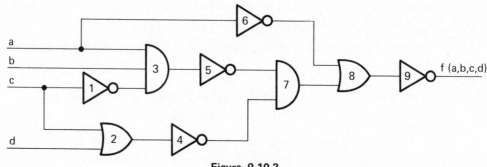

Figure 9-10-3.

9.3.4   Develop a truth table for the circuit of Problem
        9.3.1.

9.3.5   Develop a truth table for the circuit of Problem
        9.3.2.

9.3.6   Develop a truth table for the circuit of Problem
        9.3.3.

9.3.7   Design a logic circuit to realize the function
        $f(x,y,z) = x\bar{y} + x\bar{z} + \bar{x}yz$ (9.10.1)

9.3.8   Design a logic circuit to realize the function
        $f(a,b,c) = a(b + \bar{c})$.   (9.10.2)

9.3.9   Design a logic circuit to realize the function
        $f(a,b,c,d) = ac + \bar{a}\,(b + \bar{c}d)$ (9.10.3)

9.3.10 Construct a truth table for the expression of
        Problem 9.3.7.

9.3.11 Construct a truth table for the expression of
        Problem 9.3.8.

9.3.12 Construct a truth table for the expression of
        Problem 9.3.9.

9.3.13 Prove the theorem of Equation (9.3.6).

9.3.14 Prove the theorem of Equation (9.3.7).

9.3.15 Prove the theorem of Equation (9.3.12).

9.3.16 Prove the theorem of Equation (9.3.13).

9.3.17 Prove the theorem of Equation (9.3.14).

9.3.18 Use the Boolean theorems to simplify the following
        logic expressions:

        a. Problem 9.3.1

        b. Problem 9.3.2

        c. Problem 9.3.3

        d. Problem 9.3.7

        e. Problem 9.3.8

        f. Problem 9.3.9

9.4.1   Determine the complement of the following logical
        expressions:

        a. Problem 9.3.1

        b. Problem 9.3.2

        c. Problem 9.3.3

        d. Problem 9.3.7

        e. Problem 9.3.8

        f. Problem 9.3.9

9.4.2   Verify the results of Problem 9.4.1 by means of
        truth table.

9.4.3   Determine the complement of the following expres-
        sions:

        a. $f(x,y,z) = x\bar{y} + \bar{x}(y + z)$. $(9.10.4)$

        b. $f(a,b,c,d) = a\bar{b}c(a\bar{d} + \bar{a}dc)$. $(9.10.5)$

        c. $f(x,y,z) = \bar{x} + yz(x + y)$. $(9.10.6)$

9.4.4   Use the Boolean theorems to reduce the expressions
        of Equations $(9.10.4)$, $(9.10.5)$ and $(9.10.6)$.

9.5.1   Use the small circle symbol for the inverter to
        replace the inverter gates of

        a. Figure (9-10-1)

        b. Figure (9-10-2)

        c. Figure (9-10-3)

9.5.2   Identify the NOR and NAND gates of Problem 9.5.1.

9.6.1   Construct the equivalent circuit of Problem 9.3.1
        using only NAND gates.

9.6.2   Construct the equivalent circuit of Problem 9.3.2
        using only NAND gates.

9.6.3   Construct the equivalent circuit of Problem 9.3.3 using only NAND gates.

9.6.4   Repeat Problem 9.6.1 with NOR gates.

9.6.5   Repeat Problem 9.6.2 with NOR gates.

9.6.6   Repeat Problem 9.6.3 with NOR gates.

9.6.7   Repeat Problem 9.6.1 with NAND and NOR gates.

9.6.8   Repeat Problem 9.6.2 with NAND and NOR gates.

9.6.9   Repeat Problem 9.6.3 with NAND and NOR gates.

9.6.10 Repeat Problem 9.6.1 with the gate of Figure 9-6-5.

9.6.11 Repeat Problem 9.6.2 with the gate of Figure 9-6-5.

9.6.12 Repeat Problem 9.6.3 with the gate of Figure 9-6-5.

9.7.1   Design a logic circuit that produces a logic 1 at the output for the following combination of inputs: $a=0$, $b=1$ and $c=0$; $a=1$, $b=1$ and $c=0$; $a=1$, $b=0$ and $c=1$.

9.7.2   Use the Boolean theorems to simplify the expression for Problem 9.7.1. Implement the simplified expression with AND and OR gates and discuss the economy of the reduction.

9.7.3   Design a logic circuit that produces a logic 1 at the output for the following combination of inputs: $x=0$, $y=1$, $z=0$ and $w=1$; $x=0$, $y=0$, $z=1$ and $w=1$; $x=0$, $y=1$, $z=1$ and $w=1$; $x=0$, $y=0$, $z=0$ and $w=1$; and $x=1$, $y=1$, $z=1$ and $w=1$.

9.7.4   Use the Boolean theorems to simplify the expression of Problem 9.7.3. Use AND and OR gates to implement the simplified expression. How many gates were saved?

9.7.5   Use the truth table of Problem 9.3.10 to design a logic network of AND and OR gates in the form of Figure 9-7-2.

9.7.6   Use the truth table of Problem 9.3.11 to design a logic network of AND and OR gates in the form of Figure 9-7-2.

9.7.7   Use the truth table of Problem 9.3.12 to design a logic network of AND or OR gates in the form of Figure 9-7-2.

9.9.1 Use logic gates, comparators and track-store units
       to develop a program to track and store the first
       maximum of the derivative, $\dot{x}(t)$ in the step-respnse
       of a linear second-order system ($\delta=.2$ and $\omega_n=2$).

9.9.2 Use logic gates and comparators to develop a cir-
       cuit that will produce a 1 at the output when the
       step response, $x(t)$, of the system of Problem
       9.9.1 exceeds 15% of the steady-state value. Record
       the response.

9.9.3 Develop a program for Rayleigh's equation with $\varepsilon=1$,
       $x(0)=0$ and $\dot{x}(0) = -1.0$ (see Equation 5.5.1 and
       Figure 5-6-3). Add logic gates and comparators to
       determine when $x(t)\geq1$ and $\dot{x}(t)\geq1$. Record the re-
       sponse.

9.9.4 Develop a program for the example problem in Section
       6.9 with k=15. Use logic gates, comparators and
       an integrator to determine the length of time the
       response $x(t)$ exceeds 1.1.

9.11 REFERENCES FOR CHAPTER 9

(1) Krieger, M., Basic Switching Circuit Theory, The
     Macmillan Company, New York, 1967.

(2) Hill, F. J. and G. R. Peterson, Introduction to
     Switching Theory and Logical Design, John Wiley &
     Sons, Inc., New York, 1968.

(3) Marcus, M. P., Switching Circuits for Engineers
     Prentice-Hall, Inc., Englewood Cliffs, New Jersey,
     1967.

10

Sequential Digital Logic in System Simulation

10.1 INTRODUCTION

The digital logic elements discussed in Chapter 9 do not include memory. The output states are dependent only on the combination of input states at a given point in time. Previous logic states have no effect on the output. However, if the devices are capable of memory, then the output states are a function of the input combination <u>and</u> the previous states of the network. Such a system is capable of cycling through a sequence of events, and can be used to set up a desired pattern of operation.

In this chapter, the basic elements of sequential, digital logic are presented. Methods for interconnecting the elements to perform useful functions are illustrated with several examples. The chapter also discusses the use of storage elements in conjunction with comparators, switches and track-store units for interfacing with analog elements.

10.2   THE FLIP-FLOP

The basic memory element is the flip-flop. The flip-flop
is a bi-stable device with states corresponding to the two
logic levels. When placed in one or the other state, the flip-
flop remains in that state until certain prescribed input conditions are met. Thus, by controlling the input states, the
flip-flop can be used to *remember* a particular event.

In order to better understand the flip-flop and relate it
to the combinational, digital logic of Chapter 9, consider the
interconnected NAND gates of Figure 10-2-1. Assume that the

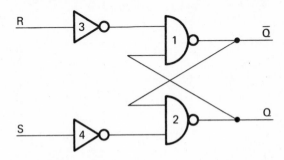

Figure 10-2-1.   Flip-flop constructed from NAND gates

input signals at the terminals labeled R–S are logic 0 and that
the output of gate two, Q, is a logic 1 and $\bar{Q}$ at the output of
gate one is a logic 0. Since Q=1 and the output of   INVERTER
three is 1, NAND gate one will have a 0 at the output, $\bar{Q}$. This
agrees with the assumed level. Since the output of INVERTER
four is a 1, and $\bar{Q}$ is a 0, NAND gate two will have a 1 at the
output. This also satisfies the assumed level for Q.

If the input at R is driven to the 1 state, INVERTER three
goes to the 0 state, causing NAND gate one to go to the 1 state.
The resulting change in the output of gate one causes NAND gate
two, Q, to go to the 0 state. Since Q also feeds the input   to
NAND gate one, the 0 on the other input of NAND gate one can go
back to the 1 state and the output of gate one will remain   at
logic 1. The flip-flop has flipped (changed state) and   will
remain in the new state. If a 1 is applied to the S input, the
input to NAND gate two goes to 0 and causes the flip-flop   to
return to the original state (Q=1, $\bar{Q}$=0). Thus, a 1 applied   to
S causes the circuit to go to the state in which Q=1 and $\bar{Q}$=0.

This will be called the *set* state. In a similar manner, a 1 on
R and a 0 on S will cause the flip-flop to go to the *reset* state
(Q=0 and $\bar{Q}$ = 1). Thus, the *set* (S) and *reset* (R) inputs are
named according to the action created by a logic 1 at the particular input.

There are several practical considerations that should be
discussed at this point. If both the R and S input terminals are
driven to 1 simultaneously, a *race* condition exists and the
result cannot be predicted. Therefore, this condition should
be avoided. The action of the flip-flop circuit of Figure 10-2-1
is summarized in the truth table of Figure 10-2-2. An additional

R	S	Q	$\bar{Q}$
0	0	No Change	No Change
0	1	1	0
1	0	0	1
1	1	Avoid	Avoid

Figure 10-2-2. Truth table for flip-flop circuit

practical consideration is the switching or transition time required for the flip-flop to change states.   As noted in previous
sections, there is a finite time required for a logic element to
change state. Since we have constructed the flip-flop from NAND
gates, there is a finite *settling time* for the flip-flop.

Most logic circuits requiring flip-flops are constructed
from integrated circuits that provide one or more flip-flops in
each package. Thus, the interconnection of two logic gates as
shown in Figure 10-2-1 to form a flip-flop is not the usual
practice. However, it is a useful circuit to remember since it
enables the construction of flip-flops from spare combinational
gates.

The flip-flop circuit introduced here is one of several
which will be discussed in the following sections. However, the
internal operating details will not be presented. The interested
reader is referred to the sources listed at the end of this chapter.

10.3 COUNTERS

One of the most popular uses of flip-flops is the construction of circuits to count pulses or level changes. Also, the discussion of digital counters will offer an opportunity to introduce another type of flip-flop. However, as noted in the previous section, no internal details will be presented.

The simplest type of flip-flop is the *toggle* or *trigger* flip-flop. Many symbols have been used and the symbol in Figure 10-3-1 will be used in this book. The normal or true

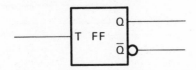

Figure 10-3-1. The *toggle* flip-flop

output is labeled Q and the inverse or false output is labeled $\bar{Q}$. The input terminal labeled T controls the action of the flip-flop. Every time the logic level on T goes from the 1 state to the 0 state, the state of the flip-flop changes (i.e., the flip-flop *toggles* or flips). If Q is a 1, prior to the change at T, it will be a zero after T goes to the 0 state. The action at $\bar{Q}$ is the inverse or complement of the signal at Q.

Toggle flip-flops can be used individually or in groups to *remember* the status of a device or several devices. They can also be connected together to form a simple counter as shown in Figure 10-3-2. To understand the operation of the counter, assume all flip-flops are in the reset (0) state (i.e., Q1 = Q2 = Q3 = 0 and $\bar{Q}$1 = $\bar{Q}$2 = $\bar{Q}$3 = 1). Also, assume that the events to

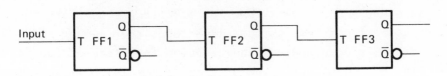

Figure 10-3-2. Flip-flop counter

be counted are represented by a change in the level of the input from 1 to 0. A typical input signal is shown in Figure 10-3-3.

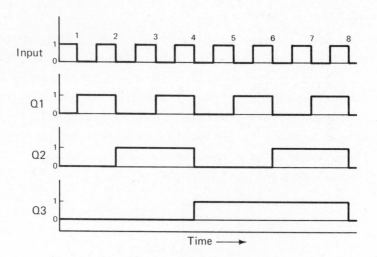

Figure 10-3-3. Counter timing diagram

When the first event occurs, the input goes to the 0 state and causes FF1 to toggle to the 1 state as shown in Figure 10-3-3. Note that although Q1 is connected to the toggle input, T2, of FF2, Q2 remains in the 0 state since T2 is sensitive only to a negative going signal (i.e., the transition from 1 to 0). Thus, after one event has occurred, Q1 = 1, Q2 = 0 and Q3 = 0.

When the second event occurs, T1 goes to the 0 state and causes FF1 to toggle. Since the transition of Q1 is in the negative direction (i.e., 1 to 0), FF2 changes state. After two events, Q1 = 0, Q2 = 1 and Q3 = 0, as shown in Figure 10-3-3. When the third event occurs, Q1 goes to the 1 state and Q2 remains in the 1 state since T2 is insensitive to positive going signals. The output combinations are now Q1 = 1, Q2 = 1 and Q3 = 0. At this point, enough events have occurred to indicate the mode of operation. FF1 will toggle on every event, FF2 will toggle on every second event, and FF3 will toggle on every fourth. Thus, by assigning values to the flip-flops, the number of events that have occurred are indicated by the state of the flip-flops. In this case, the value of flip-flop 1 is 1, flip-flop 2 must be valued at 2, and flip-flop 3 is equivalent to 4. The number of events is determined by summing the values of the flip-flops in the 1 state. It is customary to group the states of the flip-flops with the least significant state on the right.

The states and their equivalent numbers are shown in Figure 10-3-4.

Number	Q3	Q2	Q1
0	0	0	0
1	0	0	1
2	0	1	0
3	0	1	1
4	1	0	0
5	1	0	1
6	1	1	0
7	1	1	1
8	0	0	0
9	0	0	1

Figure 10-3-4. Counter state table

The counter described is a base two or binary counter and each flip-flop represents one binary digit, often referred to as a *bit*. In checking the operation of the counter, note that after the eighth event, all three bits are 0 and the cycle of counter starts over. Thus, the three bit counter will only count to eight before returning to zero. It should be noted that the settling time required when going from one number to the next will be longer whenever more than one flip-flop changes state. For example, in going from 7 to 8, FF1 changes state causing FF2 to change state which causes FF3 to change state. Thus, all three flip-flops change state, one after the other. The *rippling* of the transition through the counter must take place within the time between pulses. The addition of one more flip-flop would double the range of the counter. Also, a counter consisting of n flip-flops can count 2^n events before returning to zero.

Since it is often necessary to set a flip-flop to a desired state, two additional input terminals have been added. The extra terminals, shown in Figure 10-3-5, are designated set (S) and reset (R). This mode of operation was discussed in the previous section. Appropriately, the device is called a set-reset or RS

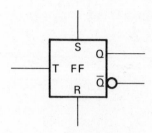

Figure 10-3-5. Set-reset flip-flop

flip-flop. When a binary 1 is placed on the set terminal, the
flip-flop is *set* (i.e., Q = 1 and $\bar{Q}$ = 0). In a similar manner,
a 1 at R *resets* the flip-flop (i.e., Q = 0 and $\bar{Q}$ = 1). Some
implementations of R-S flip-flops require a 0 on the S or R
terminal to produce the set or reset action.

As an example of the set-reset action, suppose it is desired
to transfer the state of the counter of Figure 10-3-3 (FF1, FF2
and FF3) to another group of three flip-flops (FFA, FFB and FFC).
The transfer can be accomplished with combinational logic and a
transfer circuit is shown in Figure 10-3-6. To understand the

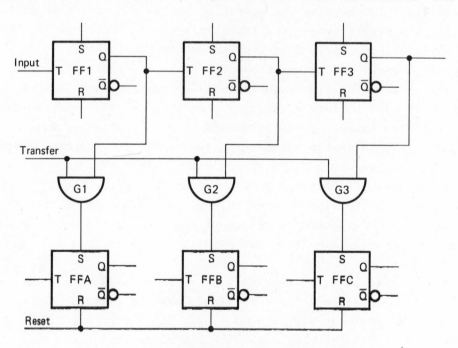

Figure 10-3-6. Transfer circuit

transfer procedure, assume that the combination in the counter is Q1 = 1, Q2 = 0, and Q3 = 1. Also, assume that the transfer line is 0 and the reset line is 0. The transfer should be initiated by reseting FFA, FFB and FFC. This is accomplished by causing the reset line to go to the 1 state long enough to reset the flip-flops (i.e., QA=QB=QC=0). The time required for the reset line to be in the 1 state depends upon the type of circuitry used and is usually specified by the manufacturer.

After the reset line has returned to the 0 state, the transfer line should go to the 1 state. From a previous discussion on the AND gate, the output of G1 and G3 will be 1 and the true outputs of FFA and FFC will be set to the 1 state. Similarly, the output of G2 is 0 and the true output of FFB is not set but remains in the 0 state. Thus, the state of the counter, 101, has been transferred to the other three flip-flops.

The flip-flops used in this example are often referred to as a *register*. Registers are used to hold or store digital signals for display (e.g., indicator lights could be driven by the flip-flops) or for transfer to another device. As an example of this utilization of flip-flops, consider the circuit of Figure 10-3-6. Once the contents of the counter are stored in the register, the counter can continue counting. In this instance, the register is referred to as a *buffer register* since it serves as a buffer between the counter and some other device that utilizes the contents of the counter.

Before leaving this example, the importance of the reset pulse should be emphasized. To illustrate this, suppose FFB were in the 1 state prior to the transfer. Since the output of G2 remains 0 during the transfer, FFB is neither set or reset, and therefore, remains in the 1 state. However, it should be in the 0 state. Thus, the buffer register (i.e., FFA, FFB and FFC) must be reset before the transfer.

In digital systems, it is frequently useful to be able to determine when a specific number of events have occurred. Assume that it is necessary to determine when the counter is at 5 (i.e., FF1=1, FF2=0, and FF3=1). An AND gate, connected as shown in Figure 10-3-7, will be in the 1 state only when all of its inputs

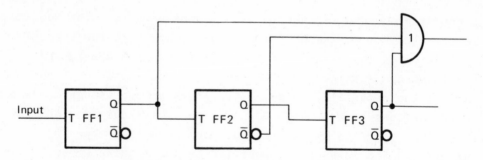

Figure 10-3-7.   Detector for counter state 5

are in the 1 state.   This will occur when Q1=1, $\bar{Q}$2=1 and Q3=1.
Thus, AND gate 1 will be in the 1 state when the true outputs of
the counter are setting at the combination 101 (i.e., a count of
5).   In order to detect a particular combination of counter
states, the true (Q) output of the flip-flop is connected to the
input of the AND gate when a 1 is to be detected.

The $\bar{Q}$ terminal is connected to the AND gate if a 0 is to be
detected.   Thus, when the flip-flops of the counter are in the
state to be detected, the inputs to the AND gate are all binary
1 and the output of the gate goes to the 1 state.   It might
appear that it is not necessary to connect the inverse output
of FF2, since the 1 from FF1 and 1 from FF3 identify the 5 state.
However, these two states also identify state 7 (i.e., FF1=1,
FF2=1 and FF3=1).

The generation of a pulse or level change when a prescribed
number of pulses or counts have occurred is a useful feature.
Most computers with patchable digital logic provide counters that
can be preset by means of special switches and when the prescribed number of pulses have been counted, the counter produces
a pulse or level change.   These counters are usually preset to
the desired number and counted down (i.e., 9,8,...,1,0) from
the preset value.   Since the last event always causes the flip-
flops of the counter to go to the 0 state, the circuits required
to detect the last event are always set in the same manner.

10.4   AN EXAMPLE PROBLEM

In Chapter 9, the use of comparators and track-store units
was illustrated with an example problem that stored the peak

value of the first overshoot in the step response of a second-order system. In order to illustrate the use of flip-flops, assume that it is desired to store the peak value of the second overshoot. A circuit to perform this operation is shown in Figure 10-4-1. The comparator goes high each time the function

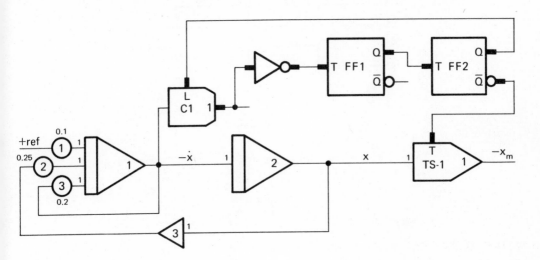

Figure 10-4-1. Storing the second over-shoot of a step response

minus $\dot{x}$ is greater than 0. The inverse output of the comparator is connected to the counter and each time the comparator goes from 0 to 1, the inverter goes from 1 to 0 and causes the counter to advance 1 state. The counter goes from state 0 to state 1 at the instant of the first overshoot and from 1 to 2 at the second overshoot. Thus, at the instant of the second overshoot, FF2 is set (i.e., $Q2=1$ and $\bar{Q}2=0$). Since the track-store unit is connected to $\bar{Q}2$, it is in Track until the occurrence of the second overshoot, when $Q2$ goes to 1 and $\bar{Q}2$ goes to 0. The counter output ($Q2$) is used to latch the comparator to prevent additional input to the counter. If the comparator is not latched, additional overshoots will advance the counter and cause the track-store to return to the track mode and store every other overshoot. The waveforms for the circuit are shown in Figure 10-4-2. There are other ways of detecting and storing the

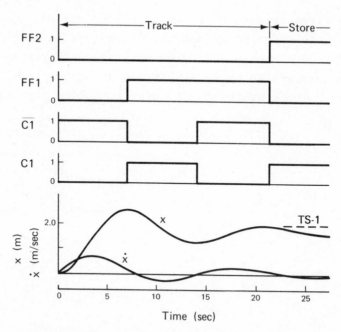

Figure 10-4-2. Waveforms from the circuit of Figure 10-4-1

value of the second overshoot and the method presented here is
included as one possible solution.

10.5 REGISTERS

In Section 10.3, a method for transferring the contents   of
a counter to another set of flip-flops was illustrated. The term
register was used to describe the group of flip-flops   to   which
the contents of the counter were transferred. Also, it was stated
that each flip-flop represents one binary digit (abbreviated *bit*)
and n flip-flops can represent 2^n different combinations or states.

Another type of register frequently encountered in   digital
systems is the shift register. The contents of a shift   register
can be shifted right or left in a prescribed manner. Before
discussing shift registers, it will be necessary to introduce the
J-K flip-flop and discuss clocked logic.

In previous sections, the race problems in digital systems
have been discussed. It was noted that whenever the state of
a device is a function of several logical variables that change
at the same instance, slight variations in the transition or
propagation times can cause the device to momentarily go to the

wrong state. In some instances, the error is of little signifi-
cance and can be tolerated. However, there are situations   in
which a momentary malfunction is quite serious and   can   cause
major system errors.

Many of the hazards cited previously can be avoided   by the
use of clocked logic. In systems utilizing clocked logic,   a
digital circuit is designed to generate a periodic pulse   train
which is used to synchronize the operation of the entire system.
A typical clock signal is shown in Figure 10-5-1.   The period,

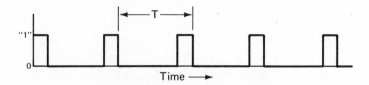

Figure 10-5-1. Typical clock pulse

T, of the clock signal is usually 1.0 microsecond for the patchable, digital logic on analog and hybrid computers.   This requires
a clock rate or frequency of 1.0 megaHertz.   The time that the
pulse stays in the 1 state is usually 10-20% of the   period   or
approximately 100-200 nanoseconds.   Some computers   provide
switches to select clock rates that are a fraction of the basic
clock rate such as 1,000 Hertz, 100 Hertz, 10 Hertz and 1 Hertz.
In addition, a manual mode is frequently included that generates
1 clock pulse each time the *step* push button is depressed.

In discussing the operation of clocked logic, it is necessary to identify certain clock periods. This can be accomplished
by subscripts (e.g., Q_n is the state of Q during the nth clock
period).   Thus, the action of a particular point can be identified
as $Q_1, Q_2, \ldots, Q_{n-1}, Q_n, Q_{n+1}, \ldots, Q_p$.

The toggle and R-S flip-flops previously discussed respond
directly to inputs on the toggle or set-reset terminals. They are
not dependent upon the operation of a clock signal.   However, the
"J-K" flip-flop is designed to operate in synchronism with   a
clock.   The J-K flip-flop derives its name from the labeling   of
the terminals shown in Figure 10-5-2(a).   The transitions of the

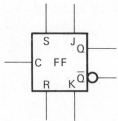

J	K	Q_{n+1}	$\bar{Q}_{n+1}$
0	0	$\bar{Q}_n$	Q_n
0	1	0	1
1	0	1	0
1	1	Q_n	$\bar{Q}_n$

(a) Programming symbol   (b) Truth table

Figure 10-5-2. The J—K flip-flop

output terminals, Q and $\bar{Q}$, occur on the trailing edge of the
clock pulse applied to the clock (C) terminal. When the clock
pulse goes from the 1 state to the 0 state, the transition determined by the logic levels at the J and K terminals takes place.
Changing the input on the J and K terminals does not affect the
output until the trailing edge of the clock pulse. As noted in
Figure 10-5-2(b), a binary 1 on J and K causes the flip-flop to
remain in the state that existed prior to the clock pulse. Thus,
the state of Q after the clock pulse, Q_{n+1}, is identical to the
state prior to the pulse, Q_n. If the input to J is a 0 and K is
held at 1 prior to the clock pulse, the output, Q, goes to 0 and
$\bar{Q}$ goes to 1 on the trailing edge of the clock pulse. In a similar
manner, J=1 and K=0 causes Q_{n+1} to be 1. If J=0 and K=0, $Q_{n+1} = \bar{Q}_n$.
This indicates that the flip-flop toggles on every clock pulse if
J and K are both logic 0. Thus, the operation of the J-K flip-
flop is a function of the J and K inputs. However, no transition
takes place until the trailing edge of the clock pulse.

The input logic levels on J and K must be present a specified time prior to the trailing edge of the clock pulse. Also,
nothing happens until the clock pulse goes from 1 to 0. Thus,
timing of the input signals on J and K is not critical. Whether
J or K reached its proper state first is not significant so long
as they have both settled to the proper values prior to the clock
transition. It should also be noted that the transition at Q
and $\bar{Q}$ cannot affect the J-K setting on another flip-flop until

the next clock pulse. Thus, clocked logic can be used to avoid most hazards in digital systems.

The R-S terminals of the J-K flip-flop in Figure 10-5-2(a) operate in the same manner as the R-S terminals of the R-S flip-flop. The logic levels on these inputs cause immediate transition of the flip-flop. Thus, the J-K flip-flop is more general and is capable of operating in the synchronous (J-K) mode or in the asynchronous (R-S) mode.

The internal circuitry of the J-K flip-flop usually involves two flip-flops – one called the *slave* and the other called the *master*. The master flip-flop is driven from the J and K inputs and determines the action of the slave at the trailing edge of the clock pulse. The outputs (Q and $\bar{Q}$) are taken from the slave. The internal operation is not of particular importance to the user. Therefore, most instruction manuals for computers with patchable, digital logic do not include these details. The interested reader is referred to the sources listed at the end of this chapter.

Now that the fundamentals of the J-K flip-flop have been discussed, it is easy to visualize several types of registers. For example, the transfer operation discussed in Section 10.3 could be achieved by having the Q and $\bar{Q}$ terminals of each flip-flop in the counter connected to the J and K terminals respectively, of the corresponding flip-flop in the buffer register. The buffer register would not follow the transitions of the counter and the state of the counter would not be transferred until a transfer pulse is applied to the clock terminals of the J-K flip-flops. This is shown in Figure 10-5-3. The transfer is initiated by a 1 on the transfer line and takes place when the transfer line goes back to the 0 state. The transfer pulse is timed to occur between the input pulses of the counter. This avoids the problems associated with attempting a transfer while the counter is changing states.

Another type of register, called a shift register, is shown in Figure 10-5-4. In order to understand the operation

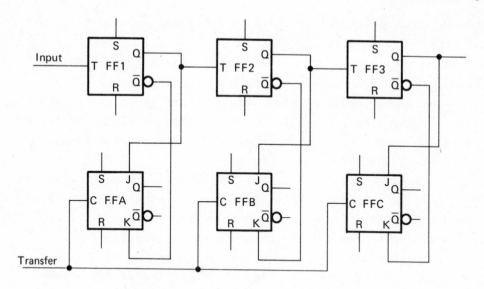

Figure 10-5-3.   Counter transferred to buffer register

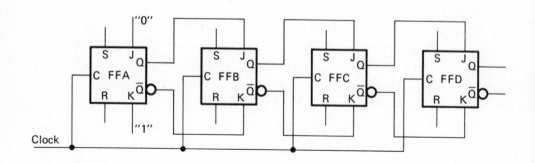

Figure 10-5-4.   Shift register

of the shift register, assume that FFA, FFC and FFD are in the
set (i.e., Q=1, Q̄=0) state and FFB is reset. The bit pattern
on the Q terminals of the register is 1011. Since the Q and
Q̄ terminal of FFA are connected to the J and K terminals,
respectively, of FFB, the state of FFB following a clock pulse
will be identical to the state of FFA prior to the clock pulse.
In a similar manner, the state of FFC will follow FFB and FFD
will follow FFC. Since a 0 is on J and a 1 is on K of FAA, it
will be *steered* to the reset state (i.e., Q=0, Q̄=1) on   each

clock pulse.   Thus, at the end of the first clock pulse,   the
bit pattern at the Q terminals of the register is 0101.   The
original 1 of FFD has been lost.   At the end of the second clock
pulse, the bit pattern on the Q terminals is 0010.   The third
clock pulse leaves 0001 and the fourth pulse leaves the register
in the state, 0000.

The shift registers of the preceding example could be made
to shift left by connecting Q and Q̄ of FFB to J and K, respectively, of FFA.   All other flip-flops are connected in a similar
manner.   In fact, the addition of the logic as shown   in   Figure
10-5-5 can make the shift register shift in either direction as
a function of the signals L and R which gate the flip-flop outputs either to the left or to the right.   The J-K flip-flops of

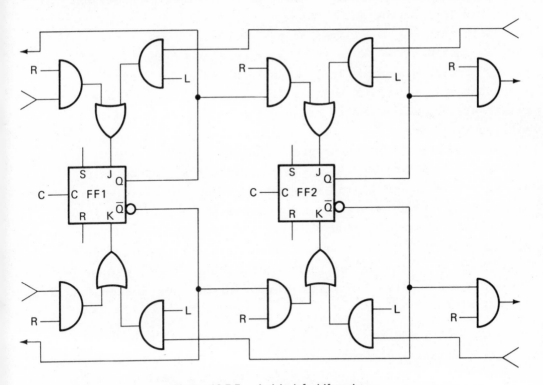

Figure 10-5-5.   A right-left shift register

Figure 10-5-4 could be connected to form a *ring* shift register
if the Q and Q̄ terminals of FFD were connected to the J   and   K
terminals, respectively, of FFA as shown in Figure 10-5-6.   A

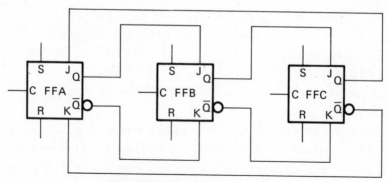

Figure 10-5-6. Ring shift register

ring shift register can be connected for any length or number
of flip-flops and used to repeat a particular binary pattern.
This is particularly useful in setting up a repetitive sequence
for a simulation program.

Note that the J-K flip-flop can be used to construct a
counter that does not have the *ripple* problem of the straight
binary counter discussed in Section 10.3.   A given state of
the counter is used to steer the flip-flops to the next appropriate state.   The examples presented here are but a few of the
many possible uses of J-K flip-flops.

Most computers which provide patchable, digital logic
include general purpose flip-flop registers that can be used
as individual flip-flops or as counters and shift registers
by applying appropriate signals to one or two control terminals.
The instruction manual should be checked for operating details.
On some computers, the set-reset nomenclature is used on clocked
flip-flops in place of the J-K designation. Thus, although
labeled S and R, the flip-flops operate in the same manner   as
the J-K flip-flop.

10.6   AN EXAMPLE PROBLEM

In order to illustrate the use of flip-flops and shift registers, consider the problem of determining the maximum value of
a function.   In Chapter 8, a circuit was developed to track and
store the maximum value in the step response of an underdamped
second-order system.   The circuit used a comparator to detect
the zero crossing of the derivative, $\dot{x}$, to determine when x is
at a maximum.   In Chapter 9, the same problem was used to illus-

trate the use of logic gates. However, in many practical applications, the derivative, $\dot{x}$, is not available and cannot be used to detect the points of inflection of the function x. Therefore, it is desirable to develop a program which will determine the maximum value of a function, x, without requiring the derivative, $\dot{x}$.

There are several approaches that could be used. The method used here involves two track-store units and a comparator. The function for which the maximum values are to be determined is the step response of the second-order system of Figure 10-6-1. This simple input was selected in order to focus attention on the maximum storing circuit. The step response, x, of the second-order system is connected to two track-store units, TS-1 and TS-2. The track-store units drive the comparator to a 1 or a 0 depending upon which track-store unit has the larger output. The state of the comparator is stored in flip-flop F. The output of flip-flop F is used to drive analog switches (ASW 1 and ASW 2) to connect the track-store unit with the larger output to amplifier 4. Thus, the output of amplifier 4 is maintained at the maximum value, X_m.

Since flip-flop F also drives the gates on the track terminals of the track-store units, the track-store unit with the larger value of x is in the Store mode and the other track-store unit is tracking. When a new value of x is found to be larger than the previous maximum the comparator changes state and causes flip-flop F to change state. This causes the output of the track-store holding the new maximum to be connected to amplifier 4. Thus, the larger value of x is always connected to amplifier 4.

The circuit of Figure 10-6-1 will not function properly without an alternate sampling of the waveform and the appropriate signals are supplied by the shift register constructed from flip-flops A, B, C, D and E. Flip-flops A and B must be set (i.e., Q=1, $\bar{Q}$=0) initially and all other flip-flops reset (i.e., Q=0, $\bar{Q}$=1). On each clock cycle, the bit pattern in the shift register shifts one position causing TS-1 and TS-2 to track or store. When a value greater than any preceding value is encountered by the track-store units, the comparator changes states causing flip-flop F to change state. Thus, the new maximum is connected to amplifier 4.

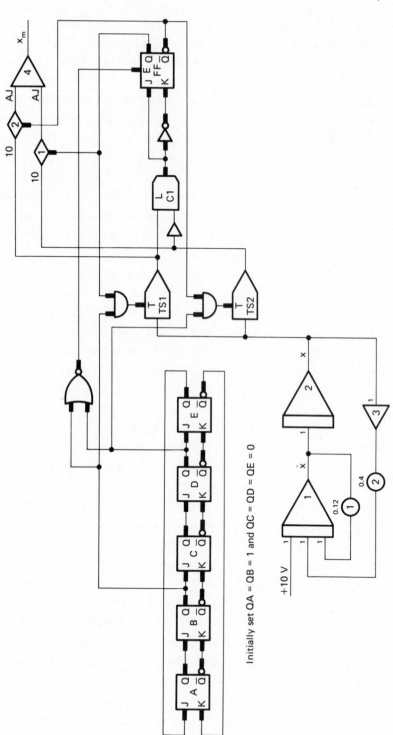

Initially set QA = QB = 1 and QC = QD = QE = 0

Figure 10-6-1. Maximum value circuit

Recordings of the step response and X_m are shown in Figure 10-6-2. The circuit was operated with a 10 Hz. clock rate and the maximum value, X_m, lagged the response X. For higher clock rates there is no discernible delay.

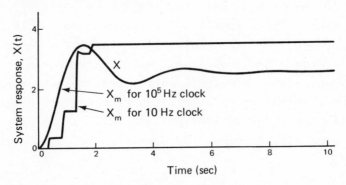

Figure 10-6-2. Step response and X_m

In order to test the circuit with a more general waveform, the signals from two sinusoidal oscillators slightly out of synchronism were summed and used as an input. The resulting waveforms are shown in Figure 10-6-3. The circuit acquired the first maximum value and held it until a larger value occurred.

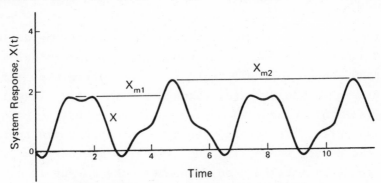

Figure 10-6-3. Maximum value circuit response

A similar circuit could be designed to store minimum values. Similar techniques can be used to determine other signal characteristics. Several examples of waveform analysis are presented in reference (6).

As stated previously, some computers have set-reset labels on J-K flip-flops. To use this approach on systems of this type, substitute S for J and R for K.

10.7 SPECIAL DIGITAL ELEMENTS

In addition to gates and flip-flops, several other digital
elements are quite useful. This section will be devoted to a
discussion of some of the special digital elements.

One of the most useful circuits is the digital mono-stable
multivibrator. The flip-flop discussed in Section 10.2 is a
bi-stable (i.e., two stable states) device often referred to as
a multivibrator. The mono-stable multivibrator has only one
stable state. The mono-stable multivibrator is also called a
one-shot multivibrator or digital differentiator. Since *one-shot*
seems to be the more widely used term, it will be used in this
book. A programming symbol is shown in Figure 10-7-1.

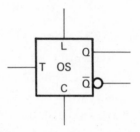

Figure 10-7-1.   One-shot programming symbol

The stable state (i.e., the state to which the device tends)
is Q=0 and $\bar{Q}$=1. A logic 1 at the T (trigger) terminal causes the
output, Q, to go to the 1 state for a predetermined time and
then return to the 0 state. Each positive going level change
(i.e., a 1 following a 0) at T causes the output to produce one
positive pulse. Therefore, the name *one-shot* seems appropriate.
Since the device senses the positive step at the input, the term
differentiator is also used. However, the output is not proportional to the slope or rise-time of the positive transition at
the input. In addition, a negative going change of state (i.e.,
1 to 0) at T does not produce a negative pulse.   Therefore, the
element is not a differentiator in the classical sense. A binary
1 on the Latch (L) terminal locks the one-shot in the 0 state
and prevents transitions to the 1 state. The output, Q, for
several input transitions is shown in Figure 10-7-2. The pulse
width, ΔT, is determined by internal adjustments.

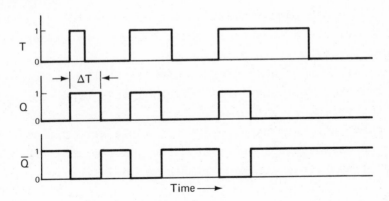

Figure 10-7-2. One-shot operating waveform

The last terminal to be discussed is reserved for the clock (C) input. The one-shot operation discussed in the preceding paragraph is asynchronous in nature. Whenever a positive transition occurs at the input, the one-shot produces a pulse at the output. Some units are capable of operating in synchronous with a clock signal. Usually, the period or length of the output pulse is one clock period. Synchronous operation is shown in Figure 10-7-3. The one-shot discussed in this section is sensitive to the leading-edge or positive transition at the input. An inverter is required if a pulse to indicate a negative transition is desired.

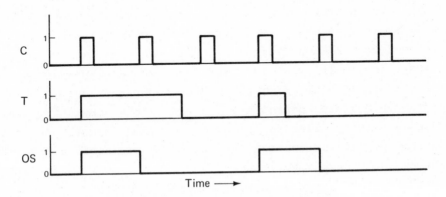

Figure 10-7-3. Synchronous one-shot

The one-shot unit can be used to sense level or logic state changes. The resulting pulse is frequently used to reset other logic circuits which end or initiate a program cycle. It is also used to advance a counter or shift register by gating the system clock to the unit to be advanced.

Another frequently used digital element is the logic push button or switch. The need for a device of this type is a result of the speed of most digital logic. If an ordinary switch or push button is used to drive a logic gate directly, the switch bounce or contact noise will cause <u>not</u> one, but several logic level transitions as shown in Figure 10-7-4. In some

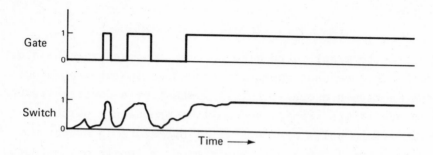

Figure 10-7-4. Switch bounce in a digital circuit

instances, the extra transitions do not affect the operation of the circuit. However, digital networks involving counters are very sensitive to *noise* of this type and special *bounce-free* push buttons or switches are provided on most computers. A noise-free switch can be constructed from a flip-flop by driving the S-R or J-K terminals from an ordinary switch. Some computers provide two push buttons for each digital switch. One push button causes the output to go to the 1 state. The other switch causes the unit to go to the 0 state from the 1 state. If the unit is already in the 0 state, depressing the *off* button causes the unit to produce a pulse similar to the output of a one-shot. Digital push buttons permit the operator to start or stop certain program phases and change functions or program configurations.

Most computers include special control circuits for the flip-flops. Each circuit can control the operation of several flip-flops and enables them to operate as a general purpose register. Appropriate patching on one or two terminals of the control circuit causes a group of flip-flops to operate as a binary counter (up or down), a shift register (right, left or ring) or as a parallel buffer register.

Most computers provide additional features and the appropriate manual should be read before attempting to use the computer.

10.8 SIMULATION OF HYBRID SYSTEMS

By definition, a hybrid system includes analog (continuous) and digital (discrete) variables. Due to the widespread use of direct digital control, many systems are hybrid in nature. Also, certain types of processes involving sequential operations are both discrete and continuous in nature (e.g., control systems containing relays, valves and switches which are bi-stable). An obvious application of the digital elements on a parallel hybrid computer is the simulation of such systems. Supposedly, the discrete events are simulated with logic elements and the continuous portion of the system is simulated with analog elements.

In order to simulate such systems, it is essential to identify all of the discrete variables and determine the sequence of operation. Quite often, the Boolean algebra techniques discussed in Chapter 9 are useful. Also, there is considerable literature available on the analysis and design of sequential systems.

Another class of systems utilizes n-level discrete variables. A signal is not simply on or off, but can occupy one discrete level or value of n possible levels. Discussion of systems of this type will be deferred until Chapter 12. A similar class of systems involves sampling. In this type of operation the variables are determined at certain intervals. An example of sampled-data systems is presented in the next section.

10.9 AN EXAMPLE PROBLEM

The analysis and design of sampled-data control systems has received considerable attention in recent years. With the widespread use of digital control for continuous systems, it is important to develop efficient methods for simulating sampled-data systems. The analog elements and patchable digital logic of the parallel hybrid computer are ideal for simulating systems of this type.

   In simulating sampled-data systems, several types of sampling
are of interest. The simplest form of sampling is the closure of
a single-pole switch for a predetermined period. This can be
simulated by the electronic switches.   A slightly more involved
form of sampling is a switch closure followed by a clamp. This is
referred to as a zero-order hold and can be simulated by the
track-store unit. The length of time for a switch closure and
the frequency of sampling can be established by an appropriate
network of digital counters and logic.   By increasing the complexity of the control network, the simulation can include variable
length and multi-rate sampling.

   In order to illustrate this type of simulation, consider the
sampled-data control system shown in Figure 10-9-1.[4]   Without
the sampling block, the system is a second-order, linear control
system. The introduction of sampling in the error return signal
can have appreciable effect on the system response.

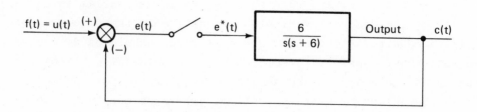

Figure 10-9-1.   Sampled-data system

   A computer diagram for the system is shown in Figure 10-9-2.
The analog portion has been time scaled by a factor of 100 ($\alpha=100$)
to facilitate recording of the waveform on an x-y plotter.   The
track-store unit is used to introduce a sampler followed by an
analog hold or clamp circuit. If a simple switch closure is desired, then the track-store unit is replaced with an electronic
switch.

   The ring counter is preset to 99 and produces one pulse
every ten sec. when driven from a 10 Hertz clock. The flip-flops
(FF 1, 2, 4, and 8) are connected as a binary counter and gate F

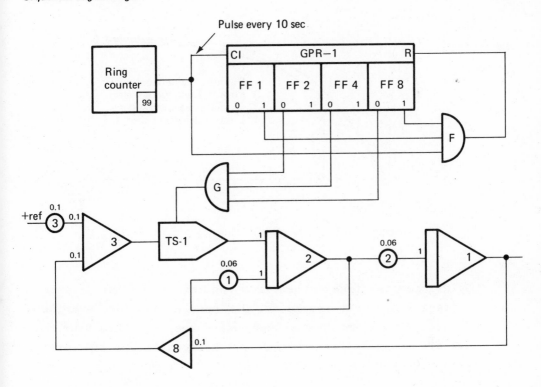

Figure 10-9-2. Computer diagram

resets the flip-flops every ten pulses or every 100 sec. Since
the analog problem has been scaled by 100, the counter changes
state once each 0.1 sec. of problem time. The binary counter
cycles every 1.0 sec. of problem time, which corresponds to 100
sec. of scaled time.

Gate F is connected to the binary counter and is in the 1
state for 20 sec. of real time or 0.2 sec. of problem time. As a
result, the track-store unit tracks the error signal for 0.2 sec.
of problem time (PT) and then holds the last value of error for
0.8 sec. of problem time (PT). At 1.0 sec. (PT) the track-store
unit returns to the track mode for 0.2 sec. (PT) and begins a new
cycle of operation. Figure 10-9-3 presents the response curves
for this simulation. The figure also contains the error and output signals for both the continuous and sampled case.

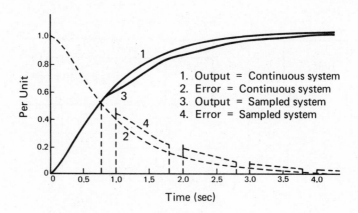

Figure 10-9-3. Zero-order hold sampling for 0.2 seconds

By driving the track-store from the inverse output of gate G, the track-store unit tracks for 0.8 sec. (PT) before storing for 0.2 sec. (PT). The system response curves for this type of sampling are shown in Figure 10-9-4. The results are similar to the continuous case.

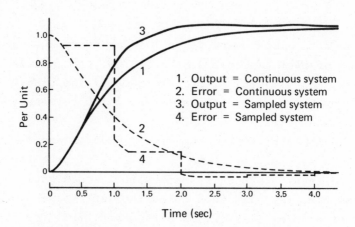

Figure 10-9-4. Zero-order hold sampling for 0.8 seconds

If the track-store unit is replaced with an analog switch (i.e., no hold circuit is involved), the response curves of Figure 10-9-5 are obtained. Note that the system is very slow in

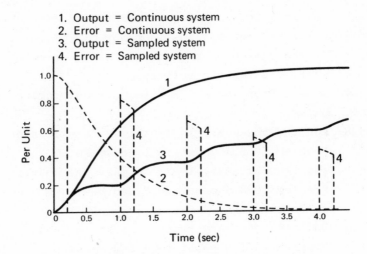

1. Output = Continuous system
2. Error = Continuous system
3. Output = Sampled system
4. Error = Sampled system

Figure 10-9-5. System response for 0.2 sec. sample

responding. This is to be expected since the error is only present for 0.2 sec. every 1.0 sec. of problem time.

Similar results have been obtained on a digital time-shared terminal using a state-space approach.[5]

10.10 PROBLEMS

Problems covering the material for this chapter are identified by sections.

10.2.1 Design a set-reset flip-flop using AND gates and inverters.

10.2.2 Design a set-reset flip-flop using OR gates and inverters.

10.2.3 Design a set-reset flip-flop using NAND gates.

10.2.4 Design a set-reset flip-flop using NOR gates.

10.4.1 Design a toggle flip-flop using NAND gates.

10.4.2 Design a toggle flip-flop using NOR gates.

10.4.3 Design a four bit down counter using toggle flip-flops.

10.4.4 Design a four bit up counter using set-reset flip-flops.

10.4.5 Design a four bit down counter using set-reset flip-flops.

10.4.6   Design a buffer and parallel transformer circuit using set-reset flip-flops for one of the counters or the previous problems. Assume a reset pulse is available for the buffer.

10.4.7   Repeat Problem 10.3.6 without requiring the reset pulse.

10.4.8   Add the necessary logic to make the counter of Problem 10.3.4 count to 6 and reset.

10.4.9   Add the necessary logic to make the counter of Problem 10.3.4 count to 6 and reset to a count of 3.

10.4.10   Add the necessary logic to make the counter of Problem 10.3.4 count to 4 and skip to 6 on the next pulse.

10.5.1   Design a J-K flip-flop using NAND gates.

10.5.2   Design a J-K flip-flop using NOR gates.

10.5.3   Repeat Problem 10.4.3 using J-K flip-flops.

10.5.4   Repeat Problem 10.4.4 using J-K flip-flops.

10.5.5   Repeat Problem 10.4.8 using J-K flip-flops.

10.5.6   Repeat Problem 10.4.9 using J-K flip-flops.

10.5.7   Repeat Problem 10.4.10 using J-K flip-flops.

10.5.8   Design a four bit left shift register.

10.5.9   Design a four bit ring shift register.

10.6.1   Develop a program to store the maximum positive value of a waveform. Test the operation of your program with a waveform generated by summing 3 sinusoidal oscillators with a magnitude of 2.5 volts and different frequencies.

10.6.2   Develop a program to store the minimum positive value of a waveform. Test the operation in the same manner as Problem 10.6.1.

10.6.3   Develop a program to store the maximum peak-to-peak value of the test waveform of Problem 10.6.1.

10.6.4   Develop a program to store the value of the minimum following the first maximum in the step response of a second-order system ($\delta=.2$, $\omega_n=1$).

10.6.5 Develop a program to store the value of the
second minimum following the first maximum
in the step response of a second-order system
($\delta=.2$, $\omega_n=1$).

10.6.6 Develop a program to store the value of the
second maximum following the first maximum
in the step response of a second-order system
($\delta=.2$, $\omega_n=1$).

10.7.1 Develop a program to count the number of times
the step response of Problem 10.6.4 exceeds an
overshoot of 10%.

10.7.2 Develop a digital program to produce a clock
pulse with a rate of one pulse per second. Use
count-down counters if available.

10.7.3 Develop a digital program to produce a clock
pulse with a rate of one pulse every ten seconds.
Use count-down counters if available.

10.7.4 Develop a digital program to produce the waveform
shown.

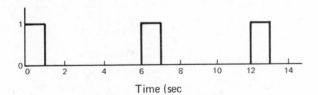

Time (sec

Figure 10-10-1.

10.7.5 Use the general purpose registers to construct
the following:

a. Four-bit right shift register
b. Four-bit left shift register
c. Four-bit ring shift register
d. Four-bit down-counter
e. Four-bit up-counter

10.7.6 Construct a four-phase clock which stays in
phases 1 and 3 for 1 sec. and phases 2 and
4 for only 0.2 sec.

10.8.1   Develop a hybrid program to produce the waveform
         shown.

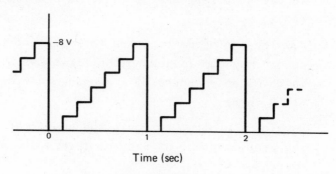

Time (sec)

Figure 10-10-2.

10.8.2   Develop a hybrid program to produce the waveform
         shown.

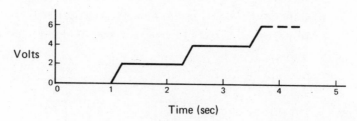

Time (sec)

Figure 10-10-3.

10.8.3   Develop a hybrid program to produce the waveform
         shown.

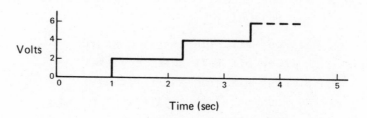

Time (sec)

Figure 10-10-4.

10.8.4　Use comparators to determine when an input is in the following ranges:

Range
1　0<x<1.5v
2　1.5v<x<3.0v
3　3.0v<x<5v

Use the comparators to drive a register to 1,2, or 3 to indicate the value of the input, x.

10.8.5　List 5 systems that are suitable for hybrid simulation. Indicate which variables would be digital or analog.

10.9.1　Simulate the example problem of Section 10.9 with a sampling rate of two samples per second with zero-order hold sampling. Sampling takes place for 0.2 seconds.

10.9.2　Simulate the example problem of Section 10.9 with a sampling rate of two samples per second without the zero-order hold on the sampler. Sample for 0.2 seconds twice each second.

10.9.3　Develop a program that will automatically vary the damping ratio of a second-order system to within some ε of the desired overshoot as set on a potentiometer. Note that it must be able to change δ in both directions.

10.9.4　Determine the effect of decreasing the sampling rate of Problem 10.9.1. What is the minimum usable value of sampling rate?

10.11　REFERENCES FOR CHAPTER 10

(1) Krieger, M., Basic Switching Circuit Theory, The Macmillan Co., New York, 1967.

(2) Hill, F. J. and G. R. Peterson, Introduction to Switching Theory and Logical Design, John Wiley & Sons, Inc., New York, 1968.

(3) Marcus, M. P., Switching Circuits for Engineers, Prentice-Hall, Inc., Englewood Cliffs, N.J., 1967.

(4) Coffey, E. L., A. W. Bennett and L. L. Grigsby, "Parallel-Hybrid Computer Simulation of Samples - Data Control Systems," ACES Application Note No.22, 1972.

(5) Kuelz, E. Jr., and L. L. Grigsby, "A State-Space Approach to System Simulation Using a Time-Shared Terminal," Second Southeastern Symposium on System Theory, University of Florida, Gainesville, Florida, March, 1970.

(6) Smith, D. W. and G. R. Foster,"Counting Peaks in Continuous Signals— An Analog/Hybrid Problem in Pattern Recognition," ACES(CoED) TRANSACTIONS, Vol. 3, No. 1, January, 1971.

11

Optimization

11.1 INTRODUCTION

The improvement of system performance is an important phase of most every engineering project. In most cases, it is a matter of varying system parameters to determine values which produce the best or *optimum* performance. This is the parameter optimization problem and a number of parameter search techniques have been developed.[1] A similar problem is concerned with the determination of the parameters of a system by varying the parameters of a model of the system to produce the "best" match between model and system performance. This is referred to as the parameter *identification* problem.[2]

Both parameter optimization and identification require the variation of parameters and an evaluation of the resulting performance. A number of criteria are used for system performance evaluation. For example, the criterion might be a certain range of values for system variables, a maximum (minimum) for a partic-

ular system variable, the minimization of an error function or
the maximization (minimization) of a function of system variables.
Obviously, the formulation of the criterion or *cost* function is an
important part of an optimization study.   In many cases, the ideal
cost function cannot be determined and the study becomes sub-
optimal in nature.

A related but more complex problem is the determination of
the optimal control for a system.[3]   The performance criterion is
usually a function of system variables and is a measure of the
cost of operating in a non-optimum fashion.   The criterion function may involve expressions which represent time, resources and/or
system error.   Also, the optimization may be subject to certain
constraints on system variables or boundary conditions.

Optimization studies are one of the most important applications of computer simulation.   By time-scaling and operating in
a high-speed repetitive operation mode, modern analog computing
elements are able to produce thousands of trial solutions or
simulation runs for a system.   The availability of hybrid computing
elements to control the simulation and make logical decisions
permits the use of sophisticated optimization techniques.   The
interconnection of analog and digital computers combine the speed
of the analog with the memory, accuracy and decision capability of
the digital to make an effective simulation device for optimization
studies.

Some of the basic optimization concepts will be introduced in
this chapter.   The first section presents techniques for implementing parameter variations.   The parameter stepping methods are
illustrated in the next section.   Other sections are devoted to
parameter optimization and parameter search techniques to achieve
known performance objectives.   These methods are extended to
multiparameter optimization.   The use of computer simulation in
optimal control is mentioned briefly.

11.2 PARAMETER STEPPING TECHNIQUES

In the previous chapters devoted to developing computer simulation programs, the system parameters are represented by
potentiometers.   In a typical simulation, the pots are set to the

appropriate values prior to each simulation run. Thus, in order
to determine the effect of parameter variations, a series of
simulation runs with different pot settings are necessary. The
time required and the likelihood of error make manual parameter
stepping prohibitive for anything except simple parameter studies.
In this section, two techniques for generating automatic parameter
variations will be presented.

The first method utilizes the electronic multiplier introduced
in Section 5.4. Basically, the typical pot-amplifier circuit shown
in Figure 11-2-1(a) is replaced with the multiplier shown in
Figure 11-2-1(b). Instead of manually setting the pot to the

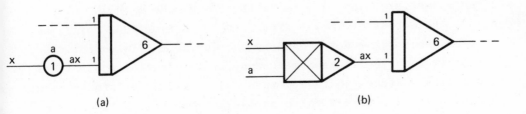

(a)   (b)

Figure 11-2-1. System parameter representation

desired parameter value prior to a simulation run, the appropriate
value is placed on the parameter input of the multiplier. There
are several ways to produce a signal which will take on a series
of values for the parameter input to the multiplier.

The parameter input to the multiplier can be supplied from a
track-store accumulator, an integrator, or several analog switches.
Consider first the use of track-store units. In Section 8.8, the
accumulation of a series of increments, Δe_i, is discussed and an
accumulator circuit is shown in Figure 8-8-3. In order to
illustrate the application of this technique, assume that it is desired to investigate the effect on system performance of a series
of parameter values, $a_1, a_2, \ldots, a_n$, where $a_{i+1} = a_i + \Delta a$. Each time the
computer is cycled to the initial condition mode, the parameter, a,
should be incremented by Δa. This can be achieved by the circuit
of Figure 11-2-2.

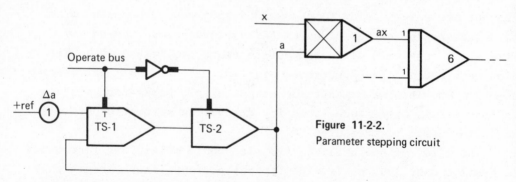

Figure 11-2-2.
Parameter stepping circuit

In order to understand the operation of the circuit in Figure 11-2-2, assume that the computer is initially in the initial condition or reset mode. For this state, TS-1 is in the store mode with an output of 0 and TS-2 is in the track mode with an output equal to the output of TS-1. Thus, the output of TS-2 will be 0 or equal to a value determined by the analog initial condition input of TS-1 or TS-2. When the repetitive operation control of the computer switches to the operate mode, TS-2 goes into the store mode and holds a constant value on the parameter input of the multiplier. At the same time, TS-1 goes into the track mode. Since the input of TS-1 is the output of TS-2 and Δa from pot 1, the output of TS-1 is equal to the present parameter input plus the increment Δa. Each time the computer goes through the initial condition/operate cycle, the parameter input of the multiplier is incremented by Δa and held constant at the new value for the next simulation run. A plot of the resulting parameter steps is shown in Figure 11-2-3. Since parameter values are influenced by

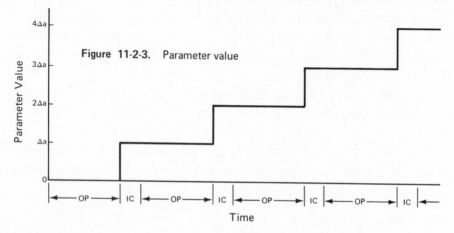

Figure 11-2-3. Parameter value

scaling, the parameter stepping circuit must be adjusted to account
for scale factor changes.

The signal for incrementing the parameter input to the
multiplier of Figure 11-2-1(b) can also be generated by an integrator. In order to understand this technique, consider the
circuit of Figure 11-2-4. First, note that the initial condition

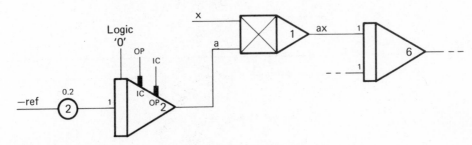

Figure 11-2-4. Parameter stepping with an integrator

bus of the computer is connected to the operate terminal of the
integrator. Thus, integrator 2 is in the operate mode when the
other integrators of the computer are in the initial condition
or reset mode. Each time the computer cycles to the initial
condition mode, integrator 2 begins to integrate. Since the
input to the integrator is from the negative reference supply,
the output will go positive at a rate determined by the pot
setting and the integrator gain. For the example of Figure
11-2-4, the integrator output will increase at a rate of 2 Volts
per second during the initial condition period. When the computer
is returned to the operate mode by the repetitive operation control,
integrator 2 is in the hold mode with a new value on the parameter
input of the multiplier. Thus, by varying the gain of integrator
2 and the length of time in the initial condition mode, the size of
the parameter step can be controlled. A negative increment can
be obtained by connecting the potentiometer of integrator 2 to the
positive reference supply. Also, the parameter values can be made
to start at any desired level by utilizing the initial condition
input of the integrator. However, integrator 2 should not be
returned to the initial condition mode unless it is desired to
repeat the same parameter value. A plot of the resulting parameter
input signal is shown in Figure 11-2-5.

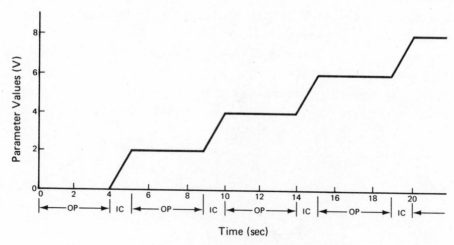

Figure 11-2-5. Parameter values

The parameter input to the multiplier could also be supplied from a circuit utilizing analog switches. For example, consider the circuit of Figure 11-2-6. In order to understand the operation of the circuit of Figure 11-2-6, assume that the computer is in the initial condition mode and that the flip-flops of the general purpose register (connected as a binary counter) are all reset (i.e., Q=0). For these conditions, all analog switches are open and the output of amplifier 3 is zero. At the end of the initial condition period, the computer goes to the operate mode and initiates a simulation run with 0 Volts on the parameter input of the multiplier. At the completion of the operate cycle, the computer returns to the initial condition mode. The one-shot (differentiator) produces a pulse which gates the general purpose counter on for one clock cycle and the counter advances to the combination 0001. The output of flip-flop 1 closes analog switch 1. The output of amplifier 3 goes to a value determined by pot 1, the resistance of the analog switch and the feedback resistor. Each time the computer cycles from the operate mode to the initial condition mode, the counter advances by 1 and a different combination of the analog switches is selected. Since the ouput of gate A will cause the Rep-Op timer to stop at counter state 1010, the effective pot settings start at 0.0 and increment to 0.1, 0.2,...,1.0.

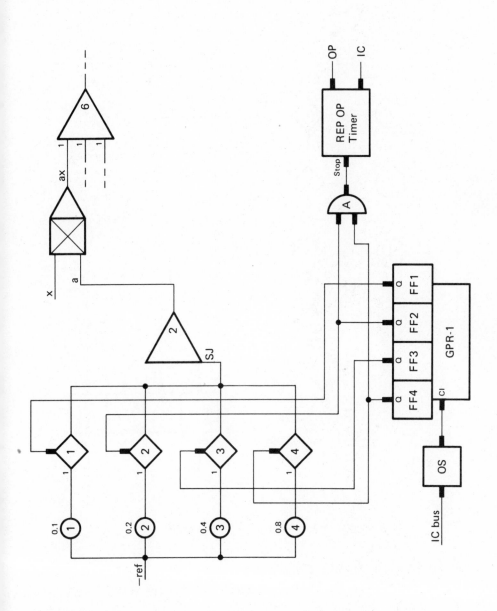

Figure 11-2-6. Parameter stepping with analog switches

The binary switching technique of Figure 11-2-6 can be used to vary the parameters without the multiplier. This method is illustrated in Figure 11-2-7. Usually, it is easier to scale and check

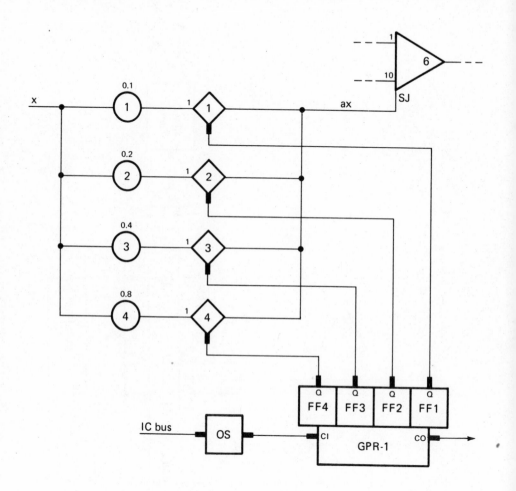

Figure 11-2-7. Digital parameter stepping

than the methods involving the multiplier. This method is also discussed in reference (5). The circuit of Figure 11-2-7 operates in the same manner as the circuit of Figure 11-2-6. The variable, x, is fed through a different combination of the four potentiometers on each successive cycle in the operate mode. As noted previously, the pots should be set in a binary sequence. The actual values will be a function of the scaling constants for the problem. Since the input to the switches may not be grounded when the switches are open, it may be necessary to use a special circuit to set the pots. Most computers have internal connections to avoid this problem.

Since most parameter sweeps are designed to cover a specific range of values, the *carry-out* signal from the general purpose register can be used to terminate the search at the end of 16 cycles. If fewer than 16 steps are desired, an AND gate can be used to produce a stop signal at any number on the counter (e.g., see Figure 10-3-7).

11.3 EXAMPLE PROBLEM

In order to illustrate the parameter stepping techniques discussed in the previous section, consider the following example problem. Assume that the effect of damping ratio on the generalized, linear, second-order system is to be determined by plotting the step response for δ = 0.0, 0.2, 0.4, 0.6, 0.8 and 1.0, with ω_n = 1.0. This problem has already been discussed (e.g., Figure 3-6-3). However, the simplicity of the problem permits full attention to be devoted to the parameter stepping features. The program for the basic equation is shown in Figure 3-6-2 and repeated in Figure 11-3-1 for convenience. Since ω_n is equal to 1, it does

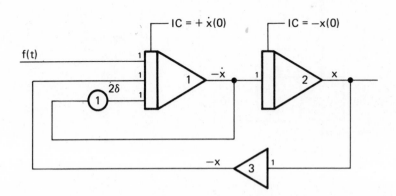

Figure 11-3-1. Generalized second-order linear system

not appear as a parameter setting on the potentiometers. The
parameter to be varied, δ, is represented by pot 1. Since the
pot setting is actually 2δ, computer runs are required for pot
settings of 0.0, 0.4, 0.8, 1.2, 1.6 and 2.0. This range of
parameter values is well suited to the analog switch techniques
shown in Figure 11-2-7. In this case, three potentiometers are
required. The settings are 0.4, 0.8 and 1.6. The resulting
circuit is shown in Figure 11-3-2.

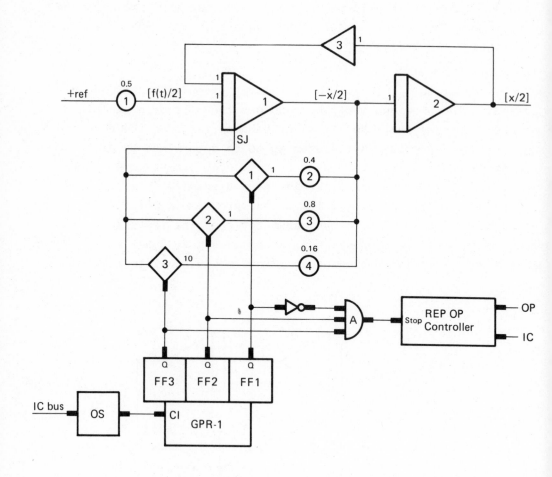

Figure 11-3-2. Damping ratio stepping circuit

In order to understand the operation of this circuit, assume that the computer is in the initial condition mode with all logic elements reset. Since the flip-flops of the general purpose register are in the reset state (i.e., Q = 0, $\bar{Q}$ = 1), the analog switches are open and the feedback path around integrator 2 is open. Thus, the damping ratio is δ=0. When the computer goes into the operate mode, the response of the circuit is determined for δ=0. At the end of the operate cycle, the initial condition bus goes to the 1 state and the one-shot (differentiator) goes to the 1 state for 1 clock pulse. This permits the general purpose register to advance from 000 to 001. The change in state of flip-flop 1 causes analog switch 1 to close and the effective damping ratio is now δ=0.2. When the repetitive operation timer causes the computer to go to the operate state, the step response corresponding to δ=0.2 is determined. When the computer returns to the initial condition mode following the operate cycle, the counter advances one state and has the output combination 010. Thus, analog switch 2 closes, switch 1 opens and the feedback produces a damping ratio, δ=0.4.

On the next initial condition cycle, the counter advances to 011 and pots 1 and 2 are connected. The resulting damping ratio is 0.6. When the computer returns to the initial condition mode following the simulation run for δ=.6, the counter advances to the state 100. This causes pot 3 to be connected, yielding a damping ratio of δ=0.8. The next initial condition period advances the counter to the 101 state and connects pots 1 and 3 for an effective damping ratio of 1.0. At the end of the operate cycle for δ=1.0, the initial condition signal advances the counter to 110. This causes gate A to go to a logic 1. The output of gate A is used to stop the repetitive operation timer in the initial condition mode (e.g., see Figure 8-11-3). The resulting waveforms are shown in Figure 11-3-3.

Similar results can be obtained by using a multiplier as shown in Figures 11-2-4 and 11-2-6. However, as noted previously, the multiplier will require careful scaling to avoid error.

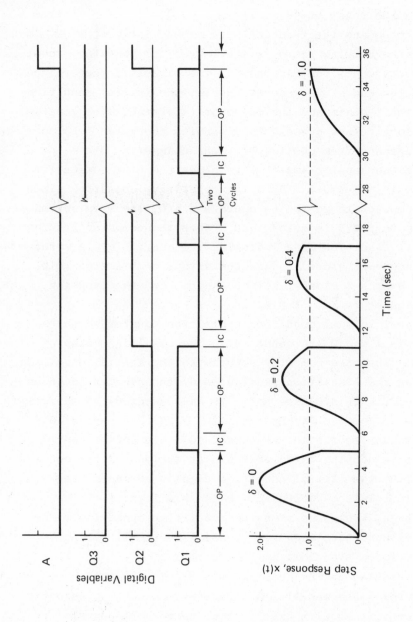

Figure 11-3-3. Second-order system response

11.4 PARAMETER OPTIMIZATION

In discussing techniques for varying parameters, nothing was mentioned about evaluating the performance or selecting the optimum parameter value. It was assumed that the range of parameter values to be studied was known and that the objective of the study was the response for the different parameter values. In some cases, this is adequate. The system designer can use the knowledge gained from the parameter sweep to improve the design and operation of the system. However, in many instances the system is too complex to permit the intuitive approach to operate efficiently. In addition, optimum performance is often achieved with parameter values which are not intuitively obvious. In response to this need, a number of optimization techniques have been developed to evaluate the performance of a system and determine parameter variations to improve the performance. Usually, the techniques operate in an iterative fashion and gradually step the system toward optimum performance.

In order to implement an optimum parameter search, an expression for the desired or optimum performance must be developed. This is often one of the most difficult aspects of parameter optimization. In some instances, the objective is to maintain a set of system variables as close as possible to a particular value or function. In other cases, optimal operation is not clearly defined. The objective is to operate the system in a manner that maximizes (minimizes) some function which is representative of the cost of operating in a non-optimal fashion. The function used as a measure of optimality is usually referred to as the performance objective, the cost function or the criterion function.

Additional understanding of the parameter optimization problem can be gained by considering a system in which two parameters, P_1 and P_2 are to be optimized. Once an appropriate cost function has been determined, it can be evaluated for all values of P_1 and P_2. A three dimensional surface can be constructed with P_1 and P_2 along the two horizontal axes and the corresponding value of the cost function on the vertical axis. The resulting three dimensional plot produces a surface similar to a contour map. If the optimum parameters minimize the cost function, then the

object of the search is to find the lowest point or "valley" of
the three dimensional surface. If the optimum set of parameters
maximizes the cost function, the object of the search   is   to
determine the parameters producing the highest peak or "mountain"
on the surface.

There are several methods for finding the maximum (minimum)
points. In a few instances, it is possible to determine an analytical expression for the optimum parameters. However, most
cases require some type of parameter search.

A variety of parameter search techniques have been developed.
The most basic is a sequential parameter search which   includes
calculation and comparison of the cost function at   each   point.
Random search methods need fewer calculations but still require
a significant number of evaluations. Variable grid   methods   use
large steps to determine ranges for possible maximum (minimum)
points. Once a region is identified as having a possible extreme,
smaller parameter steps are used. Another procedure, requiring
fewer parameter steps, is called the relaxation   method[4]   Only
one parameter is varied at a given time and that parameter   is
varied until a maximum (minimum) is found. That parameter value
is then held constant while a search for a maximum (minimum)   is
carried out on a second parameter. This procedure is continued
until the "optimum" set of parameters is found. An alternate
approach makes trial parameter changes in several directions and
then makes a parameter change in the direction of greatest improvement.

Some of the most efficient search techniques utilize the
slope of the cost function to determine which parameters   to
change and the size of the increment. Two of the   more   popular
gradient techniques are the steepest descent method   and   the
Newton-Raphson method.

All of the optimization methods discussed in this section are
subject to failure under certain circumstances. Many problems will
have several "mountains" and "valleys" and the objective   of   the
optimization is to determine highest (lowest) point (i.e., the
global extrema). Unfortunately, without an exhaustive   search,
the optimization may settle on a *local* extrema which is   not   as

optimum as the global point.   Therefore, some type of preliminary global search is required.

Each of the parameter optimization techniques have distinct advantages and disadvantages.   The method to use for a particular application should be evaluated carefully.   However, this   level of detail is beyond the scope of this book and the   interested reader is referred to the references at the end of this chapter.

11.5   SINGLE PARAMETER SEARCH FOR KNOWN PERFORMANCE OBJECTIVE

One of the simplest parameter optimization problems involves the variation of a single parameter to achieve a known performance objective.   In many cases, a cause-effect relationship   between parameter changes and system performance can be determined.   This enables the attainment of the objective with one iteration.   In other cases, the relationship is nebulous and many iterations are required.

Frequently, the objective of a parameter study is to determine the value for a particular parameter which causes a system variable to take on a specified value.   In some cases, the variable is to be maintained at or near the objective throughout the operating period.   In other instances, a particular   point   in time is specified.   For instance, a system variable   may   be required to reach a specified value at the terminal   boundary point.   In other cases, the objective may be a specified maximum or minimum value for a variable.

The parallel hybrid computer is well suited for problems of this type.   The techniques presented in Chapters 8, 9 and 10 can be used to determine the maximum (minimum) values of a variable. Track-store units can be used to hold variables for comparison with the performance objective.   These techniques, coupled   with the parameter stepping methods of Section 11.2, permit the implementation of single parameter search procedures.

Although single parameter stepping to a known performance objective is a relatively straightforward procedure, there are some difficulties that should be considered.   For example, it is usually easy to implement a variable increment stepping routine (i.e., the larger the error, the larger the corresponding parameter step).   Thus, as the objective is approached, smaller   and

smaller steps are generated and many unnecessary simulation runs
are produced. Also, if the performance objective is narrowly
defined, the parameter stepping procedure may overstep the
objective and begin to oscillate or "hunt" about the objective.
Thus, the stability of the parameter stepping system is of
considerable importance. Since the parameter selection loop is
a sampled data control system, special analysis techniques are
required.[1]

    This problem can be minimized by using a band or range about
the objective in which no further corrective action is required.
This permits larger steps and fewer simulation runs. As additional
information regarding the effect of a parameter on system performance is obtained, the range of acceptable values can be reduced.

11.6 EXAMPLE PROBLEM

    In order to illustrate the single parameter search techniques
discussed in the previous section, consider a procedure for automatically adjusting the damping ratio of a second-order system to
achieve a specified maximum overshoot in response to a step input.
A program for determining and storing the maximum value of the
overshoot was described in Section 8.10. A circuit to automatically vary the damping ratio was presented in Section 11.3.
The desired operation can be achieved by combining the overshoot
sensor with the variable damping program and adding a circuit to
compare the actual overshoot with the desired overshoot. To simplify
the discussion, the undamped natural frequency for the system will
be set at 1.0 radian per sec.

    A circuit to accomplish the objective outlined in the previous
paragraph is shown in Figure 11-6-1. In order to understand the
operation of this circuit, assume that the computer is under the
control of the repetitive operation controller and is initially in
the IC mode. Also, assume that the desired per cent overshoot has
been set on pot 1 (i.e., a pot setting of 0.75 corresponds to a
50 per cent overshoot). The flip-flops of the general purpose register can be in any state. For the purpose of this discussion,
let $Q1=1$, $Q2=0$, $Q3=1$ and $Q4=0$. Under the assumed conditions,
analog switches AS1 and AS3 are closed and AS2 and AS4 are open.
Thus, the effective feedback on the integrator producing $-\dot{x}$ is

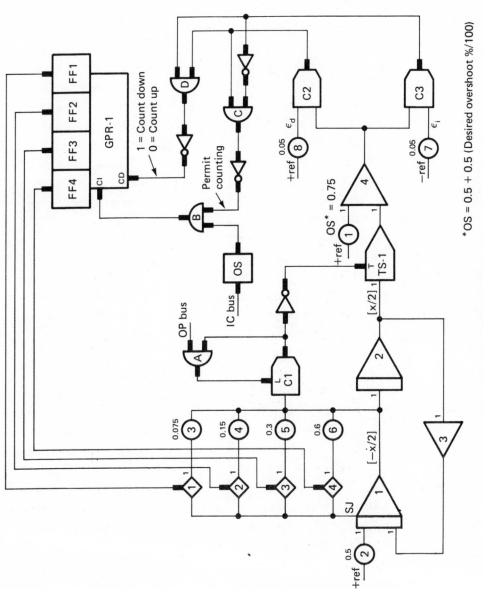

Figure 11-6-1. Overshoot adjusting circuit

0.075 + 0.30 = 0.375. Since the feedback is the term $2\delta\omega_n$ and $\omega_n=1$, the damping ratio is 0.1875.

While in the initial condition mode, comparator C1 is in the 0 state with the latch terminal at logic 0, (i.e., not latched). Since the operate bus is a logic 0 during the initial condition period, the latch terminal is held at logic 0 by gate A. The track-store unit is in the track mode with an output of 0, (i.e., the negative of the initial value of x). Amplifier 4 has a net positive input and a negative output. Therefore, both C2 and C3 are in the logic 0 state. The countdown terminal on the general purpose register is in the 1 state, and if the count input terminal (CI) is at logic 1 during a clock pulse, the counter will countdown. However, in order for the CI terminal to be a logic 1, the one-shot (differentiator) must be triggered by IC going to the 1 state when either $\overline{C2}$ or C3 are at logic 1. Thus, the counter is locked at its present state.

When the repetitive operation timer goes from the initial condition to the operate state, the integrators begin responding to the step input and AND gate A is enabled. If C1 goes to the 1 state, it will be latched by its own output. The T-S unit tracks the output, x. In response to a positive step input, the $-\dot{x}$ term goes negative initially and C1 is held in the 0 state.

When the first maximum is reached, $-\dot{x}$ goes positive and C1 goes to the 1 state. Note that C1 is latched in the 1 state by its output through AND gate A. The track-store unit goes to the store mode holding $-x_m$, the maximum value, at its output. If the overshoot is greater than the desired value, amplifier 4 will have a positive output. With a positive signal from A4, C2 will be in the 1 state and C3 will be in the 1 state if the threshold ε_i is exceeded. The output of AND gate D will be a 1 and the countdown terminal on the general purpose register is a logic 0. Therefore, the counter will count up (i.e., increase damping and decrease overshoot). In the meantime, x and $\dot{x}$ continue to change in response to the step input.

At a point in time determined by the repetitive operation timer, the computer is returned to the initial condition mode. The operate bus goes to logic 0 and the initial condition bus goes to logic 1. In response to the initial condition bus going

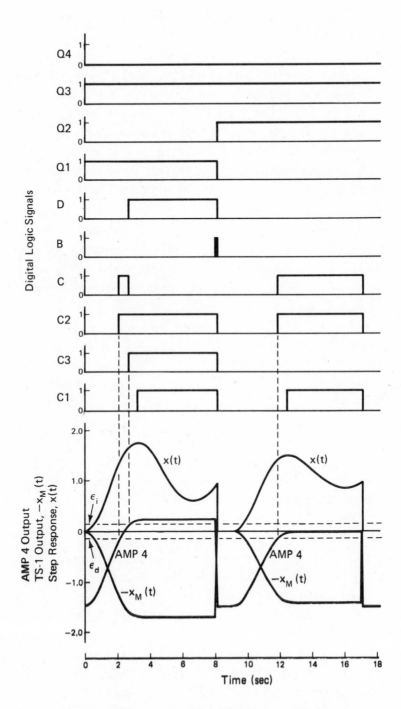

Figure 11-6-2. Overshoot adjusting circuit waveforms

high, the one-shot goes to the 1 state for one clock cycle. Since the output of gate C is 0, the count input terminal goes to the 1 state for one clock cycle and the counter is incremented by 1. The state of the counter becomes Q1=0, Q2=1, Q3=1 and Q4=0. With analog switches AS2 and AS3 closed, the feedback is 0.15+0.3=0.45, which gives a damping ratio of 0.225. In the meantime, x and $\dot{x}$ have returned to 0. The latch is removed from C1 and it returns to 0. The track-store unit returns to the track mode with an output of 0 and the output of amplifier 4 becomes negative. The output of C2 and C3 will be logic 0. The waveform for the events are shown in Figure 11-6-2.

Having incremented the damping, the system is now ready for the next operate cycle. When the computer returns to the operate mode, x and $\dot{x}$ begin responding to the step input. However, due to the increase in damping, the maximum overshoot is not as great as the previous case. As before, C1 causes TS-1 to track x to the maximum overshoot. The comparator C1 latches itself through gate A. The output of amplifier 4 does not exceed the threshold ε_i. If ε_i is not exceeded, C3 never goes to the 1 state. Therefore, even though there is a logic 1 on the count-down terminal, the one-shot pulse which occurs when the comparator returns to the initial condition mode is unable to pass through gate B to permit the counter to increment or decrement. This mode of operation is shown in the second cycle of Figure 11-6-2.

If the damping ratio is too large and the maximum overshoot is less than the desired value set on pot 1, the output of amplifier 4 remains negative. If the negative output of amplifier 4 is less than the positive threshold, ε_d, C2 and C3 are held in the 0 state. When the computer goes to the IC mode, $\bar{C}$ gates the one-shot pulse through gate B and the counter is decremented (i.e., counts down). If the output of amplifier 4 is less than ϵ_i but greater than the bias on ϵ_d, C2 goes to the 1 state and C3 remains in the 0 state. Gate C is held at 1 by $\overline{C3}$ and C2, and even though the countdown terminal is at logic 1, the count input pulse cannot pass through gate B. Thus, the counter neither advances or decreases if the overshoot is within the limits set by ε_i and ε_d.

There are other ways to accomplish the objective of this problem. For example, proportional steps in damping could be used. Since the relationship between damping ratio and over-shoot is known,[6] a direct calculation could also be used to adjust the damping. However, the simplicity of the approach presented in this section has enabled the discussion to focus on the parameter adjustment technique.

Before leaving this example, a few points are worth noting. The parameter adjustment procedure will always take a single step in the appropriate direction. In order to avoid hunting or oscillation above and below the desired value, the tolerance range set by ε_i and ε_d should be greater than the change in overshoot produced by the smallest increment in damping. Since the relation between damping ratio and overshoot is nonlinear, the system may be stable for one range of damping ratios and unstable for other values.

In selecting the pot settings for the analog switches of Figure 11-6-1, the smallest increment could be 0.1, which gives a damping increment of 0.05. For this increment size, the maximum feedback is $0.1 + 0.2 + 0.4 + 0.8 = 1.5$, which corresponds to a damping ratio of 0.75. If it is desired to vary the damping ratio from 0 to 1.0, an additional analog switch would be necessary. If an additional analog switch is used, the smallest increment can be reduced to 0.075. Since the scaling of a particular problem will also have an effect on the pot settings, the parameter adjustment circuit should be included in the scaling operation.

The parameter incrementing procedure could be made to converge to the desired value in fewer iterations if a larger increment were taken initially. Optimization schemes based on this approach use a bracketing method of adjustment. The most significant bit of the adjustment is checked first and the number of iterations required to reach the best value would be equal to the number of analog switches used. However, the digital logic required for this approach is more complex.

11.7 MULTIPARAMETER FUNCTIONAL OPTIMIZATION

In the previous sections, single parameter optimization for a known performance objective was discussed and illustrated. The

method is useful for determining parameter values which produce
a specified result in the response of a system. The method is
also effective for matching boundary conditions in the solution
of partial differential equations. However, in many instances,
optimization involves a number of parameters and the performance
objective is not a specific value of the response. In such cases,
a more complex procedure is required.

In implementing multiparameter functional optimization, the
first task is to develop an appropriate performance objective or
index. Since the performance index or criterion function is the
basis for optimization, it should incorporate a number of important considerations. First, the minimization (maximization) of the
performance index must represent optimal performance. Therefore,
any deviation from optimum performance will be reflected in the
performance index. Also, all deviations from the optimum must
produce corresponding changes in the performance index of the
same algebraic sign. The reason for this requirement stems from
the canceling effect of positive and negative deviations. Usually,
deviations from the optimal produce only positive changes in the
performance index.

With the requirements for a performance index in mind, consider the choice of terms to be included. First, the terms used
must be representative of the quantity to be optimized. For example, if energy is to be minimized, the variables of the
performance index must relate to the energy required. If the
desired system response is to match some function, $x_d(t)$, then
either the absolute value $|x(t)-x_d(t)|$ or the squared term
$[x(t) - x_d(t)]^2$ must be used. The term $[x(t) - x_d(t)]$ cannot be
used since it changes sign and the positive and negative errors
cancel each other. In most cases, the response, $x(t)$, should
match the desired response $x_d(t)$, over a certain period of time
(e.g., the first t seconds of the step response, etc.,). Since
more than one point in time or space must be considered, the
maximum deviation is usually not adequate. Therefore, most
optimizations involve integration over the interval of interest.

Thus, performance objectives of the form

$$J = \int_0^T |e| \, dt = \int_0^T |x(t) - x_d(t)| \, dt, \qquad (11.7.1)$$

or

$$J = \int_0^T e^2 \, dt = \int_0^T [x(t) - x_d(t)]^2 \, dt \qquad (11.7.2)$$

are often used. If the cost of operating in a nonoptimal fashion is represented by several variables, the cost function or performance index may take the form,

$$J = \int_0^T [e_1^2 + e_2^2 + \ldots + e_n^2] \, dt . \qquad (11.7.3)$$

In addition to the accumulative error associated with Equation (11.7.3), the optimization may also include known objectives as presented in the previous sections. Thus, the performance index can be expanded to include other terms.

Once the performance index has been defined, the parameters to be optimized p_1, p_2, ... p_j, can be determined. It is best to work first with parameters having the predominant effect. The optimization can proceed to the remaining parameters for the "fine tuning." There is no standard procedure for determining which variables to use or the order for their use. Since the value of the performance index will be a function of the parameters used and the length of time for the integration, Equation (11.7.3) should be written in the form

$$J(T, p_i) = \int_0^T [e_1^2 + e_2^2 + \ldots + e_n^2] \, dt . \qquad (11.7.4)$$

Since $J(T, p_i)$ does not reach its final value until a simulation run is terminated, it is often referred to as a "run function."

With a cost function defined and the parameters to be varied identified, the optimization procedure can be investigated. The search techniques discussed in the previous sections can be used. In this case, an exhaustive search requires a simulation run for each parameter step (i.e., all possible combinations) and an evaluation of the performance index at each point. The minimum (maximum) value of the performance index is stored along with the corresponding set of parameters. At the end of each run, the performance index for that run is compared with the minimum (max- imum) stored from all the previous runs. If the new performance index is less than (greater than) the old minimum (maximum), the old value is discarded and the new minimum (maximum) is stored along with its corresponding parameter values. For a large number of variables having a wide range of values, the exhaustive search can be quite lengthy. As a result, a number of improved techniques have been developed.[2]

One of the improved techniques, the relaxation method, was discussed earlier. A single parameter is varied (i.e., all others are held constant) until a minimum (maximum) value for J is reached. When a value for the first parameter is found which minimizes (maximizes) the performance index, it is held constant while another parameter is varied to determine a new minimum (maximum). There are certain situations in which this method fails and does not proceed to the minimum (maximum). However, the details are beyond the scope of this book.[2]

Most of the improved methods attempt to optimize the changing of parameters through the use of the slope or gradient of the performance index. This can be expressed in the following form

$$\nabla J(p) = \frac{\partial J}{\partial p} .$$

(11.7.5)

The parameter step (or combination of parameter steps) which produces the maximum improvement in the performance index can be determined by trial and error (i.e., stepping in each param- eter to determine the corresponding changes in the performance index). A similar approach calculates the gradient of the performance index and moves to maximize the decrease (increase) of the cost function. This is called the steepest descent method. Although it requires fewer simulation runs, some of the computa- tional advantage is canceled due to the need to solve for the gradient. Also, the method does not always converge to the maximum (minimum).

As indicated previously, these methods may lead to a "local" minimum (maximum). Therefore, some type of global search should be undertaken to determine if there are other local extrema which are more important. The details of most of the optimization procedures are beyond the scope of this book. Hopefully, the material presented here has introduced the subject and can serve as background of a more detailed study.

11.8 OPTIMAL CONTROL

The development of optimal control laws is another important phase of optimization. In recent years, a great deal of effort has been devoted to the optimal control problem. Control algorithms have been developed which achieve specific goals in minimum time or with minimum fuel or energy. This material is also beyond the intended scope of this book and the interested reader is referred to the references at the end of this chapter.

The state space technique introduced in Chapter 7 has been utilized quite successfully in optimal control work. The compact notation is applicable to many other areas and a couple of interesting results will be presented here. In order to describe the optimization problem in state variable form, the state vector, $\underline{x}$ represents several state variables and the targets or objectives of these variables are contained in the vector, $\underline{x}_d(t)$. The error is represented by a vector

$$\underline{e}(t) = [\underline{x}(t) - \underline{x}_d(t)]. \tag{11.8.1}$$

The quadratic form is very useful and is defined

$$\underline{e}^T \underline{W} \, \underline{e} = \sum_{i=1}^{n} \sum_{j=1}^{n} w_{ij} e_i e_j , \tag{11.8.2}$$

where $\underline{W}$ is a square symmetric matrix. The assignment of different values for the terms, w_{ij}, enables the use of different "weightings" for the error. If $w_{ij} = 0$, the corresponding error terms are ignored. The larger the w_{ij} term, the more important a particular error term is considered. If the "weighting" matrix, $\underline{W}$, is an identity matrix, the quadratic form reduces to the sum of the error terms squared. Therefore, the matrix vector form of Equation (11.7.3) can be written in the form

$$J = \int_0^T [\underline{e}^T \underline{W} \, \underline{e}] \, dt. \tag{11.8.3}$$

In going to a vector representation, the parameters can be expressed in the form

$$\underline{p}_n = \begin{bmatrix} p_1 \\ p_2 \\ . \\ . \\ . \\ p_n \end{bmatrix}.$$

(11.8.4)

Thus, Equation (11.7.4) becomes

$$J[T,\underline{p}] = \int_0^T [\underline{e}^T \underline{W} \underline{e}]dt.$$

(11.8.5)

The solution of problems of this type is beyond the scope of this book. However, this discussion has been included to illustrate another class of optimization problems.

11.9 PROBLEMS FOR CHAPTER 11

Problems covering the material of this chapter are identified by section.

11.2.1 Develop a circuit utilizing track-store units to produce waveform shown in Figure 11-9-1.

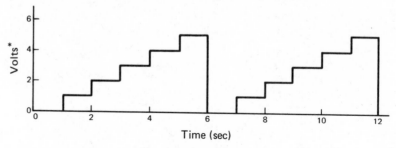

Figure 11-9-1.

11.2.2 Develop a circuit utilizing track-store units with an output that starts at the minus reference and steps to the positive reference in 1.0 Volt* steps which last for 0.5 sec each.

11.2.3 Develop a circuit utilizing track-store units with an output that starts at the positive reference level and steps down to the negative reference in 1.0 Volt* steps which last for 1.0 sec each.

11.2.4 Develop a circuit utilizing an integrator to step the output from 0 to the positive reference in 1 Volt* steps. The integrator should hold each step for 1.0 sec and go from one level to the next level in 0.1 sec.

11.2.5 Develop a circuit utilizing an integrator to step the output from the minus reference to the positive reference level in 1 Volt* steps. The integrator should hold each step for two seconds and go from one level to the next level in 0.15 sec.
*For computers having a reference ±100 Volts, use 10 Volt steps.

11.2.6 Develop a circuit to produce the waveform shown in Figure 11-9-2.

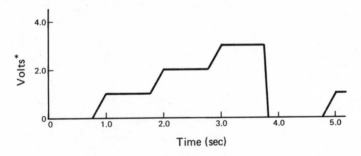

Time (sec)

Figure 11-9-2.

11.2.7 Use analog switches, potentiometers, flip-flops and a summing amplifier to produce the waveform of Figure 11-9-2.

11.2.8 Repeat Problem 11.2.2 using analog switches and potentiometers on a summing amplifier. The analog switches should be controlled by flip-flops.

11.2.9 Repeat Problem 11.2.3 using analog switches and potentiometers on a summing amplifier.

11.3.1   Develop a circuit utilizing track-store units
to solve Equation (11.9.1) for a = 0.1, 0.2,
0.5 and 1.0.   The computer should produce the
solutions on successive runs and stop at the
end of the last run.   The equation to be solved
is

$$\dot{x} + ax = 1.0, \qquad\qquad\qquad (11.9.1)$$

where x(0) = 0.

11.3.2   Repeat Problem 11.3.1 using an integrator to step
the parameter a.

11.3.3   Repeat Problem 11.3.1 using analog switches and
a multiplier to step the parameter a.

11.3.4   Repeat Problem 11.3.1 using analog switches and
potentiometers to step the parameter a.

11.3.5   Develop a circuit to solve Equation (11.9.2) for
the following parameter values: b = 1.0, 2.0,
3.0, 4.0 and 5.0.   The computer should stop at
the end of the last solution.   The result should
be recorded on an xy recorder and observed on a
CRT display.   The equation to be solved is

$$\ddot{x} + b\dot{x} + 2x = 4, \qquad\qquad (11.9.2)$$

where $\dot{x}(0) = x(0) = 0$.

11.3.6   Repeat Problem 11.3.5 for the equation,

$$\ddot{x} + 100(b)\dot{x} + 10,000x = 10,000, \qquad (11.9.3)$$

where $\dot{x}(0) = x(0) = 0$.

11.3.7   Repeat Problem 11.3.5 for the equation

$$\ddot{x} + 0.01(b)\dot{x} + 0.0001x = 1.0, \qquad (11.9.4)$$

where $\overset{\circ}{x}(0) = x(0) = 0$.

11.3.8 Develop a program to automatically solve Equation (11.9.5) for b=8 and a = 5, 10, 15 and 20. The computer should stop following the last solution. Record the solutions on an xy recorder or observe them on a CRT. The equation is,

$$\dddot{x} + 7\ddot{x} + a\dot{x} + bx = 100, \tag{11.9.5}$$

where $\ddot{x}(0) = \dot{x}(0) = x(0) = 0$.

11.3.9 Repeat Problem 11.3.8 with a=15 and b = 2, 4, 6, 8 and 10.

11.3.10 Develop a program to automatically determine the step response of the system represented by the transfer function of Equation (11.9.6). The program should automatically record the response for K = 2, 4, 6 and 8.

$$\frac{C(s)}{R(s)} = \frac{K}{s^3 + 3s^2 + 2s + K} \tag{11.9.6}$$

11.3.11 Repeat Problem 11.3.10 for the system represented by the transfer function shown in Figure 11-9-3.

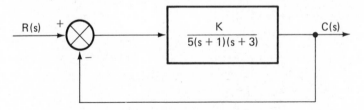

Figure 11-9-3.

11.3.12 Develop a program to automatically record the response for a system described by the state variable equation,

$$\begin{bmatrix} \dot{x}_1 \\ \dot{x}_2 \\ \dot{x}_3 \end{bmatrix} = \begin{bmatrix} 0 & 1 & 0 \\ 0 & 0 & 1 \\ -5 & -7 & -a \end{bmatrix} \begin{bmatrix} x_1 \\ x_1 \\ x_3 \end{bmatrix} + \begin{bmatrix} 0 \\ 0 \\ 1 \end{bmatrix} 1, \tag{11.9.7}$$

where a = 2, 4, 6 and 8, and $\underline{x}(0) = \underline{0}$.

11.5.1   For Equation 11.9.1, develop a program that will
         automatically determine a value for the parameter
         (a) which causes x to be equal 0.5 volts at t=1.0
         sec.

11.5.2   Develop a program that will automatically determine
         the value of the parameter (b) which produces an
         overshoot of 15 percent for the system described
         in Problem 11.3.5.

11.5.3   Repeat Problem 11.5.2 for the system of Problem
         11.3.6.

11.5.4   Repeat Problem 11.5.2 for the system described in
         Problem 11.3.7.

11.5.5   Repeat Problem 11.5.2 for the system described in
         Problem 11.3.8.

11.5.6   Develop a program which will automatically determine
         the value of K which produces a 10 percent overshoot
         in the step response of a system described by Equa-
         tion (11.9.6).

11.5.7   Repeat Problem 11.5.6 for the system described in
         Problem 11.3.11.

11.5.8   Use Equation (11.9.1) with a=0.8 and develop a
         program to automatically determine the value of
         the initial condition, x(0), which causes the
         solution, x(t) to be equal to 1.5 at t=1.0 sec.
         (i.e.,x(1)=1.5).

11.5.9   Use Equation (11.9.2) with b=1.5 and develop an
         initial condition stepping circuit which will
         determine the value for x(0) which causes the
         solution x(t) to be equal to -0.5 when t=1 sec.
         (i.e., x(1) = -0.5).

11.5.10 Develop a program which will automatically determine
         the value of K for which the system described by
         Equation (11.9.6) has zero damping (i.e., the step
         response is oscillatory). Hint: the value of the
         second overshoot is equal to the first overshoot.

11.7.1 Develop a program to determine the values for the initial condition $x(0)$ and the parameter (a) which minimized the integral of the magnitude of the error $[x(t) - x_d(t)]$ for the system of Equation (11.9.1). See Figure 11-9-4 for $x_d(t)$.

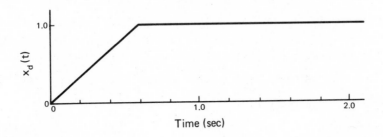

Figure 11-9-4.

11.7.2 Repeat Problem 11.7.1 for $x_d(t)$ shown in Figure 11-9-5.

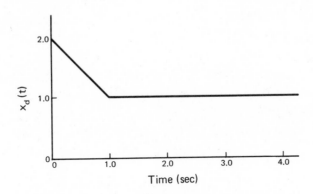

Figure 11-9-5.

11.7.3 Repeat Problem 11.7.1 using the square of the error instead of the magnitude of the error.

11.7.4 Repeat Problem 11.7.2 utilizing the square of the error instead of the magnitude of the error.

11.7.5 Assume that it is desired to model the third-order system described by the transfer function of Equation (11.9.6) with a second-order system. Determine the values of δ and ω_n for a second-order system which minimizes the integral of the magnitude of the error $|[x(t) - x_d(t)]|$, where $x(t)$ is the response of the second-order system and x_d is the response of the system described by the transfer function of Equation (11.9.6).

11.7.6 Repeat Problem 11.7.5 using the square of the error instead of the magnitude of the error.

11.10   REFERENCES FOR CHAPTER 11

1. Bekey, G. A. and W. J. Karplus, Hybrid Computation, John Wiley & Sons, New York, 1968.

2. Bekey, G. A., "System Identification--An Introduction and a Survey," Simulation, Vol. 15, No. 4, pp. 151-166, October, 1973.

3. Sage, A. P., Optimal Control Systems, Prentice-Hall, Inc., Englewood Cliffs, New Jersey, 1968.

4. Wilde, D. J. and C. S. Beightler, Foundations of Optimization, Prentice-Hall, Inc., Englewood Cliffs, New Jersey, 1967.

5. Hannauer, G., Basics of Parallel Hybrid Computers, Publication No. 00-800.3039-0, Electronic Associates, Inc., West Long Branch, New Jersey, November, 1969.

6. Gupta, S. and L. Hasdorff, Fundamentals of Automatic Controls, John Wiley & Sons, New York, 1970.

12

The Digital Computer and Hybrid Computation

12.1 INTRODUCTION

With the exception of brief comments on the classification of hybrid computers in Chapter 8, the digital portion of the hybrid computers discussed in previous chapters has been very limited. The emphasis has been on the use of digital computing elements individually instead of as components in a functional unit. Also, the digital elements operated simultaneously or in parallel with the analog elements. Thus, the *parallel* hybrid computers that have been discussed did not include a fully operational digital computer.

In answering the question "Why Hybrid?", it was stated that the hybrid computer combined the accuracy, memory, convenience and decision capabilities of the digital computer with the speed of the analog computer. The hybrid computers that have been discussed have not used digital computation in the classical sense. They have utilized only a fraction of the memory and decision capability available on the typical digital computer. In order

to complete the picture of hybrid computation, this chapter will
present the fundamentals of the digital computer and its role in
hybrid computation.

   In discussing the digital aspects of hybrid computing, digital
representation of data will be presented first. This is followed
by a discussion of the structure of the typical digital computer.
The problems associated with converting data from analog form to
digital form (ADC) and from digital to analog (DAC) are presented
next. In the remaining sections, requirements for a hybrid
interface are discussed and illustrated. Also, operating characteristics of a hybrid computer are presented and software
requirements outlined. Since the operating details of hybrid
computers vary a great deal, the chapter concentrates on general
principles. Hopefully, this overview of the hybrid computer will
provide a suitable framework to which the reader can add the
knowledge of details acquired in working with a particular hybrid
system.

12.2   DIGITAL REPRESENTATION OF DATA

   In order to carry out arithmetic operations on a digital
computer, it is necessary to format the data in proper form.
From the discussion of Chapters 8, 9 and 10, it is obvious that
the format required for the digital computer is binary in nature.
Therefore, some technique must be available to convert the numerical values of a typical problem to binary form. In this
section, methods for digital representation of data will be
presented and illustrated with several examples.

   In order to provide background for the discussion, a brief
review of number systems is presented first. There are three
requirements for a number system; a base or radix, a set of symbols and a positional notation. This format will be illustrated
with the familiar decimal number system. The base or radix is 10
and the symbols are 0, 1,...,9. Note that there are 10 distinct
symbols. The positional notation is indicated by the decimal or
radix point. The *weight* of the first digit to the left of the
radix point is the base or radix raised to the zero power. In the
decimal number system, this is 10exp(0) = 1, or the unit's position. The weight of the second digit to the left of the radix

point is the base raised to the first power. For the decimal number system, this is 10exp(1) = 10, or the "10" position. With each successive position to the left, the weighting factor increases by one power of the base. Thus, the 10's position is followed by 10exp(2) = 100, 10exp(3) = 1000, etc.

To the right of the radix point, each position is weighted with a negative power of the base or radix. For the decimal number system, the first position to the right of the decimal point is 10exp(-1) = 0.1, or 1/10. The second position is weighted 10exp(-2) = 0.01. Each successive position to the right has an additional negative power of the base in its weighting factor.

In order to evaluate a particular combination of symbols, each digit is multiplied by the weight of its position. The value of the expression is the sum of the contributions from all positions. This is illustrated in Figure 12-2-1. Thus,

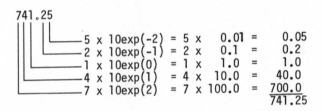

Figure 12-2-1. The evaluation of a decimal number

data is represented in the decimal number system by a decimal digit (0,1,..,9) with a weighting factor determined by its position relative to the radix point.

In the binary number system, the base or radix is two, and therefore, two symbols are required. The most widely used symbols are 0 and 1. The weight of each position is determined by the binary or radix point. The first position to the left of the binary point has a positional weight of the base, 2, raised to the zero power, 2exp(0) = 1. The second position to the left is weighted 2exp(1) = 2. The third position is 2exp(2) = 4. Each successive position to the left is weighted according to a binary sequence 1, 2, 4, 8, 16,...,2exp(n-1).

Each binary digit (abbreviated bit) to the right of the binary point is weighted with negative powers of the base. Thus, the weighting terms are; $2exp(-1) = 1/2$, $2exp(-2) = 1/4$, $2exp(-3)= 1/8,\ldots,2exp(-n) = 1/[2exp(n)]$. An example is shown in Figure 12-2-2. Thus, the binary number 1010.101 is equal to the decimal

```
1010.101
 ││││ │││
 ││││ ││└──── 1 x 2exp(-3) = 1 x 0.125 = 0.125
 ││││ │└───── 0 x 2exp(-2) = 0 x 0.25  = 0.0
 ││││ └────── 1 x 2exp(-1) = 1 x 0.5   = 0.5
 ││││ ─────── 0 x 2exp(0)  = 0 x 1.0   = 0.0
 │││└──────── 1 x 2exp(1)  = 1 x 2.0   = 2.0
 ││└───────── 0 x 2exp(2)  = 0 x 4.0   = 0.0
 │└────────── 1 x 2exp(3)  = 1 x 8.0   = 8.0
                                       ──────
                                       10.625
```

Figure 12-2-2. The evaluation of a binary number

10.625. In most situations involving the manipulation of numbers, the base or radix is assumed to be 10 and is not usually indicated. However, in problems involving several number systems, it is necessary to indicate the base. This is usually done with a subscript. In this case, $1010.101_2 = 10.625_{10}$. As an additional example, note that $1101.10_2 = 13.5_{10}$.

The procedure illustrated in Figure 12-2-2 provides a method for converting from a binary number to an equivalent decimal number. There are several ways to convert from a digital form to a binary form. The most obvious way is to determine the largest power of two present in the decimal number. For example, consider the decimal number represented in Figure 12-2-1, 741.25_{10}. First, note that the powers of 2 are: 1, 2, 4, 8, 16, 32, 64, 128, 256, 512, 1024,$\ldots,2^n$ (expressed in base 10). Obviously, 512 is present and 1024 is not. Therefore, the bit weighted 512 is needed. If the 512 bit is present, $741.25 - 512 = 229.25$ has not been represented. The largest power of 2 in 229.25 is 128. Therefore, the bit weight 256 is not needed but the 128 bit is needed. If the 128 bit is included, the remainder is $229.25 - 128 = 101.25$. The largest binary power in 101.25 is 64, which leaves $101.25 - 64 = 37.25$. Up to this point, the bits with a weighting of 512, 128 and 64 are required. In order to represent 37.25_{10}, the bit weight 32 is needed and leaves $37.25 - 32 = 5.25$. The remaining

5.25_{10} can be represented by the 4 and the 1 bit leaving only 0.25_{10} to be converted. This is obviously, $2exp(-2)$ or the second bit to the right of the binary point. Thus, 1011100101.01_2 is the binary equivalent of 741.25_{10}. This can be checked by converting back to the base 10 as shown in Figure 12-2-2.

The intuitive procedure of the preceding paragraph is too cumbersome for large numbers and a more orderly procedure is illustrated in Figure 12-2-3. The portion of the number to the

STEP I. CONVERTING THE PORTION TO THE LEFT OF THE RADIX POINT.

	Quotient	Remainder	Bit Weight
741 ÷ 2 =	370	1	1
370 ÷ 2 =	185	0	2
185 ÷ 2 =	92	1	4
92 ÷ 2 =	46	0	8
46 ÷ 2 =	23	0	16
23 ÷ 2 =	11	1	32
11 ÷ 2 =	5	1	64
5 ÷ 2 =	2	1	128
2 ÷ 2 =	1	0	256
1 ÷ 2 =	0	1	512

$$\therefore 741_{10} = 1011100101_2$$

STEP II. CONVERTING THE PORTION TO THE RIGHT OF THE RADIX POINT.

	Fraction	Whole Number	Bit Weight
0.25 x 2 =	0.5	0	1/2
0.50 x 2 =	0.0	1	1/4

$$\therefore 0.25_{10} = 0.01_2$$

STEP III. COMBINING THE RESULTS OF STEPS I AND II.

$$\therefore 741.25_{10} = 1011100101.01_2$$

Figure 12-2-3. Converting from base 10 to base 2

left of the decimal is converted to binary form by repeated division by 2, saving the remainder and proceeding with the quotient.
The fractional portion of the number is converted to binary by
repeated multiplication by 2, setting aside whole numbers that
occur and proceeding with the fractional portion. The division
process is continued until a quotient of 0 is produced, and the
multiplication process is repeated until a fraction of 0 is
obtained. Since there are fractional numbers which will never
produce a fraction of 0 when multiplied by 2, the binary representation does not always terminate (e.g., 1/3). Thus, there are
many decimal numbers for which there is no exact binary equivalent.

The techniques presented here can be extended to other radix
values. Base 8 (i.e., the octal number system) and Base 16 (i.e.,
the hexidecimal number system) are frequently used in computer
programming. However, it should be noted that these systems are
utilized for the convenience of the programmer and operator. The
computer operates in binary.

The techniques of the preceding paragraphs can be used to
convert any number to an equivalent binary form. As a result,
any number can be represented by a series of bi-stable devices.
For example, 741.25_{10} could be represented by 12 flip-flops set
to the appropriate logic 1 or 0 states. This form of data
representation is called *parallel* since all bits of the number
are available and represented simultaneously. The number could
also be represented by a single flip-flop taking on the appropriate state at a given instant. For example, each period or
cycle of a clock pulse (e.g., see Section 10.5) could be used to
time or synchronize the operation. In most cases, the least
significant (i.e., lowest weight) bit is represented first.
Thus, the sequence of logic states shown in Figure 12-2-4 represents the number 741.25_{10}. Both parallel and serial representations
are useful. Since one data path is required for each bit in
parallel representation and only one data path is required for the
serial technique, the serial form is preferred for data transmission.
However, serial transmission requires a longer period of time to
transmit the same information provided in only one clock cycle of

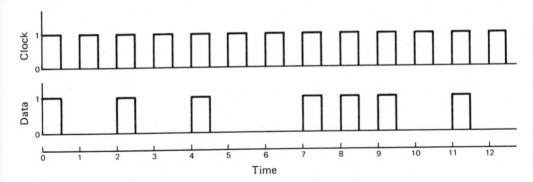

Figure 12-2-4. Sequential data representation of 741.25_{10}

parallel transmission. Most digital computers use parallel data
representation internally and communicate with peripheral devices
with serial or parallel techniques depending upon the speed required.

In Chapter 8, accuracy listed as one of the attributes of
the digital computer. It is interesting to see how this can be
achieved. First, note that a single bi-stable device such as a
flip-flop can occupy either of the two possible states. Thus, the
precision is one-part in two-parts or 50 percent. Since two flip-
flops can occupy four distinct states (i.e., 00, 01, 10 and 11),
they provide a precision of one-part in four-parts or 25 percent.
A group of three bits has eight possible states and yields 12.5
percent accuracy. When bits are grouped to represent data, the
group is referred to as a *byte* (usually 4 or 8 bits) or a *word*
(usually 8 to 64 bits). Also, a *word* is frequently subdivided
into several *bytes*. In general, n bits can have 2exp(n) distinct
states or one-part in 2exp(n) parts. Thus, an 8 bit byte (or word)
has a precision of one-part in 256 parts or approximately 0.4
percent. A 10 bit byte gives one-part in 1024 or approximately
0.1 percent, and 12 bits provide one-part in 4096 which is approximately 0.025 percent. The common word sizes available in
digital computers are: 8, 12, 16, 24, 32 and 60 bits. Also, most
machines permit the use of two words to represent a single data
point in order to increase the accuracy (i.e., double precision).
Thus, accuracy is dictated by the number of bits used in the
representation.

12.3 DIGITAL COMPUTER FUNDAMENTALS

Since most people think and work in the decimal number system, it would be convenient if digital computers operated in this manner. However, this would require elements which are capable of recognizing and operating on the 10 distinct levels representing the basic symbols. By going to a binary system, the computing elements need only to distinguish between two levels, and therefore, bi-stable devices such as magnetic cores and saturating electronic circuits can be used. By providing sufficient separation between the two levels, the tolerance for each level can have considerable latitude. Thus, all digital computer operations are carried out in binary. This section will present the internal binary operations of a digital computer along with the input/output and memory requirements. The presentation will not be rigorous or detailed. The intent is to provide an understanding of the basic operation of the typical digital computer. If additional details are required, there are numerous books on the subject and references at the end of this chapter provide an excellent starting point.

A simplified block diagram for the typical digital computer is shown in Figure 12-3-1. In most cases, data and program instructions are contained in memory. Thus, both the information

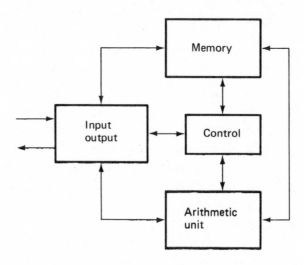

Figure 12-3-1. Block diagram of a digital computer

to be operated upon and the sequence of operations to be carried out are stored in memory. By starting the computer at the beginning of a program or sequence of instructions, the computer is capable of transferring from memory to the arithmetic unit the operand (i.e., the quantity to be operated upon) and the instruction or operation to be performed. Upon completion of a specific task, the results can be returned to a specified location in memory or maintained in the arithmetic unit for interaction with the following sequence of instructions. The input/output block enables the computer to communicate with external devices.

The basic element of the arithmetic unit is the binary adder. In order to understand the operation of the binary adder, consider the addition operation of Figure 12-3-2. In this illustration,

$$
\begin{array}{rcl}
29.25 & = & 11101.010 \\
+\ 21.50 & = & 10101.100 \\
\hline
50.75 & = & 110010.110
\end{array}
$$

Figure 12-3-2. Decimal and binary addition

29.25 is added to 21.5 in the decimal number system to produce 50.75. The addend and the augend are converted to binary and the addition is carried out in binary. The sums are equivalent as they should be.

The numbers selected for the illustration represent all possible combinations required of a binary adder. In the least significant position, 0 + 0, with no carry from a preceding addition, produces a sum of 0 and it is not necessary to carry information to the next binary position. In the second and third positions, 0 + 1 and 1 + 0, with no carry in, produced a sum of 1 with no carry to the next position. The next column (i.e., the first column to the left of the binary point) requires the addition, 1 + 1, to produce a sum of 0 and a carry of 1 to the next bit position. This is obvious since 1 + 1 = 2 in base 10 and 2_{10} in binary is 10_2.

The second position to the left of the binary point has 0 + 0, with a carry in from the previous addition. The sum is $0 + 0 + 1 = 1_2$, with no carry over to the next position. In the 4 bit position, 1 + 1, with no carry from the previous addition, produces the sum

of 0 and a carry to the next highest bit position.   In the 8 bit
position, 0 + 1, plus the carry from the 4 bit position, produces
the sum of 0 and a carry over into the 16 bit position.   In   the
16 bit position, 1 + 1, plus the carry from the 8 bit position,
produces a sum of 1 and a carry into the next higher bit position.
However, both the addend and the augend are assumed to be   0   and
the resulting sum is 1 as shown in Figure 12-3-2.   The action of
the binary adder described in the previous paragraph is summarized
in the true table of Figure 12-3-3.

Row Number	Addend A	Augend B	Carry In C_i	Sum S	Carry Out C_o
0	0	0	0	0	0
1	0	0	1	1	0
2	0	1	0	1	0
3	0	1	1	0	1
4	1	0	0	1	0
5	1	0	1	0	1
6	1	1	0	0	1
7	1	1	1	1	1

Figure 12-3-3.   Truth table for binary adder

The methods of Section 9.7 can be used to design   a   logic
circuit which produces the desired outputs.   Recall that the rows
of the truth table with a logic 1 at the output are   used   and

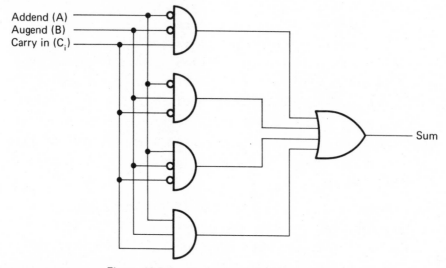

Figure 12-3-4.   Sum output of a binary adder

variables with a 1 input appear in true form, while variables with a 0 at the input are complemented. In the truth table of Figure 12-3-2, the sum column has a logic 1 in rows 1, 2, 4 and 7. The circuit for the sum output is shown in Figure 12-3-4. The circuit for the carry to the next higher bit position is designed using rows 3, 5, 6 and 7. The resulting circuit is shown in Figure 12-3-5. The sum and carry circuits can be simplified by

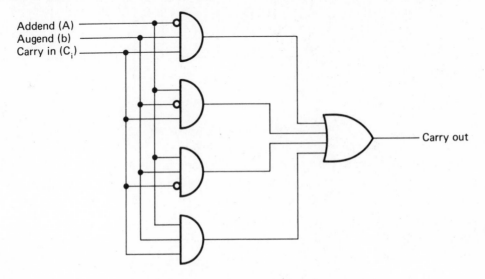

Figure 12-3-5. Carry circuit of a binary adder

applying logic minimization techniques. However, this is beyond the scope of this book and the interested reader should see references (1, 2 or 3). The sum and carry circuits are usually combined to make a *full adder* and are treated as a functional unit with the symbols shown in Figure 12-3-6.

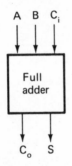

Figure 12-3-6. Binary full adder symbol

In the previous section, it was stated that most digital computers used parallel data representation and manipulation. For example, two 4 bit binary numbers could be added with the circuit shown in Figure 12-3-7. A parallel adder for any word

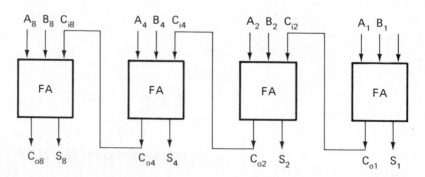

Figure 12-3-7.   Four bit parallel adder

length could be constructed in the same manner. An adder circuit, similar to the one of Figure 12-3-7, is basic to most arithmetic units.

The next arithmetic operation to be discussed is subtraction. A truth table for binary subtraction similar to Figure 12-3-3 could be constructed and a circuit design for subtracting binary numbers. However, an adder can be made to subtract by a process called complement arithmetic. Instead of gating the number to be subtracted to the adder, the complement of the number is used. The resulting output is the binary difference of the two numbers. Most computers utilize this feature and represent negative numbers in complement form. Although these details are quite interesting, they are beyond the scope of this book. See references (1, 2 or 3) for additional information.

The next arithmetic operations to be considered are multiplication and division. The truth table for binary multiplication could be constructed and used to design a circuit to multiply two binary numbers. Also, multiplication can be treated as a series of additions and carried out in that fashion. In a similar manner, the process of division can be treated as a series of subtractions. Thus, without going into details, it is obvious that the basic arithmetic operations can be carried out in binary.

In addition to the basic arithmetic operations, most computers are capable of right and left shifting (e.g., see Section 10.5) and certain logical operations. The simplified arithmetic unit is shown in Figure 12-3-8.

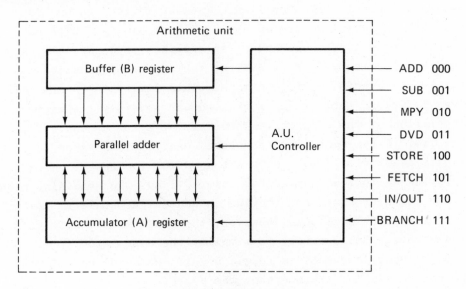

Figure 12-3-8. Simplified arithmetic unit

The A and B registers of the arithmetic unit of Figure 12-3-8 hold 8 bit binary words. Instead of an additional register to hold the result of arithmetic operations on the contents of registers A and B, most computers place the results in the A register. This is the reason for the bi-directional arrows between the adder and the A register. It is also the reason that the A register is also called the *accumulator* register. The B register holds the data from the memory and acts as a *buffer* register. For this reason it is often called the buffer register or memory buffer register.

Now that the basic operations of arithmetic units have been presented, the next block to be discussed is the control block. As noted previously, the memory contains both the data and the instructions for the computer. Therefore, for the 8 bit machine shown in Figure 12-3-8, an 8 bit word will be used to provide instructions. Most instructions provide two kinds of information: the operation to be performed and the identity of the *operand*

to be operated upon. Thus, the 8 bit word should be divided
into two parts. The first part will identify the operation and
the second portion will specify the operand. Since 8 operations
are shown, three bits (i.e., eight possible combinations) are
necessary to specify the operation. These bits are shown in
Figure 12-3-8 and called the *op code*. The remaining 5 bits can
be used to identify the operand by specifying its location (i.e.,
its address in memory). With 5 bits, the number of locations is
restricted to 2exp(5) = 32 locations. This limits the number of
storage locations that can be addressed and severely restricts
the operation of the computer. There are ways to expand this
capability. Since most computers have longer word lengths or
more bits available, 3 to 8 bits are used for the operation code
and provide up to 256 commands or instructions. The remaining bits
are used for addressing and provide an address capability in
excess of 16,000 locations. However, the small word length used
here was chosen deliberately to simplify the discussion.

Since some instructions (e.g., a shift command) do not require an address for the operand, the address portion of the
operation code is often used for other purposes. For example, in
the case of the shift command, the direction and length of the
shift can be specified with the extra bits. Therefore, the address
portion of the instruction word is utilized for a number of purposes.
Additional features are provided with the arithmetic units of most
computers. However, for the sake of simplicity, the details will not
be included in this discussion.

The next portion of the computer to be discussed is represented by the block labeled control in Figure 12-3-1. In most
computers, the control components are distributed throughout the
computer and the block diagram of Figure 12-3-1 is not intended to
imply a single control *box*. The control elements perform a number
of tasks. Perhaps the most important control function is decoding
instructions to determine the operations to be performed. The
control unit also controls the flow of information in the computer
to provide data for the operations. Additional tasks are associated with communicating through the input/output unit to peripheral
devices. Also, some type of control is needed to supervise the

fetch and store operations of the memory.   The control unit
performs many other tasks.   However, only the major features will
be discussed here.

In order to understand major features of a control unit, consider first the problem of decoding instructions. The instructions
are usually transferred from memory to the instruction register
where it is held for decoding.   Figure 12-3-9 illustrates a circuit

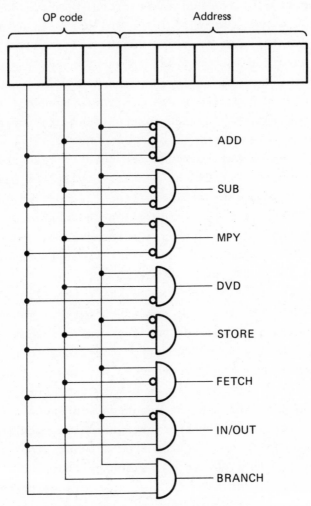

Figure 12-3-9. Instruction decoding circuit

to decode the operation bits of the simple 8-bit machine being used
as an example for this discussion. The type of instructions and

decoding techniques are characteristic of a particular computer. However, the simple example presented here is indicative of what must be done.

The address portion of the instruction is used to determine the source of data to be operated upon when the instruction is executed. For example, an add command adds the contents of the A register to the contents of the location in memory specified in the address portion of the add instruction. Thus, address bits are used to cause the memory to fetch the contents of the required address and transfer them to the B register for adding. The same procedure is used for the subtract command except that either the B register or the A register is complemented before adding. The multiply and divide operations are similar. However, the manner in which the multiply and divide instructions are implemented may require additional features.

The input and output commands are used to take information into the computer and output the results of digital computation. In this case, the address portion of the instruction is used to indicate the source of input information and the location to which output is to be directed. The data paths are controlled by the control unit with gating techniques similar to those discussed in Chapters 9 and 10 (e.g., see Section 10.3).

The shift instruction is used to shift the bits of the A register either right or left. For the eight bit machine used in this discussion, the address portion would indicate the direction of the shift and the number of positions to be shifted.

Under normal operating procedures, the instructions or commands are stored sequentially in memory and a program is *executed* by stepping through the sequence and executing each instruction in turn. The branch instruction is used to cause the memory to fetch an instruction from a point other than the next location. It is a method of switching from one program to another program. It can also be used to avoid stepping sequentially through portions of the memory utilized for data. If a data word is decoded as an instruction, serious malfunctions could be initiated.

The last function of the control unit to be discussed is
the means by which the computer steps or sequences through a
series of commands making up a program. This is accomplished
by means of a *program* or *place* register. This register contains
the address of the next instruction to be fetched from memory
when the present instruction is complete. Each time an instruction is transferred from memory, the contents of the P register
are increased by one and this determines the next instruction
scheduled for execution. The branch instruction permits the
computer to skip over a particular command or a whole series of
commands. Therefore, execution of a branch instruction causes the
machine to execute the instruction located at the address specified in the address portion of the branch command. Also, the
contents of the P register are changed to the address specified
by the branch command.

The memory block represents the portion of the computer
used to store instructions and data. The memory contains magnetic
cores or semiconductor devices capable of storing and retrieving
a binary pattern of ones and zeros. In the store mode, the memory
stores the contents of the A register in the location specified by
the address portion of a store command. Also, the memory can
fetch from storage the contents of a memory location specified in
the address portion of a fetch command. Thus, the memory fetches
and stores in response to the fetch and store commands. Also, the
memory fetches in response to the address portion of arithmetic
operations.

In order to provide additional understanding of the computer
being described, the principle registers and their interrelations
are presented in Figure 12-3-10. In Figure 12-3-10, all data
paths are parallel and identified by the heavy interconnecting
lines. The number of bits transmitted in parallel is shown next
to the lines. The narrow lines are used to indicate control
paths. The number of control bits transmitted in parallel is
shown by each of the interconnecting lines. A summary of the
machine is provided in Figure 12-3-11.

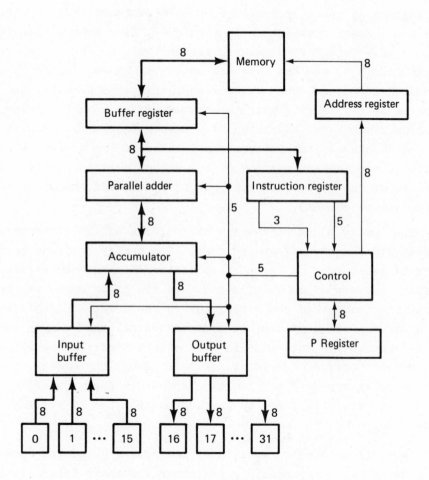

Figure 12-3-10. Computer organization

Operation	Mnemonic Abbreviation	Operation Code	Function
Addition	ADD	000	This command adds the contents of the A register to the contents of the memory location specified in the address portion of the add command. The result of the addition is placed in the A, accumulator, register. The original contents of the A register are destroyed.
Subtraction	SUB	001	The contents of the memory location specified by the address portion of the instruction are subtracted from the contents of the A register. The difference is held in the A register and the old contents of A register are destroyed.
Multiply	MPY	010	The contents of the A register are multiplied by the contents of the memory location specified in the address portion of the command. The most significant bits of the product are stored in the accumulator register.
Division	DVD	011	The contents of the A register are divided by the contents of the location specified in the address portion of the command. The quotient is placed in the A register and the original contents of the A register are destroyed.
Store	STA	100	The contents of the A register are stored in the memory location specified by the address portion of the command.
Fetch	LDA	101	The contents of the memory location specified in the address portion of the command are placed into the A register.

Input/Output	IOA	110	If the address portion of the command contains 0-15, the command is an input command and the contents of the channel specified in the address are placed in the A register. If the address portion of the command contains an address 16-31, the command is an output command and the contents of the A register are gated to the output channel identified in the address portion of the command.
Branch	BRA	111	The P register is changed to the five bits specified in the address portion of the branch command. Thus, the machine can be caused to branch to a new program and begin executing instructions in that sequence.

Figure 12-3-11.   Command summary

In order to provide additional understanding of the operation of the simple computer described here, an example problem will be presented in the next section. Before leaving this subject, it should be noted that many computers incorporate additional working registers. For more information on the organization of computers of this type, see reference (11) at the end of this chapter.

12.4   DIGITAL COMPUTER OPERATION

In order to illustrate the operation of the simple computer presented in the previous section, the step-by-step execution of a sample program will be presented in this section. For this illustration, assume that it is desired to take an 8 bit digital value from input channel 1, add to it a constant previously stored in memory and output the result to channel 16. The result should also be stored in memory. A flow chart for this simple program is shown in Figure 12-4-1. The program steps required to carry out the desired tasks are summarized as follows:

1. Input to the A register from channel 1.
2. Add a constant to the input value.
3. Output the result to channel 16.
4. Store the result in memory.
5. Go to the next task.

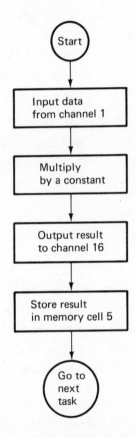

Figure 12-4-1. Program flow chart

Now that a step-by-step procedure has been developed for the desired task, the corresponding computer instructions can be determined. In order to carry out step 1, an input command is required to take data into the A register from input channel 1.

The proper command for the input operation can be determined with
the aid of Figure 12-3-11. For this particular case, the command
is

IOA,1 ,   (12.4.1)

which is the abbreviated (i.e., mnemonic) form for the command.
The corresponding binary code is 11000001.

The next operation requires the addition of a constant to
the input value now contained in A register. Before this command
can be encoded, the location in memory of the constant must be
determined. Assume that it has been assigned to memory location
3 and its value is 7. Now, using the assumed information, the
command can be written,

ADD,3 ,   (12.4.2)

where the 3 refers to the memory address. The binary code for
this command is 00000011. When this command is executed, the result of the addition is contained in the A register awaiting
further operations.

The command to output the result of the addition to channel
16 is

IOA,16 ,   (12.4.3)

which has a binary code, 11010000. Since the execution of the
input/output command copies the contents of the A register into
the buffer for output channel 16 and leaves the contents of the
A register undisturbed, a simple store command is all that is
required to put the result of the addition in memory. However,
the desired memory location for storing the result must be known.
Assume that it is desired to place the result of the addition in
memory location 5. The store command can now be written

STA,5 ,   (12.4.4)

which has a corresponding binary code, 10000101.

This completes the required sequence of commands. However,
before they can be utilized, they must be loaded into the memory.
Thus far, locations 3 and 5 have been used. In selecting the
memory location for the program, it is important to keep in mind
the manner in which the instructions are executed. The execution

of this program will be initiated by setting the P register to the
address of the first instruction of the program and initiating the
memory cycle.   The content of the corresponding location in memory is transferred to the B register.   Since the memory fetch was
in response to the P register, the data from the memory location
is transferred to the instruction register for decoding and execution.   Assume that this program is to be loaded in memory
starting at location 6.   The use of this starting address results
in the memory content shown in Figure 12-4-2.   In   the   previous

Memory Location	Contents	Comments
0	*	
1	*	
2	*	
3	00000111	Data Constant = 7
4	*	
5	*	Result Will Be Stored Here
6	11000001	IOA,1
7	00000011	ADD,3
8	11010000	IOA,16
9	10000101	STA,5
10	111xxxxx	BRA,xxxxx
11	*	

*Memory Locations May Contain Any Combination of Ones and Zeros.

Figure **12-4-2.**   Memory contents

discussion, the branch command was not encoded.   Since the P register will advance automatically from 9 to 10 when the STA 5
command is executed, the contents of location 10 will be fetched
from memory and treated as an instruction on the next memory cycle.
Therefore, location 10 should contain the first command for a new
program, or as shown, a branch to some other program.

In many cases, a program is followed by a section of core
devoted to data for the program.   It is very important to prevent
the P register from causing the computer to sequence or step into
a memory location containing a data word.   If the contents of a
data location are assumed to be an instruction (i.e.,fetched from
memory in response to the P register and not the address specifi-

cation of an instruction), the binary pattern of the data word would be decoded and treated as an instruction. Thus, it might cause the computer to execute any of the allowable instructions and cause considerable difficulties. Thus, the command BRAxxxxx has been included to cause the computer to branch to location xxxxx. Notice that a BRA,10, command would cause the computer to *hang up* (i.e., branching to its own location and executing the branch command by branching again to location 10).

In order to cause the program to be executed, the memory address of the first command in the program must be placed in the P register and a memory fetch initiated. In this case, 6 is placed in the P register and the corresponding instruction is fetched and transferred to the instruction register. The first three bits are decoded, 110 = IOA, and the address portion is used to enable a data path from input channel 1 to the A register. For this illustration, assume that the digital data available at channel 1 is 12 = 0001100. Following the execution of this command the register contents are:

A = 00001100   B = 00000000   I = 10100001   P = 00000111.

Note that the P register has advanced by 1.

A memory fetch for the next value of the P register is initiated next. The instruction stored at memory location 7 is routed through the B register to the I register and decoded as an ADD command. The command calls for the contents of memory location 3 to be added to the contents of the A register. Once the command is decoded as an ADD command, the contents of the address portion of the instructions are gated to the memory address register by the control unit. A memory fetch is initiated and the contents of location 3 are transferred to the B register and an ADD cycle initiated. The result of the ADD are placed in the A register. Following the execution of the ADD,3, command, the register contents are:

A = 00010011   B = 00000111   I = 00000011   P = 00001000 .

Again, note that the P register has been advanced by 1.

On the next memory cycle, the contents of the location 8 are fetched from memory and transferred to the I register. The command,

IOA,16, is decoded and a path from the A register to output channel 16 is established. Following the execution of this command, the register contents are:

A = 00010011   B = 00000111   I = 11001110   P = 00001001.

The P register has now advanced to 9 and the computer is ready for the next cycle.

When the command STA,5, is decoded, the contents of the A register are routed to the B register and a memory store cycle initiated. Following the execution of this command, the register contents are:

A = 00010011   B = 00010011   I = 01000101   P = 00001010.

Note that the A register still contains the information that was copied or stored into memory location 5. Memory location 5 now contains 0010011 and the BRAx command is fetched from memory and transferred to the I register. After the BRA command is decoded and executed, the register contents are:

A = 00010011   B = 00010011   I = 111xxxxx   P = 000xxxxx.

The next command to be executed is whatever is found in memory location xxxxx. Hopefully, it is the first instruction of a program to carry out the next task.

In order to illustrate the importance of branching to the proper address, assume the computer branches to memory location 3 which contains a data word. If the contents of memory location 3 are treated as an instruction instead of a data word, the decoding process would indicate that it is the command, ADD,7. This would cause the computer to add the contents of memory location 7 to whatever was contained in the A register. Since there is no way to distinguish a data word from an instruction word, this is a very important point.

One immediate reaction to the computer that has been used for this discussion is the limitation imposed by only five bits of address. Since five binary variables can represent only 32 possible combinations, only 32 memory locations can be addressed. If this were the limit of the memory capacity for this computer, the computer would have no practical value. However, by dividing

the memory into sections or pages of 16 locations, bits 4-7 could
be used to address any one of the 16 locations in a given section.
Bit number 3 is then used to indicate whether the address is in
the present section (i.e., bit 3 = 0) or in the next section (i.e.,
bit 3 = 1). Thus, the computer can be gradually stepped through
a whole series of sections, and therefore, use many more locations
than the original 32. A similar technique is used on the PDP-8
computers manufactured by the Digital Equipment Corporation[4] The
number of commands that can be executed by the computer illustrated
here is also somewhat limited. However, techniques exist for
expanding this capacity as well.

Both the computer and the example program presented here have
been kept as simple as possible. However, they should provide an
understanding of the basic organization and programming of a
digital computer.

12.5   DIGITAL COMPUTER PROGRAMMING

The program developed for the simple example in the previous
section illustrated some difficulties associated with digital
computer programming. The determination of binary combinations
required for each machine operation is very tedious and time
consuming. The process of encoding the binary instructions is
called "machine language" programming. Fortunately, a number of
aids have been developed to assist with programming.

The most basic programming aid is an *assembler*[6] Instead of
writing the binary code required for each instruction, an assembler
permits the programmer to write the mnemonic or abbreviated form
for a given command. Also, the address and number constants can
be written in decimal numbers. A form of assembly language program statements is shown in Equations (12.4.1),...,(12.4.4).   In
addition, many assemblers permit the use of names or labels for
data and points in the program. Thus, the tedium of keeping track
of addresses and locations in a program are assumed by the assembler.
Obviously, an assembler is a very useful device and programming in
assembly language is much easier than attempting to develop programs directly in machine language.

Actually, the assembler is a computer program which takes the
assembly language program as input data and produces the equiva-

lent machine language program as output data.   Thus, a program
written in assembly language is processed on the computer by the
assembler prior to the execution of the resulting machine language
program.

Although the assembler relieves the programmer of considerable
detail, computation involving equations or complicated mathematical
operations still requires a great deal of effort.   In order to
avoid this, *compilers* have been implemented[7]   A compiler permits
the programmer to work in a language more compatible with a given
field of application.   For example, the FORTRAN (formula trans-
lation) compiler is designed to assist with the development of
programs involving mathematical formulas.   Other special purpose
compilers have been developed for programming problems in other
areas.   The compiler takes as an input the program listing in
"compiler language" and produces a machine language program.

Another programming aid that should be mentioned is an
interpreter. The interpreter decodes high level language
statements and performs the indicated operations before moving
to the next statement to be interpreted.

There are many other aspects of programming that could be
discussed.   However, the terms that have been introduced will be
adequate for the discussions that follow.

12.6 DIGITAL-TO-ANALOG CONVERSION

Before a digital computer can provide an input to an analog
or continuous system, it is necessary to convert from the digital
format discussed in Section 12.2 to the properly scaled analog
form.   Techniques for digital-to-analog conversion (DAC) will be
presented in this section.   The inverse problem, analog-to-digital
conversion (ADC) will be discussed in the next section.

For this discussion, assume the digital format consists of
the 8 bit data word of the computer discussed in previous sections.
Although most hybrid systems utilize longer digital words, the
principles are identical and the shorter word length will simplify
the discussion.   If both positive and negative values are to be
considered, one bit will be required to indicate the algebraic
sign.   Usually, the left or most significant bit is a 0 for positive values and a 1 for the negative range.   With one bit set

aside for algebraic sign, only 7 bits remain to represent the magnitude. As noted previously, this permits 2exp(7) distinct combinations or 128 different levels. This enables a precision of one part in 128 parts or better than 1% accuracy. While this is adequate for some applications, most systems will have 10, 12 or perhaps 15 bits. Since 10 bits yield 1,024 distinct levels, the accuracy is better than 0.1%.

The basic approach for determining the analog equivalent of a digital value is the assignemnt of "weight" or contribution to each bit of the digital word. The contributions from the bits are then summed to determine the combined effect. For example, with 7 bits or 128 levels, a 10 volt range can be covered if the least significant bit represents 0.1 volts and all other bits are weighted according to a binary scale. Thus, the bits would be 0.1, 0.2, 0.4, 0.8, 1.6, 3.2 and 6.4 volts, where 0.1 is the weight of the least significant bit. This provides a range of ±12.7 volts. The additional range is sometimes useful and avoids errors associated with values at maximum range. If it is desired to cover the 10 volt range exactly, then the least significant bit should be evaluated at 10/128 = 0.0781 volts. If 0.1 volts is used for the least significant bit, the circuit shown in Figure 12-6-1 can be used to convert from a digital form to an equivalent analog voltage.

In order to understand the operation of the digital-to-analog converter shown in Figure 12-6-1, first note that the most significant bit determines the reference polarity applied to the converter. Positive values are represented with a 0 in the sign bit and result in the application of the negative reference. However, the resulting output is positive due to the inversion associated with the operational amplifier. The presence of a binary 1 in a particular bit closes the corresponding analog switch. This connects the appropriate pot and reference voltage to the amplifier input and its contribution is summed to produce a corresponding output. There are many circuits that can be used for digital-to-analog conversion. Hopefully, the circuit shown in Figure 12-6-1 will indicate the nature of the problem and provide an understanding of the approach.

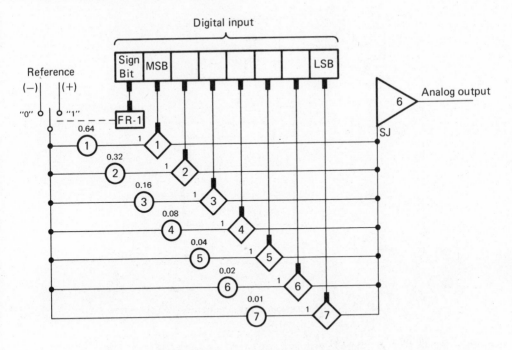

Figure 12-6-1. Digital-to-analog converter

12.7 ANALOG-TO-DIGITAL CONVERSION

Analog-to-digital conversion is more complicated than digital-to-analog conversion. In addition, there are several techniques to choose from and each method has distinct advantages and disadvantages. Thus, the technique selected for a particular application is dependent upon the required accuracy, speed and cost. In keeping with the introductory nature of this book, only a couple of the more popular methods will be discussed. There are numerous articles and books available on the subject.[9]

Perhaps the most widely used technique for analog-to-digital conversion is the successive approximation method. Although it is not the fastest method, it is faster than most techniques and is relatively easy to fabricate. It requires a comparator, a digital control circuit and a digital-to-analog converter. The operation will be explained with the aid of the block diagram in Figure 12-7-1. In order to understand the operation of the converter,

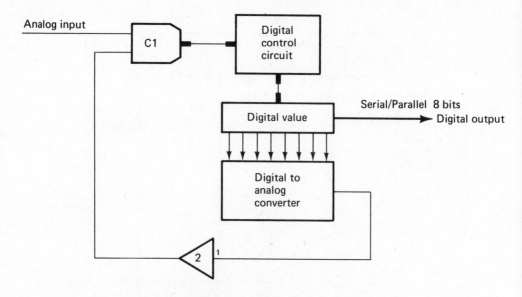

Figure 12-7-1. Successive approximation A-to-D converter

assume that the digital equivalent of an analog voltage of +4.46
volts is desired. Also, assume that the digital control circuit
initially sets all bits of the digital register to 0.

The first task is to determine the algebraic sign. With all
bits of the digital register set at 0, the digital-to-analog converter produces an output of 0 which is fed back to the comparator.
Since the net analog input is positive, the output of the comparator will be a logic 1 and this signal is used to indicate the
need of a positive digital equivalent. Thus, the sign bit remains
at logic 0. If the analog input is negative, the comparator output would be logic 0 and indicate the need to make the sign bit
equal to logic 1. For the assumed input, the sign bit will be 0.

Once the correct algebraic sign has been determined, the
conversion of the magnitude can begin. In the successive approximation method, the most significant bit is set to 1. If the bit
weights of the previous section are used, (i.e., 0.1, 0.2, 0.4,
0.8, 1.6, 3.2 and 6.4 volts), the digital-to-analog converter
produces 6.4 volts at its output. This value is inverted and
causes the comparator to go to the 0 state since +4.46 - 6.5 is
less than 0. The digital control circuit uses this signal to
return the most significant bit to 0.

Now that it has been determined that the most significant bit will not be needed, the next most significant bit will be set to the 1 state. The digital-to-analog converter produces 3.2 volts. When this is inverted and compared with the input, the output of the comparator is logic 1 since +4.46 - 3.2 is greater than 0. Thus, this bit is needed and the digital control circuit leaves it set to the 1 state. The digital output is now 001xxxxx, where an x indicates a bit yet to be determined.

This process is repeated for the bit weighted 1.6 volts. Since 3.2 + 1.6 is greater than 4.46, this bit is returned to 0 following the comparison. The bit valued at 0.8 is set to the 1 state and the test is repeated. Since 3.2 + 0.8 is less than 4.46, this bit remains set to the 1 state. In a similar manner, the 0.4 volt bit is set, tested and left in the 1 state. Thus, the digital output is now 0010111xx, where an x indicates a bit yet to be tested.

When the 0.2 volt bit is set, the comparator test indicates that the value is equal to or greater than 4.46 and the 0.2 bit is returned to 0. Thus, the output is now 0010110x. Actually, the dead-zone of the comparator would probably prevent detection of the equality and the 0.2 bit would be left on. Thus, dead-zone prevents bit chatter. If the dead zone of the comparator is adjusted to ±0.05 volts, the bit will be kept in the 1 state. This is a basic problem in all converters and the best accuracy that can be achieved is ±1/2 the value of the least significant bit. In this case, the accuracy is ±0.05 volts. Thus, the final value of the digital output is 00101110.

The successive approximation converter requires a comparison for every bit position in the digital word. A similar technique increments the least significant bit on each comparison and hence could take much longer than the successive approximation converter. However, if the increment converter is already at a value close to the analog input, only one or two comparisons may be required and the incrementing converter would produce the correct value much sooner. However, the successive approximation converter is much faster for a worst case situation.

Another approach to analog-to-digital conversion is based on simultaneous comparison. This approach requires a comparator for

each level and is expensive to construct. Another approach is
the time interval or integrating converter.[9]

In addition to the components shown in Figure 12-7-1, most
analog-to-digital converters include a sample and hold or track-
store unit on the analog input. This is necessary in order to
maintain a constant analog input during the conversion period.
It is also important to note that both digital-to-analog and
analog-to-digital conversion require a finite amount of time.
Usually, the time required to convert from analog-to-digital is
greater. In either case, the time delay or transport delay introduced by the process of conversion must be understood.   In
addition to the obvious errors in magnitude and phase, the delay
can have a destabilization effect on closed loop systems. Also,
time skew can often lead to incorrect interpretation of the
system operation.

12.8 THE INTERFACE

In order to realize the advantages of the hybrid computer,
an effective linkage or interface between the analog and the
digital computers must be available. In addition to the obvious
requirements for analog-to-digital and digital-to-analog conversion, the interface must perform several other functions.   In
this section, the interface requirements will be outlined.

Since data conversion is the most basic interface function
it will be discussed first. The fundamentals of analog-to-digital
and digital-to-analog conversion were presented in Sections 12.6
and 12.7. However, the number of inputs, the conversion rate and
the precision required for the typical hybrid system were not
discussed. The number of analog inputs to the digital system is
dependent on the manner of acquiring data from the analog computer
and the type of problems to be solved. Most hybrid systems employ
time division multiplexing and a single analog-to-digigal converter. A typical configuration is shown in Figure 12-8-1. Since
only one switch is closed at a given instance, the analog-to-digital
converter (ADC) can be used to acquire data from any number of
analog sources. For the system of Figure 12-8-1, four analog inputs are provided. The multiplexer connects channel 1 to the
converter for conversion to a digital equivalent. When this is

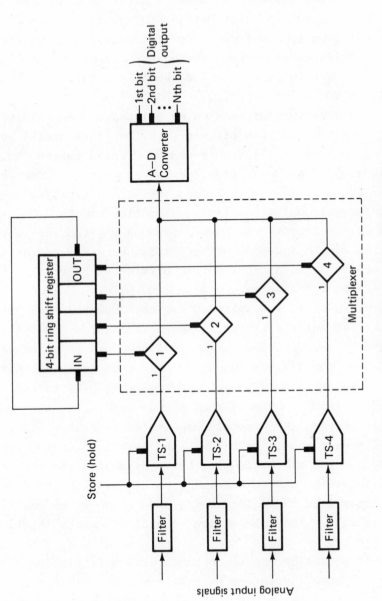

Figure 12-8-1. Multiplexer and analog-to-digital converter

complete, the switch for input 2 is closed and the switch for
input 1 opened. Following the conversion of the analog voltage
on input 2, the analog voltages on 3 and 4 are connected and
converted before the multiplexter returns to input 1.   Since a
finite amount of time is required to convert each input, there
will be a time difference or *skew* between each input. Also, the
elapsed time before input 1 is sampled again is a function of a
number of inputs to be converted.

The time skew between signals on each input can be eliminated
by utilizing a sample-and-hold circuit (i.e., a track-store) on
each input. By switching all sample-and-hold units to the hold
mode simultaneously, the value provided to the converter for all
inputs is for the same instant in time. This also provides the
constant input required for successful operation of the ADC. However, this does not improve the sample time on a given input. In
addition to the sample-and-hold units, it is necessary to include
a frequency filter at each input. This eliminates or reduces the
effect of unwanted frequencies.

The signal to close the switches for each channel can be
provided by a ring shift register as shown in Figures 10-5-4 and
12-8-1. Also, the multiplexer input   switches can be selected
by a command from the digital computer. For example, a 3 bit input address could be decoded (e.g., see Figure 12-3-8) to select
any one of eight inputs. The address decode method is the most
versatile. It enables the digital computer to determine the
order of multiplexer switching. Thus, the number of analog inputs
to be scanned and the allowable time between samples are the factors used to determine the number and type of converters required.
Recent developments in microelectronics have reduced the cost of
ADC units. It is now feasible to use several ADC units in place
of the multiplexer.

The number of analog inputs on commercial multiplexers ranges
from 4 to 128. These inputs may be terminated for patch cord connection on the analog patch panel or connected permanently to the
output or input of certain analog devices. In the first approach,
an analog signal to be converted to an equivalent digital form is
patched into the appropriate analog input connector. This value

is then converted to the digital form by addressing the appropriate input or by scanning all input points. In the latter case, frequently used analog elements are permanently connected to multiplexer inputs.

Most analog computers include an addressing system to permit monitoring of amplifiers and potentiometers by a single digital voltmeter. This system can be used to produce the digital equivalent of analog signals from these points. Thus, by dedicating a digital computer output channel to the address system of the analog computer, the analog output of any amplifier or potentiometer can be acquired. However, the conversion process must be preceded by an appropriate command for the address unit. On older computers, the addressing is mechanical and not easily adapted for digital computer selection. In other cases, relays are used for addressing and the pickup and dropout time for the relays must be considered. Perhaps the best approach is a combination of these methods. An effective analog input system can be constructed by providing a few analog inputs on the patch panel, directly connecting the most frequently used analog elements and utilizing the analog address system. If the digital computer discussed in Section 12.3 is used, 4 bits are available to address input devices. Thus, 16 different input points can be used. This is a serious limitation since many of the available addresses are needed for devices other than analog-to-digital conversion.

The specification of the ADC conversion rate determines the time required for successful conversion from analog-to-digital form. For a given system, the frequency content of the analog signals will determine the allowable time between samples on each input. Thus, the conversion time must be such that each input is sampled as often as required. Since the number of inputs is one of the determining factors for the sample time on a given input, the number of inputs and the speed of conversion are intimately related. As noted earlier, 10 samples per cycle introduces approximately 1.1 per cent error in amplitude and a phase error of approximately 18 per cent.[10] For example, if the signal to be converted contains frequencies up to 1000 Hz, then the input must be sampled at a minimum of 10,000 Hz or once every 0.1 msec. If a converter requires 5 μsec for each operation, then (0.1×10^{-3}) ÷ (5×10^{-6}) = 20 inputs can be served. If the amplitude error is to be maintained less than 0.1 per cent, then 50 samples per cycle are needed. This requires that each input be sampled at the rate, 50 x 1000 = 50,000 Hz. Thus, each channel must be sampled every 20 μsec. If the 5 μsec converter is used, the multiplexer can only accommodate 4 input signals.

The required accuracy is the primary determining factor in selecting the number of bits. As noted in Section 12.7, the minimum error is ±1/2 of the value of the least significant bit. For a 10 bit unit, an accuracy of ±0.15 per cent is typical. For 12 bits, accuracies of 0.025 per cent can be achieved. If 14 bits are used, ±.005 per cent accuracy can be expected. Most units now use 10, 12 or 14 bits.

The fundamentals of digital-to-analog conversion were presented in Section 12.6. However, there are some additional considerations that should be mentioned. In most applications, several analog outputs from the digital computer are required. There are two approaches to satisfying this need. One method uses a single digital-to-analog converter (DAC) and a demultiplexer or *distributor* to provide multiple outputs. This is the inverse of the multiplexer and ADC used for analog inputs to the digital computer. The other method involves a DAC for each analog output. Since the output from the digital computer usually comes from a single I/O buffer, a distributor is still needed to provide the digital output to the appropriate DAC.

Since it is necessary to select a particular analog output, some type of address generation and decoding is required. This is similar to the addressing used for analog inputs. Although DAC is faster than ADC, time is still important and time skew or *slew* is a factor. Also, some type of track-store or read-and-hold circuit is required on the analog outputs to maintain the signal between samples. There are many problems associated with data reconstruction and the matter should be given careful consideration.[9]

In addition to data conversion and input address selection, the interface should include a means for controlling the mode of the analog computer. If the analog computer has electronic mode control, digital mode control can be implemented easily. If relay or switch mode control is used, additional components are required to enable digital mode control. Most computer manufacturers provide special units for this task.

In order to provide efficient set-up and check-out, of analog programs, some means should be provided for setting the potentiometers under the control of the digital computer. This can be achieved with servo-set potentiometers or digital controlled attenuators. Servo-set potentiometers are driven by servo-motors which automatically turn the potentiometer to the desired setting. For digital computer control, the desired pot setting is provided by the digital-to-analog converter and a set-pot signal initiated by the digital computer. Thus, the interface must include pot addressing, a means of holding the desired pot setting and the ability to initiate a pot-set cycle.

The digital controlled attenuators are faster than the servo-set potentiometers. Usually, they require from 2 to 3 μsec for each new setting. These devices utilize FET switches and divider networks which are selected on command from the digital computer.

Since most hybrid systems include patchable digital logic, digital input and output should be provided by the interface. This enables the digital computer to sense the change in state of a logic element or the presence of a logic level. Also, the digital computer can provide set and reset pulses and change levels to drive logic elements.

One of the most complex features of this interface is intended to improve communications between the analog and the digital computer. In order for the digital computer to react to external events, some means of interrupting the execution of a program must be included. This feature is provided by the *interrupt* system. Basically, a change in level on the interrupt input causes the computer to cease executing the present program sequence and execute the instruction stored at a memory location corresponding to the particular interrupt. For example, assume that the occurrence of some event on the analog computer is to cause the digital computer to calculate a new value for a given parameter. In order to implement this feature, an interrupt would be connected to the hybrid element (i.e., comparator, etc.,) sensing the event.   The memory location for the interrupt used is set to contain a branch command to cause the digital computer to branch to the first instruction of the parameter program when the interrupt occurs. The digital computer automatically executes the instruction at the interrupt response address. This causes the computer to branch to the parameter program and sequence through the program to produce new parameter values. Upon completion of the parameter program, the digital computer branches back to the program that was interrupted or another more important task. This same technique can be used to cause the digital computer to respond almost immediately to events on the analog computer.

Since several interrupts can occur simultaneously, some means of establishing relative priority is required. Most systems including a hardware interrupt system provide a priority scheme which permits the assignment of relative priorities to the various programming tasks.

From the discussion of the interface functions, it is obvious that timing is an important consideration. The required synchronization can be established by the digital computer or by a special clock in the interface. Both approaches have distinct advantages and both types of systems have been built.   In many instances, a real-time clock is required. The features can be achieved with a frequency counter and an interrupt or special clock.

Many additional features have been incorporated in hybrid interface systems. However, the most important functions have been discussed and are illustrated in Figure 12-8-2. The important features can be summarized as follows: ADC and DAC, mode control and sense, pot set, amplifier and pot addressing, digital logic inputs and outputs, interrupts and time synchronization. These features are implemented in many different ways and the manual for a given system should be checked thoroughly before attempting to use the system.

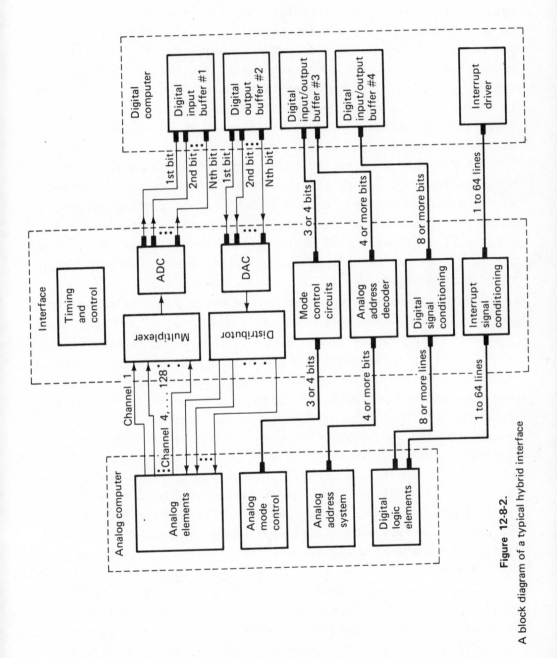

Figure 12-8-2.

A block diagram of a typical hybrid interface

12.9   HYBRID SOFTWARE

The logic, memory and computing elements of the digital computer are generally referred to as computer *hardware*. The programs which direct the operation of the computer hardware are referred to as *software*. There are two general classifications of software. The first category is called system software. This includes programs which control the computer system, facilitate the use of the system, and permit the computer to transfer from one application to another in the proper sequence. The second type of software is called application software and is made up of programs which enable the computer to perform particular tasks.

In the case of a hybrid computing system, there are system software requirements in addition to the usual digital computer system software. Also, the development of application software is more complex than straight digital or analog programming. This section will be devoted to a discussion of hybrid system software. As background for this discussion, digital system software will be discussed briefly.

There are several terms which are basic to digital system software. One of the most frequently used terms is *operating system*. An operating system consists of a group of programs which facilitate execution and scheduling of application programs. Another term, *executive program*, is used to describe a program which determines priority and controls the execution of other programs. In real-time applications, the term *monitor* is used as a label for the programming system which takes care of the real-time requirements on program scheduling and execution.

In addition to the program which keeps track of system allocation and scheduling, there are a series of routines to assist with program development and loading and input/output operations. Of these, the *bootstrap* loader is the most basic. The bootstrap program consists of a sequence of computer instructions which will automatically run a card reader, paper tape reader or magnetic tape reader. Usually, the bootstrap is not a fast or efficient loader program and is used only to load a more powerful loader program. The more sophisticated loader program contains more instructions and is often capable of *relocating* a program (i.e., loading a given program into any specified location in memory).

In addition to various types of loader programs, system software usually includes routines for checking and altering memory locations, dumping the contents of memory and transferring programs to and from bulk storage devices (i.e., magnetic disk or tape memories). System software also includes programs which allocate memory space, determine relative priority of application programs and keep track of application program status (i.e., finished, running, delayed, or interrupted). In addition, most systems include routines which test the components of the computer system and assist with system maintenance.

The programs discussed in previous paragraphs are classified as system software. Obviously, the programs are very important and usually determine the efficiency of the computer system. In smaller computer systems, these programs may occupy 30 to 50 percent of the available memory.

Since a hybrid system includes several devices not found in the typical digital computer system, hybrid system software will include additional routines. These programs are capable of testing the components of the interface and the analog computer. In addition, there are routines which supervise data communication between the analog and digital computers, facilitate operator communication and assist with system operation. These programs relieve the programmer of many of the details of hybrid system set-up and operation. In addition, some systems include programs which automatically scale the analog program. Also, the availability of fast, inexpensive analog switches has made automatic analog program patching feasible. By organizing the analog computing elements in a modular fashion and providing switches for the most frequently used combinations, a digital computer program can control the analog switches to completely patch most programs on the analog computer. Thus, much of the drudgery of analog programming has been assumed by the digital computer.

Many of the programs that assist with the check-out and set-up of the analog and interface portions of the hybrid system are classified as *interpreters*. Thus, when an operator specifies one of the allowable commands, the interpreter decodes the statement and produces the necessary sequence of digital computer instructions to perform the desired operation. These commands are then

executed to perform the required tasks. These routines can perform such operations as setting pots, identifying links to and
from the interface, changing the computer mode, performing static
checks, etc.

In contrast to system software, application software consists
of programs written for a particular use of the computing system.
These programs must be written especially for each application.
They may use routines which are a part of the system software. A
detailed knowledge of the application and hybrid system software
is required in order to develop an effective application program.
Fortunately, a detailed knowledge of the digital system · is not
required. In general, hybrid application programming requires
more system knowledge than digital application programming.

12.10 TIME SYNCHRONIZATION

The advantages of clocked logic were discussed in Chapter 10.
By providing internal synchronization, the programmer is relieved
of most of the problems associated with rise-time and "races" in
digital logic. A different type of synchronization problem occurs
in hybrid system programming. Since computation will be carried
out on both the analog and the digital computers, it is necessary
to synchronize the operation of the two systems.   The problem is
further complicated by the sampling limitations on the discre-
tization of analog signals. In addition, the serial nature of
digital computer operation and the need to execute both system
and application programs often create severe time constraints.
Thus, time synchronization for a hybrid system is of great importance.   These problems are particularly acute in simulating a
complex system with fast response characteristics.

Although each application must be studied individually, it
is possible to establish certain criteria to assist with the es-
tablishment of the necessary synchronization. In order to avoid
time skew between different system variables, the analog-to-
digital and digital-to-analog conversion of all signals is syn-
chronized by means of sample-and-hold circuits. The time between
samples (i.e., the sample period, T) is determined by the dynamics
of the system. As noted in Section 12.8, a minimum of ten samples
per cycle is required to maintain reasonable accuracy.   Thus, the

sample rate can be determined from the characteristics of the problem variables.

Once the sample period has been determined, the allocation of digital computer time must be checked. Since certain calculations must be performed on the digital computer during each sample period, the sample rate may be limited by the speed of the digital computer. In fact, this may dictate the manner in which the computations are split between the digital and analog computers. The basic sample rate and the time for the digital calculations required for each sample can be diagramed as shown in Figure 12-10-1.

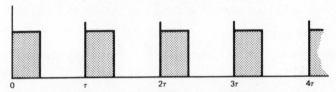

Figure **12-10-1.** Basic system sampling rate

Figure 12-10-1 gives the impression that the sample period, T, could be reduced, since the time required for computation in each step is a small portion of the total time between samples. However, the system is operated under the control of a hybrid operating system and a portion of the digital computer time must be devoted to operating system routines. They keep track of the application programs, memory allocation, etc. Thus, each sample period must include time for the operating system. In addition, certain routines of the operating system do not have to be executed during a particular sample period but must be completed periodically. These functions can be distributed over several steps. The resulting time diagram is shown in Figure 12-10-2.

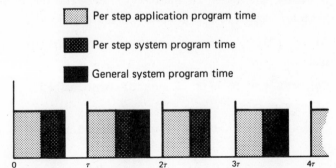

Figure **12-10-2.** Time allocation for application and system programs

Thus, it is obvious that attention must be devoted to the scheduling of digital programs and the analog/hybrid split of the
simulation.

As noted in Chapter 8 the hybrid computer has several advantages over either the analog or digital computer. However, in order
to realize these advantages an effective interface between the two
systems must be available. In addition, appropriate hybrid system
software is required in order to facilitate maintenance, programming and operation. Also, the programmer must have a thorough
knowledge of analog and digital computers and the special problems
associated with hybrid operation. An interesting challenge!

12.11 PROBLEMS FOR CHAPTER 12

Problems covering the material of this chapter are identified
by section.

12.1.1   Answer the question "Why hybrid?".

12.2.1   How many symbols are required in a base 3 number
system?

12.2.2   Given 11011.101_2, determine the equivalent base 10
number.

12.2.3   Convert the base 2 number of Problem 12.2.2 to base 8.

12.2.4   Convert the base 2 number of Problem 12.2.2 to base
16.   Use $0,1,2,\ldots,9,A,B,C,D,E$ and F as symbols in
the base 16 number system.

12.2.5   Given 137.325_{10}, determine the equivalent binary
number.

12.2.6   Convert the base 10 number of Problem 12.2.5 to the
octal number system.

12.2.7   Convert the base 10 number of Problem 12.2.5 to the
hexadecimal (i.e., a base 16 number system).

12.2.8   Given 121.5_8, determine the equivalent binary
number.

12.2.9   Convert the base 8 number of Problem 12.2.8 to
binary.

12.2.10   Convert the base 8 number of Problem 12.2.8 to base
10.

12.2.11 Convert the base 8 number of Problem 12.2.8 to base 16.

12.2.12 Determine a serial representation of the binary number of Problem 12.2.2, 12.2.5 and 12.2.8.

12.3.1 How many bits are required to address a memory containing 1000 locations?

12.3.2 How many bits are required to address a memory containing 4000 locations?

12.3.3 Convert 47_{10} and 32_{10} to binary and determine the sum of the two numbers in binary. Check your results in the decimal system.

12.3.4 Convert the numbers of Problem 12.3.3 to base 8 and determine the sum in base 8.

12.3.5 Develop the truth table for a binary substractor and design a logic circuit to carry out binary subtraction.

12.3.6 Given $A = 83.6_{10}$ and $B = 58.2_{10}$ convert to binary and use complement arithmetic to determine $C = A - B$. Check your results in the decimal number system.

12.3.7 Repeat Problem 12.3.6 for $C = B - A$. Check your results in the decimal number system.

12.3.8 Assume a 4 bit operation code and discusse the digital computer operations that might be useful.

12.4.1 For the computer discussed in Section 12.3, describe what happens when the following commands are executed.

    A. 11101111

    B. 00100010

    C. 10000010

    D. 10100010

    E. 01000010

    F. 00000000

12.4.2   For the computer described in Section 12.3, write
         the machine code for the following commands:

   A.   Add the contents of location 6 to the contents
        of the accumulator.

   B.   Substract the contents of memory location 8 from
        the contents of the accumulator.

   C.   Divide the contents of the accumulator by the
        contents of memory location 12.

   D.   Input from I/O channel 6 to the accumulator.

   E.   Branch to location 12.

   F.   Fetch the contents of memory location 10.

12.4.3   Assume that the memory of the computer discussed in
         Section 12.3 contains zeros except for the locations
         listed below.   What happens following the execution
         of a branch to location 2 command? Determine the
         contents of location 8 in memory after execution of
         the program listed below.

Memory Location	Memory Contents
0	00000000
1	00000000
2	10101000
3	00001000
4	10001000
5	11100101
6	00000000
7	00000000
8	00001001

12.4.4 Assume that the memory of the computer discussed in
        Section 12.3 contains the binary numbers shown be-
        low. Determine what happens following the execution
        of a branch to location 3 command.

Memory Location	Memory Contents
0	00000000
1	00000000
2	00000000
3	10101000
4	00101001
5	10100111
6	10000010
7	11100111

12.4.5 Write and encode a program to take 10 successive
        values from input channel 2 and store them in
        memory starting at location 2_{10}.

12.4.6 As noted in Section 12.4, the octal and hexadecimal
        number systems are frequently used to reduce the
        tedium of encoding machine commands and data. For
        the commands of Section 12.3, there are two octal
        formats that might be used. In both cases they
        are two, 3 bit bytes and one, 2 bit byte (e.g.,
        01|001|100 or 010|011|00). The resulting bits
        are then expressed in octal equivalents (e.g., 114
        or 230). Write the octal equivalent for the commands
        of Problem 12.4.3 using both formats. Which of the
        two formats is the more useful?

12.4.7 Repeat Problem 12.4.6 using the hexadecimal form
        0100|1100 = 4C, where 0,1,2,...,9,A,B,C,D,E and F
        are the symbols used for the hexadecimal code.

12.4.8 Repeat Problem 12.4.6 and 12.4.7 for the program of
        Problem 12.4.4.

12.5.1 Discuss the similarities and differences of an assem-
        bler, a compiler and an interpreter.

12.5.2 What is the advantage of using mnemonics?

12.5.3 What is the most likely application of an interpreter in a hybrid system?

12.5.4 Discuss the efficiency of a program which is hand encoded versus the program produced by the compiler.

12.6.1 Using an 8 bit digital word with the most significant bit devoted to indicating algebraic sign, determine suitable weighting for each bit if an ADC is to cover A ± 10 Volt range. Discuss the resulting accuracy.

12.6.2 Repeat Problem 12.6.1 for a 10 bit digital word.

12.6.3 Discuss the need for a track-store unit on the output of a digital-to-analog converter.

12.6.4 In Section 12.5, the multiplying digital-to-analog converter was discussed briefly. Develop a circuit using hybrid components to perform the MDAC function.

12.6.5 In order to cover a ±25 volt range, what is the minimum allowable weight for the most significant bit (exclude the sign bit)? How many bits are required to provide a 0.01 per cent accuracy?

12.7.1 Develop a parallel hybrid program to convert from an analog signal (±10 volts) to a 4 bit digital word using three comparators to determine the appropriate range.

12.7.2 Repeat Problem 12.7.1 using a successive approximation approach which checks the most significant bit first.

12.7.3 Repeat Problem 12.7.1 using an incrementing approach in which the least significant bit of the digital word is increased by 1 until the proper value is determined (i.e., counting up).

12.7.4 Discuss accuracy, word length, conversion speed and frequency range for analog-to-digital conversion.

12.8.1 List the basic requirements for a hybrid interface.

12.8.2 Given a 10 µsec, 10 bit ADC, determine the allowable frequency range for a single input.

12.8.3   For the analog-to-digital converter of Problem 12.8.2, how many inputs could be accommodated if each input is required to have a bandwidth of 1 KHz?

12.8.4   For the analog-to-digital converter of Problem 12.8.2, what is the allowable bandwidth of each input if a 128 input multiplexer is used?

12.8.5   In order to handle 8 inputs with a 2 KHz bandwidth each, what is the minimum allowable conversion time for an ADC?

12.8.6   Determine the error introduced by sampling a 1 KHz sine wave every 250 microseconds. Assume an infinite digital word length (i.e., no round-off error).

12.8.7   Repeat Problem 12.8.6 with a 10 bit converter and include the effect of round-off.

12.8.8   Discuss the advantages of having interrupts.

12.8.9   Why is an interrupt priority scheme useful?

12.9.1   List and describe the hybrid system software that would be desirable in a typical hybrid system.

12.9.2   Discuss desirable features for a hybrid operating system.

12.10.1   Given a fourth order system with time constants of 0.1, 0.25, 0.15 and 0.9 sec, determine a reasonable sampling rate.

12.10.2   If all of the state variables of the system described in Problem 12.10.1 are needed for the digital calculation at each step, determine the maximum allowable conversion time for the ADC.

12.10.3   For the system described in Problems 12.10.1 and 12.10.2, determine the basic system time frame.

12.10.4   For the system of Problems 12.10.1 and 12.10.2, assume that the application program for each step or sample requires twice as much time as the operating system programs for each step. Determine the maximum allowable time for the digital portion of the per-step calculations.

12.12   REFERENCES FOR CHAPTER 12

1. Hill, F. J. and G. R. Peterson, <u>Introduction to Switching Theory and Logic Design</u>, John Wiley and Sons, Inc., New York, 1968.

2. Bartee, T. C., <u>Digital Computer Fundamentals</u>, McGraw Hill Book Company, Inc., New York, 1972.

3. Booth, T. L., <u>Networks and Computer Systems</u>, John Wiley and Sons, Inc., New York, 1971.

4. <u>Introduction to Programming</u>, Digital Equipment Corporation, Maynard, Massachusetts, 1970.

5. Gear, C. P. W., <u>Computer Organization and Programming</u>, Second Edition, McGraw Hill Book Company, Inc., New York, 1974.

6. Wegner, Peter, <u>Programming Languages, Information Structures and Machine Organization</u>, McGraw Hill Book Company, Inc., New York, 1968.

7. Rosen, Saul, Editor, <u>Programming Systems and Languages</u>, McGraw Hill Book Company, Inc., New York, 1967.

8. Sheingold, D. H., Editor, <u>Analog-Digital Conversion Handbook</u>, Analog Devices Incorporated, Norwood, Massachusetts, 1972.

9. Beckey, G. A. and W. J. Karplus, <u>Hybrid Computation</u>, John Wiley and Sons, Inc., New York, 1968.

10. Korn, G. A., <u>Minicomputers for Engineers and Scientist</u>, McGraw Hill Book Company, Inc., New York, 1973.

C

DIGITAL
SIMULATION

13

Fundamentals of Digital Simulation

13.1 INTRODUCTION

The characteristics of analog and digital computers were presented in Sections 8.2 and 8.3, respectively. In those summaries, it was noted that the digital computer can be programmed to provide a much greater degree of accuracy than the analog computer. The large memory and ease with which a digital computer can switch from one application to another are additional advantages. Also, floating-point arithmetic operations provide a wide range of values and practically eliminate the need for magnitude scaling. All of these factors have enabled the digital computer to gain widespread use.

As noted in Chapter 8, discrete representation of numbers and sequential operation make continuous system simulation challenging on the digital computer. Digital simulation is further complicated since integration is an approximate process and subject to serious error if not programmed properly. On the

other hand, direct integration and parallel operation provide a
speed and cost advantage for the analog computer. In addition,
the direct relationship of the analog program to the system
being simulated make analog programming more natural and instructive.

As a result of the advantages cited above, considerable effort
has been devoted to developing digital simulation techniques.[1-4]
A number of approaches have been used and the purpose of this
chapter is to introduce the fundamentals of digital simulation.

Since numerical integration is basic to digital simulation,
it will be discussed first. This material is followed by a presentation of simulation techniques based on state variables. A
brief discussion of simulation of systems expressed in transfer
function form is presented next. The chapter also includes some
example problems illustrating digital simulation techniques.

13.2 A SIMPLE INTEGRATION FORMULA

A number of integration techniques have been developed for
digital simulation of continuous systems. While a thorough
knowledge of the various methods is not essential, an understanding
of the basic principles should enable more effective use of
available simulation programs.

In order to provide background for the development of integration routines, a brief discussion of digital simulation will
be presented. Instead of producing a continuous signal for each
system variable, the digital simulator will determine values of
system variables at specific points in time. Thus, instead of $x(t)$,
a continuous function, the simulation produces discrete values:
$x(t_0)$, $x(t_1)$, $x(t_2)$,...,$x(t_i)$, $x(t_{i+1})$,...,$x(t_n)$. For simplicity,
the time argument is frequently omitted and the subscripts are
used directly with the variables. The sequence becomes: x_0, x_1,
x_2,...,x_i, x_{i+1},...x_n. In most cases, the interval between
adjacent time values is a constant, $\Delta t = t_{i+1} - t_i$. For convenience, T is used in place of Δt and $T = t_{i+1} - t_i$. Hopefully,
the discrete values will be within allowable tolerances of the
corresponding values of the continuous functions being simulated.
Thus, in addition to the discrete levels or values discussed in
Chapter 8, digital simulation also discretizes time.

The simplest approach to numerical integration is based on Euler's method which uses the following approximation for a derivative,

$$\frac{dx_i}{dt} \simeq \frac{x_{i+1} - x_i}{t_{i+1} - t_i} = \frac{x_{i+1} - x_i}{\Delta t} = \frac{x_{i+1} - x_i}{T} \ . \qquad (13.2.1)$$

This is shown graphically in Figure 13-2-1. The illustration of Figure 13-2-1 can be interpreted as approximating the slope of a function at a given point with the change in the function $(x_{i+1} - x_i)$ divided by the change in time, $T = t_{i+1} - t_i$. This should be familiar since it is quite similar to the basic definition for a derivative. Obviously, the approximation is better for smaller time steps, T.

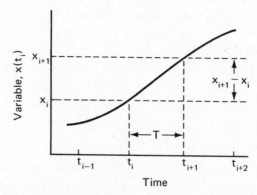

Figure 13-2-1. Graphical illustration of Euler's method

In order to illustrate the use of Euler's method, consider a system described by the equation

$$\frac{dx}{dt} + ax = 1.0, \qquad (13.2.2)$$

where $x(t=0) = x_0$. For digital simulation, the continuous variable, $x(t)$, will become $x_0, x_1, x_2, \ldots, x_i, x_{i+1}, \ldots, x_n$. Making this substitution and replacing the derivative with Equation (13.2.1) yields

$$\frac{x_{i+1} - x_i}{T} + ax_i = 1.0, \qquad (13.2.3)$$

where i = 0,1,2,...,n. This equation can be rearranged in the form,

$$x_{i+1} = x_i - Tax_i + T, \qquad (13.2.4)$$

where i = 0,1,2,...,n. Letting i=0 gives x_1 in terms of x_0, the initial condition. The next step, i=1, yields x_2 in terms of x_1. Thus, the discrete values of x can be calculated by indexing through i = 0,1,2,...,n. Equation (13.2.4) is called a difference equation and is an approximate digital equivalent of the differential equation written in Equation (13.2.2).

Programming the differential equation as expressed in Equation (13.2.4) for solution on a digital computer is quite simple. Most programming languages include provisions for looping or indexing through the values of i. This is illustrated in the Fortran program shown in Figure 13-2-2. The program was exe-

```
C       PROGRAM FOR FIGURE 13-2-2
        REAL TI(20),X(20)
C       DEFINE THE INITIAL CONDITION
        X0=0.0
C       DEFINE THE COEFFICIENT
        A=5.0
C       LET FINAL TIME EQUAL 5 TIME CONSTANTS
        FT=5*(1/A)
C       DETERMINE RESPONSE FOR 5 VALUES OF T
        DO 10 J=1,5
        FJ=J
        T=FJ*0.1
C       DETERMINE THE NUMBER OF STEPS
        N=FT/T
C       CALCULATE FIRST VALUE
        X(1)=X0-T*A*X0+T
C       CALCULATING THE VALUE OF X(I) AT EACH STEP
        DO 20 I=1,N
        AI=I
        X(I+1)=X(I)-T*A*X(I)+T
        TI(I)=T*AI
     20 CONTINUE
C
        WRITE(6,30)
     30 FORMAT(1X,4HTIME,4X,1HX)
        WRITE(6,40) TO,X0
     40 FORMAT(1X,F4.2,F7.3)
        WRITE(6,50) (TI(I),X(I),I=1,N)
     50 FORMAT(1X,F4.2,F7.3)
     10 CONTINUE
        STOP
        END
```

Figure 13-2-2.   Fortran program to solve: $\dot{x} + 5x = 1$

cuted for a=5.0 and T=0.1,0.2,0.3,0.4 and 0.5 sec. The solution
is plotted in Figure 13-2-3. Note that larger values of T

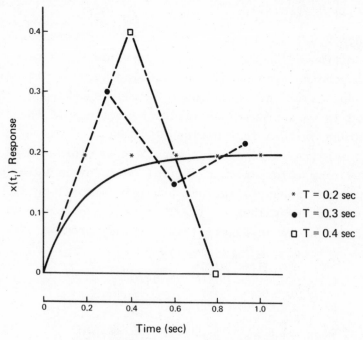

Figure 13-2-3.   Solution of $\dot{x} + 5x = 1.0$

increase the error of the approximation. However, larger values
of T require fewer calculations to cover a given period of time.
In addition to increasing the error, larger values of T can
introduce instability. In this example the integration routine
is unstable for values of T greater than 0.4 sec. This characteristic of numerical integration techniques introduces serious
errors and should be avoided.

13.3   SELECTING THE INTEGRATION INTERVAL

A knowledge of system characteristics is essential in order
to select the number of steps, n, and the integration interval,
T. The integration interval is often referred to as the sample
period and the two terms will be used interchangeably in the
remainder of this book. For the system of Equation (13.2.2), the
time constant is $1/a = 0.2$ sec. Since five time constants are
required for the system to reach steady state, the simulation
should run for at least 1.0 sec. If an integration interval of
0.1 sec is used, a minimum of ten steps is required (i.e., n=10).

If the integration interval is increased to 0.2 sec, only five
steps are needed (i.e., n=5) and the digital computer is required
to make half as many calculations. Thus, the selection of the
integration interval determines the number of computer calculations required and the accuracy of the simulation.

In selecting the integration interval for a system simulation, the upper bound will be determined by the required accuracy.
The lower bound is usually determined by the available computer
time. In some instances, considerable latitude is available and
the choice of integration interval is not critical. In other
cases, system constraints may make the selection of the integration interval extremely difficult.

In order to include the effect of every system time constant,
the integration interval should not be longer than the shortest
time constant and the simulation should run for at least five
times the longest time constant. For example, if the system
time constants are 0.1, 0.2, 0.4 and 0.8 sec, the integration
interval should be less than 0.1 sec and the simulation should
run for $5\tau_{max}$=5(.8)=4.0 sec. Thus, if T=0.1 sec, forty steps are
required (i.e., n=40). The shortest time constant should be
considered as a maximum value for T and much better results are
obtained with even shorter integration intervals. Simulation
runs with ten time intervals per time constant are not uncommon.
For this example, ten samples per time constant would require an
integration interval of 0.01 sec, and four hundred integration
steps would be needed to cover the response of the longest time
constant.

In some instances, the characteristic equation for a system
may have one or more pairs of complex conjugate roots. The
response for these terms is oscillatory and the sampling period
or integration interval should be selected to provide a minimum
of ten steps per cycle of oscillation. For example, consider a
system having a pair of complex conjugate roots with an undamped
natural frequency, ω_n=15 radians and a damping ratio of 0.5. As
stated in Chapter 6, the frequency of oscillation is $\omega=\omega_n\sqrt{1-\delta^2}$=
$15\sqrt{1-.25}$=13. Since $\omega = 2\pi f$, the highest frequency would be
$f = \omega/2\pi = 13/6.28 = 2.06$ Hertz. Thus, each cycle requires
0.486 sec and if ten samples per cycle are desired, the sampling

period should be 0.0486 sec. Ten samples per cycle will introduce approximately 1.1 per cent error in amplitude along with a
phase error of eighteen per cent.[7] If a higher degree of
accuracy is desired, more than ten samples per cycle will be
needed.

In general, the integration interval for a particular system
must be less than the interval required by any time constant or
complex conjugate pair of roots. The simulation should run long
enough to permit the response of all time constants to be
completed. In some cases, a particular time constant or a pair
of oscillatory roots are considered to be insignificant and are
not used to determine the integration interval. However, this
should be done with great care.

In many applications, it is necessary to simulate a system
in real-time. In these instances, the computer must produce the
system variables at the same rate they occur in the system being
modeled. In order to determine 1 sec of the real-time response
of the system of Equation (13.2.2), the computer must calculate
ten values of x_i if T = 0.1 sec. For this problem, each value
of x_i requires two multiplications and two additions. The arithmetic operations for each time step requires a finite amount of
computer time, t_s. If the calculation time per step (t_s) is
greater than the integration interval, T, the computer cannot
simulate the system in real-time. If the results of the digital
simulation are to interface with an external experiment in real-
time, the time required for computer input/output operations must
be added to the per step calculation time. This problem is more
acute for large systems involving many variables, since every
variable must be calculated for each integration interval, T.
Thus, the selection of integration interval determines the accuracy and the real-time capabilities of a computer.

13.4 THE TAYLOR'S SERIES

A measure of the error of the approximation given in Equation
(13.2.1) can be obtained from a Taylor's series expansion of
x_{i+1} in terms of x_i,

$$x_{i+1} = x_i + \frac{T dx_i}{dt} + \frac{T^2 d^2 x_i}{2! \, dt^2} + \cdots + \frac{T^n d^n x_i}{n! \, dt^n} . \qquad (13.4.1)$$

Equation (13.4.1) can be arranged in the form

$$x_{i+1} = x_i + \frac{Tdx_i}{dt} , \qquad (13.4.2)$$

which corresponds to the first two terms of the Taylor's series. Therefore, the error of the approximation can be represented by the sum of the remaining terms of the series. The inclusion of additional terms from the series would improve the approximation and decrease the error. Since Euler's method includes terms up to and including the first derivative, it is classified as a *first-order* numerical integration technique. Methods including the second derivative or producing values equivalent to the first three terms of Taylor's series expansion are called second-order integration formulas. The more popular integration methods match the Taylor's series expansion up to fourth-and-fifth order terms. There is little advantage in going to higher-order terms, since the coefficient T^n becomes quite small by the fifth term for $T << 1.0$ sec.

The Taylor series can be used directly for higher-order methods. However, the computational burden of calculating and storing the higher-order derivatives is unrealistic. Many other formulas have been developed that are computationally more attractive. A number of methods are compared in references (5) and (6). A stability analysis is presented in reference (7).

The following paragraph will list some of the integration formulas currently used and give a brief discussion of each.[5]

1. Predictor: Utilizes values and slopes from previous steps to predict the next value, x_{i+1}. The Adams-Bashforth method is typical of this approach.

2. Predictor-Corrector Technique: In this approach, past values and slopes are used first to calculate a predicted value, $\tilde{x}_{i+1}$. The predicted value is then used with past values and slopes to determine a more accurate value for x_{i+1}. The Adams-Moulton method is typical of this approach.

3. Single Step Techniques: In contrast to the predictor methods, single step methods do not rely on a series of values from previous integration intervals. Each

step is calculated separately. The single step
methods are necessary to get predictor methods started
since at the first interval, t_1, the necessary series
of past values is not available. The fourth-order
Runge-Kutta formula is typical of this approach and
is widely used.

4.   Variable Step Techniques: Frequently, the variables
of a system are not changing rapidly and a small
integration interval is not required to maintain
accuracy. Methods have been developed to determine
the error associated with each integration step.
This information is used to adjust the size of the
integration interval. Obviously, large integration
steps mean fewer calculations and less computer
time. However, some computer time is necessary to
make the calculations required to adjust the integration interval. In some instances, the added
complexity may not be justified.

Many numerical integration techniques have been developed and the
interested reader is referred to the references at the   end   of
this chapter.   Some of the more widely used integration techniques are as follows:

1.   Runge-Kutta
2.   Runge-Kutta-Merson
3.   Runge-Kutta-Blum
4.   Adams-Moulton
5.   Adams-Bashforth
6.   Simpson
7.   Gill
8.   Tustin
9.   State transition

The latter method will be discussed later in this chapter.

13.5   EVALUATION OF NUMERICAL INTEGRATION FORMULAS

With so many integration formulas available (reference (5)
lists and compares 42 methods), it is often difficult to select
the best approach for a particular application. This   section
will present criteria for the evaluation of numerical formulas.

The characteristic of greatest interest is error. There are two principle sources of error in digital integration: truncation and round-off. Truncation error is due to limiting or *truncating* an infinite series to a finite number of terms. For example, fourth-order methods do not include the effects of fifth-or higher-order derivatives of a Taylor series expansion. Round-off error is due to the finite word length or precision of digital computer arithmetic operations. In some instances these errors accumulate with each integration step and eventually make the solution useless.

At first consideration, it might appear that a reduction in the integration interval, T, will always produce a corresponding reduction in the solution error. However, if the integration interval becomes too small, the corresponding small changes in the system variables are lost due to round-off and the solution error increases. Thus, round-off error becomes an additional consideration in selecting the interval of integration.

The second most important characteristic of a numerical integration technique is stability. Most numerical techniques become unstable if the integration interval is made too large. The allowable range for the integration interval is a function of the time constants of the system and the integration formula used. Methods have been developed to determine exact bounds on step size.[7]

A third characteristic is the per-step solution time. This has been discussed in a previous section and is repeated here for emphasis.

The fourth consideration is ease of programming. Obviously, the more elaborate integration schemes are more difficult to use and program. Therefore, the facility of a method is an important characteristic.

As stated initially, this discussion is intended to be an introduction to numerical integration. Therefore, many details have been omitted. Also, the discussions of numerical integration have assumed time as the independent variable. This is not always true and a more general treatment would consider other variables of integration.

13.6   STATE VARIABLE TECHNIQUES

An immediate application of state variables in digital simulation is a result of the form of the state variable equations.
In Section 13.2, the rectangular rule (i.e., Euler's method) was
used to develop a difference equation to solve a first-order
differential equation. The approximation replaces the first
derivative and is quite straightforward for a first-order system.
A difference equation for a second-order system can be derived
directly. However, it is easier to convert the second-order equation into two first-order state equations and use the rectangular
rule or other numerical approximate directly in each equation.
For example, consider the system described by the equation

$$\ddot{x} + 3\dot{x} + 9x = 9 , \tag{13.6.1}$$

where $\ddot{x}_0 = \dot{x}_0 = 0$. The methods presented in Section 7.4 yield
the state variable equations

$$\begin{bmatrix} \dot{x}_1 \\ \dot{x}_2 \end{bmatrix} = \begin{bmatrix} 0 & 1 \\ -9 & -3 \end{bmatrix} \begin{bmatrix} x_1 \\ x_2 \end{bmatrix} + \begin{bmatrix} 0 \\ 1 \end{bmatrix} 9 . \tag{13.6.2}$$

Since $x_1 = x$ and $x_2 = \dot{x}_1 = \dot{x}$, the initial conditions are $x_1(t=0) = x_0 = 0$ and $x_2(t=0) = \dot{x}_0 = 0$.

Before applying Euler's method to develop difference equations, a useful simplification will be made. Instead of using
x_1 and x_2 to represent the state variables, use x and y.   This
will avoid confusing the subscripts on x_1 and x_2 with the subscripts identifying the integration step. Therefore, let $x_1 = x$
and $x_2 = y$. The state variables are now x and y and the   state
equations are

$$\begin{bmatrix} \dot{x} \\ \dot{y} \end{bmatrix} = \begin{bmatrix} 0 & 1 \\ -9 & -3 \end{bmatrix} \begin{bmatrix} x \\ y \end{bmatrix} + \begin{bmatrix} 0 \\ 1 \end{bmatrix} 9 , \tag{13.6.3}$$

with $x_0 = 0$ and $y_0 = 0$. Euler's method can be used as follows

$$\dot{x}_i \cong \frac{x_{i+1} - x_i}{T} , \tag{13.6.4}$$

and

$$\dot{y}_i \cong \frac{y_{i+1} - y_i}{T} .$$ (13.6.5)

Substituting Equations (13.6.4) and (13.6.5) into Equation (13.6.3) yields the following difference equations

$$x_{i+1} = x_i + Ty_i$$ (13.6.6)

$$y_{i+1} = (1 - 9T)x_i - 3Ty_i + 9T,$$ (13.6.7)

with $x_0 = y_0 = 0$ and $i = 0,1,2,\ldots,n$. These equations can be written in state variable form

$$\begin{bmatrix} \mathring{x}_{i+1} \\ \mathring{y}_{i+1} \end{bmatrix} = \begin{bmatrix} 1 & T \\ (1-9T) & -3T \end{bmatrix} \begin{bmatrix} x_i \\ y_i \end{bmatrix} + \begin{bmatrix} 0 \\ T \end{bmatrix} 9,$$ (13.6.8)

where $x_0 = y_0 = 0$ and $i = 0,1,2,\ldots,n$. Thus, a second-order linear, stationary differential equation has been replaced with two difference equations which are easily programmed for digital solution. As noted previously, the integration step, T, must be small in relation to the time constants of the equations.

For higher-order systems, it is difficult to use a different symbol for each state variable. A single variable with subscripts is the most popular notation. If this approach is used on the example of the preceding paragraph, Equation (13.6.8) becomes

$$\begin{bmatrix} \dot{x}_{1(i+1)} \\ \mathring{x}_{2(i+1)} \end{bmatrix} = \begin{bmatrix} 1 & T \\ (1-9T) & -3T \end{bmatrix} \begin{bmatrix} x_{1(i)} \\ x_{2(i)} \end{bmatrix} + \begin{bmatrix} 0 \\ T \end{bmatrix} 9,$$ (13.6.9)

where $x_1(0)$ and $x_2(0)$ are initial conditions and $i = 0,1,2,\ldots,n$. The state variable approach greatly simplifies the process of developing difference equations for the second-order system. In Chapter 7, it was stated that the technique is applicable to systems of any order, and in general, reduces a system of order n, to n first-order differential equations.

Another result of state variable analysis is also advantageous. In Section 7.5, the solution for the state equation of
the form

$$\overset{\circ}{\underline{x}} = \underline{A}\underline{x} + \underline{b}u ,\qquad\qquad (13.6.10)$$

was given as

$$\underline{x}(t) = e^{\underline{A}t}\underline{x}(o) + \int_0^t e^{\underline{A}(t-\Psi)}\underline{b}u(\Psi)d\Psi ,\qquad\qquad (13.6.11)$$

where $\underline{x}(0)$ is the initial condition vector. If the state equations are simplified to the form

$$\overset{\circ}{\underline{x}} = \underline{A}\underline{x} ,\qquad\qquad (13.6.12)$$

then the solution is

$$\underline{x}(t) = e^{\underline{A}t}\underline{x}(0).\qquad\qquad (13.6.13)$$

In Chapter 7, it was noted that many systems can be written
in the form of Equation (13.6.12) by including the forcing
function, u(t), as a state variable. In some cases, it is
necessary to add more than one state variable in order to carry
out the simplification. For example, the system of Equation
(13.6.1) was written in state variable form in Equation (13.6.2).
In order to write this system in the state variable form of
Equation (13.6.12), it is necessary to determine a first-order
differential equation which has a solution equal to the forcing
function, u(t)=9.0. Since the desired solution is a constant,
the derivative, $\dot{u}$, must be equal to zero. Therefore, the required differential equation is $\dot{u}=0$. The initial condition is
u(0)=9.0. Thus, the required input forcing function can be
achieved by driving the system with the output of an integrator
which has an input of 0 and an initial condition of 9.0.   Representing the output of that integrator with state variable x_3 gives
a state equation $\dot{x}_3=0$ with $x_3(0)=9.0$. This can be adjoined to
Equation (13.6.2) to yield

$$\begin{bmatrix} \dot{x}_1 \\ \dot{x}_2 \\ \dot{x}_3 \end{bmatrix} = \begin{bmatrix} 0 & 1 & 0 \\ -9 & -3 & 1 \\ 0 & 0 & 0 \end{bmatrix} \begin{bmatrix} x_1 \\ x_2 \\ x_3 \end{bmatrix} ,\qquad\qquad (13.6.14)$$

with $x_1(0) = x_2(0) = 0$ and $x_3(0) = 9.0$. A diagram for the adjoined system is shown in Figure 13-6-1.

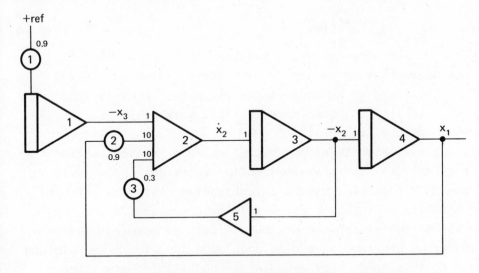

Figure 13-6-1. Block diagram for state-space system

If the input had been $u(t) = \alpha t + \beta$, instead of 9.0, the differential equation describing the input would be $\ddot{u}=0$, with $u(0)=\beta$ and $\dot{u}(0)=\alpha$. To formulate state equations, let $x_3=u$ and $x_4=\dot{x}_3$. The state equations are $\dot{x}_3=x_4$ and $\dot{x}_4=0$ with $x_3(0)=\beta$ and $x_4(0)=\alpha$. The combined state equations are

$$
\begin{bmatrix} \dot{x}_1 \\ \dot{x}_2 \\ \dot{x}_3 \\ \dot{x}_4 \end{bmatrix} = \begin{bmatrix} 0 & 1 & 0 & 0 \\ -9 & -3 & 1 & 0 \\ 0 & 0 & 0 & 1 \\ 0 & 0 & 0 & 0 \end{bmatrix} \begin{bmatrix} x_1 \\ x_2 \\ x_3 \\ x_4 \end{bmatrix} , \tag{13.6.15}
$$

with $x_1(0) = x_2(0) = 0$, $x_3(0) = \beta$ and $x_4(0) = \alpha$. Using similar techniques, most systems can be written in the form of Equation (13.6.12) which has the simplified solution of Equation (13.6.13).

The equation for the solution of the adjoined state equations can be used for any value of time (t) to determine the system variables at that point. Thus, in order to generate the solution at a series of time points or intervals, the matrix e^{At} is evaluated for each value of time (t) at which a solution is desired. Since the time intervals are usually equally spaced, the computational burden of calculating $e^{\underline{A}t}$ for each point can be avoided by evaluating $e^{\underline{A}T}$, where $T = (t_{i+1} - t_i)$, and using the relation-ship

$$\underline{x}(t_{i+1}) = e^{\underline{A}(t_{i+1} - t_i)}\underline{x}(t_i). \tag{13.6.16}$$

In this approach, the *transition matrix*, $e^{\underline{A}T}$, is calculated only once and used at every interval. The state vector at a given point, $\underline{x}_i$, is used as an *initial condition* for the transition to the next point, $\underline{x}_{i+1}$. This approach will work only for systems with constant coefficients.[8]

Since most high level computer languages include matrix-vector operations, the state transition technique is easily programmed. It is also useful in conjunction with some of the other simulation languages which will be discussed in Chapter 14. The state variable approach has been widely adopted and a number of simulation programs have been developed for simulating systems written in this form. For example, Spamod II[11] simulates systems in the form, $\overset{\circ}{\underline{x}} = \underline{A}\underline{x} + \underline{B}\underline{u}$ and $\underline{y} = \underline{C}\underline{x} + \underline{D}\underline{u}$.

13.7   EXAMPLE PROBLEM

In order to illustrate the use of the state transition tech-nique, consider the system described by Equation (13.6.1) and expressed in state variable form in Equation (13.6.3). An addi-tional state variable was assigned to describe the constant forcing function and the adjoined system is described by Equation (13.6.14). In order to evaluate the transition matrix, $e^{\underline{A}T}$, it is necessary to select a time interval. The coefficients Equation (13.6.1) indicate an undamped natural frequency of $\sqrt{9} = 3$ radians and a damping ratio of 0.5. The frequency of oscillation is $\omega\sqrt{1-(.5)^2} = 2.6$ radians or approximately 0.4 Hertz. Since reason-able accuracy requires at least ten integration intervals per cycle of system response, the integration interval should be less than 2.5/10=0.25 sec. In order to increase the accuracy, a sampling interval of 0.1 sec will be used. This will give approx-imately 25 samples or time intervals during each cycle of the oscillations in the system response. For T=0.1 sec and

$$\underline{A} = \begin{bmatrix} 0 & 1 & 0 \\ -9 & -3 & 1 \\ 0 & 0 & 0 \end{bmatrix}, \tag{13.7.1}$$

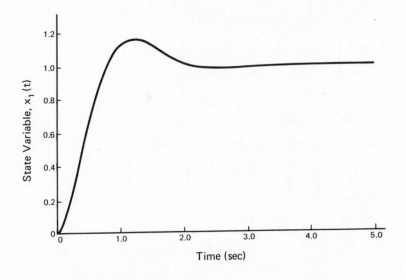

STEP	TIME	X1	X2	X3
1	0.10	0.04050	0.76601	9.00000
2	0.20	0.14456	1.27439	9.00000
3	0.30	0.28767	1.55265	9.00000
4	0.40	0.44867	1.63898	9.00000
5	0.50	0.61049	1.57643	9.00000
6	0.60	0.76044	1.40843	9.00000
7	0.70	0.89002	1.17527	9.00000
8	0.80	0.99450	0.91182	9.00000
9	0.90	1.07233	0.64628	9.00000
10	1.00	1.12441	0.39968	9.00000
11	1.10	1.15339	0.18614	9.00000
12	1.20	1.16302	0.01358	9.00000
13	1.30	1.15757	-0.11531	9.00000
14	1.40	1.14137	-0.20190	9.00000
15	1.50	1.11846	-0.25046	9.00000
16	1.60	1.09235	-0.26711	9.00000
17	1.70	1.06587	-0.25882	9.00000
18	1.80	1.04117	-0.23271	9.00000
19	1.90	1.01970	-0.19541	9.00000
20	2.00	1.00227	-0.15269	9.00000
21	2.10	0.98918	-0.10925	9.00000
22	2.20	0.98032	-0.06864	9.00000
23	2.30	0.97527	-0.03326	9.00000
24	2.40	0.97344	-0.00448	9.00000
25	2.50	0.97414	0.01719	9.00000
26	2.60	0.97665	0.03191	9.00000
27	2.70	0.98031	0.04036	9.00000
28	2.80	0.98454	0.04350	9.00000
29	2.90	0.98887	0.04247	9.00000
30	3.00	0.99294	0.03843	9.00000

Figure 13-7-1.   System response

the first five terms of Equation (7.5.11) give a transition matrix

$$e^{\underline{A}T} = \begin{bmatrix} .9595 & .0851 & .0045 \\ -.7660 & .7042 & .0851 \\ 0 & 0 & 1 \end{bmatrix}. \tag{13.7.2}$$

Therefore, the difference equations for simulating the system are

$$\begin{bmatrix} x_1(i+1) \\ x_2(i+1) \\ x_3(i+1) \end{bmatrix} = \begin{bmatrix} .9595 & .0851 & .0045 \\ -.7660 & .7042 & .0851 \\ 0 & 0 & 1 \end{bmatrix} \begin{bmatrix} x_1(i) \\ x_2(i) \\ x_3(i) \end{bmatrix}. \tag{13.7.3}$$

The response of the system is shown in Figure 13-7-1. It should be noted that an error in a given step is carried to the next step and any error in calculating the transition matrix, $e^{\underline{A}T}$ will accumulate with each step. Therefore, since the transition matrix must be calculated only once, it might be wise to include additional terms of the series.

Difference equations for the system can also be developed using Euler's Rule. The first step of the procedure is to substitute $[x(i+1) - x(i)]/T$ for each derivative term and $x(i)$ for each state variable in Equation (13.6.14). This gives

$$[x_1(i+1) - x_1(i)]/T = x_2(i), \tag{13.7.4}$$

$$[x_2(i+1) - x_2(i)]/T = -9x_1(i) - 3x_2(i) + x_3(i), \tag{13.7.5}$$

and

$$[x_3(i+1) - x_3(i)]/T = 0. \tag{13.7.6}$$

Equations (13.7.4), (13.7.5) and (13.7.6) can be written in the form

$$\begin{bmatrix} x_1(i+1) \\ x_2(i+1) \\ x_3(i+1) \end{bmatrix} = \begin{bmatrix} 1 & T & 0 \\ -9T & (1-3T) & T \\ 0 & 0 & 1 \end{bmatrix} \begin{bmatrix} x_1(i) \\ x_2(i) \\ x_3(i) \end{bmatrix}. \tag{13.7.7}$$

The elements of the coefficient matrix in Equation (13.7.7) are identical to the results obtained if the first two terms of the Taylor's series of Equation (7.5.11) are used. This is correct, since Euler's Rule is a first-order approximation. The

error introduced can be determined by substituting T=0.1 in
Equation (13.7.7) and comparing each term with the corresponding
element in Equation (13.7.3). The error can be reduced by using
smaller integration intervals or more terms of the series expansion. In the case of Euler's Rule, the only way to improve is
to reduce the integration interval. However, it should not be
reduced to the extent that round-off error becomes appreciable.

There are several other ways to evaluate the transition
matrix. There are also other methods for developing difference
equations for systems expressed in state space form.[10] However,
they are beyond the scope of this book.

13.8 TRANSFER FUNCTION TECHNIQUE

Since many of the systems being studied are derived in
transfer function form, a digital simulation technique based on
transfer functions would be useful. Considerable effort has been
devoted to this subject and a number of techniques have been developed. A great deal of the work in this area is beyond the
scope of this book and this section will only summarize some of
the results.

One approach to developing a digital simulation model from a
transfer function is based on the material in Section 7.6. In this
approach, state variable equations are developed from the transfer
function. The state variable equations can then be solved by the
Euler approximation or other integration formulas. The state
variable equations could also be solved by utilizing the state
transition method presented in the preceding section.

The other methods for developing difference equations from
transfer functions are based on substitutions for the complex
frequency operator, s, of the Laplace transform. Most of these
methods rely on the Z-transform which is beyond the scope of this
book. The complex variable, z, is related to the complex variable,
s, by

$$z = e^{sT}, \qquad\qquad (13.8.1)$$

where T is the sample period or integration interval used previously. These methods are quite useful in studying discrete time
systems. Considerable material has been written on the subject

and the interested reader is referred to reference (9) at the end
of this chapter.

The literature on Z-transforms includes some stability analysis of integration routines. Utilizing root locus techniques,
allowable ranges for the integration interval can be determined.[7]
This work has shown that the stability of numerical integration
techniques is a function of the numerical integration formula and
the system being simulated.

13.9 PROBLEMS

Problems covering the material of this chapter are identified
by section number.

13.2.1 Use the rectangular rule (Euler's method) to determine
a difference equation for the system described by
Equation (13.9.1)

$$\dot{x} + 6x = 12, \qquad\qquad (13.9.1)$$

where $x(0) = 0$.

13.2.2 Determine the time required for the system of
Equation (13.9.1) to reach steady state. How
is this reflected in the simulation?

13.2.3 Develop a computer program to solve Equation
(13.9.1).

13.2.4 Repeat Problem 13.2.1, Problem 13.2.2 and Problem
13.2.3 for the system described by the equation

$$\dot{x} + 0.1\,x = 0, \qquad\qquad (13.9.2)$$

where $x(0) = 5.0$.

13.3.1 Determine the appropriate range of values for the
integration interval, T, for Problem 13.2.1 and
Problem 13.2.4.

13.3.2 Determine an approximate integration interval, T,
and the number of integration steps required for
simulating the systems described by equations (a)
and (b),

(a) $\ddot{x} + 0.1\dot{x} + 0.01x = .02,$ \qquad (13.9.3)

where $\dot{x}(0) = x(0) = 0$.

(b) $\ddot{x} + 80\dot{x} + 10000x = 100,$ \qquad (13.9.4)

where $\dot{x}(0) = x(0) = 0$.

13.3.3   Determine an approximate integration interval, T,
         and the number of integration steps required for
         simulating the systems described by equations (a)
         and (b),

   (a) $\dddot{x} + 6\ddot{x} + 11\dot{x} + 6x = 3,$ (13.9.5)

   where $\ddot{x}(0) = \dot{x}(0) = 0$ and $x(0) = 4.0$

   (b) $\dddot{x} + 5\ddot{x} + 13\dot{x} + 18x = 2,$ (13.9.6)

   where $\ddot{x}(0) = x(0) = 0$ and $\dot{x}(0) = 2.$

13.3.4   Develop difference equations for solving the following
         differential equations:

   (a) Equation (13.9.3)

   (b) Equation (13.9.4)

   (c) Equation (13.9.5)

   (d) Equation (13.9.6).

13.3.5   Use the rectangular rule to develop an approximate
         difference equation for the system described by
         Equation (13.9.3).

13.4.1   Use the Taylor series approximation to determine the
         truncation error for a digital simulation of the
         system described by Equation (13.9.1). Assume that
         the rectangular rule is used with a sampling interval
         of 0.1 sec.

13.4.2   Develop an integration formula based on the first
         three terms of the Taylor series expansion.

13.5.1   How much is the error of Problem 13.4.1 decreased
         if a second—order integration routine is used
         instead of the rectangular rule?

13.5.2   Discuss the implementation of a scheme to adjust
         the sampling interval as a function of truncation
         error.

13.6.1   Develop state variable equations of the form
$\dot{x} = \underline{A}\underline{x} + \underline{b}u$ for the systems described by the
following equations:
(a) Equation (13.9.1)
(b) Equation (13.9.2)
(c) Equation (13.9.3)
(d) Equation (13.9.4)
(e) Equation (13.9.5)
(f) Equation (13.9.6).

13.6.2   Use Euler's method to develop difference equations
for simulating the systems of Problem 13.6.1.

13.6.3   Develop state equations of the form $\dot{x} = \underline{A}\underline{x}$ for
the systems described by the following equations:
(a) Equation (13.9.1)
(b) Equation (13.9.2)
(c) Equation (13.9.3)
(d) Equation (13.9.4)
(e) Equation (13.9.5)
(f) Equation (13.9.6).

13.6.4   Calculate the transition matrix using a sampling
interval of 0.1 sec for the $\underline{A}$ matrix shown

$$\underline{A} = \begin{bmatrix} 1 & 2 \\ 3 & 4 \end{bmatrix}. \qquad\qquad (13.9.7)$$

13.6.5   Select appropriate integration intervals and
evaluate the transition matrix for the systems
described by the following equations:
(a) Equation (13.9.1)
(b) Equation (13.9.2)
(c) Equation (13.9.3)
(d) Equation (13.9.4)
(e) Equation (13.9.5)
(f) Equation (13.9.6).

13.6.6   Write a computer program to simulate the systems
described by the transition matrix for each part
in Problem 13.6.5.

13.10 REFERENCES FOR CHAPTER 13

(1) Evans, G. W., G. F. Wallace and G. L. Sutherland, <u>Simulation Using Digital Computers</u>, Prentice-Hall, Inc., Englewood Cliffs, N.J., 1967.

(2) Chu, Y., <u>Digital Simulation of Continuous Systems</u>, McGraw-Hill Book Company, New York, 1969.

(3) Gordon, G., <u>System Simulation</u>, Prentice-Hall, Inc., Englewood Cliffs, N.J., 1969.

(4) McLeod, John, <u>Simulation</u>, McGraw-Hill Book Company, New York, 1968.

(5) Benyon, P. R., "A Review of Numerical Methods for Digital Simulators," <u>Simulation</u>, Vol. 11, No. 5, pp. 219-238, November, 1968.

(6) Martens, H. R., "A Comparative Study of Digital Integration Methods," <u>Simulation</u>, Vol. 12, No. 2, pp. 87-95, February, 1969.

(7) Bekey, G. A. and W. J. Karplus, <u>Hybrid Computation</u>, John Wiley & Sons, Inc., New York, 1968.

(8) Capehart, B. L. and D. P. Schneider, "A State Variable Integration Routine for IBM System 360/CSMP," <u>Simulation</u>, Vol. 18, No. 4, pp. 149-151, April, 1972.

(9) Tou, J. T., <u>Digital and Sampled Data Control Systems</u>, McGraw-Hill Book Company, New York, 1959.

(10) Ogata, K., <u>State Space Analysis of Control Systems</u>, Prentice-Hall, Inc., Englewood Cliffs, N.J., 1967.

14

Digital Simulation of Continuous Systems

14.1 INTRODUCTION

Since most physical systems are continuous, a great deal of effort has been devoted to developing effective techniques for simulating continuous systems on the digital computer. Analog simulation evolved first and was well established prior to the initial efforts on digital simulation. However, the advantages of the digital computer have enabled a rapid growth of digital simulation.

The purpose of this chapter is to introduce digital simulation techniques. Since the digital computer does not contain *integrating elements,* the simulation techniques rely on the numerical integration methods discussed in the previous chapter. In presenting the various digital simulation routines, programming details will be minimized since they are dependent on a particular computer. Therefore, the material of this chapter should be supplemented with appropriate documentation for the computer system to be used.

Only one of the many available simulation programs will be discussed at length. Additional programs will be discussed briefly to illustrate other approaches that have been developed. There is a great deal of similarity among simulation programs and knowledge of a particular language should enable a user to learn other methods quickly.

In discussing digital simulation of continuous systems, a brief history will be presented first. The next section introduces a continuous system modeling program along with a illustrative example. Additional sections are devoted to simulating systems expressed in transfer function form and systems involving analog and digital elements. Each technique is illustrated with an example problem.

14.2 A BRIEF HISTORY

The first efforts towards digital simulation of continuous systems were actually attempts to transfer analog computer programs to the digital computer. This led to a whole series of *digital-analog simulators* which enabled the user to program the digital computer in the same manner as an analog computer. These programs provided the summing, integrating, and multiplying blocks of analog simulation and *programming* consisted of describing the necessary interconnections on punched cards. Thus, the digital computer was used to simulate an analog computer. As a result, programs of this type are called *digital-analog simulators*.

As digital-analog simulators were expanded and improved, strict adherence to analog computer blocks was dropped. More versatile blocks were added and additional conveniences included. Thus, digital-analog simulation has gradually evolved toward continuous system simulation. Some of the more important developments are presented in the following paragraphs. A more detailed history is available in references (1), (13), (16) and (19).

The first published work on digital-analog simulation was by R. G. Selfridge in 1955.[2] The program, written for an IBM 701, uses Simpson's Rule for numerical integration. The program contains a single subroutine for each analog block and is classified as an interpreter. The program uses the block interconnection information to time share the *analog* blocks. The program did not

have an acronym. An extension of Selfridge's work was published in
1957 by Fred Lesh. The program uses a fourth-order Runge-Kutta
integration routine and is called the Differential Equations Pseudo-
code Interpreter (DEPI).

The Analog Schematic Translator to Algebraic Language, (ASTRAL)
by Stein, Rose and Parker was developed in 1958. The program uses
blocks based on the PACE analog computer. It is classified as a
compiler, and its execution generates a second program in FORTRAN.
The program uses floating-point arithmetic and Runge-Kutta-Gill
numerical integration. It was the first simulator to include
sorting, which is a process of establishing the proper order for
computing the output of each block. In order to do this, the
program determines the sequence of signal flow through the block
diagram and computes the outputs in that order.

A Block Diagram compiler (BLODI) was developed at Bell Laboratories in 1961 for simulation of sampled data systems.

In 1962, Hurley, Skiles and Rideout introduced the Digitally
Simulated Analog Computer (DYSAC) which includes a number of
functions not available as analog computing elements. The program
operates as a translator-interpreter and includes diagnostic error
messages and a graphical output.

Stover and Knudtson introduced PARTNER (Proof of Analog Results Through Numerical Equivalent Routine) in 1962. The program
is an interpreter, and as its name indicates, intended to assist
with analog simulation. However, it can be used for free-standing
simulation. Another aid for Analog Programming and Checking
(APACHE) was developed in Italy. Also announced in 1962 were
DYNASAR (Dynamic System Analyzer) and DYNAMO (Dynamic Models). They
were developed to facilitate the simulation of industrial dynamics.

In 1963, Gaskill, Harris and McKnight announced DAS (Digital
Analog Simulator) which operates in the manner of a compiler. It
uses rectangular integration and was the beginning of a whole series
of programs. DES-1 (Differential Equation Solver) was also announced in 1963 by Palevsky, Howell and Levine.

The first simulator which permitted the programmer to create
special purpose blocks was JANIS, introduced in 1963. The program
uses FORTRAN input statements and is classified as a compiler.

An outgrowth of DAS, MIDAS (Modified Integration Digital Analog Simulator) was announced in 1963 by Peterson and Sansom. MIDAS uses fifth-order Milne predictor-corrector integration and automatically varies the integration interval. It operates in the manner of an interpreter and includes a sort feature to determine the proper sequence for computing the output of the system blocks. It was the first digital simulator to gain wide scale use.

In 1964, PACTOLUS (named for the river in which MIDAS washed away his curse) was introduced by Brennan and Sano. Written for the IBM 1620, it was intended to give the programmer hands on operation similar to analog simulation. It uses second-order Runge-Kutta integration and includes nine *special* blocks which could be defined by the programmer. A larger version of PACTOLUS was written for the IBM 7090 system. A number of block oriented languages (FORBLOCK, HYBLOC, COBLOC and MADBLOC) were also developed in 1964 at the University of Wisconsin and the University of Michigan.

By 1965, the evolution of digital simulation had reached explosive proportions. A Digital Simulation Language for the IBM 7090 (DSL/90) was announced by Syn and Linebarger. Also, Sansom and Peterson introduced MIMIC (not an acronym - a synonym for simulate). Both programs are true continuous system simulation languages. MIMIC is equation oriented (compared to the block oriented digital-analog simulation) and DSL/90 provides the programmer with a choice of eight different integration routines. At about the same time, development was initiated on the IBM 1130 CSMP (Continuous System Modeling Program) and IBM S/360 CSMP.[3] The 1130 CSMP is based on PACTOLUS and is a block oriented digital-analog simulator. S/360 CSMP is equation oriented and is an extension of DSL/90.

A number of languages were developed in Europe. SAM (Simulation of Analogue Methods) and CALDAS (Kidsgrove Algol Digital Analogue Simulation) were developed in England. ASIM (Analog Simulation) was developed in Germany. SIMTRAN, a language similar to FORTRAN, was developed in Australia.

In 1966, an improved version of MIDAS, MIDAS III, was introduced by Pergin. It uses Runge-Kutta-Merson variable step integration. By this time, the number of simulation languages

was growing so rapidly that it was becoming difficult to select
the best language for a particular application. To help overcome
this difficulty, PHYSBE (Physiological Simulation Benchmark Experiment) was proposed to serve as a basis of comparison.[4]

By 1967, more than 30 different digital simulation programs
had been reported. In order to promote an orderly growth and
development of digital simulation, the Society for Computer Simulation (SCS, formerly SCI) proposed CSSL (Continuous Systems
Simulation Language).[5] The impact of CSSL has been evident in
the developemnt of CSSL III,[6] SL-1 (Simulation Language-1) and
DARE (Differential Analyzer Replacement).[7]

In the last few years, interest in digital simulation has
continued to expand at a rapid rate and many simulation programs
have been developed. No attempt will be made here to discuss or
even list the programs. A number of special purpose simulation
programs are actually compilers which generate MIMIC or CSMP programs. A great deal of effort has also been focused on interactive
and time-share systems. Special languages for simulation on minicomputers (ISL-8) have also been developed.[8]

The brief history of digital simulation of continuous systems
presented in this section is far from complete. Hopefully, it has
provided an overview of a rapidly developing field. A number of
articles have been written which compare the various techniques
and supply much more detail.[9,10,11,16,19]

14.3   THE CONTINUOUS SYSTEM MODELING PROGRAM (CSMP)

In 1965, development of the Continuous System Modeling Program (CSMP) was initiated by IBM.[3] A small system version (1130
CSMP) was developed for the IBM 1130. It is based on PACTOLUS
and includes CRT-graphic input/output. The S/360 CSMP was developed for large systems and runs on the IBM 360 family of
machines. This section will focus on the S/360 version of the
program and its use for system simulation.

The S/360 CSMP program is based on DSL/90 and incorporates
features from PACTOLUS, MIDAS, MIMIC and CSSL. It is written
primarily in FORTRAN but does not require the user to have an
extensive knowledge of FORTRAN or digital computers. It requires
approximately 100 K bytes of core storage and all calculations

are done in single-precision floating-point arithmetic.   The system to be simulated is specified in terms of 34 functional blocks or a set of equations.   It also permits the   mixing   of blocks and equations, and in addition, allows the user to define special functions in terms of FORTRAN statements.

The functional blocks provided in CSMP include the   usual analog computing elements and several functions not available on the analog computer.   The output of each block is described in terms of the inputs and parameters as shown in Figure   14-3-1.

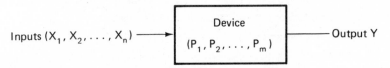

Inputs $(X_1, X_2, \ldots, X_n)$ —→ Device $(P_1, P_2, \ldots, P_m)$ ——Output Y

Figure 14-3-1.   CSMP functional blocks

Thus, the output can be expressed as

$$Y = f(P_1, P_2, \ldots, P_m, X_1, X_2, \ldots, X_n).$$ (14.3.1)

The equivalent CSMP structural statement is

OUTPUT = DEVICE (PARAMS, INPUTS),   (14.3.2)

where OUTPUT is the symbolic name of the output variable, DEVICE is the symbolic name for the block, PARAMS represents the symbolic names assigned to the block parameters and INPUTS represents the symbolic names of the input variables.   These symbolic names must start with an alphabetic character (i.e., A-Z), contain   no more than six alphameric characters (i.e., A-Z, 0-9) and contain no embedded blanks or special characters.   The constants expressed in numerical form may contain up to seven significant   decimal digits expressed directly (e.g., +17.2, -1359.1)   or   in   the exponential form (e.g., $12.2E2 = 12.2 \times 10^2$ or $-1.732E-01 = -1.732 \times 10^{-1}$).   A maximum of twelve characters can be used   to   express a constant.

The CSMP Users Manual[12] contains a complete list of the 34 functional blocks available.   They include the following analog functions: integration, differentiation, delay, dead space, hysteresis, limiter, first   and   second-order   lags,   and lead-lag elements.   Special functions include: arbitrary function gener-

ation, step, ramp, impulse and sine wave generators. Hybrid
elements include: function switches, comparators, zero-order
holds and quantizers. Digital elements include the following:
pulse generator, AND/NAND, OR/NOR, exclusive OR and NOT. In
addition, 18 FORTRAN mathematical functions are included.
Section 14.8 contains a listing of the functions available. However, before attempting to use CSMP, the Users Guide for the
particular version to be used should be obtained.

In order to carry out a simulation, the user must define
the structure of the system to be simulated, specify the value
of the system parameters and indicate the manner in which the
simulation is to be conducted. These three objectives are
achieved by means of three types of statements:

1. <u>Structural Statements</u> are used to describe the system
   in terms of functional blocks and/or equations.

2. <u>Data Statements</u> enable the assignment of numerical
   values to system parameters, constants, initial
   conditions, coordinates of arbitrary functions and
   table entries of any stored arrays to be used.

3. <u>Control Statements</u> determine the sequence of the
   simulation, the integration interval, the integration
   method, the allowable integration error and the output
   desired. The output can include printed or plotted
   values of specific variables, title information,
   minimum and maximum values on certain variables and
   conditions for terminating a run.

The first portion of a typical simulation is devoted to
setting initial conditions and problem parameters. This is
followed by a simulation run. After each run, a certain amount
of evaluation is usually required before initiating the next
run. To facilitate the sequencing of events, CSMP is divided
into three segments. The INITIAL segment is used to initialize
the model, the DYNAMIC section includes a description of the
model and actually carries out the simulation. The TERMINAL
segment is used to evaluate the results of the run and initiate
additional runs if necessary. Each of the three segments is
identified by a control statement: INITIAL, DYNAMIC and TERMINAL.

In order to illustrate the use of CSMP, the next section will present an example problem.

14.4 EXAMPLE PROBLEM

The generalized linear second-order differential equation has been used a number of times to illustrate simulation techniques (e.g., Sections 3.6, 6.3 and 7.4). It will be programmed in this section to demonstrate CSMP. The basic equation is

$$\ddot{x} + 2\delta\omega_n \dot{x} + \omega_n^2 x = \omega_n^2 f, \qquad (14.4.1)$$

with $\dot{x}(0) = x(0) = 0$. Solving Equation (14.4.1) for $\ddot{x}$ yields

$$\ddot{x} = -2\delta\omega_n \dot{x} - \omega_n^2 x + \omega_n^2 f. \qquad (14.4.2)$$

Assign symbolic names as follows: X2DOT = $\ddot{x}$, X1DOT = $\dot{x}$, X = x, ZETA = δ, OMEGAN = ω_n and FORCE = f. The following CSMP statement can be written for Equation (14.4.2),

> X2DOT = -2.0*ZETA*OMEGAN*X1DOT-X*OMEGAN**2+FORCE*OMEGAN**2
>
> (14.4.3)

where * indicates multiplication and ** signifies exponentiation. This statement is equivalent to a summing amplifier. Additional statements will be required to relate X1DOT, X2DOT and X. The CSMP equation for an integrator is

> Y = INTGRL(IC,X),   (14.4.4)

where Y is the output, X is the input and IC = Y(0), the initial condition. Thus, since $\dot{x}(0) = x(0) = 0.0$,

> X1DOT = INTGRL (0.0, X2DOT)   (14.4.5)

and

> X = INTGRL (0.0, X1DOT).   (14.4.6)

Equations (14.4.3), (14.4.5) and (14.4.6) describe the dynamics of the system.

A program to solve the equation is shown in Figure 14-4-1.

****CONTINUOUS SYSTEM MODELING PROGRAM****

*** VERSION 1.3 ***

```
 1    TITLE SECOND-ORDER SYSTEM
 2    *
 3      CONSTANT OMEGAN=2.0,FORCE=1.0,ZETA=0.5
 4    *
 5    *
 6              X2DOT=-2*ZETA*OMEGAN*X1DOT-X*OMEGAN**2+FORCE*OMEGAN**2
 7              X1DOT=INTGRL(0.0,X2DOT)
 8                  X=INTGRL(0.0,X1DOT)
 9    *
10      TIMER DELT=0.005,FINTIM=6.0,PRDEL=0.20,OUTDEL=0.20
11    *
12    PRINT X,X1DOT
13    PRTPLT X
14    LABEL X VERSUS TIME
15    END
16    STOP
```

Figure 14-4-1. CSMP program for $\ddot{x} + 2\delta\omega_n\dot{x} + \omega_n^2 x = \omega_n^2 f$

The first statement supplies a title to help document the program. The second line of the program contains only an asterisk in Column 1. The contents of a card with an asterisk in Column 1 are printed but not processed by CSMP. Therefore, statements beginning with an asterisk can be used to document the program. The asterisk on the second card generates a blank line to add space to the program listing. The third statement is the CSMP method for declaring constants. The next two statements are blank comment statements to provide space and make the program more readable. The next three statements have already been discussed. The time relationships for the program are specified on the TIMER card. The interval of integration, DELT, is set for 0.005 sec. in this example. The length of time for the run or the final time, FINTIM, is 6.0 sec. The time interval of the print-out, PRDEL, is 0.20 sec. The time interval of the print-plot output, OUTDEL, is set for 0.20 sec. The statement beginning with PRINT specifies the variables to be printed (e.g., X and X1DOT) and the PRTPLT statement indicates which variables are to be plotted by the printer. In this case, only X will be plotted.

The LABEL statement supplies a title for the plot. The END and STOP statements indicate the completion of the simulation.

Each statement is placed on a single punched card and stacked as shown in Figure 14-4-2. Usually, there are additional cards

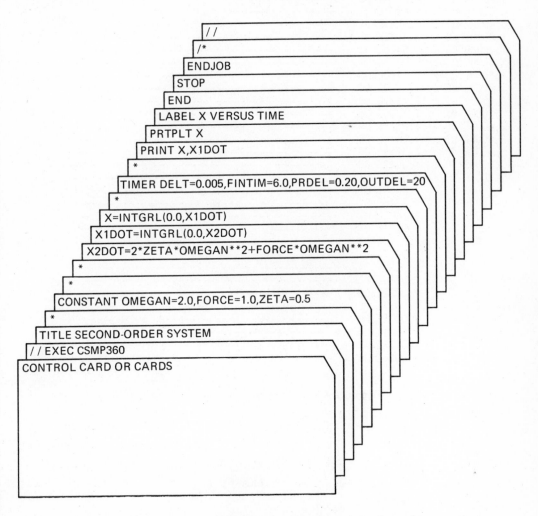

Figure 14-4-2. CSMP program for $\ddot{x} + 2\delta\omega_n\dot{x} + \omega_n^2 x = \omega_n^2 f$

at the beginning and end of the program deck. These are control statements and will vary from one installation to another. The resulting output is shown in Figure 14-4-3.

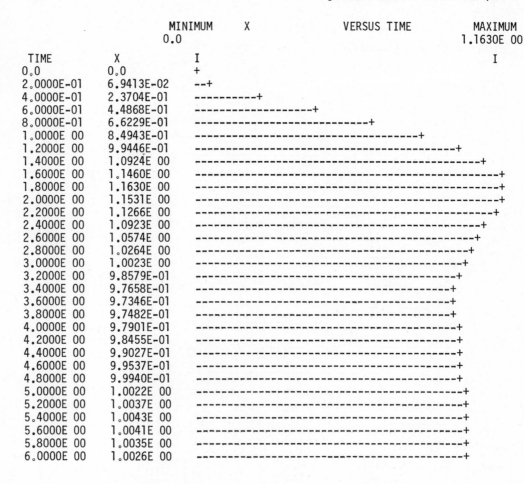

Figure 14-4-3.   Print/plot output of CSMP program

A parameter specification statement (PARAM) is required if several runs for different values of a parameter are desired. For example, if runs for δ = 0.2, 0.4, 0.6 and 0.8 are desired, the following card must be added to the program prior to the constant statement (CONST),

$$\text{PARAM ZETA} = (0.2,\ 0.4,\ 0.6,\ 0.8). \tag{14.4.7}$$

In this case, the constant statement should now read,

$$\text{CONST OMEGAN} = 2.0,\ \text{FORCE} = 1.0, \tag{14.4.8}$$

in order to permit the variation of ZETA.

Although the integration interval was specified, nothing in the program indicated the numerical integration method to be used. Eight numerical integration methods are available:

1. MILNE: Milne fifth-order predictor-corrector
2. RKSFX: Runge-Kutta fourth-order (fixed interval)
3. RKS: Runge-Kutta fourth-order (variable interval)
4. ADAMS: Adams second-order
5. SIMP: Simpson's
6. TRAPZ: Trapezoidal
7. RECT: Rectangular
8. CENTRL: Supplied by user

The type of integration used is specified by a METHOD statement. For example,

$$\text{METHOD} \qquad \text{RECT} \tag{14.4.9}$$

causes the integration to be carried out with the Rectangular Rule. In the absence of a METHOD statement, the Runge-Kutta variable integration interval (RKS) is used. Valuable insight can be gained by simulating the same problem with different integration rules and different integration intervals.

14.5 TRANSFER FUNCTION SIMULATION

The utility of a simulator that can work directly from the transfer function of a system was discussed in the previous chapter. It was noted that considerable effort has been devoted to the subject[17,18] However, most of these approaches relied on the Z-transform and are beyond the scope of this book. In Section 13.8, a procedure was presented for developing a digital model of a transfer function by means of state variables.

A number of functions for simulating systems expressed in transfer function form have been incorporated in CSMP. In addition, other expressions can be added by defining special functions. The program includes a functional block for a first-order lag (real pole) of the form

$$\frac{Y(s)}{X(s)} = \frac{1}{Ps + 1} \cdot \tag{14.5.1}$$

The equivalent CSMP statement is

$$Y = \text{REALPL (IC,P,X)}, \tag{14.5.2}$$

where IC is the initial condition and P is the real pole.   The
corresponding differential equation is

$$P\dot{y} + y = x,\tag{14.5.3}$$

with the initial condition $y(0)$.

A functional block for a lead-lag network of the form

$$\frac{Y(s)}{X(s)} = \frac{P_1 s + 1}{P_2 s + 1},\tag{14.5.4}$$

is also included. The equivalent CSMP statement is

$$Y = LEDLAG(P_1, P_2, X),\tag{14.5.5}$$

which solves the differential equation

$$P_2\dot{y} + y = P_1\dot{x} + x.\tag{14.5.6}$$

The program also includes a block for a second-order lag with
complex poles

$$\frac{Y(s)}{X(s)} = \frac{1}{s^2 + 2P_1 P_2 s + P_2^2}.\tag{14.5.7}$$

The equivalent CSMP statement is

$$Y = CMPXPL\ (IC_1, IC_2, P_1, P_2, X),\tag{14.5.8}$$

which solves the differential equation

$$\ddot{y} + 2P_1 P_2\dot{y} + P_2^2 y = x,\tag{14.5.9}$$

with $y(0) = IC_1$, and $\dot{y}(0) = IC_2$.   Thus, the second-order system of
the previous section could be solved with one statement in the
form of Equation (14.5.8) instead of three statements, Equations
(14.4.3), (14.4.5) and (14.4.6). Since the transfer functions of
most physical systems can be factored into terms of the form of
Equations (14.5.1), (14.5.4) and (14.5.7), CSMP is a useful tool
for simulating systems in transfer function form.

In addition to the functional blocks discussed previously,
the methods presented in Chapters 6 and 7 can be used to develop
a block diagram or state model from the transfer function.   The

resulting block diagram or state model can then be used as a basis for a CSMP simulation.

14.6 HYBRID SYSTEMS

In Chapters 8, 9 and 10, the use of combinational and sequential logic in system simulation was discussed. A number of advantages were noted and many physical systems involve both analog and digital elements. Since CSMP includes functional blocks for analog and digital variables, hybrid systems can be simulated.

A Track-Store or Hold function is defined by the CSMP statement

$$Y = \text{ZHOLD}(X_1, X_2) , \tag{14.6.1}$$

where $Y = X_2$ if $X_1 > 0$ and Y is in hold mode if $X_1 \leq 0$. This is equivalent to a zero-order hold and is quite useful in analog-to-digital conversion and digital-to-analog conversion. Basically, the ZHOLD statement enables the freezing or holding of the value of a variable, X_2, in response to changes in a second variable, X_1. If X_1 is considered as the track signal, the ZHOLD statement is identical to the track-store defined in Section 8.7.

The program also includes a comparator defined by the CSMP statement

$$Y = \text{COMPAR}(X_1, X_2), \tag{14.6.2}$$

where $Y = 0$ if $X_1 < X_2$ and $Y = 1$ if $X_1 \geq X_2$. The comparator can be used to compare two analog variables and change the output logic state as a function of their relative values. Section 8.10 contains an example problem illustrating the utility of comparators and track-store units.

A function switch (e.g., see Section 8.6) is also available in CSMP. The equivalent statement is of the form

$$Y = \text{FCNSW}(X_1, X_2, X_3, X_4), \tag{14.6.3}$$

where $Y = X_2$ if $X_1 < 0$, $Y = X_3$ if $X_1 = 0$ and $Y = X_4$ if $X_1 > 0$. This enables the structure of a model to be altered as a function

of a variable X_1. Note that this alteration can take place at
any point in a simulation run without interrupting the simulation.

A resettable flip-flop (e.g., see Section 10.2) is also provided by CSMP. The operation of the flip-flop is defined by the
expression

$$Y = RST(X_1, X_2, X_3),$$ (14.6.4)

where $Y = 0$ if $X_1 > 0$ and $Y = 1$ if $X_1 \leq 0$ and $X_2 > 0$. However,
if $X_1 \leq 0$, $X_2 \leq 0$ and $X_3 > 0$, then the output is $Y_n = \bar{Y}_{n-1}$. Also,
if $X_1 \leq 0$, $X_2 \leq 0$ and $X_3 \leq 0$, then $Y_n = Y_{n-1}$. Thus, the RST
function can simulate the operation of a RS flip-flop or a
clocked flip-flop. The operation of the flip-flop is summarized
in Figure 14-6-1. Note that the input X_3 is used.

Inputs			Output
X_1	X_2	X_3	Y
≤ 0	≤ 0	≤ 0	$Y_n = Y_{n-1}$
≤ 0	≤ 0	> 0	$Y_n = \bar{Y}_{n-1}$
≤ 0	> 0	≤ 0	1
≤ 0	> 0	> 0	1
> 0	≤ 0	≤ 0	0
> 0	≤ 0	> 0	0
> 0	> 0	≤ 0	0
> 0	> 0	> 0	0

Figure 14-6-1. Flip-flop operating characteristics

Since a logic 1 is greater than zero, (1>0), and a logic 0
is equal to zero, logic values can be substituted for the input
variables of Figure 14-6-1. The resulting operating characteristics are shown in Figure 14-6-2 to produce clocked operation.
The set-reset action is provided by inputs X_1 and X_2. The output
is a logic 0 any time $X_1 = 1$. Therefore, X_1 is equivalent to the
reset input. The flip-flop is set when $X_1 = 0$ and $X_2 = 1$. A number
of applications for flip-flops are presented in Chapter 10.

Logic Inputs			Output
X_1	X_2	X_3	Y
0	0	0	$Y_n = Y_{n-1}$
0	0	1	$Y_n = \overline{Y}_{n-1}$
0	1	0	1
0	1	1	1
1	0	0	0
1	0	1	0
1	1	0	0
1	1	1	0

Figure 14-6-2. Flip-flop operating characteristics

The logic functions discussed in Chapter 9 are also available in CSMP. The AND gate is defined by the functional expression

$$Y = AND(X_1, X_2), \tag{14.6.5}$$

where $Y = 1$ if and only if $X_1 > 0$ and $X_2 > 0$. The complement of the AND gate (i.e., the NAND gate) is defined by the statement

$$Y = NAND(X_1, X_2), \tag{14.6.6}$$

where $Y = 0$ if and only if $X_1 > 0$ and $X_2 > 0$. An inclusive OR gate is provided by the expression

$$Y = IOR(X_1, X_2), \tag{14.6.7}$$

where $Y = 1$ if either $X_1 > 0$ or $X_2 > 0$. CSMP also includes the NOR gate which is the complement of the OR gate. The statement for the NOR function is

$$Y = NOR(X_1, X_2), \tag{14.6.8}$$

where $Y = 0$ if either $X_1 > 0$ or $X_2 > 0$. An exclusive OR gate is defined

$$Y = EOR(X_1, X_2), \tag{14.6.9}$$

where $Y = 1$ if $X_1 > 0$ and $X_2 \leq 0$, $Y = 1$ if $X_1 \leq 0$ and $X_2 > 0$ and $Y = 0$ for all other values of X_1 and X_2. Another important logic function, NOT, is also available. It is defined by the expression

$$Y = NOT(X), \qquad\qquad\qquad (14.6.10)$$

where $Y = 1$ if $X \leq 0$ and $Y = 0$ if $X > 0$.

14.7 EXAMPLE PROBLEM

In order to demonstrate the use of CSMP to simulate hybrid problems, the example in Section 8.10 will be repeated here. The problem will illustrate the use of a comparator and a track-store unit to track and store the peak value in the step response of an underdamped second-order system. The system is defined by the equation

$$\ddot{x} + 0.5\dot{x} + 0.25x = 0.4, \qquad\qquad (14.7.1)$$

with $\dot{x}(0) = x(0) = 0$. In order to determine the maximum value of x, note that $\dot{x} = 0$ at all maximum and minimum values of x. There-fore, a comparator can be used to detect the zero crossings of $\dot{x}$ (i.e., the maximum and minimum points of x). The output of the comparator is used to cause a track-store unit to stop tracking x and go into the store mode. During the first part of the re-sponse, x is increasing and $\dot{x}$ is positive. Thus, the comparator is in the 1 state. At the instant x is at the maximum point, $\dot{x}$ goes through zero and becomes negative as x starts to decrease. A comparator monitoring $\dot{x}$ goes from the 1 state to the zero state at this instant. The output of the comparator causes a track-store (ZHOLD) unit to track during the rise of x ($\dot{x}$ is positive) and switch to the store mode at the instant x is a maximum.

A CSMP program for the equation would have the following structural statements:

$$X2DOT = -0.5*X1DOT - 0.25*X + 0.4, \qquad (14.7.2)$$

$$X1DOT = INTGRL(0.0, X2DOT), \qquad\qquad (14.7.3)$$

and

$$X = INTGRL(0.0, X1DOT). \qquad\qquad\qquad (14.7.4)$$

Equations (14.7.2), (14.7.3) and (14.7.4) could be replaced with Equation (14.5.8) with P_1 = 0.5 and P_2 = 0.5. A CSMP statement for the comparator to detect the zero crossing of X1DOT is

$$MAXPOX = COMPAR(X1DOT, 0.0), \tag{14.7.5}$$

where MAXPOX is the symbolic name of <u>max</u>imum <u>p</u>oint <u>of</u> X. From the term for a comparator in Equation (14.6.2), MAXPOX will have a value of logic 1 initially and change to logic 0 when $\dot{x}$ (i.e., X1DOT) goes negative. Since a logic 1 is required to make the ZHOLD function of Equation (14.6.1) track its input, the output of MAXPOX can be used directly. When X passes through a maximum point, X1DOT goes negative causing MAXPOX to go to the 0 state. Thus, MAXPOX can be used to cause a ZHOLD function to go into the hold mode and store the maximum value of X. The CSMP statement for the hold function is,

$$XMAX = ZHOLD(MAXPOX, X). \tag{14.7.6}$$

A CSMP program incorporating statements (14.7.5) and (14.7.6) is shown in Figure 14-7-1. The CSMP program is equivalent to the

```
        ****CONTINUOUS SYSTEM MODELING PROGRAM****


TITLE SECOND-ORDER SYSTEM
*
   CONSTANT OMEGAN=2.0,FORCE=1.0,ZETA=0.5
*
*
        X2DOT=-2*ZETA*OMEGAN*X1DOT-X*OMEGAN**2+FORCE*OMEGAN**2
        X1DOT=INTGRL(0.0,X2DOT)
            X=INTGRL(0.0,X1DOT)
*
     MAXPOX=COMPAR(X1DOT,0.0)
        XMAX=ZHOLD(MAXPOX,X)
*
   TIMER DELT=0.005,FINTIM=6.0,PRDEL=0.20,OUTDEL=0.20
*
PRINT X,X1DOT,XMAX
PRTPLT XMAX
LABEL XMAX VERSUS TIME
END
STOP
```

Figure 14-7-1. CSMP program with hybrid elements

hybrid program shown in Figure 8-10-1, (i.e., the latch connection is
removed from the comparator). The response curve for the simulation is shown in Figure 14-7-2.

```
                        MINIMUM     XMAX          VERSUS TIME        MAXIMUM
                          0.0                                       1.1630E 00

TIME          X            I                                              I

0.0          0.0          +
2.0000E-01   6.9413E-02   --+
4.0000E-01   2.3704E-01   -----------+
6.0000E-01   4.4868E-01   ---------------------+
8.0000E-01   6.6229E-01   -------------------------------+
1.0000E 00   8.4943E-01   ----------------------------------------+
1.2000E 00   9.9446E-01   -------------------------------------------------+
1.4000E 00   1.0924E 00   ------------------------------------------------------+
1.6000E 00   1.1460E 00   --------------------------------------------------------+
1.8000E 00   1.1630E 00   ---------------------------------------------------------+
2.0000E 00   1.1630E 00   ---------------------------------------------------------+
2.2000E 00   1.1630E 00   ---------------------------------------------------------+
2.4000E 00   1.0630E 00   ---------------------------------------------------------+
2.6000E 00   1.0630E 00   ---------------------------------------------------------+
2.8000E 00   1.0630E 00   ---------------------------------------------------------+
3.0000E 00   1.0630E 00   ---------------------------------------------------------+
3.2000E 00   1.0630E 00   ---------------------------------------------------------+
3.4000E 00   1.0630E 00   ---------------------------------------------------------+
3.6000E 00   1.0630E 00   ---------------------------------------------------------+
3.8000E 00   9.7482E-01   -------------------------------------------------+
4.0000E 00   9.7901E-01   -------------------------------------------------+
4.2000E 00   9.8455E-01   --------------------------------------------------+
4.4000E 00   9.9027E-01   --------------------------------------------------+
4.6000E 00   9.9537E-01   --------------------------------------------------+
4.8000E 00   9.9940E-01   --------------------------------------------------+
5.0000E 00   1.0022E 00   ---------------------------------------------------+
5.2000E 00   1.0037E 00   ---------------------------------------------------+
5.4000E 00   1.0043E 00   ---------------------------------------------------+
5.6000E 00   1.0043E 00   ---------------------------------------------------+
5.8000E 00   1.0043E 00   ---------------------------------------------------+
6.0000E 00   1.0043E 00   ---------------------------------------------------+
```

Figure 14-7-2.   Print/plot output of CSMP program

With the statements in their present form, the ZHOLD function
will track when X1DOT is positive or zero and hold when X1DOT is
negative. This would cause the ZHOLD function to acquire and hold
briefly each successive maximum value of X. If the peak value of
the first overshoot is desired, additional elements are required

to cause ZHOLD to lock in the hold mode and remain there even when X1DOT goes positive following negative excursions. This can be achieved by adding a flip-flop to the simulation diagram between the comparator and the hold (track-store). The flip-flop should be connected in a manner such that it is set when X1DOT goes negative and remains set even when X1DOT goes positive and negative at other maximum and minimum points.

As an illustration of combining analog, hybrid and digital elements in a single CSMP program, consider the example problem of Section 9.9. The example problem used analog elements to simulate a dynamic system, hybrid elements (comparators) to detect certain ranges of variables and digital elements (AND or OR gates) to determine if certain combinations of system conditions have occurred. A CSMP program to carry out a similar simulation is shown in Figure 14-7-3. A printed output listing for the program variables is shown in Figure 14-7-4. A plot of the problem variables is shown is shown in Figure 14-7-5. Note that the values for this example differ from those of Figure 9-9-1.

```
****CONTINUOUS SYSTEM MODELING PROGRAM****


TITLE        HYBRID SYSTEM
*
   CONSTANT OMEGAN=2.0,FORCE=1.0,ZETA=0.5
*
            X2DOT=-2.0*ZETA*OMEGAN*X1DOT-X*OMEGAN**2+FORCE*OMEGAN**2
            X1DOT=INTGRL(0.0,X2DOT)
               X=INTGRL(0.0,X1DOT)
*
            C1=COMPAR(X1DOT,0.1)
            C2=COMPAR(-X1DOT,0.1)
            C3=COMPAR(X,1.0)
*
            GA=IOR(C1,C2)
            GB=AND(C3,ORG)
*
   TIMER DELT=0.005,FINTIM=6.0, PRDEL=0.2,OUTDEL=0.2
   PRINT X, X1DOT, C1, C2, C3, GA, GB
*
END
STOP
```

Figure 14-7-3. CSMP program with analog, hybrid and digital elements

HYBRID SYSTEM

TIME	X	X1DOT	C1	C2	C3	GA	GB
0.0	0.0	0.0	0.0	0.0	0.0	0.0	0.0
0.200000	6.9412E-02	0.64196	1.0000	0.0	0.0	1.0000	0.0
0.400000	0.23704	0.98875	1.0000	0.0	0.0	1.0000	0.0
0.600000	0.44868	1.0925	1.0000	0.0	0.0	1.0000	0.0
0.800000	0.66229	1.0200	1.0000	0.0	0.0	1.0000	0.0
1.00000	0.84943	0.83857	1.0000	0.0	0.0	1.0000	1.0000
1.20000	0.99446	0.60786	1.0000	0.0	0.0	1.0000	1.0000
1.40000	1.0924	0.37411	0.0	0.0	1.0000	1.0000	0.0
1.60000	1.1460	0.16874	0.0	0.0	1.0000	1.0000	0.0
1.80000	1.1630	9.11456E-03	0.0	0.0	1.0000	1.0000	0.0
2.00000	1.1531	-9.90690E-02	0.0	0.0	1.0000	1.0000	1.0000
2.20000	1.1266	-0.15870	0.0	1.0000	1.0000	0.0	1.0000
2.40000	1.0923	-0.17801	0.0	1.0000	1.0000	0.0	1.0000
2.60000	1.0574	-0.16780	0.0	1.0000	1.0000	0.0	1.0000
2.80000	1.0264	-0.13911	0.0	1.0000	1.0000	0.0	0.0
3.00000	1.0023	-0.10178	0.0	0.0	0.0	0.0	0.0
3.20000	0.98579	-6.35142E-02	0.0	0.0	0.0	0.0	0.0
3.40000	0.97658	-2.95965E-02	0.0	0.0	0.0	0.0	0.0
3.60000	0.97346	-3.00928E-03	0.0	0.0	0.0	0.0	0.0
3.80000	0.97482	1.52044E-02	0.0	0.0	0.0	0.0	0.0
4.00000	0.97901	2.54351E-02	0.0	0.0	0.0	0.0	0.0
4.20000	0.98455	2.89832E-02	0.0	0.0	0.0	0.0	0.0
4.40000	0.99027	2.75900E-02	0.0	0.0	0.0	0.0	0.0
4.60000	0.99537	2.30658E-02	0.0	0.0	1.0000	0.0	0.0
4.80000	0.99940	1.70317E-02	0.0	0.0	1.0000	0.0	0.0
5.00000	1.0022	1.07709E-02	0.0	0.0	1.0000	0.0	0.0
5.20000	1.0037	5.17302E-03	0.0	0.0	1.0000	0.0	0.0
5.40000	1.0043	7.47747E-04	0.0	0.0	1.0000	0.0	0.0
5.60000	1.0041	-2.31542E-03	0.0	0.0	1.0000	0.0	0.0
5.80000	1.0035	-4.06684E-03	0.0	0.0	1.0000	0.0	0.0
6.00000	1.0026	-4.71098E-03	0.0	0.0	1.0000	0.0	0.0

Figure 14-7-4. Printed output for CSMP program

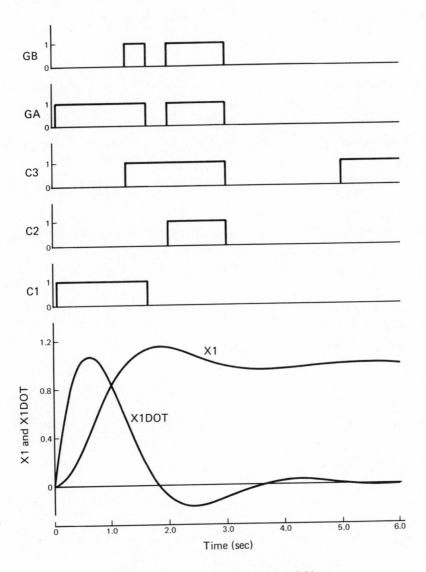

Figure 14-7-5. Plot of program variables

14.8   SUMMARY OF CSMP FUNCTIONS

The more commonly used CSMP functions are presented in this section. The functions are classified in the following categories: analog, hybrid, digital and forcing functions.

ANALOG FUNCTIONS

Name	Form	Comment
Function Generator (Linear Interpolation)	Y=AFGEN(FUNCT,X)	Permits user defined functions
Function Generator (Quadratic Interpolation)	Y=NLFGEN(FUNCT,X)	Permits user defined functions
Second-Order Lag (Complex Pole)	Y=CMPXPL(IC1,P1,P2,X)	$G(s)=1(s^2+2P1*P2s+P2^2)$ $=Y(s)/X(s)$
Dead Space	Y=DEADSP(P1,P2,X)	P1 = LEFT LIMIT P2 = RIGHT LIMIT
Hysteresis Loop	Y=HSTRSS(IC,P1,P2,X)	P1 = LEFT LIMIT P2 = RIGHT LIMIT
Integrator	Y=INTGRL(IC,X)	IC = INITIAL CONDITION X = INPUT
Dead Time (Delay)	Y=DELAY(N,P,X)	P = DELAY TIME N = POINTS IN INTERVAL P
Derivative	Y=DERIV(IC,X)	IC = INITIAL CONDITION X = INPUT
Integrator	Y=MODINT(IC,X1,X2,X3)	X1 = OPERATE, X2 = RESET X3 = INPUT
Lead-Lag	Y=LEDLAG(P1,P2,X)	$G(s)=(P1s + 1)/(P2s + 1)$ $=Y(s)/X(s)$
Limiter	Y=LIMIT(P1,P2,X)	P1 = LEFT LIMIT P2 = RIGHT LIMIT
First-Order Lag (Real Pole)	H=REALPL(IC,P,X)	$G(s)=1/(Ps + 1)$ $=Y(s)/X(s)$

HYBRID FUNCTIONS

Name	Form	Comment
Comparator	Y=COMPAR(X1,X2)	Y=1 if X1 $\geq$ X2
		Y=0 if X1 < X2
Function Switch	Y=FCNSW(X1,X2,X3,X4)	Y=X2 if X1 < 0
		Y=X3 if X1 = 0
		Y=X4 if X1 > 0
Input Switch Relay	Y=INSW(X1,X2,X3)	Y=X2 if X1 < 0
		Y=X3 if X1 $\geq$ 0
Output Switch	Y1,Y2=OUTSW(X1,X2)	Y1=X2,Y2=0 if X1 < 0
Quantizer	Y=QNTZR(P,X)	P=Quantitization Increment, X=Input
Zero-Order Hold	Y=ZHOLD(X1,X2)	X2=Input, X1=Track

DIGITAL FUNCTIONS

Name	Form	Comment
And	Y=AND(X1,X2)	Y=(X1 and X2)=(X1·X2)
Exclusive Or	Y=EOR(X1,X2)	Y=(X1 EXOR X2) $=(\bar{X}1 \cdot X2 + X1 \cdot \bar{X}2)$
Inclusive Or	Y=IOR(X1,X2)	Y=(X1 or X2)=(X1 + X2)
Nand	Y=NAND(X1,X2)	$Y=\overline{(X1 \text{ and } X2)}$ $=\overline{(X1 \cdot X2)}$
Nor	Y=NOR(X1,X2)	Y=(X1 or X2)=(X1 + X2)
Not	Y=NOT(X)	$Y=\bar{X}$
Resettable Flip-Flop	Y=RST(X1,X2,X3)	Y=0 X1 > 0
		Y=1 X2 > 0, X1 $\leq$ 0
		Y=0 X1 $\leq$ 0, X2 $\leq$ 0, X3 > 0
		Y=1 X1 $\leq$ 0, X2 $\leq$ 0, X3 $\leq$ 0

FORCING FUNCTIONS

Name	Form	Comment
Random Number Noise Generator (Normal Distribution)	Y=GAUSS(P1,P2,P3)	P1 = Odd Integer P2 = Mean P3 = Standard Derivation
Random Number Noise Generator (Uniform Distribution)	Y=RNDGEN(P)	P = Odd Integer
Impulse Generator	Y=IMPULS(P1,P2)	P1 = Start Time P2 = Period
Pulse Generator	Y=PULSE(P,X)	Start When x > 0 P = Duration
Ramp Function	Y=RAMP(P)	P = Start Time
Sine Function	Y=SINE(P1,P2,P3)	P1 = Delay P2 = Frequency in Radians P3 = Phase Shift
Step Function	Y=STEP(P)	P = Start Time

14.9 NONLINEAR EQUATIONS

The techniques introduced in this chapter can be applied directly to solve nonlinear equations. The analog functions provided by CSMP are capable of simulating the more common nonlinearities directly. In instances in which the available functions do not apply, the function generation capability may be used. In other cases, it may be necessary to define a function in terms of a FORTRAN routine. The approach is straightforward and will not be illustrated here.

14.10 INDUSTRIAL SYSTEMS

In going from analog-digital simulation to general purpose simulators considerable flexibility has been achieved. In addition to simulating the operation of the classical analog elements, digital simulation languages can be used to study the operation of all types of dynamic systems. Thus, continuous system simulation languages have been widely used in the study of industrial dynamics, a field devoted to the study of relationships between the performance of a business and its organization. This is beyond the scope of this book and the interested reader should see references (14) and (15).

14.11 PROBLEMS

Problems covering the material of this chapter are identified by section number.

14.4.1 Verify the solution of the example problem of Section 14.4 by preparing a CSMP (or other digital simulation) program.

14.4.2 Alter the program to make repeated runs for $\omega_n = 1.0$, 2.0, 4.0 while holding $\delta=0.5$.

14.4.3 Develop a program to solve the state equation

$$\begin{bmatrix} \dot{x}_1 \\ \dot{x}_2 \end{bmatrix} = \begin{bmatrix} 1 & 2 \\ 3 & 4 \end{bmatrix} \begin{bmatrix} x_1 \\ x_2 \end{bmatrix} + \begin{bmatrix} 0 \\ 1 \end{bmatrix} 2 . \qquad (14.11.1)$$

14.4.4 Develop a program to solve the equation

$$\dddot{x} + 15\ddot{x} + 30\dot{x} + 60x = 90, \qquad (14.11.2)$$

where all initial conditions are zero.

14.4.5 Develop a program to solve the equation

$$\ddot{x} + 0.008\dot{x} + 0.001x = 0, \qquad (14.11.3)$$

with $\dot{x}(0) = 2.0$ and $x(0) = 0$.

14.4.6 Use CSMP (or equivalent) to solve the equation of Problem 4.3.1.

14.4.7 Use CSMP (or equivalent) to solve the equation of Problem 4.3.5.

14.4.8 Use CSMP (or equivalent) to solve the equation of Problem 4.3.10.

14.4.9 Use CSMP (or equivalent) to solve the equation of Problem 4.3.13.

14.4.10 Use CSMP (or equivalent) to solve the equation of Problem 4.7.11.

14.4.11 Use CSMP (or equivalent) to solve the equation of Problem 4.10.1.

14.5.1 Develop a program to simulate the transfer function

$$T(s) = \frac{3.5}{s + 1.2} . \qquad (14.11.4)$$

14.5.2   Develop a program to simulate the transfer
         function

$$T(s) = \frac{0.001}{s + 0.01}.$$ (14.11.5)

14.5.3   Develop a transfer function for the equation

$$\ddot{x} + 3\dot{x} + 2x = f(t),$$ (14.10.6)

         where $\dot{x}(0) = x(0) = 0$ and $f(t)$ is arbitrary.

14.5.4   Develop a program to simulate the system of 14.5.2
         for a unit step input, $f(t) = 1.0$.

14.5.5   Develop a program to simulate the system of Problem
         6.3.1.

14.5.6   Develop a program to simulate the system of Problem
         6.3.2.

14.5.7   Develop a program to simulate the system of Problem
         6.3.3.

14.5.8   Develop a program to simulate the system of Problem
         6.4.1.

14.5.9   Develop a program to simulate the system of Problem
         6.4.2.

14.5.10 Develop a program to simulate the system of
         Problem 6.4.3.

14.5.11 Develop a program to simulate the system of
         Problem 6.6.1.

14.5.12 Develop a program to simulate the system of
         Problem 6.6.2.

14.5.13 Develop a program to simulate the system of
         Problem 6.6.3.

14.5.14 Develop a program to simulate the system of
         Problem 6.8.1.

14.5.15 Develop a program to simulate the system of
         Problem 6.8.2.

14.8.1   Use a parameter statement to solve Problem
         8.7.2 using CSMP or equivalent.

14.8.2   Use CSMP to do Problem 8.10.3.

14.8.3   Use CSMP to do Problem 8.10.4.

14.8.4   Use CSMP to do Problem 8.11.5.

14.8.5   Use CSMP to do Problem 8.11.6.

14.8.6   Use CSMP to do Problem 8.11.7.

14.8.7   Use CSMP to do Problem 8.11.8.

14.8.8   Use CSMP to do Problem 9.9.1.

14.8.9   Use CSMP to do Problem 9.9.2.

14.8.10 Use CSMP to do Problem 9.9.3.

14.8.11 Use CSMP to do Problem 9.9.4.

14.8.12 Use CSMP to do Problem 10.2.1.

14.8.13 Use CSMP to do Problem 10.5.1.

14.8.14 Use CSMP to do Problem 10.6.1.

14.8.15 Use CSMP to do Problem 10.6.2.

14.8.16 Use CSMP to do Problem 10.6.3.

14.8.17 Use CSMP to do Problem 10.6.4.

14.8.18 Use CSMP to do Problem 10.6.5.

14.8.19 Use CSMP to do Problem 10.6.6.

14.8.20 Use CSMP to do Problem 10.7.1.

14.8.21 Use CSMP to do Problem 10.7.2.

14.8.22 Use CSMP to do Problem 10.9.1.

14.8.23 Use CSMP to do Problem 10.9.2.

14.8.24 Use CSMP to do Problem 10.9.3.

14.9.1   Use CSMP to do Problem 5.3.1.

14.9.2   Use CSMP to do Problem 5.5.1.

14.9.3   Use CSMP to do Problem 5.5.3.

14.12   REFERENCES FOR CHAPTER 14

(1) Linebarger, R. N., and R. D. Brennan, "A Survey of Digital Simulations: Digital-Analog Simulation Program," *Simulation*, Vol. III, No. 6, pp. 22-36, Dec. 1964.

(2) R. G. Selfridge, "Coding a General-Purpose Digital Computer to Operate as a Differential Analyzer," Proceedings 1955 Western Joint Computer Conference.

(3) Brennan, R. D. and M. Y. Silberberg, "The System/360 Continuous System Modeling Program," *Simulation*, Vol. 11, No. 6, pp. 301-308, December, 1968.

(4) McLeod, John, "PHYSBE-A Physiological Simulation Benchmark Experiment," *Simulation*, Vol. 7, No. 6, pp. 324-329, Dec. 1966.

(5) SCi Software Committee, "The SCi Continuous System Simulation Language (CSSL)," Simulation, Vol. 9, No. 6, pp. 281-303, Dec. 1967.

(6) Control Data Corporation, CSSL III Users Guide, Publication No. 17304400, 1971.

(7) Korn, G. A., "Project DARE: Differential Analyzer Replacement by On-Line Digital Simulation," Proceedings of AFIPS Fall Joint Computer Conference, pp. 247-254, 1969.

(8) Benham, R. D.,"Interactive Simulation Language - 8 (ISL-8)," Simulation, Vol. 16, No. 3, pp. 116-129, March 1971.

(9) Martem, H. R., "A Comparative Study of Digital Integration Methods," Simulation, Vol. 12, No. 2, pp. 87-94, February 1969.

(10) Benyon, P. R., "A Review of Numerical Methods for Digital Simulation," Simulation, Vol. 11, No. 5, pp. 219-238, November 1968.

(11) Tiechroew, D., F. W. Lubin and T. D. Truitt, "Discussion of Computer Simulation Techniques and Comparison of Languages," Simulation, Vol. 9, No. 4, pp. 181-190, October 1967.

(12) System/360 Continuous System Modeling Program (360A-CX-16X) Users Manual, H20-0367-2).

(13) Gordon, G., System Simulation, Prentice-Hall, Inc., Englewood Cliffs, N.J., 1969.

(14) Ansoff, H. I. and D. P. Slevin, "An Appreciation of Industrial Dynamics," Management Science, Vol. XIV, No. 7, pp. 383-397, March 1968.

(15) Clancy, J. J. and M. S. Fineberg, "Digital Simulation Languages: A Critique and a Guide," Proceedings, Fall Joint Computer Conference, 1965.

(16) Fryer, W. D. and W. C. Schultz, "A Survey of Methods for Digital Simulation of Control Systems," Cornell Aeronautical Laboratory Report No. ZA-1691-6-1, July 1964.

(17) Corrington, M. S., "Simplified Calculation of Transient Response," Proceedings of the IEEE, Vol.53,
No. 3 , pp. 287-292, March 1965.

(18) Chu, Y., Digital Simulation of Continuous Systems,
McGraw-Hill Book Company, New York, 1969.

(19) Nilsen, R.N. and W.J. Karplus, "Continuous-System
Simulation Languages: A State-of-the-Art Survey,"
Proceedings of the International Association for
Analog Computation,Vol.XVI, No. 1, pp. 17-25, Jan
1974.

15

Digital Simulation of Discrete Systems

15.1 INTRODUCTION

The variables of many physical systems are not continuous and are known to operate only at discrete values. For example, studies of vehicular traffic, supermarket customers, inventory systems, manufacturing processes, etc., involve the flow and interaction of distinct units or entities. The purpose of this chapter is to introduce the subject of discrete system simulation and give a brief overview of some of the programs that have been developed. Although an example problem is included, the material of this chapter is not intended to serve as a complete guide to discrete system simulation. If detailed information on a specific simulation program is desired, an appropriate user's guide should be obtained.

The first part of this book is devoted to analog simulation of continuous systems. In the second part, digital signals are characterized and hybrid computing elements introduced to

link analog and digital systems. The resulting hybrid computers
are used to simulate systems involving continuous and discrete
variables. In later chapters, the digital computer is introduced and used to simulate continuous systems by means of
numerical approximations. This chapter will concentrate on
techniques for simulating discrete systems on the digital
computer. Thus, both continuous and discrete systems can be
simulated on either type of computer.

Before discussing discrete system simulation, it would
be beneficial to compare continuous and discrete systems. The
variables of a continuous system undergo transition from one
value to another value in a smooth *continuous* manner, occupying
all intermediate values. In contrast, the variables of a
discrete system *jump* from one point to another point and do not
necessarily occupy intermediate values. Most continuous systems
are described by differential equations, while discrete systems
are often characterized by difference equations. Also, many
discrete systems are stochastic or random in nature. Actually,
most systems involve both continuous and discrete elements and
are usually studied in terms of the predominant characteristic.

In both continuous and discrete simulation, time is usually
the dependent variable. In the case of digital simulation of
continuous systems, time is usually subdivided into uniform intervals and the simulation is *clocked* in terms of the basic time
interval. In contrast, discrete system simulations are often
event oriented and time is not necessarily advanced in uniform
increments.

In continuous system simulation, the dynamics of the system
are characterized by equations stating the interrelations of
system variables. Simulation is the process of producing the
time history of the system variables. In discrete system simulation, system variables are *entities* interacting with elements
of the system. Discrete simulation is the process of producing
a time history of these *transactions*.

The methods for digital computer simulation of continuous
systems are quite similar to analog computer simulation techniques. These concepts are common to most all computer languages
for continuous system simulation. Therefore, a programmer can

switch from one language to another without a great deal of difficulty.   Discrete system simulation is based on a different
type of mathematics and there are several distinct approaches
to describing systems.   Therefore, the transition   from   one
discrete system simulation language to another is more difficult.

Some of the basic concepts of discrete system simulation
will be presented in the next section.   This information   will
serve as background for a discussion of discrete system simulation languages in the following section.   The remaining sections
of this chapter are devoted to an example problem   illustrating
discrete system simulation and some additional discussion   on
the more popular discrete system simulation languages.

15.2   FUNDAMENTAL CONCEPTS

As noted in the previous section, discrete system simulation
often involves the flow and interaction of distinct   units   or
entities.   Traffic flow, inventory and manufacturing   processes
were cited as examples of systems of this type.   In general,
there are two types of action involved.   The first   is   simply
the flow of entities through the system (i.e., the   number   of
entities at various points in the system).   The second type of
action involves the processing of the entities by components of
the system.

In order to illustrate the operation of a discrete system,
consider a manufacturing process.   Typically, raw materials from
several   ources external to the manufacturing system flow   into
the system.   The raw materials are processed sequentially at one
or more work stations to become components for   final   assembly.
At some point in the manufacturing process, the parts are assem-
bled to produce the *end* product.   Each of the   process   steps
requires a finite amount of time.   However, the   exact   time
required at each step cannot be predicted.   Observation over a
period of time can be used to determine the shortest, longest
and average time for each step.   However, this information cannot
be used to determine a precise time for producing   a   particular
element.   Thus, knowing the number of elements waiting to   be
processed at a certain station does not enable the determination
of the precise number of processed elements available at   a

later point in time. Thus, the production rate is a *random* variable. Systems characterized by random variables are called *stochastic* systems. This is in contrast to *deterministic* systems in which a precise output can be determined from the input and the nature of the system.

In addition to the random or stochastic operation of the system elements, the arrival of elements to be processed is subject to uncertainties and is also random in nature. With random inputs and random operation, the deterministic methods of previous chapters are not adequate to describe or model the operation of such systems. Fortunately, a number of methods from theoretical statistics can be used to model the operation of stochastic systems. The remainder of this section will be used to present the basic concepts needed to model discrete systems.

The first concept needed is an understanding of *probability*. Stated simply, the *probability* of the occurrence of a particular event or condition in the course of N chances, is the ratio of the number of times (n) the event can occur, to the number of chances or opportunities (N) for the event to occur. Thus, the probability of a particular event is the fraction (n/N) indicating the likelihood of the occurrence of the event.

If the probability of each occurrence is plotted versus all possible occurrences, the resulting curve is called the *probability distribution* function or *probability density* function. The distribution function indicates the range of possible values and their respective probability of occurring.

Another important statistic is the average or *mean* value of a random variable. This is also referred to as the *expected* value of the variable. The nature of a random variable is also indicated by its *variance* and *standard deviation*. Without going into the mathematical details, the variance is an indication of the shape of the distribution or density function. For example, consider the two probability functions shown in Figure 15-2-1. In both cases, the smallest value of the variable x is 2 and the largest value is 6. The mean or average value (i.e., the expected value) for both cases is 4. However, the probability of

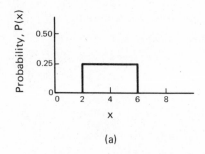

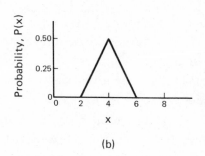

(a)   (b)

Figure 15-2-1.   Probability distribution functions

x taking on values near 2 or 6 is much greater for the distribution in Part (a) than for the distribution of Part (b).   Also,
the variable x is more likely to take on values near 4 for the
distribution of Part (b) than in that of Part (a).   Therefore,
the variance or standard deviation of Part (b) is smaller than
the variance or standard deviation of Part (a).   (The standard
deviation is the square root of the variance).   Thus, the probability distribution or density function is an important indicator
of the nature of a random variable.   In a similar manner, the
standard deviation and variance are useful for describing the
characteristics of the probability distribution or density function.

As an example of modeling a discrete system   component,
consider an operation in a manufacturing process.   The operation
can be described in terms of the length of time required   to
carry out the desired tasks.   An upper bound on time can be
determined along with a minimum time and an average time.   If
sufficient observations are made, the nature of the time required can be described by a probability distribution   function.
The resulting distribution function will have an average value,
a variance and a standard deviation.   A small variance would
indicate a tendency for the time required to perform the operation to be near the average or expected value.   A large
variance would indicate a wider variation in the time required
to carry out the operation.   The development of similar models
for each operation of the manufacturing process   would   enable
computer simulation of the entire system.   However, the simulation would have to be repeated many times in order to account

for the many possible variations in the system characteristics. This will be illustrated with an example problem in Section 15.4.

Certain distribution or density functions occur frequently and have been used to describe many processes encountered in discrete systems. The Poisson, normal, exponential and rectangular distribution functions are some of the more popular terms. Thus, in addition to basic probability concepts, an understanding of probability distribution functions, probability transform theorems and random number generation is important. These and other concepts important to discrete system simulation will not be presented in this chapter since they are available in a number of other books.[2,3,4] However, the concepts that have been discussed should enable a basic understanding of the techniques utilized for discrete system simulation.

15.3 DISCRETE SYSTEM SIMULATION LANGUAGES

The development of discrete system simulation languages closely parallels the implementation of continuous system simulation languages discussed in Section 14.2. The techniques utilized in discrete system simulation can be traced to the work on game theory by operational researchers in the 1920's. This effort was accelerated with the development of digital computers and by 1966 more than 20 simulation programs had been reported.[5] The development of programming techniques for discrete system simulation has been reported in several books and a number of articles. A partial list of these references is presented at the end of this chapter.

The earlier work on discrete system simulation languages was devoted to systems characterized entirely by discrete variables. More recently, languages have been developed which permit the inclusion of both continuous and discrete variables. The more popular discrete languages are:

GPSS (General Purpose Simulation System)

SIMSCRIPT (a Simulation Programming Language)

GASP (General Activity Simulation Program)

SIMULA (Simulation Languages)

SOL (Simulation Oriented Language)

These languages require different levels of programming experience
in order to use them. For example, GPSS is intended to require
a minimum of programming effort. On the other hand, SIMSCRIPT
requires considerable more programming experience.   It   should
be noted that several general purpose languages such as Fortran,
Algol, PL-1 and APL have also been used to simulate discrete
systems.

     In most of the discrete system simulation languages, the
system to be simulated is described in terms of the *world view*
of the language being used.   There are several approaches to
describing the *world view* of a language.   For example, the
language may focus on the entities or particles which flow
through the system.   This approach was adapted for GPSS and
the system is described in terms of blocks which operate on or
interact with the entities as they flow through the system.
The opposite approach focuses on the events, and describes the
operation of the system in terms of the events occurring as
system time progresses.   In either approach, the common factor
is the passage of time, whether it is keyed on particular activities or event occurrences.

     As noted previously, considerable effort has been devoted
recently to simulation languages which permit characterization
of continuous and discrete systems.[19]   This activity has led
to GSL (General Simulation Languages),[20][21], GASP IV (General
Activity Simulation Program IV)[22], and SMOOTH.[23]

     Unlike continuous system simulation languages, the programs
developed for discrete system simulation do not have a high degree of similarity.   Several approaches have been used and a
detailed discussion of these methods is beyond the scope of
this text.   However, the remainder of this chapter will contain
a brief introduction to one of the more popular languages and
a few comments on other approaches. Hopefully, the discussions
will enable the reader to understand the basic approaches and
provide background for further study.

15.4   INTRODUCTION TO GPSS

     GPSS is a block oriented language with 43 types of blocks
available to describe discrete systems.   The blocks are repre-

sented by a set of symbols and a symbolic name describing the type of action performed by the block. The operation of the system is determined by the movement of entities or *transactions* from block to block. Transactions begin or originate at *generate* blocks and leave the system at *terminate* blocks. Each block is assigned a *location* number which is listed in sequential order with other location numbers. Transactions normally move from generate to terminate blocks in sequential order unless a *transfer* block is encountered. The transfer block provides a *branching* capability and is used to provide alternate paths for transactions. Time is incremented by means *advance* and *generate* blocks. The action time is defined by the *mean* and *modifier* assigned to the block. The *mean* determines the average action time required to carry out the functions of the block. The *modifier* is the maximum positive and negative deviation from the mean. A rectangular distribution (e.g., Figure 15-2-1(a)) is assumed. If the modifier is 0, all transactions take place in the time interval specified by the mean.

The basic concepts discussed in the preceding paragraph can be illustrated with specific examples of GPSS statements. For example, a block to generate transactions is represented symbolically by the drawing in Part (a) of Figure 15-4-1. The program

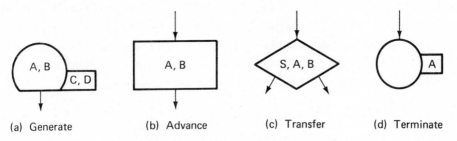

(a) Generate   (b) Advance   (c) Transfer   (d) Terminate

Figure 15-4-1. GPSS block diagram elements

statement for a generate block is

GENERATE 4,0   (15.4.1)

where the 4 indicates the generation of a transaction on the average of every 4 units of time (i.e., seconds, minutes, hours, etc.,). The 0 indicates a tolerance or modifier of 0. Thus, a new transaction will be generated every 4 units of time. If a

variation in the time for generating a transaction is desired, it
would be specified in place of the 0. For example, a variation
in generation of plus or minus 1 time unit would be produced by
the statement

GENERATE 4,1   (15.4.2)

This statement creates a transaction on the average of every 4
time units with the shortest interval between transactions being
3 time units and a maximum interval of 5 time units.   Note that
the probability distribution is uniform or rectangular (i.e.,
equal probability of values between 3 and 5). The third field of
a generate block specifies the time for the first transaction.
If the third field is blank, the first transaction occurs at T=1
time unit. The fourth field of a generate command indicates the
total number of transactions that will be generated. For example,
the command

GENERATE 4,1,2,5   (15.4.3)

will generate a total of 5 transactions on an average of every 4
time units with a minimum interval of 3 time units and a maximum
interval of 5 time units. The start time is set for 2 time units.

The processing of a transaction is indicated by the *advance*
block shown in Part (b) of Figure 15-4-1.   The program statement
for an advance block is shown in Equation (15.4.4). The entry in
the first field of the advance statement indicates the average
action time and the second field is used to specify the deviation
or modifier of action time. For example, the command

ADVANCE 5,2   (15.4.4)

provides an action time of 5 time units with the minimum action
requiring 3 time units and the maximum time required being 7 time
units. Note that all times between 3 and 7 occur with equal probability.

The flow of transactions can be directed from the normal
sequence by the insertion of a transfer block shown in Part (c)
of Figure 15-4-1. Transactions are transferred to the symbolic
location specified in the field of the transfer statement.   The
first field of the transfer statement indicates the selection

factor. The selection factor indicates the percent of transactions transferred to the symbolic location specified in the third field of the transaction statement. The remainder of the transactions are transferred to the symbolic location specified in the second field of the transfer statement. For example, the statement

$$\text{TRANSFER .200,x,y} \qquad (15.4.5)$$

causes 20 percent of the transactions to be transferred to location y and the remainder (i.e., 80 percent) are transferred to symbolic location x.

Transactions leave the system by means of a terminate block shown in Part (d) of Figure 15-4-1. The field of the terminate statement is used to indicate the rate of incrementing the terminal counter for each transaction. If a terminate block is assigned a terminate count of 0, transactions terminating at the particular block are not counted. If the termination count is set to 1 as shown by the statement

$$\text{TERMINATE 1} \qquad (15.4.6)$$

each transaction increments the termination count by 1.

The utilization of facilities is indicated by *seize* and *release* blocks shown in Parts (a) and (b) of Figure 15-4-2. This feature

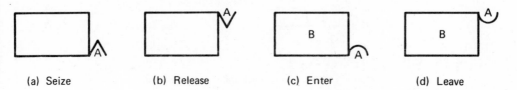

(a) Seize (b) Release (c) Enter (d) Leave

Figure 15-4-2. GPSS block diagram elements

permits the simulation of systems involving facilities that are not available for other transactions while they are in the process of carrying out a given transaction. The statements for these blocks are

$$\text{SEIZE 2} \qquad (15.4.7)$$

and

$$\text{RELEASE 2} \qquad (15.4.8)$$

where the number 2 identifies a particular facility.

The program includes the ability to simulate storage facilities by means of *enter* and *leave* blocks shown symbolically in Parts (c) and (d) of Figure 15-4-2. The program statement for simulating the enter block is

ENTER 4   (15.4.9)

where the number 4 identifies the facility being entered. The statement for a leave block is

LEAVE 5   (15.4.10)

where the number 5 indicates the block from which the transaction is moved. The second field of the seize, release, enter and leave statements is used to indicate the change in the contents of the block occurring with each transaction. If the second field is blank, each transaction increments the block count by 1.

In order to illustrate the use of GPSS, consider a data channel of a computer system with an error rate of 10 percent. Assume that the time to transmit a record ranges from 1.0 to 3.0 minutes. Also, assume that there is a need to transmit a record at intervals of time ranging from 1 minute to 5 minutes. A GPSS model of the channel is shown in Figure 15-4-3. The *generate*

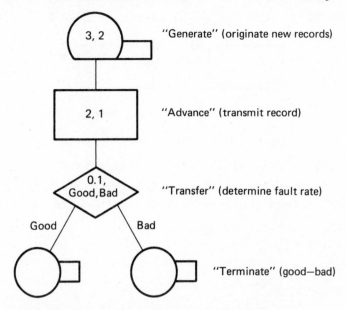

Figure 15-4-3. GPSS diagram for a communication channel

block with field entries of 3 and 2 will cause a new transaction (i.e., a data record in this case) to be generated on an average of every 3 minutes with a modifier of 2 minutes. Thus, the minimum interval between data records will be 1 minute and the maximum interval will be 5 minutes. The *advance* block with field entries of 2 and 1 indicates the average time to transmit a transaction (i.e., a data record) is 2 minutes with a modifier of 1 minute. Thus, the minimum time for transmitting a data record is 1 minute which corresponds to a data record 1 minute in length. The maximum time to process a transaction is 3 minutes. The *transfer* block is used to simulate the 10 percent failure rate of the channel. The *select* field entry of .100 causes 10 percent of the transactions to be routed to the *bad* termination. The remaining 90 percent of the transactions are sent to the *good* termination. Both *terminate* blocks have termination counts of 1, indicating an increment of one count for each transaction terminating at that block.

A computer program for the system is shown in Figure 15-4-4.

```
*        GPSS EXAMPLE PROGRAM
*
*    COMPUTER DATA CHANNEL SIMULATION
*
         SIMULATE
         GENERATE    3,2
         ADVANCE     2,1
         TRANSFER    .1,GOOD,BAD
GOOD     TERMINATE   1
BAD      TERMINATE   1
         START       1000
         END
```

Figure 15-4-4.   Coding statements for GPSS program

A single computer card is required for each block. Additional cards are used to document the program and control the simulation. The first card is a comment card providing a title. Comment cards are identified by an asterisk in Column 1. The second card is a blank comment card inserted to provide space for the titles. The next two cards are also comment cards providing additional title information and spacing. The fifth card is a control card with "simulate" beginning in Column 8. This is used to specify that a simulation is desired for the system described. The next 5 cards describe the blocks of the model. The symbolic names

"good" and "bad" are in Columns 2 through 6. The block type is
specified beginning in Column 8. The describing fields for the
block start in Column 19 and are separated by commas.   Comments
for each block can be added beginning in Column 45.

At this point, the model of the system has been specified
but no entry has been made to indicate the number of trial transmissions.   This can be established by means of a GPSS control
command,

       START 1000   (15.4.11)

which is the command to initiate 1000 trials.   Other GPSS control
statements are *clear* which initializes the system, *end* which
signals the end of a GPSS program and *simulate* which indicates
the desire to simulate the system described by the GPSS statements.   The *start* and *end* cards are the last two cards.   The
complete program deck is shown in Figure 15-4-5.

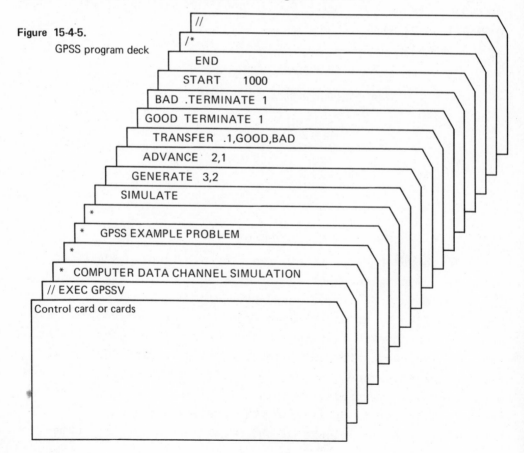

Figure 15-4-5.

    GPSS program deck

```
                                    //
                                /*
                            END
                        START     1000
                    BAD .TERMINATE 1
                 GOOD  TERMINATE 1
                  TRANSFER  .1,GOOD,BAD
                ADVANCE  2,1
              GENERATE  3,2
            SIMULATE
          *
        *   GPSS EXAMPLE PROBLEM
      *
     *  COMPUTER DATA CHANNEL SIMULATION
   // EXEC GPSSV
 Control card or cards
```

The output resulting from the example program is shown in Figure 15-4-6. Note the program is relisted with a sequence

```
*       GPSS EXAMPLE PROGRAM
*
*    COMPUTER DATA CHANNEL SIMULATION
*
        SIMULATE
1       GENERATE    3,2
2       ADVANCE     2,1
3       TRANSFER    .100,4,5
4       TERMINATE   1
5       TERMINATE   1
        START       1000
```

RELATIVE CLOCK		3019 ABSOLUTE CLOCK		3019	
BLOCK COUNTS					
BLOCK	CURRENT	TOTAL	BLOCK CURRENT	TOTAL	BLOCK CURRENT
1	0	1000			
2	0	1000			
3	0	1000			
4	0	903			
5	0	97			

Figure 15-4-6. Output from GPSS simulation

number added for each block. Also note that the symbolic names have been removed and the appropriate sequence number substituted. The output also includes a record of the transactions handled by each block. Note that 97 of the 1000 trial transmissions were classified as "bad." This is the result of assigning a 10 percent select rate on the transfer block. However, since the specification is random, the resulting assignment is determined statistically and will not result in exactly 100 or 10 percent "bad" transmissions.

The example problem presented here could be expanded to illustrate other features of GPSS. A similar example is developed in reference (6) and includes many of the additional features. References (25, 26 and 28) also include excellent examples.

15.5 OTHER DISCRETE SYSTEM SIMULATION LANGUAGES

As noted previously, a number of languages have been developed for simulating discrete systems. The three most popular languages appear to be GPSS, SIMSCRIPT and GASP.[24] In the previous section, the salient features of GPSS were outlined and an example problem presented. In order to provide some information on SIMSCRIPT and GASP, a brief outline of these languages will be presented in this section.

The approach to discrete system simulation used in SIMSCRIPT is quite different from that of GPSS. Instead of blocks operating on transactions flowing through the system, the particles of the system are represented by *entities*. Each entity has *attributes* and interacts causing *events*. The events characterize the operation of the system. Thus, SIMSCRIPT utilizes *entities* and *events* to simulate the operation of a discrete system. The entities of the system are classified as either temporary or permanent. Temporary entities are created during simulation and destroyed in the course of execution. Permanent entities are present at all times. The events may originate within the system (i.e., endogenous) or as a result of an external action (i.e., exogenous). For example, the messages to be transmitted on the communications channel of the example in the previous section would be temporary entities. However, the communication channel itself would be treated as a permanent entity.

The entities have attributes which describe the entity and its capacity to interact with the system. Simulation is then a process of scheduling and executing the events in their proper sequence.

In general, programming in SIMSCRIPT requires more experience than required to use GPSS. Additional information on SIMSCRIPT is available in reference (15).

The other popular simulation language is GASP.[14,17] A number of versions of GASP have been developed and the most recent is GASP IV.[22,27] In a manner similar to some other languages, GASP uses entities and attributes to describe the activities of a system. The program codes the activities taking place at event times and the corresponding effects on the entities and their attributes.

State variables (e.g., Chapter 7) have been incorporated in GASP IV to enable the program to simulate both continuous and discrete variables. Since it is necessary to schedule events at regular intervals of time and events that occur at particular states, simulations of this type are more complicated.

Additional details on programming in GASP can be obtained in references (14), (17), (22) and (27).

15.6 PROBLEMS

Problems covering material of this chapter are identified by section number.

15.2.1 List 5 systems which include random variables.

15.2.2 List 5 systems having both continuous and random variables.

15.2.3 Determine the probability of obtaining either 7 or 11 on 6 successive rolls of a pair of dice.

15.2.4 Determine the probability of drawing a king from a deck of cards on the first draw.

15.2.5 Determine the probability of getting one head and one tail if two coins are tossed simultaneously on three different trials.

15.2.6 Determine the mean or expected value for distribution shown

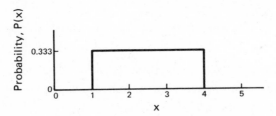

Figure 15-6-1.

15.2.7 Determine the mean or expected value for distribution shown

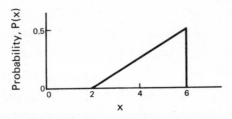

Figure 15-6-2.

15.2.8 Determine the mean or expected value for the distribution shown

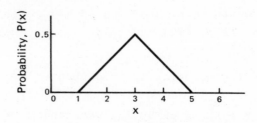

Figure 15-6-3.

15.2.9 Determine the mean or expected value for the distribution shown

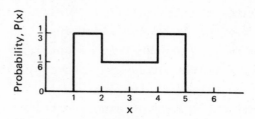

Figure 15-6-4.

15.2.10 Discuss the variance or standard deviation of the distributions shown in Problems 15.2,6, 7, 8 and 9.

15.2.11 Discuss the requirements for simulating a two elevator system in a public building during the hours 9 a.m. to 5 p.m.

15.2.12 Discuss the requirements for simulating a bank lobby with 3 windows for tellers.

15.3.1 Using the references at the end of this chapter as a starting point, prepare a discussion on the development of discrete system simulation languages similar to the discussion of continuous system simulation languages in Section 14.2.

15.3.2 Discuss the type of events and the time schedules required for a discrete system simulation of two automobile ferries providing transportation across a river.

15.4.1   Use GPSS or another simulation language to model a
portion of a manufacturing process. Assume that
the process has a 20 percent failure rate, requires
from 3 to 7 minutes to complete and raw materials
arrive at intervals ranging from 4 minutes to 6
minutes.

15.4.2   Using the model developed in Problem 15.4.1, simulate
the operation of the system for 1000 trials.

15.4.3   Using the model developed in Problem 15.4.1 determine
the operating characteristics of the system in producing 1000 good parts.

15.4.4   Use the model of Problem 15.4.1 to determine the
characteristics of the system in producing 50 bad
units.

15.4.5   Develop a GPSS model for a spray paint unit requiring
from 2 to 6 minutes per job with a failure rate of
0.1. Assume an arrival rate ranging from 3 to 5
minutes and determine the following:
a) the time required to paint 1000 units
b) the time required to paint 1000 acceptable units
c) the time required to paint 50 bad units
d) the time spent waiting for a new job

15.7   REFERENCES FOR CHAPTER 15

1.   Freeman, D. E., "Discrete Systems Simulation...A Survey
and Introduction," Simulation, Vol. 7, No. 3, pp. 142-148,
September, 1966.

2.   Mosteller, F., R. E. K. Rourke and G. G. Thomas, Probability and Statistics, Addison-Wesley Publishing Co.,
Inc., Reading, Mass., 1961.

3.   Bowker, A. H. and G. J. Lieberman, Engineering Statistics,
Prentice Hall Inc., Englewood Cliffs, New Jersey, 1959.

4.   Lee, Y. W., Statistical Theory of Communications, John
Wiley and Sons, Inc., New York, 1960.

5.   Tocher, K. D., "Some Techniques for Model Building,"
Proceedings of the IBM Scientific Computing Symposium,
IBM Data Processing Division, pp. 117-154, White Plains,
New York, 1966.

6. Gordon, G., <u>Systems Simulation</u>, Prentice Hall Inc.,
    Englewood Cliffs, New Jersey, 1969.

7. Evans, G. W., G. F. Wallace and G. L. Sutherland,
    <u>Simulation Using Digital Computers</u>, Prentice Hall, Inc.,
    Englewood Cliffs, New Jersey, 1967.

8. Schmitt, J. W. and R. E. Taylor, <u>Simulation and Analysis
    of Industrial Systems</u>, Richard E. Irvin, Inc., Homewood,
    Illinois, 1970.

9. Buxton, J. N., <u>Simulation Programming Languages</u>, North-
    Holland Publishing Company, Amsterdam, 1968.

10. Chu, Y., <u>Digital Simulation of Continuous Systems</u>,
    McGraw-Hill Book Co. Inc., New York, 1969.

11. Dahl, O. J.,"Discrete Event Simulation Language,"
    <u>Programming Languages</u>,F.Genuys, Ed., Academic Press, New
    York, 1968.

12. Emshoff, J. R. and R. L. Sisson, Design and Use of Com-
    <u>puter Simulation Models</u>, MacMillan Co., New York, 1970.

13. Forrester, J. W., <u>Industrial Dynamics</u>, John Wiley and
    Sons, Inc., New York, 1961.

14. Pritsker, A. A. B., P. J. Kiviat, <u>Simulation with GASP
    II</u>, Prentice Hall, Inc., Englewood Cliffs, New Jersey,
    1969.

15. Markowitz, H. M., B. Hausner and H. W. Kerr, <u>SIMSCRIPT</u>:
    <u>A Simulation Programming Language</u>, Prentice Hall, Inc.,
    Englewood Cliffs, New Jersey, 1963.

16. Teichroew, D. and J. F. Lubin, "Computer Simulation-
    Discussion of the Techniques and Comparison of Languages,"
    <u>Communications of the ACM</u>, Vol. 9, pp. 723-741, October,
    1966.

17. Kiviat, P. J., "Development of Discrete Digital Simu-
    lation Languages," <u>Simulation</u>, Vol. 8, No. 2, pp. 65-70,
    February, 1967.

18. Robinson, L. F.,"How GASP, SIMULA and DYNAMO View a
    Problem,"<u>Progress in Simulation</u>, 1. M. Kay and J. McLeod,
    Eds., Gordon and Breach, New York, 1972.

19. Fahrland, D. A., "Combined Discrete-Event/Continuous-
    Systems Simulation," <u>Simulation</u>, Vol. 14, No. 2, pp.
    61-72, February, 1970.

20. Golden, D. G. and J. D. Schoeffler,"GSL - A Combined Continuous and Discrete Simulation Language," <u>Simulation</u>, Vol. 20, No. 1, pp. 1-8, January, 1973.

21. Golden, D. G. and J. D. Schoeffler, "Problems in the Implementation of a Combined Continuous-Discrete Simulation Language," <u>Simulation</u>, Vol. 20, No. 2, pp. 49-52, February, 1973.

22. Pritsker, A. A. B. and N. R. Hurst, "GASP IV: A Combined Continuous-Discrete FORTRAN Based Simulation Language," <u>Simulation</u>, Vol. 21, No. 3, pp. 65-75, September, 1973.

23. Sigal, C. E. and A. A. B. Pritsker, "SMOOTH: A Combined Continuous Discrete Network Simulation Language," <u>Simulation</u>, Vol. 22, No. 3, pp. 65-73, March, 1974.

24. Kleine, H., "A Second Survey of User's Views of Discrete Simulation Languages," <u>Simulation</u>, Vol. 17, No. 2, pp. 89-94, August, 1971.

25. GPSS/360 Introductory User's Manual, IBM Corporation, Form No. H20-0304-4.

26. GPSS/360 V User's Manual, IBM Corporation, Form No. SH20-0851-1.

27. Pritsker, A. A. B., <u>The GASP IV Simulation Language</u>, Wiley Interscience, New York, 1974.

28. Greenberg, S., <u>GPSS-Primer</u>, Wiley Interscience, New York, 1972.

Index

†